VENTURE CAPITAL INVESTING

VENTURE CAPITAL INVESTING

**The Complete Handbook
For Investing In Small Private Businesses
For Outstanding Profits**

David Gladstone

Prentice Hall, Englewood Cliffs, New Jersey 07632

Library of Congress Cataloging-in-Publication Data

Gladstone, David.
    Venture capital investing.

    Includes index.
        1. Venture capital—United States—Handbooks, manuals,
etc.   2. Small business—United States—Finance—
Handbooks, manuals, etc.   I. Title.
HG4965.G575 1987   332.6'722   87-14414
ISBN 0-13-941428-2

Editorial/production supervision: **Cheryl Lynn Smith**
Cover design: **Ben Santora**
Manufacturing buyer: **Lorraine Fumoso/Paula Benevento**

Dedicated to L.G.,
with love

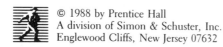

© 1988 by Prentice Hall
A division of Simon & Schuster, Inc.
Englewood Cliffs, New Jersey 07632

The publisher offers discounts on this book when ordered
in bulk quantities. For more information, write:

> Special Sales/College Marketing
> Prentice Hall
> College Technical and Reference Division
> Englewood Cliffs, NJ 07632

Printed in the United States of America

10 9

ISBN 0-13-941428-2 025

Prentice-Hall International (UK) Limited, *London*
Prentice-Hall of Australia Pty. Limited, *Sydney*
Prentice-Hall Canada Inc., *Toronto*
Prentice-Hall Hispanoamericana, S.A., *Mexico*
Prentice-Hall of India Private Limited, *New Delhi*
Prentice-Hall of Japan, Inc., *Tokyo*
Simon & Schuster Asia Pte. Ltd., *Singapore*
Editora Prentice-Hall do Brasil, Ltda., *Rio de Janeiro*

CONTENTS

PREFACE AND ACKNOWLEDGMENTS

After more than a decade in the venture capital investment business, I have not been able to find one book that covers the subject of venture capital investing in small private businesses. Many books, including my own **Venture Capital Handbook** from Prentice Hall, advise the entrepreneur on how to raise money from venture capitalists, but no book tells the whole story on how to invest in small private businesses. Although a number of books start out in that direction, almost all of them end in philosophical dialogue about small businesses and entrepreneurs.

The National Association of Small Business Investment Companies operates a school called the Venture Capital Institute. I have taught at that institute and know that it provides an excellent introduction to the venture capital investment process. One of the teaching aids at the institute is a large three-ring binder filled with articles by various faculty members. Each contributor has had extensive experience in venture capital investing, and each contribution is a gem in its own right. (For those interested in the institute, write NASBIC, 1156 15th Street, N.W., Washington, D.C. 20005.)

However, the institute's book lacks a uniform style and unifying theme. Like so many teaching manuals, it is great for teaching a group, but it does not suffice as a reference book. In addition, it is quite large and not portable. So, with pen in hand, I set out to write the definitive book on venture capital investing.

Venture Capital Investing is *not* the definitive book that I had hoped to write. I soon learned that one could easily write a ten-volume work on the subject of investing in small private businesses,

vii

but that I would have to sacrifice comprehensiveness in the interest of size. Thus, this book should be considered a primer on venture capital investing. It will provide the reader with a good basic understanding of the subject.

Those who have been in the business for a while may find some of the material familiar and perhaps even too simple, whereas beginners may find it difficult. Whatever the case, there is abundant information here for all business people and investors who want to invest some of their money in venture capital situations.

If, after reading this book, you decide that venture capital investing is too difficult, there is some good news. An outstanding mutual fund that specializes in investing in small companies can do the work for you. It has an outstanding track record. You can get its annual report by writing to Allied Capital Corporation, 1666 K Street, N.W., Suite 901, Washington, D.C. 20006, or by calling (202) 331-1112.

Experience

After receiving my M.B.A., I thought I knew almost everything about business. After only a few months of working in the venture capital area, I realized how little I actually knew about the world of small business. Without question, the case book method that was pioneered by Harvard Business School is the best education that anyone can obtain before entering the venture capital investment business. But that training only gives you a "mind set" that enables you to approach each business problem as you would a case, and this makes it easier to solve venture capital business problems.

In reality, as many writers before me have observed, the classroom is far removed from the practical aspects of investing in small business. Venture capital investing is the last of the apprentice trades. One must be involved in the industry for a considerable length of time before one can expect to have enough knowledge to invest in the venture capital area. Up to now, the only way to develop this knowledge was through experience. This book represents an effort to remedy the situation - it is a reference guide that one can use again and again.

Over many years of investing in venture capital I have developed a system of approaching venture capital investing problems. Although the system is not foolproof, it has worked well for me all this time.

I have reviewed thousands of business plans using a methodology that has helped me avoid pitfalls and make astute investments. These methods of analyzing business plans are revealed in this book.

There are virtually hundreds of "tricks" to investing in the venture capital business. Many of them have been taught to me by my friends in the industry, others I have learned in the school of hard knocks. I have tried to pass on many of these small dos and don'ts of investing in the venture capital area in this book.

It is my sincere hope that the readers of this book will be able to avoid many of the disasters that can easily befall the investor who is putting capital into small business. With this book as a guide, an investor should be able to improve the odds of making a fortune by investing in a small growing business.

Acknowledgments

Many people have made this book possible - most of them are in the venture capital industry. It is important that some of them be given credit here. Obviously the mistakes and problems of this book are not theirs, but mine alone. I will forever be indebted to all the people who have taught me so much about the venture capital business. I hope that those whose names I don't mention will forgive my oversight.

Many employees at Allied Capital Corporation played an integral role in the outcome of this book. George C. Williams is indirectly, and perhaps even directly, responsible for this book because he has been teaching me about the venture capital business since 1973. Jon Ledecky and Brooks Browne have unknowingly played a large role because they challenged my assumptions on many occasions. Clyde Garrett, Cabell Williams, and Kathleen Ryan have played a similar role, and have also pointed out many critical aspects of small business lending.

Harry Brill has shown me how the numbers really stack up in a small business. David Parker's legal expertise has kept me out of trouble many times and taught me countless good lessons. Betsy Erickson helped me begin this book, Jane Drury finished it. To these two, I owe everlasting indebtedness. No words can ever thank them enough for all the help they gave.

Members of the Board of Directors of Allied Capital Corporation, all venture capitalists in their own right, have unknowingly contributed to this book. To the founding directors of Allied Capital Corporation - Curtis Steuart, Murray Toomey, Henry Kaufman, and Walter Green - I want to express my thanks for establishing the value system that has made Allied the strong company it is today. Those values are the cornerstone of this book. Special thanks go to Bob Long and Wallace Holladay, who joined the company later on and helped continue its growth. My deepest thanks go to three investors who came in about five years ago- Willem de Vogel, Ray Lee, and Joe Clorety, all of whom were willing to risk their money at a time when Allied Capital Corporation was at a turning point. Not only did they invest their money, but they invested their time and attention to help the company grow even greater. The information they brought to the company appears in this book. To three later directors - Guy Steuart, William Walton and Warren Montouri - I say thank you for all the help you are giving me today.

Many people in the venture capital industry have helped to shape my thinking about this book and deserve to be mentioned by name:

Robert Allsop	R.W. Allsop Capital Corp.
Steve Austin	Metropolitan Capital Corp.
Richard Bannon	Cardinal Development Fund
Thomas Barry	North Riverside Capital Corp.
Frederick Beste	NEPA Venture Fund
John Blackburn	Orange Nassau Capital Corp.
David Blair	White River Capital Corp.
Frank Bonsal	New Enterprise Associates
Robert Braswell	MCA New Ventures
Earl Brian	Biotech Capital
Greg Bultman	R.W. Allsop Capital Corp.
Ian Bund	MBW Management Inc.
Donald Burton	South Atlantic Venture Fund
William Cannon	Capital For Business, Inc.
Frank Chambers	Continental Capital Ventures
Morton Choen	Clarion Capital Corp.
Don Christensen	Greater Washington Investors
Patricia Cloherty	Fifty-Third Street Ventures, L.P.
Floyd Collins	First Southern Capital Corp.
William Comfort	Citicorp Venture Capital
Joseph Conway	Michigan Capital & Service
John Crabtree	First Southern Capital Corp.
David Croll	T.A. Associates
Michael Cronin	First SBIC of California
Robert Davidoff	CMNY Capital Co.
Barry Davis	Alliance Business Investment
Kenneth DeAngelis	Rust Capital Ltd.
David C. Delaney	First SBIC of Alabama
J.B. Doherty	TDH Capital Corp.
Cyril Draffin	Greater Washington Investors, Inc.
David Dullum	Frontenac Capital Corp.
Thomas du Pont	First Tampa Capital Corp.
Bruce Duty	Capital Southwest Venture Corp.
Daniel Dye	First SBIC of California
David Engelson	First Connecticut SBIC

Philip English	Broventure Co.
A. Hugh Ewing	Hillcrest Group
Raichard Farrell	The Venture Capital Fund of New England
H. Wayne Foreman	Marine Venture Capital, Inc.
John Foster	J.H. Foster & Co.
Bondurant French	First Chicago Investment Advisors
Richard Frisbie	Battery Ventures
Jeffrey Garvey	Rust Capital Ltd.
Stanley Golder	Golder, Thoma & Cressey
Gary Granoff	Elk Associates Funding Corp.
Andy Greenshields	Pathfinder Venture Capital Fund
Robert D. Gries	Gries Investment Co.
Jeffrey Griffin	Greater Washington Investors, Inc.
Samuel Guren	William Blair Venture Partners
William Gust	Broventure Co.
Daniel Haggerty	Norwest Growth Fund, Inc.
Patrick Hamner	Capital Southwest Venture Corp.
David Harkins	Massachusetts Capital
Thomas Harvey	Carolina Venture Capital Corp.
Timothy Hay	First SBIC of California
James Hebenstreit	Capital For Business, Inc.
James Hellmuth	BT Capital Corp.
E.F. Heizer	Heizer Corp.
John Hines	Continental Illinois Venture
John Hoey	Beneficial Capital Corp.
C.L. Hoffman	Southeast Venture Capital
David Howe	Peachtree Capital
Tom Jahl	Three Cities Research
Brian Jones	First SBIC of California
David Jones	InterVen Partners
Joseph Kenary	First Mayland Capital, Inc.
Mark Kimmel	Columbine Venture Mgmt., Inc.
David King	Sovran Funding Corp.
Wayne Kingsley	InterVen Partners
Eugene Landy	Monmouth Capital Corp.
William Lanphear	The Early Stages Co.
Charles Lee	Abacus Ventures
Janice Leeming	Fund of New England
Arthur Little	Narragansett Capital Corp.
Troy McCrory	NCNB SBIC Corp.
James McGrath	Hutton Venture Investment Partners
Herman McManaway	Heritage Capital Corp.
James McManus	Market Corp. Venture Associates
Andrew McWethy	Irving Capital Corp.
Robert Manchester	Narragansett Capital Corp.
Brian Mercer	American Security Capital Corp.

Steven Merrill	Merrill, Pickard, Anderson & Eyre
Jane Morris	Venture Economics, Inc.
Irwin Nelson	Nelson Capital Corp.
Charles Newhall	New Enterprise Associates
Thomas Noojin	Invesat Corporation
Martin Orland	AMEV Capital Corp.
John Oxendine	Broadcast Capital, Inc.
John Padgett	First SBIC of California
Charles Palmer	North American Company
Alan Patricof	Alan Patricof Associates
Milton Picard	Financial Resources, Inc.
Martin Pinson	Greater Washington Investors
P.S. Prasad	Falcon Capital Corp.
Robert Pratt	Atlantic Venture Partners
Stanley Pratt	Venture Economics, Inc.
Brent Rider	Union Venture Corp.
Kinsey Roper	Heritage Capital Corp.
Donald Ross	Rand SBIC, Inc.
Alan Ruvelson	First Midwest Capital Corp.
Stephen Schewe	Norwest Growth Fund, Inc.
David Schroder	MorAmerica Capital Corp.
Sanford Simon	Ferranti High Technology, Inc.
Max Simpson	Crosspoint Investment Corp.
Harold Small	M & T Capital Corp.
Barry Solomon	Irving Capital Corp.
Edwin Spina	North American Company
William Starnes	Heritage Capital Corp.
John Sterling	Reedy River Ventures
Tony Stevens	First SBIC of California
Richard Tadler	Orange Nassau Capital Corp.
G. Jackson Tankersley	The Centennial Fund
Don Taylor	Corp. for Innovation Development
Carl Thoma	Golder, Thoma & Cressey
William Thomas	Capital Southwest Venture Corp.
Noel Urben	BT Capital Corp.
Franklin Van Kasper	VK Capital Corp.
Peter Van Oosterhout	River Capital Corp.
Patrick Welsh	Welsh, Carson & Anderson
Harvery Wertheim	Harvest Ventures, Inc.
Alex Wilkins	Delta Capital, Inc.
Walter Wilkinson	Kitty Hawk Capital, Ltd.
Martin Witte	Marwit Capital Corp.
Robert Zicarelli	Norwest Growth Fund

My thanks to the many entrepreneurs who have suffered through my education in the venture capital business. God bless you all for all of your help.

A special apology is extended to women who read this book. Common usage of the English language provides for the use of masculine pronouns. The use of masculine pronouns is not meant to diminish the contributions of females nor to discourage females from becoming venture capital investors.

VENTURE CAPITAL INVESTING

CHAPTER 1

KEYS TO SUCCESSFUL INVESTING

Every person is the total of his or her experiences. Each of us brings to every situation intellectual "baggage" in the form of prejudices and preferences, inherited and learned from past experiences. Therefore, in order to understand what this book is about, the reader needs to know something about the background of the writer.

All of my experience with small business has come from my years at Allied Capital Corporation. Allied Capital has a lending group that lends only to small businesses and an investment group that invests only in small businesses. At Allied Capital, I have reviewed thousands of business proposals and I have met hundreds of entrepreneurs. While my formal knowledge of business comes from obtaining my M.B.A. from Harvard Business School, my practical knowledge of investing in small business comes from my experiences at Allied Capital Corporation. If you can understand the philosophy behind Allied Capital, you will understand this book's approach to venture capital investing.

Allied Capital Corporation

Allied Capital Corporation is a public company that was established in 1958. It went public on a best efforts offering in 1960 and raised $1,000,000. I joined the company on January 2, 1974. At that time, it had four employees and about $12,000,000 in assets. Since then, the company has increased its assets and earnings significantly. I would like to believe that Allied Capital's outstanding success has been due to my being with it, but in reality those responsible for its growth are the many good associates who joined with me to build the firm.

Allied Capital Corporation has paid regular quarterly cash dividends and an annual extra cash dividend since 1964. The company's philosophy is that the stockholder must receive a tangible return every year. Since 1974, the company has increased its total cash dividend payout each year.

Allied Capital has a highly diversified investment portfolio. Over the years, the company has tried investing in just about everything. It has chosen not to concentrate on any one industry or any one stage of development of the companies it invests in. In recent years Allied Capital has not been seeking start-up companies, but it invests in a few of them every year. Nor does it seek to invest in turnaround companies (companies in trouble), although it sometimes get involved in them. Over the years, Allied's "bread and butter" has been of second- and third-round growth financings for existing businesses and leveraged buyouts of profitable companies.

It is interesting to note that Allied Capital has specialized in debt financings even with its equity arm. While the lending group at Allied Capital makes only small business loans, the venture capital group invests primarily in convertible debentures and loans with warrants. This debt orientation has been one of the reasons for Allied Capital's success and has permitted Allied to pay dividends each year.

As already mentioned, Allied has pursued a broad range of investments, from companies with mundane products to those offering high technology. However, the one type of company Allied seeks most aggressively is the "marketing-driven company." It constantly seeks companies that are driven to capture a share of the market.

If any readers would like an annual report of Allied Capital Corporation, they should write to Allied Capital Corporation, 1666 K Street, N.W., Suite 901, Washington, D.C., 20006, or call (202) 331-1112, and a copy will be sent. I hope that after reading this book you will be interested in becoming a stockholder of Allied Capital Corporation. If you would like more information in this area, see *Venture Capital Handbook* by David Gladstone, published by Prentice Hall.

WHAT ARE THE BASIC ITEMS TO LOOK FOR IN A BUSINESS PROPOSITION?

This book is about the "due diligence process." That is, it describes the steps that an investor should take in checking out an investment opportunity. This is a detailed process that takes weeks of work. It begins when an investor is confronted with a business proposal and must decide whether the idea warrants further investigation. There are six critical components to look for in this first stage of evaluation.

1.   The Numbers Should Be Properly Presented

Everybody in the investment business lives and dies by the "numbers." This means that the investor cannot proceed without accurate figures on a company's past performance. Anything less than accurate and detailed (and in most cases certified financial statements) will lead the investor into a business risk that is probably not worth the business opportunity. To repeat, no investor should make an investment without accurate figures.

In addition, **current** financial statements are an absolute must. All too often, investors are given old financial statements that are ancient history. The older numbers do not reflect how the company is doing now. You should not accept any statements older than three months. Make the entrepreneur give you current financial statements or don't invest. Any entrepreneur who sends you poorly prepared or stale financial statements does not deserve financing.

Another thing to look for is the entrepreneur's knowledge of the financials. You must make sure that your entrepreneur is able to explain the numbers in detail. If he can't, it is a sure sign that he does not live and die by the numbers and therefore will be a poor match for you because, as an investor, you must live and die by the numbers.

In addition, the entrepreneur must provide accurate and detailed projections for at least three years, but preferably five years. As an investor, you cannot assess how much money you can make without good projections. I remember asking an engineer for some projections on his small business and being told that he couldn't supply them because this involved "sheer speculation" and engineers don't guess about things; they only report what is known. Needless to say, I did not invest in his company. Projections are important because they reflect the company's financial plan. A company without a financial plan is a company without financial direction.

Another point is that if the company has not reached breakeven, it should provide you with a month-by-month financial analysis indicating when the company will reach breakeven. An investor needs to know when a company will finally reach cash flow breakeven and no longer need money.

If a small business person cannot produce accurate financial projections, it should hire an accountant to do so. However, if the entrepreneur does hire an accountant he should still know most of the numbers by memory if he intends to live and die by the numbers. If you ask the small business person about the financials and he answers, "these financials were put together by my accountant" and cannot tell you why certain projections do certain things, the small business person does not understand the numbers. This is a clear sign that you will have problems in the future.

As an investor, I cannot afford to deal with entrepreneurs who do not understand the financial projections for their company. A good entrepreneur must know the operating plan and the financial plan. A good manager has a deep appreciation of accounting. He knows that without accurate and timely information he cannot manage his company. This sounds obvious, but many entrepreneurs are "concept people." An entrepreneur who lives by the numbers is the one you want to back.

2. The Deal Must Make Lots of Money

Usually one does not have to tell an entrepreneur that the projections must go up. Every set of projections that I have ever received from entrepreneurs go up. If they didn't go up, no one would be interested in investing.

Unless the projections go up significantly, then no venture capitalist is going to be interested in investing. Venture capitalists look for a return on investment of at least 25%, and in many situations they expect to see as high as 50% to 100% return on investment per year.

When you look at the projections, you should be asking, "What will the company be worth in three to five years?" Using that projection and the expected value of the company in three years, the investor should calculate how much of the company he will have to own in order to receive a high return on investment. If the projections don't go up significantly, the investor will have to own a very large share of the small business. Once doing this calculation, I determined that to make the type of return that I thought was commensurate with the risk, I would need to own 150% of the company. I didn't make the investment. It was a nice little business, but there was little possibility of a high return.

3. The Acid Test of a Deal Is Management, Management, Management

Some years ago I attended an industry seminar in which we were asked what attributes might indicate that a business was going to be successful. There were ten slots on the blackboard, and within a minute the first six slots were filled with the word **management**. Over and over again, venture capitalists say that the acid test of any deal is its management.

4

But what exactly does management mean? It is very easy for an investor to blame poor management for a loss, but the reverse is also true: One makes a lot of money when management is good. Well, then, what management qualities should an investor look for? Here are a few.

Honesty and Integrity. One criterion that every investor uses to test management is honesty. If the entrepreneur team is not honest, almost "honest to a fault," then it is unlikely that the lender or venture capitalist will invest. A friend of mine tells about touring a plant with a group of venture capitalists and stopping for a moment to watch a lady at a drill press. He happened to ask her what she was making. She replied, "Oh, nothing. I was hired just for the day. I was told there were some big shots coming through and that I should look real busy." Management's credibility (and that of others in the plant) was gone. As a result of that one incident, the company never raised the money it needed. The news of its actions went flying through the venture capital community and killed all hopes of raising cash.

Experience. Every lender and venture capitalist wants to back an entrepreneur who has extensive experience in the industry in which the business is operating. If the entrepreneur is a white-collar government worker who is going to buy a meat-packing plant, for example, the investor should have serious reservations about that person's qualifications for work in the industry. Would the entrepreneur know how to run a meat-packing plant? I remember one of the questions I asked a man who owned a meat-packing plant when I was fresh out of business school and filled with a new concept called "management by objective," or MBO. I asked the owner if he used MBO to run his plant. He was a fairly burly fellow puffing on a big cigar and he quickly informed me, "No, sonny, I don't use MBO in my plant. I use MBI." "Oh," I asked, "What is MBI?" To which this husky fellow replied, "Management by intimidation." This gruff entrepreneur knew how to work in his business. He knew that objectives were best left in the office and that management by objective would not work inside his meat-packing plant. He had the experience necessary to operate the plant.

Achievement. Solid achievements in the entrepreneur's background are a big plus. Every investor should look for achievements. The chances of success increase when the entrepreneur is an achiever. Look at the entrepreneur's background. What did he achieve in college? In business? Achievers are what make the world go round. During the 1950s, a social scientist studying achievers and nonachievers made some interesting discoveries about their backgrounds. The background factor having the highest correlation with the achievers was that they had been an Eagle Scout. The lowest correlation was between achievers and pipe smokers. There is a lesson here for anyone looking at an entrepreneur trying to raise money: Bet on a high achiever. They have the spark that will light the fire. They want to win. They have achieved in the past and most likely will continue to achieve.

High Energy Level. What most investors look for in a management team is a high level of energy. Being an entrepreneur is tough. I have the greatest respect for all entrepreneurs. They work long hours. Personally I have worked only a few seventy-hour weeks and I don't like them. Your entrepreneur will have to be one who can accept the long hours and the grinding pace. Creating a great business is 1% inspiration and 99% perspiration.

Your entrepreneur must therefore be in good health and of sound mind. His health will be put to the test as he deals with the daily stress of his work and physical exhaustion. Make sure your entrepreneur is a strong person with plenty of energy. He must have the energy to be successful. Good management will not only possess the strength to work long hours, but will actually put in the long hours to make the business successful.

Motivation. Many entrepreneurs work long hours week in and week out. So, when I am talking to an entrepreneur, I often ask, "Why do you want to do all of this, knowing it is going to take time out of your life. Why is it you want to get involved in this difficult situation?"

The wrong answer to this question is, "I want to be my own boss. My current boss doesn't understand me. I just want to get out on my own." Investors should not be solving the personal or psychological problems of entrepreneurs. The right answer to this question is "It is a great opportunity for us both. If you will invest in the company, we can make a lot of money."

Of course, there are plenty of greedy people in the world who want to make money. But it is my experience that the winners are rarely greedy! Business profits are a way of measuring one's success. It is a moral judgment to select business profits as a measure of self-worth. Every achiever selects some standard to be measured by. A doctor measures success by the lives saved or the diseases cured. A clergyman measures success by the souls saved. An inventor by the useful inventions created. When one selects a business career, one accepts as the ultimate measure of success, the sales and profits made. You want to back an entrepreneur who measures success by profits.

4. The Situation Should Be Unique

One basic question every venture capitalist asks is "Why is this situation special?" Every investor knows that in the business world, big businesses "beats up" little businesses. Therefore, if a small business is to survive, it must have something special, such as a patent, a proprietary process, a two-year lead time on the competition, or a good location (for example, in the case of a restaurant). What does the small business bring to the marketplace that will make people want to buy its product or service? The business must have something unique if it wants to win in the competitive environment.

At the same time, most venture capitalists are "afraid" of products that are too unique. The product or service should not be revolutionary; rather, it should be evolutionary. I suspect most venture capitalists would not have backed Edison's new invention, the electric light bulb because it was much too revolutionary. Revolutionary products change the way human beings live on this earth. As a result, they take many years to gain public acceptance and the return on investment is stretched out over such a long period of time that the **annualized** return on investment is too low for most investors. Venture capitalists don't want to wait twenty to twenty-five years. Their normal time horizon is five to ten years. So, the product cannot be revolutionary; it should be a follow-on product.

5. The Proposed Venture Should Be Oriented toward the Market

Every successful business must take its direction from the marketplace it addresses. Some say, "Build a better mousetrap and the world will beat a path to your door." Very unlikely! Mousetraps are sold not bought. The world belongs to those who understand the marketplace. Good entrepreneurs do not introduce a product because it is a nifty product. They introduce a product because their analysis of the marketplace shows a new product will sell.

Some people praise Henry Ford for creating mass production. He should be given more credit for his market analysis. He believed that the average person would purchase a cheap stripped-down car if it was available. Instead, most cars were like the high-priced and beautifully made Stanley Steamer or Pierce Arrow. His market analysis concluded that people would buy a low-cost, shaking, rattling, "tin lizzie." That contraption is marketing history. It changed the way we live.

A good entrepreneur starts not with a product idea, but with a vision of what the marketplace needs and wants. A market division entrepreneur loves the action of making sales. He is not in the lab to create a new product, but to find a solution to a problem or develop a product that people will want. Make sure you back a market-oriented company.

6. The Deal Must Have An Exit

The final element of a business proposition that every investor should look for is the exit. This refers to the way to get one's money back, or to cash in on the investment. Every venture capitalist is looking at cash flow and how the money will come back. Venture capitalists spend a great deal of time reviewing a business situation to make sure that they will get their money back as well as turn a good profit.

There are only three basic ways to get your money out of a small business: (1) it can go public (this is the normal way venture capitalists reach liquidity); (2) a large conglomerate or other business group may want to buy the entire business and pay off its debts and give its stockholders a good return on investments (Allied Capital has fared extremely well in this area); or (3) the company can simply buy out the venture capitalist by refinancing the company out of cash flow. Although this last exit is an unusual way for venture capitalists to make money, Allied Capital has been very successful over the years in triggering buyouts. The point here is this: Make sure there is a way out before you get into an investment.

IT'S NOT AN INVESTMENT, IT'S A PARTNERSHIP

Every person who reads this book, and especially those who intend to put money into a small company should be absolutely sure that the relationship between you, the investor, and the entrepreneur is a strong partnership, in reality a "marriage." It must be a trusting relationship in which neither party is trying to get the upper hand. Both parties must be working together to make money. Therefore every investor should get to know the management of the company before investing any money in it. I usually try to spend extra time with the management team so that I feel comfortable with them.

I remember some years ago talking to a group up North who had three "Doc-in-the-Boxes". This is slang for a medical delivery system that compares the medical delivery system to the fast food business. In place of a "Jack-in-the-Box," where one goes for a quick meal, you have a Doctor-in-the-Box, which refers to an accessible unit that provides quick, efficient, and cheap medical service. In this case, three individuals owned three Doc-in-the-Boxes and wanted a large investment so they could continue to expand. After meeting with them for a full day and after being convinced that I should make the investment, I was persuaded to join them for dinner. After a few drinks, they began to tell me how they really operated the business.

First they described (and these are their terms) how they were going to "screw" the IRS and not pay their taxes, then they described how they were going to "screw" their suppliers and not pay them, how they were going to "screw" Medicare and Medicaid to get higher payments, and how they were going to "screw" a few of their patients by overcharging them. I knew before that dinner was over that if I made the investment, someday in the future one of those "screws" would have my name on it.

PREPARE A WRITTEN SUMMARY BEFORE YOU BEGIN TO INVEST

I firmly believe that every investor should prepare a written summary before formally investigating the situation. A summary of one or two pages can crystallize your thinking about why this is such a great investment opportunity. It will also put in a concrete form what you want to discuss with your friends, your banker, your accountant, and others. All of them can help you to determine whether it is a good investment opportunity. After reading this book you should be able to prepare such a summary. This summary should be a response to the following questions:

What Are You Investing in?

Here you are trying to define the entity that you are investing in. For example, specify whether it is a partnership, a subchapter S company, or a corporate entity. Usually, I put down the name, address, and telephone number of the business. Many times this information does not appear in a conspicuous place on the proposal. Before you go any further, you should wade through the proposal and who you would be investing in. This information will also be handy in the future when you want to talk to the company's people.

Who Is Your Contact at the Business?

Many proposals list a number of contact people in the firm, but as an investor you need to know who you will be dealing with directly during the due diligence process and during the monitoring after you have invested in the company. Usually it is the president of the company, although sometimes the vice-president of finance will be your contact. Find out immediately who this person is and make sure you have a clear channel for gathering information from this person. If your initial contact is a broker you should ask the broker to introduce you to the person who is going to be your contact at the business. Don't let all of the information filter through the broker. Get it from the "horse's mouth."

What Kind of Business Are You Investing in?

Here, I try to describe in ten words or less the type of company I am investing in. Describe the industry, describe the stage of development, such as a start-up. Try to pinpoint the kind of business you will be investing in.

Summarize the Business Situation

Prepare a thumbnail sketch of the company's situation. Emphasize the strong points that draw you toward this investment. You should be able to do this in one paragraph, or perhaps two. But, it should be brief, and it should crystallize in your mind the business situation that you are getting involved with.

Who Is on the Management Team?

Although management is the most important section in the entire analysis, you don't need to cover the entire background of the individuals who you are considering investing in. Do hit some of the highlights that make you want to invest, such as the entrepreneurs' experience, their past achievements, their "go-power." Make sure you put down the names and the credentials of the top two or three people. You only need to highlight in two or three sentences what aspect of their background sets them apart from other management teams that you have seen.

What Are They Selling?

In a very brief paragraph, describe the product or service the company is selling. State why the product or service is unique and, if it is not unique, explain why this product or service will succeed over other products and services that are offered by the competitors. You need not discuss the competition in detail, but it is important to differentiate the company in summary form from others in the industry. More than a paragraph here would be too much.

What Is So Unique about the Situation?

In two or three sentences state why this situation is unique. You may have covered this adequately in the preceding paragraph, but if not, elaborate here.

How Much Money Are They Raising and How Much Are You Considering Investing?

Every business proposal tells you how much money its principals are looking for, but the amount should not be expressed in ranges. For example, the business proposal should not say $500,000 to $1,000,000. The company should know how much money it needs to do the job and should state that figure. In addition, you will want to know the type of money it is raising. Is it selling common stock, preferred stock, convertible debentures, loans with warrants? What structure and format will be used in raising this money? If management hasn't set that out, then determine what you would prefer and put it in this section. Keep in mind the type of structure of the investment, such as stock, warrants, and convertible debentures.

Is There Any Security for Your Investment?

Every banker looks for collateral when making a loan to a company. Even though you are an investor, your investment can be in the form of debt with collateral security. You may take a second mortgage on the assets of the business or you might have outside collateral such as a mortgage on the person's house. Venture capital takes many forms, but whatever the form, your prime consideration should be how to lower your risk.

How Will the Money Be Used?

The proposed use of proceeds is not always set out in great detail in the business plans. However, after investigating and discussing these plans with the entrepreneur, you should have a good idea of how he is going to spend the money. You should be able to state in one short paragraph where the money is going. You should not have to use such broad terms as "working capital" but should be able to specify where the funds are to be used.

What Is the Past Financial Performance?

In this section you want to summarize the sales, earnings, assets, liabilities, and net worth of the company. In three or four columns you ought to be able to sketch out where the company has been and what kinds of trends it is setting. You may be surprised by what you can learn dredging through the business plan and placing these items in your summary.

What Are the Projections?

As a venture capitalist taking a long-range view of the situation, you should look at the five-year projections for the company. Even though the fifth year is highly speculative, it gives you a clear idea of how the company will grow and, in essence, how much money you stand to make if it meets the projected goals. Without a summary projection in the same format as the financial history, you will not be able to develop a basic understanding of the company.

How Will You Cash in?

As I mentioned before, no venture capital company wants to remain a minority stockholder in a company forever. Every venture capitalist must realize the capital gains on his money. Even though your horizon may be three to seven years, you must have a clear perception of how you are going to get out of the investment before you go into it. You should be able to state in three or four sentences how you plan to get out of this situation.

How Much Can You Make?

The expected profit is the final test of a promising business proposal. If you own a certain percentage of the company, what will it be worth when you cash it in? I like to set out in a tabular format the cash that I will be expected to put into the company over the next seven years and the cash that I can expect to receive back. This format enables me to summarize clearly the cash in and cash out. There are probably a thousand ways to determine this, but I use a calculator that gives me internal rate of return. If a company can't show a 25% internal rate of return and the situation entails all of the typical risks of a venture capital investment, then it doesn't deserve any more of your time.

What Do You Like about This Situation?

List in point form three to five reasons for making the investment. What is it that you like about the situation and that is compelling you to invest? If you can't express it now, then you probably will never be able to do so.

What Do You Dislike about This Situation?

No investment opportunity is perfect. Every one of them seems to have some "warts." You should be able to explain those dislikes in three or four lines. You should know exactly what you don't like about the situation. If it goes bad, you will know what to avoid in the future.

WHAT DOES A SUMMARY LOOK LIKE?

What follows is a useful summary format. This format is a composite of many that I have seen. The figures are based on an actual investment, but the numbers and names of the people involved have been changed. The investment made a tremendous amount of money for everyone.

Company: Electronic Press, Inc.
          8888 Avenue of the Americas
          New York, N.Y. 10005
          Telephone: (212) 555-1212

Contact: Joseph Entrepreneur, president.

Type of Business: Electronic preparation of camera-ready copy and printing of materials requiring quick turnaround.

Company Summary: A new company has been formed to purchase the assets of an ailing printing company. The company uses the method of setting type known as "hot type." The company will write computer programs to drive a special machine that will produce camera-ready copy for printing. This unique method will make "hot type" obsolete. All existing customers will be serviced with "hot type" until the new system is ready.

Management: Joe Entrepreneur, president, has been in printing for twelve years. He has worked in all phases of the business. He has been working with computer programs to set type for the past year. He has a B.A. from a New York university in accounting. He is thirty-two years old.

Jim Executive, vice-president, has been in the computer field for eight years. He has been a programmer, systems analyst, and management consultant on computer applications. He has been working on a computer program to set type for one year. He has an engineering degree from a large Boston college. He is thirty-one years old.

Product/Service and Competition: Electronic Press will begin by continuing to offer conventional typesets and printing. Once the computer can be used to set type, the company will offer the customer five-hour turnaround or better for typesetting and printing. Customers can use the actual camera-ready copy for corrections and can make corrections quickly.

Funds Requested: $600,000 in common stock for a 40% ownership.

Collateral: None.

Use Proceeds: $200,000 as down payment of the business; $200,000 accounts payable; and $200,000 to carry the company's research and development budget to develop the computer program. The purchase price is $600,000: $200,000 in cash, and $400,000 in a five-year 8% note.

Financial History:	*Actual,* *2 Years Ago*	*Actual,* *1 Year Ago*	*Actual,* *Last Year*
Revenues	$2,109,000	$2,989,400	$2,460,500
Net loss	(79,000)	(43,100)	(11,600)
Assets	2,279,500	2,700,100	2,870,000
Liabilities	1,956,400	2,420,100	2,601,600
Net worth	323,100	280,000	268,400

Financial Future:	*Projected,* *This Year*	*Projected,* *Next Year*	*Projected,* *2 Years Out*
Revenues	$2,900,000	$3,800,000	$6,000,000
Net income	10,000	160,000	800,000
Assets	3,970,000	4,770,000	5,570,000
Liabilities	3,601,600	3,731,000	3,372,000
Net worth	878,400	1,039,000	1,839,000

Exit: The company will go public in three years. If the company does not go public in five years, then the investors can exchange their ownership for three times their investment and be paid out over three years.

A SECOND SUMMARY

To give you more food for thought, here is a second summary. In this case (again, the information is disguised), Allied Capital barely got its money back. It was not a pleasant investment because the owner lacked entrepreneurial abilities.

Company: TT5 Corporation
123 Main Street
McLean, Virginia 22101
Telephone: (703) 555-1212

Contact: Joe Entrepreneur, president.

Type of Business: Manufacturer of switching gear for telephone equipment.

Company Summary: TT5 Corporation was founded three years ago by Joe Entrepreneur, an individual with seven years' experience in the communication and switching-gear industry. The company's first product was a multipurpose switching unit attached to PBX systems that permit the buyer of the unit to use several low-cost telephone services. The company will reach profitability in one year and estimates show that it will be very profitable in three years.

Management: Joe Entrepreneur, with seven years' experience in manufacturing PBX and related equipment, founded the company and has served as president. He previously worked for a large communications network conglomerate and several other corporations in the communications field. He is a graduate of a Boston technological university with a degree in electrical engineering.

John Executive, vice-president, has been with the company for one year. He has had seventeen years of experience in the field of PBX and related equipment. He has written two books on the subject and has been granted six patents for work in telecommunications. Currently he guides the company in all of its marketing operations. He has an M.B.A. degree from a large university in Maryland.

Product/Service and Competition: TT5 Corporation manufactures a unique electrical switching box that can be adapted to all forms of PBX and telephone equipment. At present no companies other than TT5 Corporation are in the business of manufacturing these add-on communication boxes. It is doubtful that anyone will enter the business in the next two years. If competitors do enter, TT5's patents should give it a monopoly on certain types of PBX installations.

Funds Requested: $500,000 convertible subordinated debentures at 15% interest and convertible into 20% ownership of the company.

Collateral: Second secured interest in the assets of the business subordinated to a local bank debt of $1,750,000.

Use of Proceeds: The company has currently outstripped its line of working capital at the bank ($750,000) and its low equity base prevents the bank from increasing the line of credit beyond the current status. Initially, the company will use the $500,000 to pay down the bank loan and negotiate a larger line of credit ($1,750,000) with the bank so that more working capital will be available to the company.

Financial History:

	Actual, 2 Years Ago	Actual, 1 Year Ago	Actual, Last Year
Revenues	$100,000	$ 450,000	$ 979,000
Net loss	(226,000)	(443,000)	(62,000)
Assets	443,000	1,002,000	1,200,000
Liabilities	232,000	1,402,000	876,000
Net worth	211,000	(232,000)	(170,000)

Financial Projections:

	Projected, This Year	Projected, Next Year	Projected, 2 Years Out
Revenues	$1,425,000	$3,260,000	$8,350,000
Net income	90,000	224,000	790,000
Assets	1,500,000	2,000,000	2,900,000
Liabilities	900,000	1,230,000	1,800,000
Net worth	(80,000)	144,000	943,000

Exit: The company will attempt a public offering on the basis of earnings in three years. If there is no public market and no prospect for a public market in the near future, then the company will offer to buy back the stock owned by the venture capitalist.

What Makes It Exciting?

There are three reasons why such summaries excite the venture capitalist. First, the product is unique. As discussed under "Product/Service and Competition," the product is manufactured only by this company, and there appears to be no potential competition on the horizon. The second bit of information that is music to the venture capitalist's ears is the fact that the individuals have had previous experience in this area, as well as long experience in the industry. This background usually makes the venture capitalist more comfortable about the operation and about the prospects for the future. The crowning touch is the financial projections. Not only has the company turned the corner from its actual financial statements, but it is now projecting strong earnings. Obviously the venture capitalist will be led to believe that in the years ahead the company will go public or be sold to a large company. When the public offering occurs, the investor (as well as the entrepreneurs) will reap huge capital gains.

OBJECTIVE OF YOUR SUMMARY

Whether or not you wish to use the format suggested here, you must try to summarize and crystallize your thoughts about why you are making this investment. If some nonmonetary items begin to creep into your thinking, it is the first sign that you are making a mistake. For example, if you are making the investment in order to help a friend, why not just help him find a bank loan instead? Are you making the investment so that you will be famous and recognized as the person who backed this great investment? There are better ways to become famous. You may turn out to be famous for backing a crazy idea that failed. Are you making the investment because the entrepreneur is the same race, religion, or sex? A very poor barometer for success. Are you making the investment for some social goal? Why not make a cash gift to some charity? That will look better than an investment in a failed company. Are you investing so you can be on the board of directors? Being on the board of directors will carry some substantial liabilities beyond your investment - you might find out one day that IRS is looking to the directors for past due payroll taxes.

If you are making the investment because you will get some free merchandise, it would be much cheaper to go out and buy the product. Too many people have ended up losing a great deal of money this way and the product has turned out to be far from free. In your summary you should keep coming back to the key points, that is, good management, good profit potential, unique product, and great exit opportunity. If these things keep popping into your mind while you are writing the summary, then you are on the right track.

Once you have finished your summary, you should pass it to a few friends and let them read it. An accountant should definitely look at it and so should your banker. Both are very conservative people and would probably advise you not to invest, but make sure they understand what you see in the business and why you are interested. If your summary churns up their desire to invest in the business, you know you are on the right trail.

SOME WORDS ABOUT FRANCHISING

Just because someone is starting a franchise that at first glance looks like the next great fast food concept in your area, don't automatically jump at the idea. Franchising is just another means of operating a business. Before you invest in a franchise, you have to be sure that some very important characteristics are present.

Sound Concept

When you look into the history of a franchise, investigate the uniform franchise agreement that it must file in many of the states. In that filing you will find the failure rate of the franchisor. If you discover that the number of failures exceeds 3%, the franchise that you are about to invest in is above the national average. You may want to read the entire uniform disclosure agreement in order to learn about the franchisor.

Well-Financed Franchisor

One of the things that you will be looking for when you review the uniform disclosure agreement is the financial statement of the franchisor. If the franchisor is not well financed and is living hand to mouth, he is not going to be able to give your franchisee a great deal of help. Study the franchisor as well as your franchisee. Unless the franchisor has the wherewithal to give a great deal of assistance to your franchisee, in all probability the franchisee that you are investing in will fail.

How Does the Franchisor Make Money?

Every franchisor has an orientation in one direction or another toward the franchisee. By this, I mean that the franchisor is either trying to make a great deal of money out of the franchising fee or he is content to break even on the franchise fee and make his long-term money on the royalties. It is by far better to select a franchisor who is oriented towards long-term royalty payments than one who is betting on a quick up-front fee of the franchisee. The franchise fee should not exceed the amount of the service that is being given to the franchisee. In good franchisor relationships, the franchisor charges a fee sufficient to cover his expenses for delivering the training and other assistance to the franchisee.

Good Relations

You may want to call a large number of the franchisees of the franchisor in question to see if they are happy with their relationship with the franchisor. If, after a few phone calls, you find a group of unhappy franchisees, you may want to invest elsewhere. If the chain of franchisees is unhappy with their franchisor, in all probability your franchise is not worth what you are being charged.

STANDARDS OF VENTURE CAPITAL INVESTING

People use various criteria when making decisions about venture capital investing. Although everybody has their own ideas about what to look for, here is some sound advice from an individual in the business who seems to have made a few bucks: Look for people who are hard working and honest; look for a growth industry with strong opportunities; and make sure the company has an adequate capital base. Those three simple rules have helped this sage of the venture capital industry to make a great deal of money.

On a more analytical level, one of the large venture capital pools has identified four common characteristics of the investments that have made money for this pool. First, there is a barrier to entry in the business. That is, each company has some kind of franchise that others are unable to have. It may be a proprietary situation or patent or something that prevents someone else from entering the business.

Second, each of the companies is leverageable. That is, the company is able to borrow money on the assets of the business so that it need not have an inordinate amount of equity capital in the business. Leverage is like buying stock on margin. You put up only part of the equity and the rest you borrow on the assets of the business.

Third, the venture is repeatable. That is, if you have only one location or one situation in which this business opportunity works, then it is basically a one-time shot. This major venture capital firm looks for things that can be done over and over again as a basis for a business.

Fourth, each company is able to pay low taxes or no taxes at all. This venture capital firm found that the companies it invested in were better able to generate internal capital by using depreciation of their assets quicker than the useful life or have some other way of sheltering income in order to pay off the leveraged portion of the finances, as set out above. If you are going to have leverage, according to this group, you must be able to pay it back with pre-tax dollars rather than paying tax and then paying back the debt on an after-tax basis.

These four are the keys to success in the eyes of this company. What do you think are the keys to success? The harder you work at analyzing and learning as much as possible about your investment opportunity, the easier it will be to identify the keys to success in the investment that you are looking at.

Chapters 2 through 7 of this book explain how to investigate a small business. Obviously investigating a new idea for a business is entirely different from investigating a business that is already thriving and needs growth capital. You will have to adjust the questions you ask according to the stage of development of the business in question.

CHAPTER 2

ANALYSIS OF MANAGEMENT

In analyzing management the investor has one basic objective, to determine if management is entrepreneurial. There are virtually hundreds of thousands of small businesses in the United States today. Some have management that is entrepreneurial; most are not. But, let's understand the term, entrepreneur.

The term *entrepreneur* has undergone a change in meaning since the late 1800s, when it was used to refer to "the director or manager of a public musical institution" (see *The Oxford Universal Dictionary*). *Entrepreneur* derives the French verb *entreprendre* (to undertake), which, however, had already entered English many years earlier in the form of enterprise, from *entrepris*, the past participle of *entreprendre*. *Enterprise* first appeared around 1430 and was commonly used to refer to an undertaking of bold and arduous nature. The person carrying out the enterprise was known as the enterpriser but eventually this term lost ground to *entrepreneur*, the primary meaning of which became "one who organizes, manages, and assumes the risk of a business or enterprise" (see *Webster's*). *Enterpriser* referred primarily to persons taking up a cause, usually warfare for personal gain.

In most instances, the enterpriser was someone who led a small band of men, perhaps a small army, in an attack on a town, usually to pillage. Enterprisers were also known for their ingenuity. Interestingly, some of these original meanings have not been lost. Today's entrepreneurs set out to capture markets, to beat the competition, and to obtain profits.

The Study of Entrepreneurs

Entrepreneurs have been studied at some length over the past thirty years. However, researchers have been hard-pressed to differentiate between small business owners and entrepreneurs. They have had difficulty in differentiating managers in large companies and entrepreneurs. Indeed, researchers have had difficulty in identifying the characteristics of an entrepreneur. One book (which shall remain nameless) has described entrepreneurs as people of small physical stature who have experienced some kind of physical illness in their childhood, had acne as adolescents, and grew up poor and without a good education. Some entrepreneurs are said to have overcome these problems. While it is wonderful to read about those entrepreneurs who have overcome their physical problems and built a business, one must think of all those people who have those same physical attributes but who simply grew up to be average human beings and didn't happen to become entrepreneurs. The book in question strained desperately to name people who were short, had suffered physical illness, and who had overcome all of these in order to build a great business. So it seems to me that the physical attributes that some writers keep pointing to, have little to do with entrepreneurial activity. While I found that book very entertaining; I found very little on which to base future judgments for selecting entrepreneurs. How would you apply this "new knowledge" if you were an investor? Think how silly it would be to measure your entrepreneur's height, to ask if he had a history of personal problems, to check his skin for acne scars, to ask about his physical health as a child, and to use all that as a selection process for backing an entrepreneur. Nothing could be further from good investment management.

Another book that I have read (it shall also remain nameless) sees entrepreneurs as being loaded with guilt and having experienced great deprivation. They are also said to identify strongly with their mothers. I always enjoy reading these psychological evaluations; they are good for a laugh. This same book described entrepreneurs as mostly divorced people. In addition, the writer described their wardrobes and indicated that entrepreneurs would only be happy with shirts that did *not* have button-down collars (so you could get them on and off easily) and shoes that had very thin soles. Those individuals who wore wingtip shoes with very thick soles could not be entrepreneurs. (Women come out well on this one!) Imagine then, how you would analyze the entrepreneur from the investor's point of view. First you would need to do some psychoanalysis to determine if the entrepreneur is loaded with guilt for not accomplishing those goals that his parents or peers seemed to expect of him. Also you would need to determine the degree of deprivation he has undergone to decide if he had risen from sufficiently low ranks. Finally, you would need to know if the individual identified closely with his mother. After you analyzed the "inner being" of the entrepreneur, you would be ready to look at his clothes to see if he had the proper attire, that is, thin-soled shoes and shirts without button-down collars. How ridiculous this approach is for an investor of serious money.

All of these descriptions of entrepreneurs are disastrous simplifications. If anyone used them as investment guidelines, the investor would soon be quite poor. One could just as easily determine that there are not many black entrepreneurs or women entrepreneurs and therefore, that we should not invest in them because they are high-risk propositions. Such oversimplifications will only lead you down the wrong trail. Your best bet is to develop your own knowledge base and apply it to the people you meet who have succeeded as entrepreneurs. Determine what characteristics you think are important for an entrepreneur.

CHARACTERISTICS OF ENTREPRENEURS

Many "scientific" studies of entrepreneurs have been conducted by social scientists. Most of this work has been reported in the trade press. Despite their problems, these studies have produced some very interesting results. The characteristics that they have discovered are the ones that you should look for in the individual you are backing in an enterprise. These are broad characteristics.

In general, social scientists study two sets of characteristics: (1) mental characteristics (such as the need for achievement, need for power, belief that one is in control of one's own destiny, and risk preferences) and (2) behavioral characteristics (such as determination, resourcefulness, a sense of urgency to get things done and a realistic approach to facts). Generally speaking, the mental characteristics have been studied more than the behavioral traits. This is unfortunate because the average person finds it easier to identify the behavioral traits than the mental ones.

Certain physical attributes of entrepreneurs are important as well, such as physical energy level, a better-than-average ability to speak and communicate, and mental stamina.

Finally, there are some other characteristics you *as an investor* will want in an entrepreneur, such as honesty, partnership orientation, and a desire for fair play.

Now let us turn our attention to the attributes most studied because they seem to be present in successful entrepreneurs.

Need for Achievement

Every study of entrepreneurial individuals has demonstrated that entrepreneurs need to achieve. They are competitive to a fault. They must be first. This basic trait makes it very easy to identify entrepreneurs in a business. Start looking at their background. Does the entrepreneur have achievements in his past? Where has this so-called entrepreneur been spending the past few years? Has the entrepreneur been trying to accomplish something? What accomplishment is the entrepreneur proud of? Go through his background in detail and try to determine what achievements have been made. Ask references if the entrepreneur is an achiever and a self-starter. If you cannot demonstrate to your satisfaction that the so-called entrepreneur is driven to succeed, dump him quickly.

High Need for Autonomy and Power

One of the outstanding characteristics of every entrepreneur is a drive to be independent. The entrepreneur wants to be autonomous. He doesn't need the support of any group, he doesn't need to belong to a club or a group or a clique. Most entrepreneurs do not need any nurturing by a mentor. Entrepreneurs need to dominate the situation, need to be in control and to direct others. As a result, many entrepreneurs have poor personal skills. They believe that everyone is motivated in the same way and that employees and associates do not need the kind of personal motivation that most skilled managers recognize they must instill in others. Some entrepreneurs, of course, have excellent people skills.

It will be difficult for you to see the entrepreneur's drive for independence without knowing something about his performance. That is why it is important to talk to the people acting as references and the employees of his firm. Also, if you continue to talk with the entrepreneur and see how he has behaved in the past, you will soon get a clear fix on whether the individual you are talking to has a strong desire for autonomy.

High Degree of Self-Confidence and Need for Control

Most entrepreneurs are very confident about what they are doing. They seem to be emotionally stable and have very high self-esteem. Sometimes this is confused with self-centeredness, but most often their high self-esteem is merely an outward manifestation of their personal self-confidence. Because of this, most entrepreneurs exhibit good leadership and have the ability to set goals and work toward them.

24

In addition, entrepreneurs strongly believe that they can control their own destiny. They believe that fate is responsible for little in their life. Although they may say that luck played a part in their success, they will also state that they took advantage of an opportunity that happened to come along. Some people believe fate will determine who they are and what they will be. This is not how entrepreneurs think. The responsibility for their destiny rests squarely on their own shoulders.

High Tolerance for Ambiguity

Most tests of entrepreneurs have shown that they have a high tolerance for ambiguity. As a result, they are nonconformists by nature and have no strong aversion to change as long as it suits their objectives. Most entrepreneurs are creative when measured on any creative scale, and they are generally curious and interested in almost everything. They are able to judge risks accurately and thus are perceived as risk-takers. Whereas most people would perceive something as a high risk, most entrepreneurs would have the good sense and analytical skill to see through the high risk to a safer way of accomplishing the goal. In doing your background work on the entrepreneur, you should look at his ability to judge risk and his ability to take seemingly ambiguous situations and make sense of them.

Need to Assume Only Moderate Risk

In fact, entrepreneurs are not high risk takers. That is, given the opportunity to (a) take no risk whatsoever and have a small gain, (b) take moderate risk and have a moderate gain, and (c) take a high risk with high gain, entrepreneurs will opt to take moderate risk. In many circles, entrepreneurs are equated with high risk takers. However, many researchers have noted that entrepreneurs are moderate risk takers. Those researchers who have classified entrepreneurs as high risk takers fail to understand that entrepreneurs are analytical by nature and thus are usually able to perceive risk better than most people. This means that where an average person might see high risk, an entrepreneur might perceive only moderate risks. When you are studying your entrepreneur, try to determine his risk profile. If you sense that the entrepreneur is a gambler, don't bet any money on him or you will find a sure loser. If you are interested in high risks, you may as well go to a gambling casino and place your money on the roulette wheel.

High Degree of Determination

Entrepreneurs are a determined lot. They all seem determined to succeed. They want to accomplish things, and their desire to do so is strong. They are able to fix on a goal and reach it. This attitude can be seen in athletes, who become "psyched up" on winning. A sports competitor will imagine that he has won an event and in this way puts himself into a winning frame of mind. Entrepreneurs also exhibit this sense of determination and ability to see a clear win for themselves. Make sure that your entrepreneur is a determined person.

High Degree of Resourcefulness

Entrepreneurs are very resourceful. When problems occur, they are geniuses at finding solutions. When a situation presents itself, they become the consummate problem solver, looking at every area and finding a way to win. They are resourceful to the point of making the rest of us look silly. With their creativity and inquisitiveness, they won't rest until they find a solution. Make sure you know how resourceful the entrepreneur is.

Sense of Urgency

Most studies of entrepreneurs indicate that they have a strong sense of urgency. They are constantly trying to beat the clock. They try to squeeze as many things as possible into each hour of the day. They seem to be in a race against time. They must achieve such and such by a certain deadline. Some entrepreneurs are driven to squeeze so many things into a single day that they end up being late for meetings and don't accomplish everything. These entrepreneurs are out of control and you should avoid them. Any entrepreneur who can't be on time for meetings is most likely "out of control" and is not doing the job right. Make sure you have an entrepreneur who knows his limits, but who also has this sense of urgency to get things done.

Knowing What Is Real

One of the striking characteristics of entrepreneurs is their sense of what is real. Entrepreneurs rarely fool themselves into accepting bad situations. They know they have a marketing program and a sales job to carry out and they do it. But, they are not caught up in their own sales hype or their own promotional fever. They know that the real facts will determine the outcome of events. They have a keen understanding of what is real and what is fabricated. As a result they can get to the bottom of an issue very quickly. When you are discussing projections with entrepreneurs, see if they are blowing smoke or if they have their feet on the ground. A good long discussion about their projections will demonstrate whether they are in touch with reality or are on "cloud nine."

High Level of Energy

Entrepreneurs must have a high level of energy in order to succeed. Being an entrepreneur involves enormous amounts of time and energy. Every successful entrepreneur I have financed has had tremendous energy. If the person you are looking at doesn't have a high energy level, then you may not want to be his backer. The health of the individual is therefore important. If the person is not healthy, he may break under the stress of being an entrepreneur. In order to determine the state of his health, ask the entrepreneur if he is insurable. Ask how his health is, ask him if he's been sick in the recent past. You can easily determine the health of your entrepreneur by inquiring about a life insurance policy. He will need a physical to have the insurance. What you will have trouble determining is the energy level of the entrepreneur. However, in your reference checks you can find out about his energy level.

One of the things that I routinely do is to call entrepreneurs early in the morning. I happen to be an early riser and I call to see if they are at work early in the morning. I also call late at night to see if they are still working. Entrepreneuring takes many hours of the day, and if your entrepreneur is a late riser or an early quitter, he probably will not be successful.

Strong Communications Skills

Most entrepreneurs have good social skills and are adept at persuading and conversing with people. You can spot these skills in conversations with the entrepreneur. If the entrepreneur is able to explain his proposal in a winning style, this will be an outward manifestation of self-confidence and social persuasiveness. If he seems to have an outgoing personality and good presence, this, too, will indicate his great self-confidence. And if he seems to be emotionally stable, this will be evidence of his strong self-confidence. Some writers think that entrepreneurs come from broken families, are riddled with guilt about things in their past, come from divorced families, and usually end up divorced themselves. According to my own perception of the world, as well as the reports I've read on entrepreneurship, none of this is true. It is a common myth that an entrepreneur is so driven that he inevitably destroys his own family. In reality, divorce among entrepreneurs is no

27

greater than in corporate America, where people are under stress. As far as guilt is concerned, none of the entrepreneurs I have backed appeared to be guilt-ridden, felt that they had to achieve to satisfy their mother or father, or seemed bent on overcoming some past problem in their lives. All of the entrepreneurs I have known have had their own reasons for success, but it's usually been something that comes from within and has not been based on some incident in their childhood. They have decided to be measured by business success and are driven to make a good showing.

Mental Stamina

In addition, most entrepreneurs have tremendous mental stamina. That is, they can think about problems for hours on end without getting tired or giving up. It is not unusual for an entrepreneur to work long, long hours on mental problems. This mental stamina is a key skill of entrepreneurs and it is used to their advantage. You will soon have an idea of the entrepreneur's mental stamina after you have "interrogated" him about the many issues of his business for a day. If, at the end of the day, the entrepreneur is physically exhausted and is unable to give you satisfactory answers, you will have your answer. He may not be the type of entrepreneur you will want to back.

High Degree of Integrity

Most entrepreneurs are honest in their approach to the world. Of course, a number of entrepreneurs have cheated and lied their way through life. As an investor, you want to make sure that your entrepreneur is honest and straightforward. If you invest in a dishonest entrepreneur, somewhere along the way you will be done in; the entrepreneur will get rich but not the investor. In order to determine an entrepreneur's honesty, during your interview you can ask the same question twice, but do it at different times in the interview and see if he answers the same way both times. Sometimes an entrepreneur who is lying will trip up in answering the same question. Also during the interview, you may find an entrepreneur avoiding a question. Question avoidance is a sure sign that the entrepreneur is hiding something he doesn't want to reveal.

In checking the references of entrepreneurs, one of the questions I always ask is, do you think the person is honest? Although the more conservative references will avoid answering the question directly if they think the individual is dishonest, you can usually tell whether the reference is giving the entrepreneur an unqualified recommendation in the area of honesty. Credit records, too, will reflect his honesty. If the entrepreneur has a history of not paying his bills, what makes you think he's ever going to give you any money back? As an investor in a venture capital situation, you can never be too careful with entreprencurs. It's much better to have an entrepreneur who is honest than one who cheats and lies.

However, it's not unusual for an entrepreneur to use what business schools call "constructive deceit" during negotiation. This means that the entrepreneur and you as the investor have the right to "tell white lies" in order to advance your negotiation position. In discussing subjects with an entrepreneur you may not want to give the real reason why you don't want to do something, for if you told him that you didn't want to do it because you didn't like it, you might destroy the relationship between you and the entrepreneur. So, as a negotiating position, you use constructive deceit. That is, you tell the entrepreneur that your board of directors would not approve of such a thing and therefore you can't go forward. In this way, you can avoid a confrontation with the entrepreneur and maintain your personal relationship with him.

You should also expect the entrepreneur to use the same kind of constructive deceit to protect his position. Don't be surprised when you find the entrepreneur hasn't been honest to a fault and you have caught him in a little white lie. It's usually harmless and not worth mentioning. Studies have shown that telling white lies does not prove that the person is a thief or a crook.

Another term used in this regard is "intellectual honesty." This means that the person only expresses views and examples that he believes in. There are, of course, those who will say or do things in order to sway your opinion. For example, a car salesman may tell a woman that she looks terrific in a red car, when he doesn't think so. Or, the salesman may say that a product is the most beautiful ever made, when he really believes it is quite ugly. In our society, we expect salespersons to be intellectually dishonest when they offer subjective opinions. We know they must sell a product to earn a living and so we expect them to be intellectually dishonest when giving their opinions on the product they are selling. You should expect your entrepreneur to be intellectually dishonest about his business in the same way. His product may not be judged the best product by others, but the entrepreneur will "think" it is the best.

Intellectual dishonesty becomes a more serious matter when it applies to the performance of the product or to facts that can be proved. For example, the car salesman who tells a prospective buyer that a six-cylinder engine is as good as an eight-cylinder engine can be proved wrong. Sure, it may be just as good in stop-and-go traffic, but not on the freeway. The entrepreneur who tells you the performance of his product is as good as that of his competitor's product in the face of objective evaluations that say otherwise is lying. Don't fault your entrepreneur for trying to convince you of the worth of his product, but do avoid those people who can't accept reality and continue to tell you they are right and all others are wrong.

Seeking Partnership Status

The entrepreneur you are backing should see you as a partner and not as an investor. Investors as such don't usually fair well in the venture capital environment. Investors need to become partners. You can do this by spending a good deal of time with the entrepreneur so that you become friends and establish that you are both seeking the same goals - to make him rich and to make you rich. In this partnership your side of the equation is as important as the entrepreneur's. You must do your part in the partnership and not try to sandbag the entrepreneur with some special legal provision that reduces his equity or places him in a weak position. You need to maintain your relationship as partners and work with the entrepreneur. Make sure your entrepreneur wants to be a partner. It is the best kind of relationship in venture capital deals.

Seeking Fair Play

Also make sure that your entrepreneur is seeking fair play from you and that he knows you are seeking fair play from him. Explain any problems that arise or any situations that come up that might suggest you are not playing fair. If you pull a surprise on the entrepreneur along the way, then he will believe that you are not working in good faith. If you ever find yourself pitted against the entrepreneur, remember that he has most of the tricks up his sleeve and that henceforth you will have a hard time working with him. Seek out the entrepreneur who has a high sense of fair play and honesty and you'll be on stronger ground.

In reviewing an entrepreneur's background, it will be hard for you to determine whether he has all of the characteristics mentioned above. To get a proper perspective of the entrepreneur you will have to adopt a special way of thinking.

HOW WE SEE ENTREPRENEURS

The problem with the venture capital business is that when we analyze people, our perceptions of others are usually wrong. Perhaps not entirely wrong, but at best the judgments we make of entrepreneurs are vague and unverifiable. Unfortunately, we tend to tag people with traits that summarize past behavior or current observations that we believe will predict future behavior. The problem is *specific* behavior may not necessarily be repeated and therefore cannot be used to generalize or to predict future behavior in other areas. We observe a single incidence of a person's behavior and try to generalize from that one incident. We try to place a general trait tag on an individual after observing a few specific instances.

The classical example of a trait that people are often tagged with is honesty. We say a person is honest or dishonest on the basis of a few observations. The label implies that the person will be honest/dishonest in *all* future relationships. Trying to determine whether an entrepreneur is honest is difficult because there are so few opportunities for us to observe the entrepreneur's behavior. We dig into his background and references looking for clues. But most often we lack enough data to determine whether an entrepreneur is honest or will be in the future.

Even when we do have more data, there is usually conflicting evidence. The problem with trying to test someone's honesty is that, according to most studies, we all have done things that could be used to tag us as dishonest. Most people are not honest to a fault. They do some things that could be considered dishonest, but will not do other dishonest things. For example, a person might keep an article he has found but might not lie about his athletic achievement. Some people might lie about their athletic achievement, but might not cheat on an exam. In the retail trade, there are employees who might take store merchandise home, but might not take cash from the register. How many people take their employer's paper and pencils home for personal use? How many people actually give the company a full eight hours of work (not goof-off time) every day? So, who is completely honest? How can we judge anyone to be honest? How can we predict they will be honest in the future?

Other traits - like persistence, dependency, conformity, aggressiveness, and so on are just as difficult to measure as honesty. Furthermore, some traits we decide to look at in entrepreneurs don't have much predictive value at all. I have noticed in my own description of one entrepreneur terms like *good*, *kind*, *fair*, and *nice*. With these vague words I am not really describing the person; rather I am expressing my approval of the person, saying that I like him or her. This type of personal opinion doesn't have much predictive value.

How We Make Judgments

When we judge people we are indicating what standard of behavior we expect or what standard we live by. We develop these ideas about how people should behave through years of experience. In making our judgment, however, we do not analyze the pros and cons of someone else's behavior at great length. Normally, we react spontaneously and depend on intuition to be our guide. But intuition is fallible. Yet it is the way most of us apply traits to various people. In essence, intuition is a skill that has been so thoroughly learned that we use it unconsciously. Thus, when someone lies about his athletic skills, we judge him to be *not* honest. When another person keeps a lost pen without asking who lost it, we may approve that action and not brand that individual as dishonest. All of us subconsciously consult a particular list of behavior traits to test "honesty," and we apply it intuitively, without questioning our underlying assumptions.

Intuition rapidly evaluates the data that we receive and forms an opinion. Some people require more data than others before they are ready make a judgment; others are quick to reach a decision, sometimes on the basis of only one event (a snap judgment). Most people take written information, references, interviews, and any other information they pick up, and feed it into their minds, where they match it against the set of tests that they use in judging people.

The problem is that as we learn more facts about an entrepreneur, it is *unlikely* that all of these facts will point in the same direction. For example, some information may suggest the person is honest, whereas a small amount may indicate dishonesty in certain situations. So we begin to weigh each piece of information for its predictive value. Intuitively, we set up a checklist and put pluses and minuses alongside each item according to whether it's a good point, an irrelevant point, or a bad point. Then we add the points to see if the entrepreneur has passed our test. We may even use a very complex system wherein certain items are given much more weight than others on the grounds that they are much more important to the prediction of behavior or for this investment situation. We use these pluses and minuses intuitively because we have done it many times in our daily interaction with others. Although intuition may be a reliable guide for someone who has interviewed thousands of entrepreneurs, it is to be trusted by the rest of us. We need to approach our evaluation of entrepreneurs analytically.

Analytical Approach to Evaluations

What makes evaluation more complex is that every venture capitalist has his own separate system of judging entrepreneurs, which is based on personal experience. One venture capitalist may decide a certain entrepreneur is honest, whereas another might *not* give the entrepreneur the tag "honest" because he failed on one point that the venture capitalist considered critical. The way to handle this situation is simple. After you have investigated and interviewed an entrepreneur a number of times, you should make a list of items that you have observed about the individual and see if you can use them to reach a logical conclusion about the traits reflected by these items. Appendix 4 lists examples of traits that a venture capitalist would be concerned about.

Look at the traits in Appendix 4 and decide whether you agree or disagree that each is descriptive of the entrepreneur. Make sure you have a basis for tagging the entrepreneur with each trait; question each judgment. Once you do this, you will better understand the individual. If two venture capitalists have interviewed the entrepreneur, compare trait lists. Talk about the entrepreneur to get a good feel for the individual. As soon as you think you understand the entrepreneur, try to answer the following three sets of questions below:

1. How will the entrepreneur treat you and your venture capital company? Will he try to do you in? How will he treat you if the company is in trouble? How will he treat you if the company is going to make a ton of money? Give you a screw job? Or will he be happy that you are making money too?

2. Are the traits of the entrepreneur the ones needed to be successful in the industry he is in? How will the industry react to this person? Do these traits match up with the keys to success in the industry?

3. Are these traits the ones that will make this specific business successful? Will these traits be accepted by employees? Will they be accepted by professionals like lawyers, bankers, and accountants?

This approach should help you put some thought into the judging of entrepreneurs. It is not scientific but it is a logical approach that is bound to be more reliable than snap decisions.

INTERVIEWING ENTREPRENEURS

One of the venture capitalist's greatest sources of information is the interview with an entrepreneur. However, interviewing won't produce much in the way of information unless it's done correctly. Here are a few pointers on how to improve your interviewing skills so the interview will yield more information.

Be Prepared

Make a list of the information you want to learn from the entrepreneur during the interview. What precisely are you looking for? An interview that rambles through a person's background and business situation won't reveal nearly as much as one that has a specific focus. So make notes as you read the materials supplied to you by the entrepreneur and organize your questions around these notes before you meet with the entrepreneur.

Clear Mind

All good interviewers approach the interview with a *clear mind*. Research shows that an individual who has a clear idea of what he's trying to determine and whose mind is not cluttered with other problems or situations around him will come away with a great deal of information.

So, enter the interview with a clear mind. If you are worried about missing a plane or another meeting, or if you have other things on your mind, your questions will be less effective and the answers less informative than if you are "tuned up" with sharp questions and "tuned in" to each answer.

Conducive Environment

An interview should not be constantly interrupted or conducted in an environment of distractions. Hold telephone calls, stop people from barging in, and don't break into the interview to do something else. Don't hold the interview in a public place like a restaurant. An uninterrupted interview will yield much more than one punctuated with interruptions.

Always go into an interview with more than enough time. One long interview per day is about all that anyone can accomplish, so don't plan more that. An interview can't be completed well if you are in a hurry or have something else on your mind. Also, make sure the entrepreneur has plenty of time and has scheduled the interview as *the* major event of the day. Plan your interviews well, and they will yield golden nuggets of information.

Be an Effective Listener

Effective listening means encouraging the candidate to talk openly about his situation. Candidates who feel encouraged will provide better information than those who do not. Also, an interviewer who can see a candidate accurately can encourage him in the proper direction. During the interview, try to establish an atmosphere in which both you and the entrepreneur are in the right frame of mind. Be sure you have enough time to get to know each other. When the entrepreneur is talking, *don't interrupt.* Don't try to show how smart *you* are, let the entrepreneur show you how smart *he or she is.* Talk just enough to get the entrepreneur to open up and tell you what he really means. A nice joke will often show that you are friendly and let the entrepreneur "open up." Use silence constructively; that is, don't feel you have to keep the air full of questions. Let the room fill up with silence and usually the entrepreneur will volunteer more information. When the entrepreneur talks, pay attention, and look as though you are paying attention. If you aren't listening, it will show and the entrepreneur will say less.

Keep on Your Toes during the Interview

A very unusual process takes place when you interview an entrepreneur. You carry out several mental tasks simultaneously and switch from one to the other. A good interviewer focuses on specific points and has a rational approach to things. At times, an interviewer might let intuition come into play in order to pick up on some nuances or rationalizations made by the entrepreneur and bring those back into the question-and-answer session.

At other times, you might need to step back and see the whole interaction in order to determine whether additional questions are needed and where holes need filling in. You may ask the same critical question twice in an interview just to see if it is answered the same way both times. Inconsistency may be a sign of dishonesty. Interviewing is tough work. It can be a tremendously complex event marked by both strain and exhilaration as you push forward looking for information.

Types of Interviews

There are two types of interviews. The first type is a panel or *group interview.* That is, a group of venture capitalists may interview one entrepreneur or an entrepreneur and two or three of the top management. In this situation, the entrepreneur is facing several interviewers at once and may be more formal and less open. On the other hand, when a group of questions is being asked, the interviewers tend to be sharper and more focused and are able to probe into the situation owing to the interaction of the panel members.

The second type is the *individual interview.* It can be more intimate and offers the entrepreneur an opportunity to open up and provide personal information that one doesn't talk about in groups.

35

Usually you can get more personal information in a one-on-one interview.

Both of these types of interviews are useful, but the individual interview is a must. It is the only way to really get to know that person.

Document Your Work

After every interview, you should document your discussion. Keep a piece of paper handy while you are interviewing and make notes to yourself. Later, you may want to dictate a memo for the file. I usually make copious notes during the interview, although I find it advisable to keep the paper on which I'm making notes out of sight of the entrepreneur. When people see you taking notes, they tend to be more formal.

In summary, you should enter an interview with a clear and extremely alert mind. You can't have distractions. Also, you've got to review the entrepreneur's material beforehand so that you will know what you're looking for. You should have read the business plan and looked through the person's resume. You have to be prepared. Walking in and wandering through the business situation is a very inefficient use of time.

The cardinal rule for an interviewer is to be an effective listener and to encourage candidates to continue to talk.

ASSESSMENT OF ENTREPRENEURS

In assessing the abilities of an entrepreneur, we can gain information about the effective techniques from some of the industrial psychologists. At my venture capital firm, we've never used psychological tests or industrial psychologists except in one situation, and that was a special one. For your enjoyment, the second part of Appendix 4 includes a psychological assessment of the current president of a major company.

The industrial psychological approach does not try to tell you why people act the way they do, it tries to tell you how able a person is. The industrial psychologist tries to avoid relying on many of the outward appearances of the individual. There is a considerable body of evidence that in some situations people are motivated either consciously or unconsciously to present themselves in what they believe to be a favorable light. This kind of "play acting" can lead you to misread a person. Therefore industrial psychologists try to identify factors that truly reflect the individuals character. For example, an expert will not automatically rate a lively outgoing conversationalist higher than the shy introvert, or consider the highly educated person more clever than those who may not have had the same educational opportunities. And the successful business record is not taken at face value by a probing expert. Like the industrial psychologists, investors need to hone their techniques so that they are not misled by outward appearances.

The aim of the industrial psychologists is to discover not only how intelligent a person is, but also how effective that person is in applying his abilities to various contexts. Most of us do not have the skills of industrial psychologists, but we can learn from the things they do. They try to construct an oversimplified model of the person that can be used to predict how he or she will behave in doing the required work. In applying this model, industrial psychologists are not trying to discover the causes of any particular behavior but are simply hoping to predict behavior. In essence, they are trying to predict how the person (in the most important job in the company) will react to various situations.

Industrial psychologists usually administer a large set of written tests to an entrepreneur. Although such tests have been used by some venture capitalists, they are not fully accepted and are probably not something that venture capitalists can use to any extent. This leaves us with the interview and conversation with the entrepreneur. An important point to remember is that people normally speak at 125 words a minute, but we can think and comprehend conversation at 500-600 words per minute. This means that we have ample opportunity during interviews and discussions with the entrepreneurs to pick up many of the subtle clues and basic information that will lead us to a sound decision about the person.

The first thing to do when you are spending the day with an entrepreneur is to outline what you expect to do during the day. This may put him at ease and give you more information about his approach to life. One of the things industrial psychologists ask the entrepreneur to do is to describe his life history. Initially the entrepreneur may be a little slow, but after a little encouragement most people enjoy talking about where they grew up, their parents, their outlook on life, and how they arrived at the position they find themselves in now. Most people will give you a detailed history of their business experience. It is very important to listen. Often, I must stop myself from interrupting an entrepreneur while he is talking. I find I must tolerate the pauses he makes in order to let him think out what he is going to say. Industrial psychologists frequently use open-ended questions and encourage the entrepreneur to talk about himself freely. In this kind of open and friendly interview, attitudes and opinions of the entrepreneur will inevitably emerge as well as many facts about the person's behavior. If you are a good listener, evidence in the form of recurring themes and patterns of behavior will reveal themselves. For example, the person who has consistently made major decisions for himself in the past is likely to continue to do so in the future, and the person who has always led an essentially solitary life is unlikely to change into a highly gregarious person.

The industrial psychologist usually concentrates on three basic areas which I briefly review below as they will enlighten you about some of the things you should be looking for.

1. **Intellectual Effectiveness.** Here, you are trying to compare the manager with the entire management population you've ever known in order to determine whether this manager is in the top 5% of those you have worked with. The following questions will help you establish his intellectual effectiveness:

   Is the entrepreneur a quick learner? A conceptual thinker? Can he work quickly and accurately with numbers? Does he have good verbal skills? Does he have the ability to communicate orally as well as in writing? Is he an objective thinker or is he strongly influenced by his emotions (there is now a considerable body of evidence that successful executives are able to be more logical and objective than are the less successful ones)? Is he really a critical thinker or does he let his preconceived notions set the pace? Is this person able to produce original ideas? Is he imaginative or strictly conventional?

2. **Work Approach and Style.** Is the entrepreneur a generalist or is he detail-minded? Does he believe in having a thorough knowledge of minor matters or does he dismiss detailed items as irrelevant? Does the entrepreneur recognize priorities and know which things are important and should be put first? In his decision-making approach, is he impulsive or cautious, slow or confident? Just how does he go about making decisions? What kind of strategist is the entrepreneur? Is he a long-term planner? A short-term tactician? How energetic is the entrepreneur? Is he restrained or explosive? Is he vigorous, efficient? How does he tolerate pressure? Is he stable, or is he easily pushed off the edge? How would the entrepreneur react to emergencies? Is he calm or frustrated? How would you measure his ambitions, and how important is his success to him? Will he sacrifice the interests of others? Will he sacrifice Allied's interest to his own objectives? Are his aims realistic? How flexible is he? Can he handle a number of tasks in parallel? How adaptable is he? Can he adjust to different environments?

3.   **Personal Relationships**. What kind of relationships does the entrepreneur have with his superiors? Is he frank, stubborn, loyal, amenable? What relationship does he have with his peers? Is he friendly, cooperative, tolerant, a team person, highly competitive, a loner? What relationship will he have with subordinates? Is he domineering, protective, decisive, sensitive? Is he willing to delegate responsibilities? And what relationship does he have with outsiders? Is he confident, careful, courteous, disdainful?

When an industrial psychologist is finished, he usually summarizes the person's traits and lists the positives and the negatives. For example, the psychologist might say that the person is industrious and energetic, that he is flexible and can adapt to change, that he is decisive, above average in his ability to communicate clearly, and imaginative, and that he makes a good first impression. The psychologist might also list the individual's limitations: For example, his basic intellectual power may be a little below average, his judgment of emotionally toned situations suspect, and analytical skills below average; he may unstable and insecure, hypersensitive and quick to take offense, unable to sustain a seemingly cheerful and friendly manner, and not be at his best on a team.
This does not suggest that you should employ an industrial psychologist or that you should try to become an amateur industrial psychologist. However, it is interesting to see how professionals go about their tasks. I believe that all venture capitalists can learn something from these situations which will help them become better at judging entrepreneurs. Although industrial psychologists can give us a general understanding of the individual, they cannot determine whether that individual will perform well in his chosen field or area. We can look for general characteristics in entrepreneurs, but by themselves these will not indicate whether the individual is going to be successful in his chosen field. What we have to do is determine the keys to success in the business situation and in the industry that we're looking at and determine if the individual has the matching personal traits. Entrepreneurs should have certain general traits. However, some specific traits are also required for success in each industry.

WHAT VENTURE CAPITALISTS SEEK IN ENTREPRENEURS

Since 1974 I have been working with venture capitalists and asking them what they look for in an entrepreneur. Generally speaking, the answers fall into two categories. The first category concerns individual characteristics and the second the experience of the individual.

The Entrepreneur's Individual Characteristics

Staying Power. Venture capitalists want an entrepreneur who is capable of intense effort over a long period of time. Venture capitalists know that 90% of every venture success comes from perspiration not inspiration. They know that if a small business is to succeed, the management team is going to have to work long hours to compensate for the lack of employees at the company.

Handle Risk. Venture capitalists look for an individual who has the intellectual power to evaluate risk and know what to do after the evaluation. Every small business twists and turns many times during its life, and the early years are the most traumatic. An entrepreneur must be capable of analyzing situations, evaluating the probability of success, and implementing a plan. Unless they are able to evaluate risk and analyze complex situations, small businesses usually remain small businesses.

Verbal Ability. Venture capitalists need an entrepreneur who can articulate an idea. Many people have tremendous minds but lack the ability to explain their thoughts to the outside world. Without the ability to speak accurately and convincingly, most small businesses will fail. In the early years, an entrepreneur must persuade vendors to give him credit, persuade banks to give him money, persuade employees to work long hours, and persuade government authorities to let him do something that no one else can do. It is this verbal ability that sets most entrepreneurs apart from scientific inventors and small business people. If your entrepreneur lacks the ability to persuade, you are probably making a mistake by investing in him.

Detail Orientation. Some find it almost contradictory that venture capitalists want an entrepreneur who knows the details. Most of us think that good entrepreneurs worry about the big picture and hire other people to handle the details. This perception couldn't be further from the truth. An entrepreneur must carry an inordinate amount of detail around in his mind and be able to use it all to the best advantage of his company. Details about numbers as well as the situation will need quick reactions and an individual with the ability to do it. Without this attention to detail and knowledge of the specifics, most small businesses can't grow.

Compatible Personality. Believe it or not, venture capitalists most often invest in an entrepreneur who has a personality that is compatible with their own. Compatible personalities may not be at the top of anyone's list, but entrepreneurs are not financed unless they are compatible with their venture capital source. It is indeed like a marriage. Most people don't get married unless they like each other. Venture capitalists don't "marry" entrepreneurs unless they like them. Even if an entrepreneur is capable of meeting many of the problems in a situation, a venture capitalist will not invest unless he can stand "living with" the individual. I remember reviewing a restaurant situation some years ago in which I liked the investment opportunity, but found the entrepreneur obnoxious. I knew I would not be able to stand working with him over the ensuing years and therefore we didn't make the investment.

Experience of the Entrepreneur

Market Knowledge. Venture capitalists don't have the time to learn about a marketplace in detail. For this reason, venture capitalists want to know above all that the entrepreneur has a thorough knowledge of the marketplace. It is rare that a venture capitalist will back an entrepreneur who has little or no experience in a business area. It is common knowledge that an individual needs at least two years to understand an industry. No one wants to finance on-the-job training for an entrepreneur.

Track Record. Venture capitalists would like to back people who have a track record, especially a track record relevant to the situation. Ten years ago we were about to back an entrepreneur who wanted to buy a business that was a "turnaround." The individual seemed to have the proper background, in that he had turned around several businesses and made a substantial profit for his investors in the past. The difficulty was that he had not been involved in a turnaround in this particular industry and therefore we felt we should not invest. The track record of an entrepreneur is something that a venture capitalist will investigate time and time again. He will look for achievements in the individual's background and he will look for achievements in the specific industry in which he is about to invest. This is a key point for every venture capitalist.

Leadership. Every venture capitalist is looking for a leader for the company. Any time a venture capitalist backs an entrepreneur without leadership, they have inevitably had trouble and had to replace the entrepreneur. Therefore, venture capitalists look for entrepreneurs who have been in leadership positions in the past and who have demonstrated their abilities conclusively. Without leadership, the company is probably not going to go anywhere.

Reputation. Venture capitalists are looking for entrepreneurs with outstanding reputations. They want trustworthy people. They are about to give a great deal of money to these people and they want to be sure the recipients are above reproach. Every venture capitalist in the business can give you a long lament about some entrepreneur who took money. If there is any hint that the reputation of the entrepreneur is not 100% solid, experienced venture capitalists will not invest.

CHARACTERISTICS OF SMALL BUSINESS PEOPLE

In trying to differentiate a small business person from an entrepreneur, one thing usually shines through. Although a small business person wants to build the business, he has a more immediate concern: to take as much cash out of the company as possible. He will usually run it as a subchapter-S corporation. He will have a big car and a great many perks and other items of self-aggrandizement. All of these factors indicate that the individual is interested in taking money out of the company rather than reinvesting it in the growth of the company. This usually means that, as soon as the business starts to grow, the company will run into a cash crunch. This is usually when they end up on the doorstep of a venture capitalist, seeking additional capital to do the things that they should have been doing with their money earlier.

I remember one situation in which two individuals had come up with a unique line of cosmetics. It was a product that could be duplicated by others but this group probably had a two- or three-year jump on the competition. They enjoyed a great reputation after making this cosmetic discovery. Instead of using the huge profits that the company generated in the initial years to hire a chief marketing person, an outstanding sales manager, a good controller to keep the books accurately so an audit could be taken, and staff who could provide good quality control, these two entrepreneurs began to draw such enormous salaries that the company's main purpose became to pay their salaries. At the end of three years, they approached my company for investment capital. Having each taken over $1,000,000 out of the business and invested it personally, they felt secure. The only problem was that by the time they had reached me, three major competitors were offering the same product and a giant cosmetic company had just introduced a similar line. Instead of having a two-year time horizon in which to build the business into a great company, these two were staring with a hopelessly small company with little or no chance of growth. They were eagerly pawing over a registration statement that had raised $20,000,000 for 25% of a small cosmetic company. The other company had started two years after they had begun their operation and had copied their concept completely about a year before. The difference was that the entrepreneurs behind this second company had plowed everything back into the business and built it into a money machine. Sales had more than tripled in three years, whereas in the company that had come to me sales had remained flat. It was a sad sight to see two individuals who could have been worth $30,000,000 or $40,000,000 who instead had only their nest eggs of $1,000,000 locked away. They had missed a great opportunity.

In reviewing small business people and entrepreneurs, and trying to differentiate between the two, you will find that the immediate need for cash and status is a sign of a small business person, whereas the desire to plow money back into the business and take a long-term outlook toward capital gains on sale of the stock at some future date is a characteristic of an entrepreneur.

CONCLUSIONS ON ENTREPRENEURS

When you are analyzing the entrepreneur you should first record five things you like about the entrepreneur and five things you dislike. As you begin your relationship, you will find the numbers in the "like" column add up. Most of them should be in the areas outlined above. If you find a lot of comments in the "dislike" column, you should not make the investment. Every investment that my company has ever made in which we had reservations about the entrepreneur has turned into a very difficult situation for us. When you find something negative about the entrepreneur, try to understand the circumstances and ask yourself whether you would have done the same thing the entrepreneur did in that situation. If the answer is yes, you probably have to overlook it and continue your analysis.

If, however, you find a situation in which you don't believe you would have done the same thing as the entrepreneur, outline what you would have done differently. Then confront the entrepreneur with the situation and ask why he didn't go forward in that manner. Sometimes in a relationship with an entrepreneur you will uncover things that seem to be quite negative. If you don't ask about these negatives and just go your merry way without making the investment, you may have missed a great opportunity. I know several situations in which potential negatives came out in the reviewing process. After confronting the entrepreneur with these situations, we heard the answers, which straightened things out, and we made the investment. If we had not spent the time confronting the entrepreneur with the problems we were having with the situation, we would have missed a good opportunity. Appearances are not always what they seem. You need to dig behind almost everything, especially the negatives in an entrepreneur's background.

DEVELOPING BACKGROUND INFORMATION

Now you need to develop the background information on the entrepreneurs in an organized fashion. To this end, we have the following areas to analyze and develop information.

Personal References

Ask the entrepreneur to supply references, beginning with personal references. These will be people who know the entrepreneur, but are not part of his business relationships. They are usually friends, relatives, and teachers. They may know a great deal about the individual, but not much about his business.

These references should supply information about the personality of the individual and about the entrepreneur's personal habits. You are trying to discover if the entrepreneur indulges in alcohol or drugs or is involved in nonsocial behavior that will be detrimental to your business. For example, in checking one personal reference, we determined that the individual was highly asocial. When we asked him about this, he admitted that he had a problem and was understanding when we declined the investment because he knew that if the business community learned about it the business would be destroyed. This kind of risk was far greater than the expected return on this investment. Once you have finished a personal reference, you should prepare a written record of the inquiry, indicating how that person answered the questions you asked.

Business References

You also want to ask the entrepreneur for a number of business references. These are people who have been in business situations with the entrepreneur and know how he operates. There are three basic groups to consult for this information.

The first group consists of **inside references**. These are people such as superiors, associates, or subordinates in his current business position or past business positions. Someone who was the entrepreneur's boss for ten years may give you great insights into this individual's past. A cohort with whom he worked five years ago can also be helpful in determining the entrepreneur's business ethics. I remember asking one business reference about an entrepreneur and being told: "I don't know why the little S.O.B. gave me as a reference. He worked for me for two years and did nothing more than ride around in his car and got nothing done. He was a disgrace to my organization." It's not often that you will find such references, but, every now and then even a good entrepreneur makes the mistake of giving a bad reference.

The second group of business references are **outside references**. These are people such as competitors, suppliers, or buyers of their product. They are the ones who come into contact with the entrepreneur in a business relationship that is not inside the business. Quite often the competition will know a great deal about the entrepreneur, especially if he has moved from one competitor to another. This kind of inside information can be very revealing.

The third type of business reference comprises **professional references**. These are bankers, accountants, and lawyers who have worked with or for the entrepreneur in some business relationship in the past. Sometimes the entrepreneur will give you the name of a consultant who he has used as a reference. Consultants can tell you whether an entrepreneur used their services efficiently, or ignored their recommendations. This information will tell you whether an entrepreneur is willing to take advice from experienced people in the business. Some references may not give all the information that you want, but nonetheless will speak in reasonably positive terms about the entrepreneur. You should therefore ask each reference who else might know the entrepreneur well. In this way, you can generate other references on the entrepreneur and find out if they think the same way as the primary reference. Sometimes an entrepreneur will use a boss who he merely reports to, but does not work for directly, as his reference. If possible, you should try to determine who the direct supervisors are and seek them out. They may be left off the reference list because they have some good information that the entrepreneur doesn't want you to know.

Credit Reports

Credit reporting agencies can be used for obtaining additional information on the entrepreneurs. Some, such as the credit bureau, specialize in personal reports. These give you information on an individual's personal credit. They can be quite interesting to read, especially if you find the entrepreneur has borrowed lots of money and has been extremely slow in paying back personal debts. Also, the bankruptcies occasionally show up in these credit reports.

In addition, reports put out by agencies such as Dun & Bradstreet can be used to evaluate entrepreneurs who have had previous small businesses. These can give you very insightful information on the payment history of the small business that the entrepreneur worked for. You can see how the entrepreneur ran the past small business from a financial viewpoint.

In addition, you can hire agencies such as Bishops Reports to collect detailed information about entrepreneurs, for example, from county courthouses where the entrepreneur has lived. Although this is a more expensive approach, it will provide you with a detailed credit history of the individual.

Private Investigators

Private investigators are not hired to check out the background of an entrepreneur. However, from time to time one is forced to use this method of obtaining information. If you are thinking of hiring a private investigator to check out an entrepreneur, it most likely means some basic things are wrong and that you probably shouldn't invest in the entrepreneur. However, private investigators can be used. One who helped us once determined that the entrepreneur had had a drinking problem in a past job and that he had been fired for being an "alcoholic." However, when we confronted the entrepreneur with the situation, he explained that at the time he was going through a divorce. It was an extremely emotional and stressful experience and he had turned to alcohol for a short period. He demonstrated conclusively that he was no longer alcohol dependent and had only been involved in this life-style for a short period in his career. This was an acceptable answer and it checked out with later investigations. The investment was subsequently approved by a board of directors.

Psychological Assessment Test

We've talked about psychological tests and hiring industrial psychologists to conduct them. Some of these tests have proved quite fruitful in reviewing middle management in large corporations, and even upper management to some degree. They have been used on a very limited scale by venture capitalists. I don't know why they haven't been used, but basically most venture capitalists believe that they are adept enough at assessing entrepreneurs to do without psychological tests. It's also quite demeaning to ask entrepreneurs to take psychological tests in order to determine if they are good entrepreneurs.

Written Information

The entrepreneur will provide you with reams of written information, some of it containing details about the entrepreneur. There will be brochures about the business and blurbs about the entrepreneurs, along with copies of articles they have published in newspapers and trade magazines; these articles will also describe the business and the entrepreneurs. These sources contain information about the individuals that you should not overlook. Reviewing them will give you inside scoop on the entrepreneur.

In addition, you should ask the entrepreneur to provide a detailed resume on each of the key people in his organization, including himself. This resume will summarize the history of the entrepreneur and the other key principals in the company, from early schooling through the current period. The resume should lay out in chronological order where the entrepreneur has been most of his life. If it doesn't, ask the entrepreneur to do a resume in that manner. In this way you can make sure there are no unexplained gaps in the entrepreneur's background.

I remember one entrepreneur who presented me with a resume that hadn't covered three years of his background. All other credit references had checked out completely and everything seemed to be in good order. However, as I pressed the entrepreneur for more information about this three-year period, he grew vague and said he must have put the wrong dates down. Since this was more than ten years ago, he was not sure of the dates and would have to get back to me on that. This intrigued me, and I checked further on the individual's background. After talking to a lawyer in a town where he had been located, I found that the individual had been involved in a fraud and had been sent to prison for three years. None of this information had been revealed in credit reports or any of the other references that I had checked. It was only by closely examining the entrepreneur's background year by year that I was able to detect this fact about the entrepreneur's background.

Nor should you take the written information presented by the entrepreneur at face value. Entrepreneurs have been known to "exaggerate" their achievements. In telephoning colleges and universities to confirm an entrepreneur's credentials, I have only once uncovered a false statement in this regard. This along with other factors helped to kill the deal.

There is also the story about an entrepreneur who presented a detailed resume to a group of venture capitalists. Records at his high school and everywhere else indicated that he had graduated from that school, that he had worked, that he had gone to college in a good midwestern town, and that he had graduated from the college named. He had also taken an advanced degree from that college and had worked for a good number of years at a solid midwestern company. The venture capitalists decided to invest in this new west coast company. To their utter amazement, a few days later the entrepreneur disappeared with the money they placed in his bank account. After checking with the FBI, they were told that the individual had been a two-bit mobster from New York who had ratted on organized crime and sent a number of them to prison. The authorities had provided him with a false background as part of

47

their witness protection program. This crook had used his pristine background to lure venture capitalists into his new business and took off with their money. He was never found.

Information from the Entrepreneur

In your conversations with the entrepreneur, you will will be able to pick up things that will help you evaluate his past performance and your future trust in him. Encourage the entrepreneur to talk about his past, where he grew up, the type of parents he had, whether he had a paper route, and what type of high school he attended. All of these details provide background information that you should write down at your earliest convenience and put into your file. This kind of information will help you determine whether the individual has the characteristics that you are looking for in an entrepreneur for this business.

At some point in interviewing the entrepreneur, I say, "Look, during the next days we are going to conduct a detailed check on your background and will specifically look for bad points. If there is anything out there that we are likely to pick up, would you tell me about it now so it won't come as a surprise?" By being candid with entrepreneurs about your background checks you can often induce them to open up about their past. I remember one individual turning bright red and telling me that he had been arrested. I said, "Oh, what for?" He looked back and said, "When I was in college, I was in a bar one night and got pretty drunk and tore up a piano." From the other details on his record, it looked as though he had sewn all his wild oats on this one night. It was an act that had no bearing on this person's ability to run the company.

Local People

Many times when we are investing in a small business that is not located in our home town, we call upon a venture capitalist in the city in question or someone else who we know there. We ask them to find out whether anyone has heard anything good or bad about this individual. It is generally easier for someone who lives in the same town to find the contacts who can tell you what kind of person you are dealing with. They may have heard something in their business dealings or they may have seen something about the individual in the local newspapers some years back. They can supply you with local information about the entrepreneur that you would otherwise be unable to obtain.

Public Information

If the individual who you are investing in has been involved in a public company, then SEC files can provide additional information on the individual. If the person has been involved in radio or television, the FCC will have files on the stations that the individual has worked for, and there may be some information about the person in those files. This public information can usually lead you in the right direction.

Customers

When you are talking to the customers of the business, be sure that you ask about the entrepreneur. Many customers will know the entrepreneur because he has been helping the company sell the product. They may give you some insight into the entrepreneur's personality, ethics, and reputation.

Investors

Other investors in the company can also give you some background information on the entrepreneur. You will want to contact other investors and find out why they invested in the company and if they are happy with their investment. Also, ask them what, if they could change anything, they would want to change, what problems they have had with the entrepreneur, and what they liked about the entrepreneur. Get to know these investors and find out what they think about the entrepreneur who you are about to invest in.

Employees

Finally, ask employees of the company about the entrepreneur. What is it that they like about the chief executive officer? What is it they dislike? Don't despair if most of the employees say that they like the CEO and do not have any criticism. At some point you will find the one who is willing to give you an earful. You will find the "mole" who will give you the inside information you need on the company and the CEO.

MANAGEMENT TEAM

Usually it takes more than one person to make a corporation go. You will want to investigate the number two and number three people in the firm almost as closely as you will investigate the CEO. It is important for you to know if they can fill the shoes of the CEO if the CEO should die or become disabled. You will also want to determine if there are any disagreements among the management team. Find out if any problems are brewing. Review the experiences of the management team to see how they fit together. Are they the same age, do they have the same background and experience, or do they have a diverseness that will let them handle a multitude of problems? Do they work well together or is there constant bickering and conflict? Be sure to ask all of them how they feel about the chief executive officer. Also ask each one of them how he feels about the others.

Organization Structure and Decisionmaking

It is very important to understand who exercises the authority. Is the CEO making the decisions or does he share them with the board of directors and his management team? Does the board of directors function as a committee or is it merely a sounding board for decisions that have already been made.

Determine the duties and responsibilities of each person on the management team. Who has defined these duties? Who has determined whether they are carried out correctly? Has there been sufficient delegation of authority? Have the authority limits been defined adequately? Does the organization depend only on one or two people on the team? Could it function without several of the key employees? Make sure you understand the decisionmaking process in the company.

DOCUMENTATION

When you have finished asking questions, you should document in detail all the significant points you have uncovered. Also make sure that you have all of the items that you want or that management will be sending them to you. Appendix 1 contains a list of items that you should probably have on any company that you plan to invest in. What I find particularly interesting are the reports used by management to manage the business. Once I have those, I feel I can see the business the way the entrepreneur sees it. If I see it in that light, I will probably have a better understanding of the business.

Strengths and Weaknesses

At the end of the day, I always try to list the strengths and weaknesses of the CEO and the management team. I find it important to put them down on a piece of paper. This helps me to assess the risk that lies behind every deal because the management team counts for so much. I believe that management counts for at least 20% of the business, and in most circumstances 50% of the business. In essence, if you do not have a good management team you will probably not succeed, no matter how good the product or the production process.

FINAL JUDGMENT

At the end of all your investigations, you are going to have to sit back and think about your entrepreneur. Is this person the type of leader who can make the projections happen? This judgment is the final one. I wish you the best of luck in making it.

CHAPTER 3

REVIEWING PERSONNEL
AND COMPENSATION

From an investor's viewpoint, a company is little more than the people who work for it. Companies succeed because the people make the company succeed. A company usually fails because the people fail. An entrepreneur alone cannot carry a company very far; there must be a group of people dedicated to the success of the corporation. An entrepreneur can be a cheerleader and a coach. The entrepreneur can be a quarterback and can call some extremely good plays, but without the complete team, all the employees working together, no company can succeed.

One of the most important areas for an investor to investigate is company personnel. What is the true work ethic inside the company? What is the group culture? How does the company's personnel shape up in comparison with the competition? In this chapter we look more closely at the due diligence involved in checking out the personnel of a corporation.

HOW IS THE COMPANY ORGANIZED?

Academicians have studied company organizations for years. The academic and popular press has reported revelation after revelation regarding the corporate culture. Each season a new group of buzzwords seems to appear to describe corporate organizations. If you are to understand the company and how it operates, you must understand how the company is organized.

Corporate Organization Chart

Organization charts are necessary in even the smallest corporations in order to delineate the relationships between various people and to spell out each staff member's responsibilities. Organization charts give a clear visual presentation of the corporation's hierarchy. Every organization chart should indicate who is at the head of production, of marketing, and of finance. In the early stages of the company, one individual, usually the president, may play several of these roles, but it is understood that somewhere in the life of the company a person will be hired to perform each function.

Some small companies don't have organization charts, and when they don't, as part of the due diligence you should construct one while talking to the entrepreneur. Draw a chart and put people's names on it. Determine who reports to whom and exactly who is responsible for what functions in the company. This will give you a very clear understanding of how the people interact and how the corporation functions. Although some academicians argue that organization charts are not necessary, or, at least, that they rarely reflect the total interaction in the company (and I concur with the latter criticism), I still think a chart is a good beginning. It may be that one individual reports to two people for certain jobs in which that individual is currently carrying out two functions. It is rare, however, to find that job functions have not been delineated in a larger organization. When they have been delineated, it's fairly easy to construct an organization chart.

I remember a company in which the entrepreneur was adamantly opposed to having people's names on an organization chart. He fervently believed that the team could work together to solve any problem and that, although certain people had certain jobs to do - for example, the accountant had to prepare the financial statements - it was a team effort and everyone should work together. At the time I thought this was a fairly novel idea and believed it might succeed. After the company failed, I revised my appraisal of this entrepreneur's team approach to things. There are a number of nitty-gritty jobs that need to be done in every corporation and they should be assigned to specific individuals, who are charged with completing them in a timely manner. These people should have someone to report to so that when those tasks are not completed on time the person responsible can be reprimanded, and when they are completed on time the person can be rewarded. Any corporation that lacks this hierarchical structure is likely to experience growing pains, if not outright failure.

Many in the business world disagree about hierarchical organizations. Most critics question not the structure itself, but the height of the structure. In other words, an organization chart that has a high pinnacle with one entrepreneur at the top and many people at the bottom will be less effective in the marketplace than one in which the pinnacle is less high and is spread out and features a strong middle-management team. I have seen descriptions of organizations that had task force groups or associates with sponsors for each associate. These are almost the same as hierarchical organizations except that the hierarchy does not have a steep pinnacle. Decisionmaking has been pushed down to lower echelons so that the employees on the floor are more involved in deciding how to get the job done. Regardless of whether the entrepreneur wants a hierarchical organization, he will be involved in one and he should be able to prepare an organization chart for you to review.

Officers and Directors

In every company you study, always get a complete list of the officers and directors, with their names, addresses, and telephone numbers. You will want to talk to all of them. Also obtain a list of people who have over 5% ownership in the company, with their addresses and telephone numbers. It may be important to contact them and if you have the information in the file it's easier than having to get it at a later date. In particular, anyone who owns such a large block of stock should be contacted to determine why they made such a large investment in the company.

Stockholders

Have a list of all stockholders prepared for you. Ask that the list indicate the amount each person paid for his ownership and the percentage of ownership. Determine when each person purchased his equity. Call several of them to see what they know about the company.

Characteristics of Management

When you make a list of the officers, directors, and large stockholders, you should include the following information: the title or position of the person, age, years in present position, years with the company, prior business experience, education, compensation, and whether he or she has a written or unwritten employment agreement with the company. All of these details are important to the investor because they will say something about the management team. When you are looking at the management team you will want to ask these types of questions: Is there a strong management team to carry out the plans? Or, does everything depend on one key entrepreneur? What would happen to the company if one of the key employees was not available for an extended period of time? Is the group of key employees of the same age, experience, and background or does it consist of a blend of youth, experience, and different backgrounds? Does the key group of employees work together as a team? Are there identifiable lines of authority? Does management use an integrated approach to problems? Is there a great deal of bickering within the team?

Does the CEO dominate the operations of planning and projections or does the group decide where the company will go? Is there either a written or understood developmental plan for each of the key executives in the company to follow? How will they make a great deal of money if the company is successful?

Can the company develop from within the required middle management people to carry out the business plan? What strategy does the group use to fill key positions? Do they use outside consultants or headhunters? What is the past experience of the company in filling key jobs?

Is the current compensation system for key executives designed to retain them and attract others to the company? Are these compensation levels in line with the industry norms?

HOW ARE PEOPLE COMPENSATED?

For many years sociologists and psychologists have been studying employees of large and small companies. They have determined that people work for companies for many reasons and that money is only one of them. People look for many ancillary benefits when they work for a company, from the ambience of the offices to the camaraderie of the personnel. Each of these factors has some effect on how hard people work and how much they enjoy their jobs. Compensation in its broadest sense involves all of the rewards people receive in a work environment. Compensation as we know it is primarily the money and other material benefits received by employees for performing their duties.

Employee Compensation

Another part of the due diligence process consists of asking for a complete list of the payroll and W-2s for the preceding year. This will show you how much people are being paid and also single out those who are being paid a great deal. You will want to find out why they are being paid so much. In addition, you should determine what kind of wage increases have occurred over the past years. If pay has risen dramatically in recent years, you will want to know why. If wages increase quickly, employees may expect salaries to continue increasing rapidly over the next few years. If the company is going to leverage itself with high debt or spend an additional amount of money in a new area, it may not have the cash to give employees the kind of raise that they have been expecting. As a result, employee morale may slump and employees may not make the contribution to the company's progress that is needed to make the company a winner.

Compensation System

The compensation system that a company sets up for its employees is all-important. It must reward people for performance. You should study it to see how well it achieves this objective. Usually, one starts with written procedures for determining beginning salaries, raises, promotions, and dismissals. If the company has no written procedures, then spend time with the management team asking questions about their procedures for determining these changes in employee status. I can't stress enough how important it is for a small company to implement (early in its life cycle) a compensation scheme that rewards not only the top management team but all employees for their good work. The company should have an entrepreneurial spirit at the top and at the bottom. An employee at the bottom who makes an extra contribution to the company's well-being should be rewarded. When these types of incentives are installed in a company, performance among the work force is more likely to improve. We're all aware that people don't work for money alone; however, money is a good motivating force for most people. In addition, it is a tool by which many people, both entrepreneurs and workers, measure themselves against other people. An hourly worker who makes 10% more than another gains status and recognition among his peers.

As part of the due diligence, you should determine the average salary of hourly wage employees, supervisors, and officers. Determine whether employees of this company are paid less than the norm for the area as well as the norm for the competition. The less mobile, nonsupervisory personnel must have salary parity with others in their category in the same geographic area if the company is to keep its trained work force. Training an hourly worker is not cheap, and once an hourly worker has a skill that is marketable at an amount above the compensation he is receiving, the temptation to make another $0.25 per hour is usually more than he can resist. So, compensation at the lower end must be on parity with the local organizations.

The pay rate of supervisors and management must also be commensurate with people in the same field in the general region and perhaps, for upper-level management, in the nation. Although management has become less mobile over the years, anyone who can get a 20% to 30% increase in salary would be a prime candidate for a headhunter or someone else wanting that manager to move to a different city. Good management is hard to find. Management that works long hours and achieves for the good of the company is even harder to find. Those managers who achieve for the company need to have "golden handcuffs" to prevent them from leaving the corporation. There are myriad methods of compensating both management and supervisors. One of the most effective is a large salary, but there are others, such as pension and profit-sharing plans, retirement plans, stock options, time off with pay, and other perks that would give an individual a reason to stay with the company.

It's very hard for a small company to compensate management at the same rate that larger businesses can. However, small businesses have the tremendous advantage of being able to reward good management with a piece of the pie in the form of stock options. Direct ownership in the company is one of the strongest motivators and one of the best golden handcuffs that can be used in any small business. Part ownership in the company gives the manager an opportunity to make money if the company does well. In a small company, there is a direct correlation between the output of the general management team and the success of the business. Any manager with an entrepreneurial spirit knows that he can make a significant amount of money from the stock options if he does a good job. As an investor, you should make sure that the key managers as well as those workers below the key managers have adequate incentive to stay with the company and make it a success. If the compensation system of the company is not adequate and doesn't look as though it's going to be changed, one should probably not put money in the company. The compensation system is a key component of every company.

Pension Plan

In investigating a company, one should also review the pension plan. You should obtain a copy of the pension plan to make sure it is adequate. In addition, you should determine if the plan has been fully funded for the past few years. If the company owes any unfunded liability to the pension plan, this is like a debt owed to any other institution and could have a direct impact on the cash flow of the company. A company that is barely breaking even and has a huge unfunded pension liability is a candidate for bankruptcy. At a minimum, it would take a great deal of earnings to come out of this problem, and future earnings would go to contributions to the pension plan rather than to building up the company's assets.

In investigating the pension plan, find out who handles the pension side of the business and if it is fully funded.

ERISA is an organization that reviews pension and profit-sharing plans. You should ask the expert who handles the pension and profit-sharing plan if he is aware of any ERISA violations. If the plan needs to be updated, you should know when that is going to happen. In addition to reviewing the ERISA plan, you should determine what the contributions have been for the last five years. This may give you an insight into the company's ability to generate cash. It also may show you, if the contributions have been small, why the team running the business now feels that it is getting a raw deal because its pension plan is not being funded.

Sometimes in reviewing pension and profit-sharing plans you are suddenly greeted with a surprise. You may find that the company has overfunded its pension plan and can take some money out for corporate purposes. This is a very exciting moment in the due diligence process; to find an overfunded pension plan is to find a hidden asset.

Profit-Sharing Plan

If the company has a profit-sharing plan, obtain a copy of it and determine the formula for making contributions. I believe that a profit-sharing plan is a significant part of compensation in any company. If the company does well, a contribution is made to the profit-sharing plan and all employees share in it. Nothing could be simpler in tying an individual's interests directly to those of the company. In reviewing the profit-sharing plan, find out if all the contributions have been made for the past few years. If they haven't, find out why not. This may be another liability because the company must make contributions to the profit-sharing plan. You should determine what contributions have been made to the profit-sharing plan have been over the past five years.

In addition, ask whether the profit-sharing plan can be terminated or amended at any time. The plan may have been set up by a retiring management team and thus may have been designed to take the maximum amount of cash out of the company. Unless the profit-sharing plan is changed, some of the cash that may be needed to build the company will have to be set aside for profit sharing. It may be necessary to change the plan.

Bonus Plan

Early in the investigation of compensation, one should determine if the company has a bonus plan and, if so, how it is computed. Many companies have a Christmas bonus plan that offers employees goods, services, or actual cash. More often, the company's bonus plan for employees is based on its profits. If a performance-type bonus plan exists, you should obtain a copy and make sure you understand how it works. Again, a bonus plan that is based on the profits of the company, in which an individual gets a big bonus if the company does well, is a great plan because it directly rewards people who have made the company successful. It is central to every business operation.

Sometimes an entrepreneur will set his sights on large bonuses. In the early years, as an investor, you should discourage top management that owns a large percentage of the company from taking large bonuses. The fact is, investors want to stimulate management's interest in making the stock worth a great deal rather than in taking cash out of the company. As an investor, you own stock in the company but do not get a bonus. Investors want the entrepreneur to be on the same footing and to be working for the company in a way that will build up the worth of the stock as opposed to the size of the entrepreneur's bonus. For those individuals who depend on the company but who do not have large stock ownership, a bonus plan is definitely in order. In virtually every investment agreement, compensation is discussed in detail and is limited for those who have large stock holdings; for those who don't have large stock holdings, a strong incentive program is set out.

Stock Option Plan

Many companies have set up stock option plans to reward employees, especially key employees. If the company has a stock option plan, get a copy of it and determine whether the plan is effective in holding key employees. See how many options are available, how many have been awarded, and how people feel about the plan.

Other equity incentives available as rewards include "phantom stock option plans" in which stock is never really issued, but management gets a bonus on the basis of how well the company's stock performs. These are most often used in large public companies.

Stock incentives and stock options are one of the most important reward systems any small business can establish. You should make sure you understand how the small business you are reviewing is using its stock ownership plan in order to reward employees. What vesting policy does the company have? What happens to the option when the employee leaves? What happens to the stock that the employee has gained under the stock option plan if the employee leaves? If the company has the right to purchase the stock back, what price does the company use to repurchase the stock? Sometimes companies become involved in stock ownership plans on the theory that employees who own a tiny bit of the company will feel like an owner. Usually this is a myth and management should pay no attention to it. Management should shut down the stock option plan for those employees further down the ladder, and should institute a good profit bonus plan. This has much more effect than a stock option plan on employees who want to own a little bit of the company.

Other Benefits

Other benefits are also used to hire and retain employees. I remember asking an entrepreneur how he was able to hire a top engineer away from a major computer company. The entrepreneur explained that the engineer would not even take his telephone calls until he asked his secretary to put a note in front of the engineer with only two words on it: Laguna Beach. The big computer company had stationed the engineer in upstate New York, whereas the entrepreneur's company could offer to transfer him to its headquarters in Laguna Beach.

Look at this company to see what other reasons might be used to hire and retain top employees.

WHAT EMPLOYMENT CONTRACTS EXIST?

In every medium-sized and large company, employment contracts exist between the top management team and the company they are running. Smaller companies usually do not use employment contracts. These contracts are becoming more commonplace as top managers try to make sure that the company treats them fairly and the company tries to make sure that the employees know what is expected of them. As an investigator of a company, you need to review all employment contracts.

Employment Contracts and Special Compensation Arrangements

Employment contracts can be extremely detrimental to companies. Some years ago, an investor tried to sell a company in which the president had a ten-year irrevocable employment contract that based his salary on his performance. The formula turned out to be ludicrous and the company found it was paying most of its profits to the president. No one wanted to buy the company with such an onerous contract in place. Employment contracts that cannot be amended or changed under certain circumstances can spell disaster. When you are investing in a company, make sure you understand the employment contracts for all individuals.

Termination agreements with employees should also be checked out. In recent years, these termination agreements, sometimes called "golden parachutes," have provided ridiculously high payments to top management regardless of the reason for their termination. Sometimes the agreements are negotiated when a person is hired; most often, they are put into place when the company becomes very profitable.

Employment contracts and termination agreements can also work to the disadvantage of the employee. I know two young men who spent three years as virtual slaves because they had signed employment contracts that said they would have to give all their time and attention to the company's efforts as long as they were paid a specific salary. A new owner bought the company and made these two young men perform the most incredible jobs. They were threatened with lawsuits if they didn't comply. As a result, they wasted years of their lives doing things that most of us wouldn't do.

Noncompete Agreements

Noncompete contracts are usually signed by key employees and those with special knowledge about the company. These agreements make it illegal for the employee to leave the employment of the company and work for a competitor or to start up his own company. The employee is thereby precluded from competing directly with the company.

However, in recent years noncompete contracts have been voided by many state and federal courts on the grounds that "you cannot preclude an individual from being gainfully employed." As a result, most noncompete contracts are good only in the city in which they are signed; an employee could go to another city and be gainfully employed and thus become a direct competitor with the company.

Nondisclosure Contracts

In order to avoid having a noncompete contract voided by the courts, many employers make their employees sign a nondisclosure contract. This means that the employee will not disclose proprietary information about the company to his new company. Although the employee may go to work for another organization in another town, supposedly he will not use proprietary information to aid his new employer. Where possible, an investor should review both the noncompete and the nondisclosure contracts to see if they have any teeth in them. Otherwise you might find yourself with the entire sales team leaving one afternoon, joining a competing company down the street, and destroying the company you have invested in.

WHAT IS THE WORK FORCE STRUCTURE?

The structure of a work force can determine how well the company operates. If the work force is primarily a blue-collar union work force, the company will be quite different from a white-collar nonunion company. You need to understand the structure of the work force.

Unions

Does the company have a union that represents the employees? If so, what is the name of the union? Who controls the membership, the national or the local union? How long has the union been in place? How many employees are covered? When does the contract expire? Describe the terms of the contract, including (a) escalation clauses, (b) regular rate increases, (c) promotions, (d) retirements, (e) production requirements, (f) hiring, (g) firing, (h) hours worked per week, and (i) other benefits. Get the name of the union head so you can talk to him.

List the grievances filed and the arbitration awards that have occurred during the last five years. Are labor contract problems anticipated for the next time the contract arises? Are significant increases anticipated for the contracts as they come due?

Have there been labor strikes during the past ten years? If so, give the date of the strike, the union involved, the duration of the strike, the cause of the strike, and the settlement involved in resolving the strike.

If the company does not have a union, has there been union activity in the past? Is there a pending election? Does the company have a formal anti-union plan?

Like everything else in this world, there are good unions and bad ones. Some unions become bureaucratic and unchanging, while others are flexible and progressive. You need to understand the type of union that controls the work force at the company.

Work Stoppage

It is important to determine if the company has had a work stoppage of any kind. If the company has had strikes, then find out why and get all the details, as mentioned above. It is also important to know if work stoppages or work slowdowns have been due to equipment failure, inventory shortages, or other reasons during the past three or four years. Any work stoppage is serious and it will tell you what operating problems the company is having.

Training Program

Does the company have a formal training program for its employees? If it does, obtain a copy of the teaching materials and review them. If there is no formal program, describe the procedure for training new employees and for transferring employees. Every company should have a training program for bringing new skills into the company.

Determine who is responsible for ensuring that the company has well-trained employees. Spend time discussing employee training with this person. Determine how much money is spent on training each year, broken down by departments, if possible.

Determine if any cross-training has occurred, that is, if people have been trained to do different jobs so that if an employee is absent someone else can step into that job.

Morale of the Work Force

What effort is expended by the company in trying to determine the morale and attitude of its employees? Has a consultant ever come in and discussed attitude and morale? Do employees believe in giving the company an honest day's work or do they try to do as little as possible for the company?

WHAT PERSONNEL RECORDS ARE MAINTAINED?

Most companies maintain personnel records regarding wages. However, quite often small companies keep poor personnel records. If there are personnel records, you should go through them in order to evaluate the way the company handles its personnel and its record keeping.

Maintaining Internal Records

Hiring and firing of employees is an important process, but keeping up with them while they are in the company and determining how well they are performing is also important. You should review the records created for hiring employees as well as for evaluating, transferring, promoting, and demoting them; changing compensation; reprimanding them or taking disciplinary action; and for training, absenteeism, tardiness, and any terminations.

In today's litigious society, you should determine what procedures have been laid down by the company for building legitimate cases for employee termination. In addition, you should find out what requirements the union has imposed on the hiring and firing of employees. One good method of reviewing this area is to obtain a copy of each form used to monitor employees, and if possible review several actual employee files to see how well they are maintained.

Payroll Records

As a check on the other information you've been gathering about employees, obtain a copy of the weekly or monthly payroll records for all employees, both full- and part-time. Also get a copy of the annual salaries that were reported on the employees' W-2 forms for the previous year. This kind of information can give you an overall view of the general payroll and employment practices of the company. Divide the employees by their departments in order to see which departments have the most people expenses. It may be that you will determine an imbalance in one department or another, or a shortage in one department that is critical to the company. This can be an illuminating exercise.

Employee Books and Manuals

You should determine if the company has a corporate policy handbook for employees. This would be a book that is given to each new employee to acquaint him or her with the company. If one exists, obtain a copy and read it. Also determine if the company has an employee benefit handbook. If it does, get a copy and read it to see what benefits the company tells its employees they have.

Determine if the company has a "Standard Operating Procedures Manual" for the various departments or job functions. If it does, obtain a copy of each one of the department manuals.

Reports from the Personnel Department

Get a copy of the reports the personnel department directs to other areas of the company and assess their value. Some memorandums and reports will give you an insight into the way personnel works.

In addition, determine what reports are generated from outside the personnel department and given to the personnel people, and see what they do with them. Assess the value of these reports.

Hiring Procedures

Bringing in a new employee to a company is a serious step. Every time a new employee comes into the company, he or she brings a new set of values and goals. It is critical that the people hired strengthen the company's goals and aspirations. You should review in detail the procedures used for soliciting, interviewing, screening, evaluating, and conducting reference calls and credit checks in the hiring of new management personnel as well as other employees. Determine what technique is used in hiring people. A lie detector test? A written examination? Do industrial psychologists evaluate employees? How does the company screen candidates and determine who will best fit into the company?

Motivating Employees

In this section you are trying to determine what specific methods or techniques the personnel department has applied to motivate the employees. What motivation techniques does the company use?

Personnel Files of Management

Quite often the personnel files on management are kept in a different area and perhaps under the control of a different group. One of the things you should do as an investigator is review the personnel files of all the officers, directors, and department heads, as well as some of the supervisors in order to determine what kind of people are running the company.

Employee Litigation

In any organization with a substantial number of employees, an employee now and then files suit against the company. Get a copy of the litigation and determine what kind of accusations have been made. Determine if there are any actions threatened or pending. How serious are the actions and do they give any indication of how the company is operated?

Regulatory Agencies

Numerous local, state, and federal agencies regulate the way employees are to be treated and how they are to be paid. The question you must answer is, has the company experienced any regulatory problems from these agencies in the last two or three years? Have any complaints been filed? If so, find out what they are. This may also give you an insight into the company's employee practices. In addition to the normal employment agencies, there are other agencies that regulate an employee's relationship with the firm. There are safety and health regulations, consumer product safety regulations, and environmental regulations pertaining to air, water, waste treatment, and land. Are there any actions threatened or pending? Have there been any actions along these lines during the last two or three years? If there have been any such actions, get as much information on them as possible to see if they might create a problem in the future.

Obtain a summary of the company's rating for unemployment and workmen's compensation. If the company has very large claims in this area, they will be a giveaway on how it treats its work force.

PERSONNEL CONSULTANTS

Sometimes a small business will hire a personnel consultant. Determine whether the company has hired an outside personnel consultant during the past two or three years. Get the consultant's name, address, and telephone number and talk to him or her. Find out what problems the consultant was called in to solve and if they were actually solved.

OTHER EMPLOYEE BENEFITS

Indirect benefits to employees are also of interest. You should describe the vacation and holiday policies as well as the leave policies available to top management. You should understand the policies relating to travel and entertainment expense. Sometimes corporations are quite generous with travel and entertainment expenses and an employee is permitted to buy all kinds of things on his expense account. After all, historians will remember, George Washington accepted no pay in his leadership of the Continental Army. He asked that the Continental Congress pay only his expenses. Well, his expense account is a classic. He ran the Continental Army through his personal expense account. This included clothing, guns, and other necessities such as food and military paraphernalia needed to fight the British.

Does the company pay for automobiles, airplanes, limousines, and boats? These kinds of off-the-balance-sheet perks can be enormously rewarding to management.

Health Insurance

One of the largest line items on major corporation's profit-and-loss statements is a line item called health insurance. General Motors pays more for health insurance than it does for any other single line item on its profit-and-loss statement, even more than it pays for steel and metal. You should review the medical and life insurance cost for the company. It may be that the company's health and life insurance costs are out of line with the norm in the industry.

SUMMARY

Hiring and retaining good employees is of paramount importance to the growth of any company. A company that doesn't hire the best will ultimately be unable to compete. A company that does not fire employees who are not performing well will ultimately have troubles. I have seen this happen in many a small business that has let "dear old Uncle Joe" or perhaps a spouse handle the financial records. Because of the family relationship, that person cannot be replaced and no one can be hired over them. If this individual is not capable of doing the job, the company may suffer. This kind of favoritism will ultimately hurt the company and hurt your investment.

Another thing you should think about, after you have gone through the personnel department and understand it thoroughly, is whether would you like to work for this company. Is there some place in the company that you would like to work? Does it seem to be a pleasant place? Does it have the esprit de corps of a winning company? Is it an exciting and dynamic company in which employees are motivated to do their best? You need to concentrate on this item in order to come to a final judgment on the personnel area.

Major Strengths and Weaknesses

You should determine the five major strengths the company has with regard to personnel. You should write these points down for future reference. In addition, you should identify its five major weaknesses in the personnel area and you should confront management with these weaknesses to see how they plan to deal with them. If they don't have a solution, it may not be a good company to put money into.

When you are reviewing the company for its strengths and weaknesses, try to determine how the company must change or upgrade its benefits programs or its salaries to be on par with the competition and to be in a position where it can adequately compensate those people who are going to be needed to make the company go. It is extremely important that you understand what needs to be done to a company's compensation system before you invest.

Ratio Analysis

A number of ratios in the personnel area can give you a good feeling of what is going on. These ratios can be calculated over time by using prior financial statements. Those for the future can

68

be computed by using projections to determine what is happening with the company. These ratios will indicate how the company has performed historically and what it might be expected to do in the future.

Average Salary. Calculate the Average Salary over time by dividing the Total Payroll by Total Number of Employees. This will tell you whether average pay has gone up or down per employee over a given period of time. If salaries are going up, can the company maintain its growth and have salaries increase at the same rate?

Average Sales per Employee by Division. Calculate the Average Sale per Employee by Division such as the sales division or the production division. This ratio will show which divisions have high labor costs. Calculate this by dividing Total Payroll Expense for that division by the Number of Employees in that division.

Total Payroll as a Percentage of Sales. Calculate the Total Payroll as a percentage of sales by dividing Total Payroll and Benefits by Net Sales. This can show you whether labor costs are going up relative to sales. This is a good gauge, over time, of the way the company is going.

Benefits as a Percentage of Payroll. Calculate the benefits as a percentage of payroll by dividing Benefits by Total Payroll. This will tell you if benefits are going up as a percentage of payroll and if the company is spending more than it should on benefits.

Employee Turnover. Calculate the Employee Turnover by dividing the Total Number of Employees who left in a year by the Average Number of Employees. This will measure the stability of the work force and perhaps even reflect employee satisfaction. It is quite common in the fast food industry to have a 100% turnover of employees in a year, but in other companies with a highly professional work force, the turnover is extremely low.

Sales per Employee. Calculate the sales per employee by dividing Net Sales by the Number of Employees. This will give you a measure of the efficiency of the company. If, as the company goes forward, it has fewer sales for the number of employees, this will be a sign that the company is not getting as much out of its total labor force in terms of sales as it should. This could be a key indicator of inefficiency.

Checklist

The checklist in Appendix 1 contains a number of questions to help you gain information about the personnel area. Pay special attention to the section on documentation. You should follow it in collecting information on all aspects of personnel.

CHAPTER 4

ANALYSIS OF MARKETING
AND SALES

Before you start with your due diligence on the marketing and sales function it's best to know the cast of characters who will be carrying out the marketing plan. This approach to the marketing area - that is, to look at the people first - is a carryover from the investigation of people set out in Chapters 2 and 3. If there are some marketing people you haven't interviewed, do so as part of this section.

Marketing is a critical aspect of any company. Marketing-driven companies are usually high-growth companies. You should be trying to determine if this company is market driven.

WHO ARE THE PEOPLE WHO SELL?

The people who sell the product may run the gamut from someone selling directly for the company to an outside representative. All of these people help to move the product to the consumer. It is important to understand who these people are and how they sell.

Personnel

Study each of the key marketing people to determine what mental assets they bring to the company, what kind of experience they have in marketing this kind of product, and what knowledge they have of this particular industry. Without skilled marketing people, there is little chance that a product can make it. You have probably heard the saying, "If you build a better mousetrap people will beat a path to your door." Nothing could be further from the truth. The adage should read, "If you build a good marketing group, they will beat a path to the customer's door." With very few exceptions, products and services are sold, not purchased. It is the salespersons of the company who must convince the purchasers to buy. Therefore, you must perform exceptional due diligence on the personnel who are responsible for marketing. This detailed analysis should follow the guidelines set out in Chapters 2 and 3.

Salesman Analysis

You should obtain a short resume on each of the salesmen. If there are too many salesmen then a resume on the top ten will do. You should review the resumes and look for a pattern. Meet some of the salesmen and discuss how they sell the product. It is important to get to know the sales force and try to understand how they view the marketplace.

In order to assess the abilities of the salesmen, you should have a list of them and their dollar volume of sales for the last three years. In addition, find out what management expects them to sell in the future. Does this expectation exceed what the salesmen themselves are saying they can sell? This is an important point, because if management is setting quotas that the sales force cannot meet, management is probably being unreasonably optimistic. You are trying to understand all the aspects of a sale in order to judge the reasonableness of the sales projections being made by management.

Outside Representatives

Many companies do not have a direct sales force, or they may have a small sales force that calls on representatives or distributors. If this is the case, you need to find out who these outside representatives and distributors are. You need a list of these representatives by dollar volume sold and by unit volume sold for each product. You will need the names, addresses, and telephone numbers of these outside representatives so that you may call them and talk to them about the product. See Chapter 7 for the types of questions to ask manufacturing representatives.

Motivation

Describe in some detail the technique and methods used by the marketing department to motivate its salespersons and the representatives of the company. Is monetary reward the only motivation? Or does the marketing department use other items to motivate employees and representatives? It is critical to find out what will make employees and representatives of the company sell more of the product. Motivation should not be treated lightly.

Once you understand the motivation being used, ask yourself whether this motivation is sufficient to sell the product. How does it compare with the industry or the competition? Do the salespeople feel sufficiently motivated? You are trying to determine if the sales projections can be met. If you find the motivation of the employees quite low, you might begin to think that the sales projections being made by management cannot be met.

Terminations of Employees

Make a list of the salespersons or other representatives who have been terminated during the past three years. You will want to know how long they were with the company and the reasons they left. Frequently, you can get the names and telephone numbers of past salesmen and representatives and ask why they left or why they were terminated. Needless to say, some terminated employees may have an axe to grind and they may tell you things that are untrue. On the other hand, they may give you some insight into the company that will not come through from loyal employees. It behooves you to track down several of these people and make sure you understand why they left.

WHAT ARE THEY SELLING?

The age-old question that every company asks itself is what are you selling? This may seem obvious in a product-oriented company, but after some analysis you may determine that the product is not the only thing the company is selling. It may be selling service, a new idea, or a whole new approach to a problem. There are many items to be sold in addition to the product. Be sure you understand what the company is selling.

Products

The best way to begin analyzing the marketing side of the business is to identify the products or services being sold by the company. List the products by category and then list the specific products in each category. This list should include the dollar volume in sales of each product and the number of units sold for earlier periods. I usually go back three years in determining units and dollar volume. In addition, you need the same information for each of the products that are projected in the future, that is, the number of units to be sold in the following five years and the dollar volume for those units.

This will be discussed in greater detail in both the production section and the financial section, but for now remember that the marketing people should know their gross margin on each product. Beside each product put down the percentage gross margin that the company will have as indicated by the marketing people. It is important to check this with the information you get from others. Marketing people are normally optimistic on both gross sales and gross profit. When it comes to cutting prices and making the sale, the marketing people are most likely to cut the price and reduce the gross margin in order to make the sale. They do this because they are usually being paid on a percentage of gross sales and not on gross profit.

Product Descriptions

Within each of the product categories (or, if the product list is not too long, each of the products) describe the product in detail and emphasize its distinguishing features. For each of the products ask the basic question: What benefits will the user derive from this product or service? What makes this product or service different from the competitor's? This is a key question that you will spend more time on later when we discuss the consumer.

Seasonality of Products

Each of the products should be analyzed as to seasonality. In both the historical data and the projections, one may be able to see evidence of demand seasonality. Seasonality is common in most industries, and, if severe, it can be disastrous to the cash flow of a company. Obviously, a candy maker will have tremendous seasonality, particularly around Halloween and to some extent Christmas and Easter. You should look for the seasonality of the product in order to make sure you understand how it's being sold and what it does to cash flow.

Product Literature

Also collect all the sales literature and sales brochures you can find on each of the products. This will help you become familiar with the product and the claims being made by the company concerning product quality or performance. You should also obtain a price list outlining what the company is charging for its products or services. Sometimes price lists are called by a different name. For example in the radio and TV business, they're called rate cards. This tells you how much an advertising "spot" will cost on radio or TV.

Product Development

What new products are being discussed by the marketing department? How is it planning to implement these new products? When do staff think they might be available? What marketing studies have been completed to validate the new product? What marketing studies were completed for the existing products? Get a copy of each marketing study.

What product would the marketing department introduce into the market next if it had sufficient funding? Is the next product a "missing product," that is, one that is needed to fill out the product line? If so, ask the marketing department to describe this new product.

WHO BUYS THE PRODUCT OR SERVICE?

The customer has been studied extensively in business research. The marketing department should know its customers inside and out. It's important to understand who the customer is. Sometimes you will be surprised. For example, although men are the consumers of men's underwear, most often it is the wife who buys the man's underwear. Thus, the customer of the product is not the man who wears it but the woman who buys it. That is why advertisements for underware show the "Mr. Macho" male model. Every company should know who buys its product or service, and your research should confirm what management tells you.

Customers

Now that you are acquainted with the product or service and how it's sold, you want to understand the customers. First, get a complete list of the customers, if possible. By all means, get a list of the ten largest customers. You will want to make a list of the customers by sales volume and unit volume in order to understand which customers are buying the most units and the most dollar value. The marketing management should have this list on hand.

If it is a retail business, ask management to prepare a customer survey. You should know the demographics of the retail customer and who the product is aimed at.

Contracts with Special Customers

One needs to determine if there are special arrangements with major customers. In some instances, the company will not sell its product outright, but merely place it on consignment. Consignment is very popular in many businesses such as clothing and book publishing.

Although the retail store "purchases" the product from the manufacturer, the contract may allow the store to return the merchandise for full or partial credit. Sometimes, in order to get a major account, a manufacturer will produce enough goods so that it can place them on consignment with the retail outlet. This places a tremendous burden on the manufacturing outlet as it must carry, in its inventory, the investment that is normally carried by the retail outlet.

You should get copies of any contracts between the company and its customers. If there are no contracts, get a detailed explanation of the relationship between the seller and customer.

A dress manufacturer I investigated once had tremendous sales, and each year at the New York City show, buyers would come to New York to look at the new line. Orders would be taken during a relatively short time each season. What I didn't realize was that after all of the bookings were placed in the company and the products were shipped, the company still had not "sold" the merchandise. One had to wait through the season to see if those clothes had actually been sold by the retailer. If they hadn't been sold, the contract between the manufacturer and the retailer allowed the retailer to return the merchandise and get back 80% of what he had paid the manufacturer for them. In essence, there was a huge contingent liability not recorded on the balance sheet of the manufacturing company, and it was one that did not go away for approximately six months. The frightening thing was that if the dress manufacturer happened to produce a whole line of "doggy rags," the company could become bankrupt. The company risked the entire operation every six months.

Loss of Customers

You should determine how many customers have been lost during the last two years, and, if any major customers have been lost, you should get their names, addresses, and telephone numbers so that you may later contact them. In addition, you should ask the company why it lost those customers and if there is any opportunity to regain them.

Some time ago while studying a small computer company, I learned from the marketing department that the company had lost several good customers. Upon contacting one of the customers, I found that the printer of the product they had been shipped had numerous problems. The printer had to be returned many times, the input device did not work properly, and the computer program itself had several "bugs." When I confronted management with these problems, it maintained that this was unusual and that all problems had been corrected. However, upon further analysis I found return

76

slips from numerous other customers and then realized that the computer system did not work. If it hadn't been for the one or two customers that had been lost by the company, I probably would not have uncovered all the other problems regarding their computer system.

Customer Complaints

List the five most common complaints received from customers regarding the product or service. It is necessary to discover what customers are complaining about. Some may be minor problems and may be fairly random in nature, but if you see a pattern of complaints about the product, this shows a vulnerable point that the competition can jump on. It may also indicate why people aren't buying the product.

List the five most serious or costly complaints received from customers regarding the product or service. Here you are not worried about why people are complaining, but what it is costing the company to overcome these complaints. It's important to know how much the company is spending to handle complaints. I remember a company that had very strong sales on the march upward; however it was spending an inordinate amount of money fixing the product so it would meet its advertised attributes. This was a costly method of handling customer complaints. Ultimately it dragged the company into bankruptcy.

You should determine who handles company complaints and how they formulate a strategy for handling such complaints. For example, is the customer always right, or does the company spend time and money proving the customer is wrong and that the product is o.k.? A skeptical or negative attitude toward all customer complaints is going to lose the company sales in the long run. Research has determined that a customer will spread the work of a bad experience with a product to fourteen other people, whereas a good experience with a product will only be related to three other people. This means that the company must hustle in order to avoid too many complaints in the marketplace. Ask the marketing people if there is a set procedure for handling complaints. Is there a written description of how complaints are to be handled? If so, obtain a copy and find out how the company handles its complaints.

Is there a monthly or cumulative list of complaints? Are the complaints logged in so someone can follow them? I know of one very large hotel company that mails all complaints to the chairman of the board. Some afternoons the chairman of the board can be seen opening complaints and reading them. It's a very effective method. Every employee knows that all the complaints go to the chairman, that someone in full authority is reading them. This encourages employees to handle customers in an exemplary fashion.

Order Backlog

It's extremely important to determine the present backlog for each of the customers and for each of the products. This will give you a quick overview of where the company stands with its customers and products. For purposes of comparison, you should try to determine the company's backlog at the end of the last two years. This will enable you to see whether the backlog is actually building or if the company is eating into its backlog and not being able to replace it.

It's also important to determine when the backlog can be produced and shipped so that it can be turned into an account receivable or cash. For each product, list the backlog and see when it is to be delivered and how many dollars are involved in the shipment. For example, you might list the current backlog by product and then look at backlog for three months, up to six months, up to nine months, and up to twelve months or more. Within each of those categories you would look at the dollar volume for each of the products. If some of the products go into the distant future, you may want to discount the likelihood that they will ever be delivered. By aging the backlog, you can get a quick idea of how likely the company is to produce profits in the near term. If it has a tremendous backlog but most of it is not deliverable for over a year, you might start asking yourself what the company is going to do for the next twelve months. Verifying the backlog can be very important, especially if there is a large current backlog.

Customer Credit Approval

One of the most critical elements of any business selling program is the extension of credit to customers. This can facilitate sales but it can also be a disaster if customers don't pay. You need to understand the credit facility in detail. Who establishes the credit limit for the customers? What is the credit approval process? How do they go about determining whether a customer is creditworthy? Do they run credit reports? What special credit arrangements do they have with certain customers? Do they extend credit longer to some customers than to others? If so, why?

To understand the marketing department, you must understand how it determines which customers qualify for credit. If setting credit lines were left entirely up to the marketing department, I suspect that almost everyone would get credit. After all, the marketing people are paid on the basis of sales rather than on collections. If you are paid by sales, you want to extend credit to the world so that everybody will buy the product.

Customer's Credit Terms

In understanding the credit terms given to customers, you should try to understand what role the marketing department has in collecting the accounts receivable. If intimately involved with the credit collection and paid accordingly, it's highly unlikely that it is going to extend credit indiscriminately. Nonetheless, you should establish the normal terms of a sale and exactly how the marketing department fits into the overall scheme of setting credit limits and collecting from credit customers.

Disputed Invoices

Determine if there are any sales invoices with material disputes. It is important to know why they're in dispute and, if necessary, you may want to call the customers and discuss why they are not paying their bills. That call may give you tremendous insight into the business. On the other hand, you may just end up talking to a deadbeat who should not have been shipped on credit.

WHAT IS SAID TO THE CUSTOMER?

Public relations runs the gamut from the spunky ads we all watch on TV to the industrial manuals that are given to potential consumers of industrial products. Communicating with the outside world is a delicate part of the process of selling the product, It's important to understand what is being said to the customers about this product and this company.

Public Relations

In general, all information about the company comes under the heading of public relations. What articles have been written about the company? What research has been done by industry analysts? Has the company been mentioned in any studies of the industry? All of these types of information should be gathered. Usually the company gathers articles that are flattering and will hand these out. The company doesn't give out the ones that aren't flattering. If possible, ask for the company's public relations file and go through it to see all articles that mention the company.

Advertising

Some small companies don't have advertising or public relations agencies, but most large companies do. Advertising agency here means someone hired by the company to promote its product. You should obtain the name, address, and telephone number of the agency and the names of the individuals who work on the company's account. You will later want to call them and discuss in detail their relationship with the company.

Formal Advertising Program

The company should be able to outline its formal advertising program and explain how it intends to inform the consuming public about its products or services. A fairly detailed media plan should be used to disseminate this information. It is important that the company gain recognition in the marketplace, and the advertising agency is supposed to be instrumental in gaining this recognition. If it has media samples, get copies of the print advertisements and be sure to listen to and watch the radio and television ads.

Advertising Budget

You should determine what the advertising budget has been for the last three years. You should also determine what the company intends to spend for the current year and its projected advertising budget for the next five years. In addition to finding out how much money will be spent, you should try to learn what the money has been spent on in the past and what the money is earmarked for in the future.

I remember talking to a company once that wanted $1,000,000 (a nice round number). When I asked what it was going to spend this amount on, the reply was "advertising." When pressed even further as to what it intended to do with the money, the company representative said it would all be spent on TV time. Needless to say, this seemed to be a fairly reckless approach to promoting the company's product, since TV is not the best medium through which to advertise all products, especially those of an industrial nature. You must understand in detail the advertising program being put forth by the company so that you can determine if it is spending the money wisely.

Questions for the Advertising People

When you talk to the people at the advertising or public relations agency that works for the company, you will want to ask some specific questions. First, find out how long it has been the the company agency. If it's only been a short time, then obviously you are going to have to find out the name of the previous agency and why a switch was made.

In addition, you should determine how often the company advertises. Perhaps it has been rather spotty, and the advertising people may be able to explain why that is a good approach. Ask about the average size of its printed ads to get a feel for whether they are adequate. Does the advertising agency have a standing order to place certain ads in certain publications? If so, find out how much longer and why it will continue to advertise in that specific periodical. What is the cost of advertising and what is the average amount the company is spending? How does that compare with others in the field?

Has the advertising agency always been paid on time? His it ever had to contact the company for failure to pay? If the company is not paying the advertising people and you find this a persistent trait of the existing management team, it may mean that you will never be paid either.

Will the advertising agency continue to run the ads for this company? Does it think the company is making the right moves in its marketplace? Who is the contact person at the company? If the agency deals with someone other than the person you've been talking to in marketing, you will want to talk to the agency's primary contact to see why that person thinks the agency is good. In addition, you should solicit any general comments from the agency regarding the company. How would it change the ads to make them better? What could the company do to capture more market share? These kinds of general questions can yield more information about the industry, the competition, and the company you're analyzing.

WHAT IS THE MARKETPLACE FOR THE PRODUCT OR SERVICE?

By defining the marketplace for the product you can tell how much money the company can make. If the market is small, you cannot expect sales to go beyond a certain point. The size and strength of the competitors in the marketplace will also determine how much of the marketplace can be obtained by a company. It is very important to understand market growth, market size, and the strength of the competition.

Market

You must analyze the market that each one of the products is sold into. You need to know the total dollars and the total number of units that are sold in this marketplace. Are there geographic limitations to the marketplace? You should determine the market share of each of the companies, or at least the market share of the major companies. For example, Competitor A might have 20% of the marketplace and Competitor B might have 10% of the marketplace. Your company, because it is new, may have only 2% of the marketplace.

It is very important to know what kind of market you're selling into. If it is dominated by one financially strong competitor (e.g., who has 70% of the marketplace), you must use a completely different strategy than when selling into a marketplace in which the largest competitor has 10% of the market. A highly fragmented market versus a highly segmented market means a different marketing strategy and different chances for success.

Competitors

You must investigate the competitors thoroughly. You can often understand the company you are dealing with much better if you understand the competition. You should go through all of the products that you have listed and note the competition for each one. Next, gather information on the financial strength, the name recognition of the product, and the general standing in the marketplace for each one of the competitors. You should describe in detail the competition's strengths and weaknesses and any significant differences between it and your company.

An important thing to look for in the competition is sales tie-in. Do they sell this product as part of a whole list of products? If they're selling brake systems in general and one of the components of the brake system happens to be the brake pad, then how will your company, which manufactures only brake pads, compete with this fully integrated competitor?

Market Growth

You should study the market and determine its annual growth rate. Certainly the marketing department should understand how fast its product market is growing. It should know how much the market grew for each of the last three years and should be able to project growth for each of the next five years. It is very important to establish whether you have a growing market or a stagnant market. For example, if you have a market that is stagnant and management is projecting growth at the rate of 15% per year, this means that it will have to take market share and sales away from competition. This is an entirely different marketing strategy from one that would be appropriate when the market is growing at 30% per year and your company is projecting a 20% growth rate. Understanding the growth rate of a marketplace is critical to any long-term projections and strategy.

Market Information

Be sure to ask where the market information is coming from. If someone says the market is growing at 35% per year, you will want to know the basis on which they are making those projections. Sometimes the information is merely based on hunches and guesses. On the other hand, some industries are studied in detail and the information available on the market is very good.

Substitutes in This Marketplace

Many products have substitutes. In the food business for example, when beef prices go high people switch from beef to chicken or pork. Try to determine if there are any substitutes for the product that the company is selling. If there are substitutes, then the company will not only have to worry about the competition in its industry, but also the competitors who manufacture the substitute product. You must understand how substitution can work, who the substitute competition is, and how they can affect your product.

Marketing Objectives

Ask the marketing people what their objectives are. What are the marketing objectives in a general sense? Sometimes a marketing person will say the objective is to obtain a larger share of the market. At other times marketing people say the objective is to gain geographic coverage, that is, to have the product sold nationwide. When they talk about market coverage, they often talk about their marketing roll-out, as they roll out from one corner of the United States to the other. They may even talk about penetrating foreign markets. All of these can be important marketing objectives, and sometimes a short-run strategy to cut price and gain market share can be a great benefit to the company in the long run. However, market share and geographic distribution are not nearly as important as generating gross profits for the company. If the marketing people are interested in generating profit for the company rather than pursuing goals that are not strictly related to profit, the company is more likely to be successful than it would be if they had other objectives in mind.

Marketing Strategies

In addition to obtaining a list of objectives, you need to ask the management team to explain in detail their specific strategy for accomplishing the objectives. They may be relying on seven or eight strategies to achieve their basic objectives.

HOW IS PRICE DETERMINED ?

The price of the product or service is directly related to the sales a company will make. It is important for an investor to understand how the price of the product was arrived at. The price of a product will determine its position in the marketplace with respect to products of a similar nature. Price is the single most important attribute to determine in trying to define where a product or service fits in the marketplace. Companies often talk about price points. These are the imaginary lines between the higher-priced and lower-priced items that determine the price category in which a product will be classified. Most companies talk about their high-priced, medium-priced, and low-priced lines. Each one of these particular items has a price point and companies place their product in one of these price quadrants. For example, they may have a product that is priced on the high end of the mid-price range. You should find out why the company is pricing its products in this range and how it arrived at the various price points and positionings of its products.

Pricing Policies

This brings us to one of the most important questions for any company, that is, what price should it sell the product for? In my years of working with entrepreneurs I have found that the pricing question has received little attention. As a result, some big mistakes have been made in pricing products. For some strange reason entrepreneurs approach pricing in a very unsophisticated fashion. I remember one group whose whole reason for being was to beat the competition's price. It ignored service, failed to have good salesmen, ignored good packaging techniques, and gave little attention to the distribution channels because its sole concern was to have the lowest price. It believed that the market was so price sensitive that if a product could be sold for less, customers would demand it. This company's product was never accepted in the marketplace and the company was soon liquidated.

Other companies seem to price their products according to the competition's prices. For example, in the computer industry, most hardware is priced according to the computer industry leader. The large market share being held by the leader is a pricing umbrella under which all of the smaller companies must price their products. It's important for an investor to determine whether a small business has arrived at the price of its product logically.

Pricing Process

You should ask the marketing people to describe in detail the pricing process they follow. Who establishes the price? Who has input into setting the price? How do they determine the proper price? Who is authorized to sell the product at a price that differs from the approved price list? Can any salesman cut the price? Who is in charge of setting the price?

A retail organization that I know has a basic floor price that no one can go beyond. However, its advertised prices are in excess of that amount. Snappy ads are used to entice customers into the showroom. The ads say, in essence, "Come in and make us an offer." This company allows salesmen to sell the product for practically any price above the floor price. This often creates a rather bizarre approach on the selling floor, especially if two salesmen are selling the same product next to one another and you can hear different groups haggling for different prices. It also leaves many customers disgruntled because they aren't sure if they are getting a bargain basement deal or being ripped off. Prices float from high to low and salesmen are compensated more as the price goes up. Their percentage of the total sale grows with the price. This company is flourishing!

Price Changes

How often does the company revise its prices? Does it change prices frequently or does it try to keep them more or less stable Does it respond to the competition's price changes quickly? Or does it wait a while to see if the price will stick? Is there a price leader in the industry that everyone else follows? Understanding how prices change and who changes them is of critical importance to every business operating in the industry and to you as an investor. Price changes can be an indication of a rapidly changing industry where one can have big losses.

Product Warranty

Does management describe in detail the present warranty policy? What kind of warranty actually exists? Get copies of the warranty for the product and review it, carefully.

What warranty expenses has the company had for each of the last three years? What warranty expenses does the company expect to have for each of the next five years? How did the company calculate the amount it expects to spend in warranty expenses?

What amount does the company have as a warranty reserve? That is, what amount of sales has been placed on the balance sheet as a reserve against future warranty claims? Is this warranty reserve adequate? Since the warranty reserve is basically an accounting entry, does the company have the cash or credit line it would need to honor a large warranty claim? Is a warranty claim one of the reasons it needs money from an investor?

WHAT INTERNAL REPORTS ARE MADE?

Every company should record its marketing and sales endeavors. This is one of the key activities of any business. You should be able to review the company's marketing reports and determine from them what is going on both in the company and in the marketplace.

Marketing Reports

Get a list of the reports generated by the marketing department and assess their value to the company. Try to determine how the marketing department uses them. Also review them for information about how the marketing department is being run and for details about the products and customers.

Determine if any other reports from the company are shared with the marketing department. For example, does the marketing department know what is happening in the production area? Does the marketing department know what is happening in the financial sphere? Does the marketing department understand the problems in collecting accounts receivable? If it does not, it may be selling the product to people who don't pay. As a result, the finance department may be clogged up with an inordinate number of slow-paying or nonpaying customers. The marketing department should not allow this kind of situation to develop.

Is there a report that charts any of the activities in the marketing department. For example, does it have a sales chart showing monthly or weekly sales?

Sales Projections

How often, and for what forecast period, does the marketing department project sales and expenses for its department? Get a copy of the marketing forecast and determine how it is put together.

Go through the marketing forecasts with the marketing managers and review how they are put together. What assumptions have been made? How often do the assumptions change and with what frequency are the projections changed?

Get copies of actual financials for the past three years and compare them with the sales department's projections for the past three years. If they diverge substantially, the new sales projections may be of little value in assessing the company's promise. In determining how accurate the sales projections have been in the past, you will obviously be making a statement about what degree of accuracy projections should attain in the future.

Discuss in detail the results for the company as projected by the marketing department for this year. Probe to determine how well it understands the marketing budget and sales projections. The marketing department that puts together sloppy projections probably does not understand the marketplace very well.

Procedures Manuals

Does the marketing department have a manual on procedures? If so, get a copy and review it. If not, ask why not. Determine from talking to people in the marketing department if they follow the procedures manual or if it's just an out-of-date binder that's never used. Determine when the last entries were made in the manual and the date it was last reviewed. This will give you an indication of how well-organized the marketing department is. The fact that a marketing department does not have a procedures manual is not the kiss of death, but it should have some kind of document that encourages the people in the marketing department to work together as a team.

WHAT EXTERNAL INFORMATION IS AVAILABLE?

By developing external information, you will have an opportunity to check the accuracy of the information being supplied by the company. You will also be able to develop a clearer understanding of how the industry views itself as well as its position in the overall marketplace. Trade associations and trade publications are key information sources. Quite often, research institutions supply this type of information.

Industry Associations

Is the company a member of any trade or industry association? If so, get the names and addresses of the associations and, if possible, the names of the managers of those associations. It will be important to contact the manager of the major trade association for industry statistics and for other information on the industry. Many times an association is small enough to know the inside scoop on the activities of both your company and some of the other companies in the industry. You should also determine if there are other ancillary trade associations or perhaps some that are somewhat similar in nature that could give you an understanding of the industry.

Trade Shows

Does the company participate in any industry trade shows? If so, list them and determine how this helps sell the product.

Does the company attend conventions that might enhance its stature in the industry? If possible, attend a convention and see what type of people are there.

Trade Publications

Obtain a list of the names and addresses of the most important trade periodicals in the industry. Get recent copies and find out what the contributors consider to be the pressing issues of the industry. If you make an investment in a company, you should subscribe to one or two of the trade periodicals in order to follow the industry. Many trade periodicals are published by the trade association itself, and most trade associations have newsletters. Make sure you review past publications and also get on the mailing list if you put money in the company.

BASIC INFORMATION

Ratio Analysis

You will have to undertake a number of marketing ratio analyses if you are to understand the company's performance in the marketing area.

Calculate the *Sales per Salesman* by dividing the Total Sales by Number of Salesmen out during the year. This will measure salesman productivity in terms of their ability to produce sales for the company. If you see this figure declining over the years, it will indicate that the company is not producing per salesman what it has in earlier periods and may indicate that there is a problem.

You should also calculate *Selling Expenses as a Percentage of Sales,* by dividing Total Selling Expense by Sales. This will measure the cost related to obtaining each sale. If you see this cost going up, you should investigate why.

Another useful calculation is *Salaries and Commissions as a Percentage of Sales*. This can be calculated by dividing Total Salaries and Commissions by Total Sales. Again, this percentage will give you an indication of what cost is incurred for each sale, that is, the human cost. If you see this human cost going up, you need to ask why.

Calculate *Gross Profit per Salesman* by dividing Gross Profit by the Number of Salesmen on the average during the past year. This will let you measure the ability of a salesman to contribute to the gross profit of the company. If you see this number going up, you should be happy.

Also calculate the *Gross Profit as a Percentage of Marketing Expense* by dividing Gross Profit by Total Marketing Expense. This will measure the effectiveness of the marketing team with respect to gross margins per marketing dollar spent.

Another area of analysis is *Marketing Expense as a Percentage of Sales*. Here you divide the Total Marketing Expense by the Total Sales in order to measure the total cost of the marketing programs relative to the sales being generated. You should include all marketing expenses such as advertising and promotion.

Another useful ratio to analyze is the *Returns as a Percentage of Sales*. You may do this by taking the Total Dollar Returns and dividing this figure by Sales before Returns, but after any discounts. This will measure to some degree the customer satisfaction and the product's quality.

The final area to review is the *Discounts as a Percentage of Sales*. You may calculate Discounts as a Percentage of Sales by taking the Discounts Given and dividing by Gross Sales. This will indicate the amount the product must be discounted in order to gain sales. This is a key figure in the retailing business.

What Are the Strengths and Weaknesses

Once you've gathered as much information as possible about the marketing department, you should write down the five major strengths that you see in this corporation. In addition, you should identify the five major weaknesses in its marketing department. Once you've done this, you should assess how critical these five strengths and weaknesses are to the success of the business.

Conclusions on Marketing

Finally, you must formulate some basic conclusions about the marketing area. Is this the marketing team that can implement the marketing strategy? Can this marketing team make the company successful in this sales arena? Is this the marketing program that best fits this industry? Can this marketing strategy really work? At the end of the day, you should write down your conclusions on the marketing area before proceeding to other areas.

Checklist

Appendix 1 contains a long list of questions to guide you in analyzing the marketing area. It also provides numerous documentation sections to refer to and suggests references to call in regard to marketing. Make sure you call them.

CHAPTER 5

INVESTIGATING THE PRODUCTION
PROCESS

Every business involves production. Even a service company follows some production process in order to deliver the service to the customer. Every investor should understand the process by which the product or service is produced for the customer. Most of this chapter deals with the manufacturing process. However, the investor should become familiar with all the stages of production in order to understand this area. The production process also includes purchasing. Here you will identify the suppliers for the business. In addition, there is usually a shipping and a receiving area; both of them need to be examined. Usually customer services pertain to the production area. That is, after the product has been shipped to the customer, if the customer complains then the production department has to make good on what it has shipped to the customer. Finally, research and development is critical in every growing business and must be understood by the investor if he is to determine whether the investment is suitable for the long term.

THE FACILITY

You should also examine the facility where the production takes place, even if the property is leased or owned. A number of basic questions need to be asked. First of all, what is the exact address of the production area? If it is on property, then what is the square footage of the land? If it is owned, what is the cost of the land? Also, if it is owned, what is the assessed value for tax purposes and the fair market value today? If you have an appraisal, what is the date of the last appraisal and what was it appraised at?

The building size is another important item along with the age of the building and any expansion that has been done. The condition of the building and the possibility for expansion should also be investigated. In order to understand the value of the assets, you should determine the assessed value of the facility for tax purposes; and the fair market value from an appraiser plus the date of the last appraisal.

Here you are trying to determine if the plant is adequate for the company. If it is not, a move in the near future may be necessary. Your analysis should also determine if the facility is a "good deal"; or if it is an albatross around the company's neck.

I remember a nice little business that was doing $5 million a year, but unless they could crank the operation up to more like $15 million in a year, their facility would remain too large. They were investing a great deal of money in a huge facility in hopes that sales increases would soon fill up the plant. Sometimes entrepreneurs don't understand real estate. They take on far too much real estate and let it drag the company down. Entrepreneurs should also realize that they are not in the business of investing in real estate. Ownership of real estate may be nice for a mature company that needs to invest its money. However, for an entrepreneur company, owning your own real estate is not nearly as important as having enough working capital to produce the product.

This is a good time to ask questions about the insurance coverage on the building. Does the company have fire and hazard insurance? Does it have insurance against floods and hurricanes?

Also, you should ask questions about the amount of the mortgage on the property and the monthly payments. If the property is leased, of course, you should make notes on the amount of the monthly payments, when the lease is to expire, and if there are any renewal options.

Plant Moves

As part of your due diligence you may determine that the company will have to move its plant. This is perhaps the single most traumatic event any company can experience. Moving a company will be extremely disruptive and will take up a great deal of management time in the planning process, the actual move, and the adjustment period. Many management groups can be hired to help with the move, and so most entrepreneurs believe that a move is a fairly simple process and will not engage them. The truth is that moves usually cause considerable disruption in production, as well as in the overall management of the business. I have reached a point in my investment career where I don't want to invest in any company that has to move in the near future. I have seen so many companies go through such difficulties and have witnessed my investment upside dwindle so rapidly that I avoid them wherever possible.

EQUIPMENT

Once you have an understanding of the facility itself, it's time to move onto the machinery and equipment. Ask some basic questions such as the age of the equipment and current repair costs per annum. It is also important to know if new replacement equipment is available as well as spare parts. I remember visiting a firm once that was started in 1920s and finding that the very specialized equipment used by the firm was no longer being manufactured. This meant that every time a part was broken, the company had to make the item itself. This is a very time-consuming process and could interfere with production for some time if a major piece of the machinery was broken.

As an investor, you should know what kind of new equipment appearing in the marketplace might make this company's equipment obsolete or put it at a competitive disadvantage. It's been reported that the new steel mills in Europe and other parts of the world are much more efficient and better able to utilize the new technologies than the old steel mills in America. As a result, American steel has suffered.

You should ask the production people what kind of production equipment is used by the competition. Do they have more modern equipment? Is their plant better laid out? What does the production process at the competition look like and how can it be emulated here? If the company has a poor process, perhaps a different method of production will have to be invented.

You should ask if the company has a formal preventive maintenance program for repairing machinery on a regular basis. If so, investigate the program and determine if staff are maintaining the equipment adequately or if they are just running it constantly, and if you can expect huge maintenance costs to show up as soon as you make your investment.

Be sure you meet the person who is in charge of preventive maintenance and talk to him about what kind of reports are prepared on the maintenance of the equipment.

Make sure to ask whether the company anticipates any major repairs or reconditioning work to the equipment in the next twelve months. Get an idea from this person of what kind of repairs are going to be done in the future and see if this amount corresponds to the figure being used by the financial side of the business in its projections.

The Need for New Equipment

Ask the person in charge of equipment if he needs new capital equipment or new production space during the next 12 months. If the answer is yes, you should try to determine how much more space or equipment the company will need. You should review these items and amounts with senior management and compare them with the company's capital expenditure budgets for this year and several years to come.

I always ask people in production the following questions: If you had no money constraints, what pieces of equipment would you replace? What new equipment items would you add to improve efficiency? This usually gives me a pretty good idea of what items are needed in the production process.

I also ask which piece of equipment is responsible for the current bottleneck in the production process? Or looking to the future, I ask which area of the production process will need to be increased as the number of units produced increases.

Another factor to consider is what pieces of equipment can cause a production stoppage for any significant period of time, for example, anything over four hours. How many times has the production process been shut down in the past because of equipment failures? What plan exists if a certain piece of equipment fails and shuts down the production process? What will management do if production is shut down by this one piece of equipment?

It is important to know how easily production can be shut down. If it seems a likely event because the company only has one piece of critical equipment, this means that the risk in investing in this company is fairly high, since there is no backup. I remember a company that was in the business of making jackets for records. As the company developed, it decided to purchase a special piece of equipment for making record jackets from Germany. Although the company did spend a great deal of time making sure that the German equipment worked properly, it was not until the company had actually installed the equipment and began operation that it discovered a serious problem. To begin with, it took hundreds of hours to get the equipment to operate. Countless numbers of Germans flew to the company's plant to help the management team make the piece of equipment work. After months of working on the equipment, it was found that the equipment was not much better than some of the other items already on the market. Even though the piece of equipment handled the entire operation from start to finish, it was no faster than two smaller American-made machines operated by seven people. The savings in labor were not realized, because when all was said and done, it took seven people to keep the new German machine in operation, three in actual operation and

94

four as a support group handling software tapes and other aspects of the machine after some months of operation.

Surplus Equipment

Here are some other important questions to ask about equipment: Do you have surplus equipment and, if so, is there a plan to sell off this equipment?" Do you have any surplus or idle building area that could be subleased? These kinds of questions should tell you whether the company is overcapitalized from the standpoint of machinery, equipment, and building. If there is a substantial amount of excess equipment, perhaps it should be sold off.

In this world of fast-changing technology, it is critical to understand that a company's equipment must be modern enough to prevent the company from sinking to a competitive disadvantage. This may take some snooping among people (other than management) in the production area so that you can understand what they are thinking. If they constantly complain about not having the latest equipment, you can be sure that they are at a disadvantage.

Capital Expenditures

You should establish whether a formal procedure exists for approving capital expenditures. You should also determine that equipment can't be purchased just because the production crew wants to have the latest gadget. I remember a company involved in high technology video production in which the management was in love with new equipment. They bought every new "gizmo" that came on the marketplace, and they were constantly changing every part of the production process. This created havoc in the process itself and it also drained the company of the capital needed to do the marketing, even though it had the most modern, beautiful equipment.

In purchasing equipment, management should look at this as a return on investment. When the company is about to buy a piece of equipment, it should calculate the return on investment on the basis of the expenditure of funds. If the company buys a $30,000 piece of equipment and the return on investment is 10%, then the company probably should not buy it. As an investor in the company, you will want to know how the company calculates the return on the money it invests.

PRODUCTION CAPACITY

All of the questions above were oriented toward determining the capacity of the facility. It is important to know how much it can produce. If you are investing in a company that is near its capacity and none of the investment capital is going to be used to increase that capacity, obviously the company will have to obtain financing for new equipment before it can expand capacity.

You should also compare the capacity with the backlog. If the plant cannot chew up the backlog for several months or even a year, then perhaps management should consider increasing its capacity so that it can catch up with the backlog and deliver it to the customer.

Production Employees

Even though you have already spent a lot of time investigating the employees of the firm, you still need to look at another aspect of the employees. What you are looking for now is the really tough jobs in the production process. You need to identify the key production positions and determine what personnel backups you have for each of these key positions. If there is an extremely high-skilled job and there is only one person doing it, what happens to the firm when that person is out sick?

You must recognize that the people involved in the production process can be a limiting factor. If it is extremely hard to find a critical person such as a qualified machine operator to operate certain types of equipment, obviously the production process can reach capacity quickly and be difficult to expand.

Training is the key to the growth of any company. You should review the company's training manuals and determine how it is training employees to help increase its capacity and its productivity. Find out how production management selects and trains individuals as well as new supervisors. Determine who does the training and how it is carried out. Here you are looking for a logical approach that will show employees how to be highly productive and get the job done. A haphazard approach to production training will be a deterrent to growth.

Motivating Employees

Employees must be motivated, whatever the production process. You need to understand specifically how management measures employee productivity and efficiency. You also need to know whether the employee understands the importance of this productivity and efficiency. Try to get a handle on the specific techniques that management uses to motivate the employees.

If you have the opportunity, review several employee evaluation forms and see if the management is making a conscientious effort to spur the employees on through regular evaluations.

Review the written wage rate schedule for employee positions and determine the last date of the last revision. Try to determine from this whether the wage rates are high or low or average in relation to the industry, the competition, and this area. Are they training people only to have them leave shortly thereafter for a higher-paying job down the street? These are all key things to know. If the turnover rate is high because the pay is not very high, you can be sure this company is going to have to increase its pay before it can grow. One question that I always ask is, Does the company have a formal procedure for reporting employee absences, reprimands, promotions, and transfers? There should be a file that follows employees as well as the whole work force.

Ask production management to classify the production employees into production staff, supervising shipping, quality control, receiving, research and development, and management. Then, break down the payroll by these categories. Ask management where people need to be added and where they need to cut.

Ask the head of production to name five major personnel problems at the present time. The answers may be revealing.

Unions

If you have an opportunity, make sure you talk to the production people about the union and activities. Ask for their grievance log and talk to the labor lawyer for the company.

If the company is not unionized ask what specific plans the company has for reducing the possibility of any of their employees becoming unionized.

Retirement Plans

You should talk to the production people about the retirement plan to determine if they are satisfied with it. If they are not satisfied, find out what they would like to change. Also make sure that the retirement plan is treating the people well or find out if people are afraid to retire because the plan is so poor.

Staff Meetings of Production People

Do the production people meet regularly with all the supervisors in order to determine what problems are going on in the plant? What regularly scheduled meetings does the company have for each of the department heads? The company should be holding meetings that allow the production process to learn from its many activities.

REGULATORY AGENCIES

Every production process seems to be regulated by a myriad of governmental regulations. The most prevalent of these emanate from the Equal Employment Opportunity Commission (EEOC). Ask management if it has received any EEOC reports concerning discrimination based on age, race, sex, or color. What kind of grievances have been filed with federal regulatory or state regulatory agencies regarding equal opportunity employment.

The occupational safety and health laws are stringent in every state. The Occupational Safety and Health Administration (OSHA) is usually handled by the Environmental Protection branch of the state government. Determine what kind of OSHA regulations are required of the company, whether the company has been audited by OSHA, and whether they are in compliance. Review the file from OSHA and make sure you understand what risks are involved with this company and OSHA.

Other federal, state, and local laws and regulatory agencies have an impact on companies. For example, for radio stations it is the Federal Communications Commission. In this regard, you should contact the agency directly and determine if the company has any problems at that agency. With regard to the FCC, you can actually go to the agency and review the records on the company that are in the public reading rooms.

SUBCONTRACTING WORK

Determine if part or most of the work is subcontracted out to other companies. If it is, get the names, addresses and telephone numbers of the subcontractors so that you may contact them to determine what kind of subcontracting work is being carried out.

There are really two kinds of entrepreneurs when it comes to subcontracting work. Some entrepreneurs are marketing oriented and subcontract out every piece of work possible. They have someone else make the product that they are selling. In doing so, they sometimes miss having the flexibility to control their own destiny. When they make big sales, they are unable to deliver the product because they don't have the ability to command the production process so as to meet the demand. They also miss some tremendous profits they could gain by producing some parts of the process themselves. These entrepreneurs loathe the production area and don't want to deal with the headaches. You need to make sure that subcontracting is the best strategy for the company.

The second type of entrepreneur is more manufacturing oriented. He may be a scientist who loves dabbling in research and development and tinkering with the production equipment to make it work better. This type of entrepreneur wants to manufacture everything. He also wants to control the entire process from the time it comes in the door until the finished product goes out. Some of these entrepreneurs have their drawbacks because often they produce items that have no margins to speak of. For example, they might manufacture a product that they could buy for 5% or 10% over their manufactured cost. These entrepreneurs are tying up their own time and working capital in order to make a very small profit.

In discussing the production process with management, you should determine why it has decided to "make or buy" each component in the production process. There is a very straight-forward, simple analysis on make or buy that should be carried out by those in charge of production before they make a product and before they buy it. By performing such an analysis, it is very easy to determine whether one should be using subcontractors. (See Chapter 7 for the questions for subcontractors.)

INVENTORY

You need to ask the production people about the inventory levels. That is, is their current level of inventory at an optimum level? Is it too little, or too much? Who establishes the optimum inventory level and who do they have to answer to if they increase inventory? Ask how they determine the optimum inventory level for finished goods and for raw materials as well as work and process. You want to make sure that the production people are sensitive to the amount of inventory carried by the company. After all, a large amount of inventory means capital tied up in that inventory. Unfortunately, a company can't operate without inventory. You need to know that the production people are conscientiously trying to reduce the inventory level at all times.

Determine whether any of the company's inventory items require long delivery lead times. If anything has to be scheduled sixty to ninety days out, then you need to find out who that supplier is. This will be discussed later in the supplier section.

What inventory items, if any, have only one source of supply? You need their names, addresses, and telephone numbers because these suppliers are as critical to the company as any of the bottlenecks in the plant. If, for some reason, one of these suppliers were unable to deliver, the company could come to a standstill. You will want to investigate these sole sources to see if they are stable businesses.

Find out whether any items in inventory are obsolete, outdated, out of style, subject to markdowns, or have become unsellable in any way. If so, make a list of them and determine their value. You will want to compare this with the value they carry on the balance sheet. Some companies try to carry obsolete inventory on their balance sheet. A good accounting firm will usually catch this, but sometimes they don't.

QUALITY CONTROL

Does the company have specific employees in charge of quality control (QC)? You should determine who is in charge of quality control and make sure you speak with them. What quality control standards, if any, are followed by the QC department? Ask management to describe in detail the company's quality control program and to provide to you with any procedures manual that is used by the quality control people. A specification sheet for each product that is produced should also be available. The manufacturing process is like putting together tinker toys or cooking a pie. There should be a recipe for each product that is produced. It should be written down in straightforward language so that anyone can produce it. The quality control people will use this book to measure quality. If it is not produced by the book, the quality is probably not good.

PRODUCTION COSTS

It's always intriguing to talk to the production people about cost. I am always surprised to learn how few production people know what money is involved in what they are producing. The production people should have a detailed worksheet for determining the direct labor costs, the indirect labor costs, and the labor content of each one of their products. If they don't, management will never know how much labor cost goes into producing anything.

Usually the production process involves a standard cost system. If it does, this will be all the more confusing to those who don't have an accounting background. It is essential to know that the standard cost program is frequently updated in order to make sure it does not get completely out of sync with reality. You should know who is monitoring and controlling the various costs of production, especially the cost of labor. Frequently reports are put together on the direct and indirect costs going into every product being produced. You should get a copy of any of these reports on costs.

PRODUCTION LEVELS

Is there a daily, weekly, or monthly production schedule? The production people should have a schedule and you should know how they determine what will be produced and the quantity. There should also be a log of the production process that summarizes each of the production runs. In addition, records of the production stoppages should be available. Whenever the company experiences a shutdown for more than four hours, the reason should be documented so that it doesn't happen again. Always ask about production levels and why they are not higher.

Back to Capacity

Now you should be able to determine the production capacity of the firm. You have to determine how many shifts and days it is operating, and from that you should be able to walk through the production capacity, assuming that no new plant or equipment is being added. From that you should calculate what percentage of the capacity they are currently operating at.

STRENGTHS AND WEAKNESSES OF THE PRODUCTION PROCESS

You should make a mental note of three major strengths and three weaknesses in the production area of the company. I often ask management to list them for me and then I try to draw my own conclusions from what I have seen, heard, and read.

PURCHASING PROCESS

In small companies, purchasing is usually handled by one person. As the size of the company grows, the purchasing work increases and a team may be used. You need to analyze the purchasing process. Here you want to ask the purchasing people some questions to check on what you have heard before. Do they have any inventory items where less than two suppliers are available? In other words, do they have any sole source suppliers?

Are there any contracts between the company and any suppliers? If so, obtain copies so you can find out whether they are locked into a high-cost supplier because of a stupid purchasing mistake. Determine the company's objective in maintaining inventory levels. How many months of production are they supporting in their inventory?

I ask the purchasing person if any inventory items have delivery lead times in excess of sixty days. If they do, then you should make a list of these items. It may be critical to have certain products in stock in large quantities rather than having to order them frequently, especially if lead times are in excess of sixty days.

What are the normal credit terms that the company is getting from suppliers? Does the company take advantage of purchase discounts? If it doesn't, the company may well be losing a substantial amount of money by not taking the discounts offered.

How often is a physical inventory taken? Who takes the inventory and what procedure is used to take it? When an inventory is taken, are the numbers often incorrect?

Who establishes the specifications for the items to be purchased? Before something is purchased, what purchasing requisition or approval procedure is followed? Is there a procedures manual for purchasing items? If so, you may want to take a look at it to see if it is actually a current working book.

How much theft goes on in the business? How much "shrinkage" is involved in the inventory area? What system is in place to reduce the possibility of theft, both internal and external? What has been the company's experience in inventory shortages during the past few years?

When it comes to reordering, does the company have a formal reorder policy? That is, when a certain item that is to be used in the production process reaches a certain level, is it automatically reordered? Does the purchasing agent have to receive a formal command before he can reorder something.

SUPPLIERS

You need to obtain the names, addresses, and telephone numbers of the major suppliers to the company. You need to know the number of units purchased from them during the last time period, for example the last twelve months. You should know the dollar volume of the products being purchased.

Once you have this list, you will need to begin calling suppliers. Questions to be asked of suppliers are the to be found in Chapter 7.

RECEIVING

Once a product has been ordered, it will be received by the company and brought into inventory. Receiving goods should follow a regular procedure. Ask the people in receiving what procedure is followed for receiving products and what kind of procedures manual is available. They should be able to describe the procedure for receiving goods and services. There should also be a method for requisitioning and receiving tickets being reconciled so that those items that have been purchased are received. You should determine who is authorized to sign a receiving ticket. Is there a regular procedure for signing and completing a receiving ticket for every item that is received? You should understand how the company is handling its receiving because a great deal of money can be lost in the receiving process.

A common problem here is that the items received are improperly recorded from the company's records. Some items received are never logged into inventory and therefore aren't used until they are found. This could take a number of months.

It is also important to determine what system is in place to reduce the possibility of internal theft at the receiving process area.

There should be a procedure for determining that the goods and services received meet the specifications and quality of those ordered. You should identify the company's three major strengths and three major weaknesses in the receiving area. Usually management can name these very quickly.

SHIPPING

Once the product has been manufactured, it needs to be shipped. There should be some kind of shipping procedure and perhaps even a shipping manual. There should be someone to sign the shipping tickets to make sure the accounting department knows goods were shipped out the door. When the product is received by the customer at the other end, there should be some way of determining that the customer has signed your shipping ticket so that you can prove that the merchandise was received. I remember one instance in which the company that we had invested in had a computer failure and did not know which items had been shipped. Fortunately, we had notices indicating that the customer had received the items and could use them to reconstitute the accounts receivable and rebill the clients accurately. However, another company that didn't have a good shipping policy or keep good records went out of business because it couldn't reconstitute its accounts receivable.

As an investor, you need to know what checks and balances are in place at the company to reduce the possibility of theft at the shipping level. It is important to understand the method of shipping as well. Is it by trucks, a delivery service such as UPS, or by common carrier? In emergencies, what kind of air freight service does the company use?

CUSTOMER SERVICE

Frequently customer service is placed in the marketing area, but for larger items customer service becomes part of production. The customer service people are part of the production area and are responsible for making sure that customers get the product that they ordered. As part of your due diligence, determine how many employees are in the customer service department and who precisely performs the customer service work. Sometimes the employees of the firm prepare the product for reshipping to the customer. At other times, service reps in the field handle customer service. You need to delve into the customer service side to understand how the customer is kept happy. You should ask staff to identify the most frequent customer service problems. List the top ten. This will give you a good idea of what the customer service people are up against. I remember one company that had to rework a complete order because of a production process and this caused a great deal of overtime and extremely frustrating working experience for the people in customer service. They did it and the company saved face even though it lost a great deal of money on the order.

The customer service people should be able to describe the product warranties and guarantees provided by the company and the cost of these warranties and guarantees to the company. It is important to understand the customer service area because it will give you a sense of how the product is being accepted in the field.

Sometimes the company contracts out the customer service work. If it does, you need to know who is providing this customer service and what it is costing the company. You also need to have a copy of the customer service contract with this service agency. You should determine the names, addresses, and telephone numbers of any of these contractors.

Here are some questions to ask about customer service that is contracted out.

How long have you performed the customer service work for the company?

How many customer service calls do you have on a monthly basis?

What is the basic nature of the customer service calls that you get?

What specific items have you been asked to fix that pertain to customer satisfaction?

If you could fix one item in the company, what would you want to fix so that it would make customer service easier?

How much does the company pay you to perform customer service?

On the amount that you are being paid? Can you make a profit?

Will you continue to do the new customer service in the future?

How would you change your customer service contract if you could change it today?

You should ask management to identify the three major strengths and three major weaknesses in its customer service area.

RESEARCH AND DEVELOPMENT

The final section of this chapter is about research and development (R&D). It is extremely important to know what research and development goes on in the company. First, you should identify the people responsible for research and development. Are they tied in with production or separate from it?

What has the research and development budget been for the last five years? What kind of money is the company going to spend on research and development in the next five years? Once you have these figures, you can ask the following questions about financings.

What specific projects are in progress? Why were those projects chosen? Who made the decision to proceed on these projects? Usually the market where the products are to be sold has been carefully studied. Entrepreneurs in some of the smaller companies claim to have "intuitive" knowledge of what the market is looking for. Usually these intuitions are incorrect. Every product that is being brought to the marketplace should have been market tested. You should look at the past to see what kind of formal research projects were completed by the company before it instituted research and development programs for those products.

Often an outside consultant will be used to help the company determine what products it should go after or to evaluate products that the company has determined are the best. One of the critical aspects of the research and development area is secrecy. You need to determine how these projects are protected from being stolen by the competition. You should describe the company's procedure for capitalizing or expensing its R&D budget. If it is being placed on the balance sheet, this may artificially inflate the value of the company because the product has not proved itself. Find out who the people in research and development report to. If they report to the production area, research and development most likely amounts to adding items that have been enhanced in some minor way to the existing product line. If those in research and development report to the marketing people, you probably see all kinds of items being added to the existing product to make it sell. Many of them may be little more than bells and whistles. If R&D individuals report directly to the president of the company, the company is probably charged with a long-term vision and is coming up with good products for research and development.

Review any reports that are coming out from research and development staff. If there are no reports, you may ask top management how they know that the research and development people are doing their job.

When reviewing a product that is being researched and developed, you should ask the company's management if there are any patents or patents pending around the new product. Sometimes new products are produced under a patent license. If there is a license for the patented products, you should review it in detail. I remember reviewing the patent license for one company and finding that it was about to expire. I asked the company what it intended to do if the individual who owned the patent would not license it again. I was stunned to hear that management hadn't even thought about it.

Research and Development Strengths and Weaknesses

You should identify the five major strengths and weaknesses of the company's research and development section. Management should be able to give you some help in this area.

BASIC INFORMATION

Production Reports

Ask middle management to show you the reports they are generating and sending to top management. If they have no reports at all, ask them why not. What value does top management place on these reports? Determine who receives the production reports.

Also, determine if reports are made at the change of each shift and also if a production log report is made out regularly to keep up with what is being produced.

Ratio Analysis

Although a number of critical ratios need to be examined in a manufacturing company, we will only mention a few key ones. If you want to develop this further, obtain a good book on production processes and make sure you study the rations used by manufacturing personnel.

Compute the *Hours Needed to Produce a Unit* by dividing Direct Labor Hours by the Number of Units produced. This will measure the units of labor it is costing for each unit to be produced and indirectly will measure employee productivity.

Next calculate *Labor Cost as a Percentage of Total Production Cost* by dividing Labor Cost by Total Production Cost. This will give you a measure of the total labor cost to the total production cost and show the labor required to produce each item. If you see this labor content going up over the months and years, you need to determine why.

You should calculate the *Material Cost to Total Production Cost* by dividing Cost of Materials by Total Production Cost. This too will show you the percentage of total cost going to materials. If you see the cost of materials going up, then you should ask why.

You should calculate the ratio of *Manufacturing Overhead to Total Production Cost* by dividing the Total Manufacturing Overhead by Total Production Costs. This will give you the percentage of total production costs that is consumed in overhead. If you see the overhead percentage going up over of periods of time it will be a clear indication that something is wrong.

You should also calculate *Idle Time as a Percentage of Total Time Available* by dividing the Total Idle Time by the Total Available Direct Labor Hours. This often a hard number to get to, but if you can, it will measure the efficiency of the company in achieving and keeping all of its employees busy and productive.

An interesting, but difficult calculation to make is the Percentage of Total Factory Hours taken up by Direct Labor Hours. You can obtain this figure by dividing the Direct Labor Hours of people on the production floor by Total Hours of all the Factory Personnel. This will measure the amount of support personnel needed to complete the production process and will also show you what percentage is direct labor. If you see direct labor going down and support labor going up, there may be a problem.

Calculating *Overtime as a Percentage of Total Hours* can also give you a measure on the company's costs. To calculate, divide the Total Overtime Hours Worked by the Total Hours Worked. You will see how often people have to be brought in on overtime. If this number is large, it may mean that the company is having to schedule overtime to catch up with work that was not completed during the regular shift. You will need to investigate this in detail. Overtime hours are paid at a higher rate than regular hours, so it is costing the company considerably more to produce the product in overtime hours.

Machine Utilization is another interesting figure. You can compute this by dividing Productive Machine Hours Used by Total Available Hours on the Machines. This will measure the efficiency with which the equipment is utilized and perhaps give you an indication of a scheduling problem. If the machines are not being used efficiently, it may mean that the company is buying excess equipment instead of getting the efficiency out of its existing machine base.

Finally, calculate the *Scrap Rate* by dividing the Number of Units Scrapped by the Total Units Produced. This will be a good measure of efficiency of the production process as well as the quality control of the company.

Conclusions on Production

Once you have analyzed the production process in detail, you need to determine the efficiency of the overall plant. Does the company use its assets (such as land, building, machinery, equipment, employees, supervisors, etc.) efficiently? You need to come up with a general idea of whether the company is efficient or inefficient, or falls somewhere in between.

You also need to reach a basic conclusion about the management of production. Are these people able to manufacture the product efficiently? Are they able to meet the production schedule as set forth in the business plan? Can they maintain the production process like a well-oiled machine? Are you confident that they will be able to achieve the production goals that they have projected?

As part of the production analysis you should evaluate research and development. Do you think the company is engaged in the proper research and development? Is it on the forefront of technology or merely following the leader in the industry? Does it seem to know what it is doing in research and development? Do you believe management is capable of handling research and development? By the end of the day, you should have an overall feel for production management, the production process, and the research and development area. If you come out feeling uneasy or negative about this area, you definitely want to turn down the investment opportunity.

Checklist

Appendix 1 contains a list of questions about the production process. You should ask yourself many of these questions. You will want to pay particular attention to the checklist provided under the documentation area and make sure that you receive many of the items listed.

CHAPTER 6

ANALYSIS OF THE FINANCIALS
AND PROJECTIONS

Who are the people who count the beans? For many years now financial people have been known as "bean counters." Although the term is belittling, these people play an important role in the company. If the numbers are not correct, there is no way to manage the business. If the financial side is in the hands of incompetent people, then the business is doomed to failure. The safety of your investment depends on these bean counters and how they keep the books of the company.

The procedure in analyzing this area is the same as it was for the areas we have already discussed. You will need to analyze the financial people before you analyze the financial area. You need to know the individuals who will carry out the financial plan. You need to know who has computed the projections for the company. If you haven't yet interviewed some of the financial people, you should do so now.

Personnel

You should first concentrate on the background and experience of the people in the financial area. Obtain a short resume on each of the key financial people and look for experience in the small business area, specifically in helping small business companies grow and managing the financial function of small companies. These are key attributes of anyone in the small business area. You should analyze the financial people in depth, as you did the personnel carrying out the marketing function and the production function.

ANALYSIS OF THE NUMBERS

All of the qualitative analysis accomplished in the previous chapters now needs to be transposed into a financial analysis. That is, all the qualitative data must be verified in its quantitative form. All the achievements of the marketing and production department must now be stated in terms of financial achievements. At this point of the analysis, you must turn all of your thoughts to numerical concerns.

It is wise to start with the year-end numbers and then go to the interim financials. Usually the year-end numbers will have been prepared by an auditor and should have been certified.

Financial Analysis

The first place to begin the financial analysis is to study the historical financial statements of the company. One must first verify that these financial statements are accurate and current. Frequently a small business will try to skimp on financial data by not preparing regular financial statements. This is a sure sign that the company is not being run by the numbers and should give you a clear indication that the company is not serious about using the financials to guide the management team. Before you begin investigating the financial section of a company with old historical financial statements, you may want to have the accountants come in and review the situation. Accountants call this a businessman's review of the numbers. Every time I have asked accountants to review companies with old financial statements, the accountants have come back with horror stories. Frankly, I am down on companies that can't keep current financial statements and I do not invest in them. Old or sloppy financials usually mean business problems.

Hundreds of books have been written about financial analysis, about how to "walk through" the balance sheet and profit-and-loss statement in order to determine whether the company is operating well or is in trouble. Anyone who is in the venture capital business should have been schooled in depth in financial analysis. Therefore, this book does not try to elaborate on the various areas of financial analysis. This kind of analysis is indeed important, but you will also be concerned with the venture capital analysis, which should include the other items mentioned in this chapter. But before discussing these other items, let's consider some of the major items you should look for in the financial statements.

ANALYZING THE PROFIT-AND-LOSS STATEMENT

I always begin by looking at the company's sales and trying to understand how they recognize revenues. I have seen so many companies recognize sales in so many different ways that I no longer trust a mere number in the sales column. I need to understand what is behind it. For example, in the publishing business, a book is sold by a publisher to a bookstore and the revenues are recognized by the publishing company. However, the book can be returned by the bookstore to the publisher for full credit, so that a sale does not occur for the publisher until the retail store has sold the book to a retail customer. Recognizing revenue in the book publishing business can be difficult because a company may have several of its books take off and make sales look extremely good until the reviews come in and the books are sent back to the publisher. Verifying the sales figures from companies is necessary for investors.

Percentage of Completion

In other companies, such as government contractors, large contracts are recognized on a "percentage of completion" basis. This means that the project can be one-half finished and the contractor can recognize half or maybe more than half of the contract as revenues, even though progress payments of cash to the business may fall behind the amount of the contract that has been completed. This can "front load" sales of the contractor and make it look as though it is having a fantastic year, when in fact it is experiencing a severe cash shortage.

Loss Leaders

In other situations, a contractor may bid on the initial part of a contract and the bid may be so low that the contract constitutes a loss to the company. According to accounting principles, it can then bury those losses as investments in future contracts. That is, they never show up on the income statement. They are booked on the balance sheet as an asset in order to substantiate the theory that the government, after an initial contract, usually comes back for a larger follow-on contract. The loss that was incurred on the initial contract can be amortized over the second long-term contract. It was the small company's loss leader. I have seen several companies in which losses of this nature were on the balance sheet as an asset. In analyzing the company, you should become familiar with the way it recognizes revenues. Both the losses and revenues will tell you how the cash flows of the company will occur.

Research and Development

Expensing research and development can also give rise to assets on the balance sheet. The income statement may show no expense for research and development because the expense is being capitalized. This new asset is then taken off the balance sheet and expensed through the income statement over a five- or ten-year period. The company has spent the money and run out of cash but the income statement may show they a profit!

Standard Cost

How the company recognizes its costs of production can also be tricky. Some companies measure costs on the basis of "standard costs." At the end of the year, they adjust the "standard cost" and bring in the real costs of production. However, standard costs do not recognize any reworking of the product. If the product doesn't meet the specifications of the client, more cost will be incurred in making the product right. This may mean that the company will produce an item, recognize a standard cost, show a profit on the product, then later in the year have to recognize either (a) an expense for reworking the product to make it sellable or (b) additional expenses in order to bring the standard cost in line with reality. Both of these can be extremely disconcerting to an analyst because it is not until the end of the year that things pop out. I remember a small public company that always showed good revenues in its first, second, and sometimes even in its third quarter, only to have all of those profits blown away by the audit, which took into account the real costs. Imagine an analysis of a company that showed good profits after its third quarter. Imagine further that after looking at those financials, you invested. Then comes the fourth quarter and the audit. The audit has such large adjustments that the year ends with a big loss. This happened to me. I was left wondering whether this was a deliberate deception by management or just the result of a poor accounting system. In any case, it was a direct indictment of management.

CASH FLOW ANALYSIS

The first thing to do in cash flow analysis is to check the cash in the bank. How much cash does the company have and how does it flow in and out of the company? Make sure you understand how the company gets its cash. Critical questions to ask are: How many collection points does the company have for its cash? How many depository bank accounts does it maintain? What kind of cash balances does each account have? Of the cash that is collected,

112

what amount cannot be used because it is in the financial float? What procedure does the company have for minimizing the transfer time for collecting cash balances?

Also look at the number of disbursement points. Who authorizes payments from the company's funds and what amounts are they authorized to disburse?

What procedures are used to ensure the proper disbursements by authorized people? To transfer funds and ensure the timely payment of its bills? Does the company take advantage of discounts when they are available? How does it avoid missing discounts when payments are late? If the company is missing discounts, what does this cost the company per year? Quite often companies come to venture capitalists asking for financing to take care of discounts. Obviously if this is the only reason someone comes to you for venture capital, it is a mistake to put your money in. You will not get the kind of return on investment that you are looking for if the cash is only going to be used for making timely payments of bills in order to take advantage of discounts.

ANALYSIS OF THE BALANCE SHEET

Cash flow analysis naturally leads you to the balance sheet. One source of cash is accounts receivable. You need to understand how receivables are recognized and how frequently receivables are not paid. That is, the company may have a receivable booked and income recognized, but the buyer of the product owing the money may not have recognized it as a payable and may not believe it owes anything to the company you are looking at. Looking behind accounts payable is a must.

You should determine what percentage of the company's sales is cash and what amount is credit that will be recognized as accounts receivable. What credit terms is the company giving its customers and how do those terms compare with those offered by the competition and the industry in general? What credit information is used to make the credit analysis and who in the company determines which customers will get credit? Is the procedure for extending credit coordinated with the sales activity? How frequently do the financial people update the customers' credit information? The small business world is strewn with failures from small companies that extended credit to uncreditworthy customers who did not pay their bills. Like any other assets, an accounts receivable is no good unless it can be turned into cash.

Inventory

What dollar amounts are tied up in inventory? How does management explain the money in inventory? How is this inventory coordinated with the management of production? What are the tradeoffs between the flexibility of having a maximum inventory and the advantage of keeping a minimum inventory to reduce working capital? How is the responsibility for inventory control divided between the finance people and the production people?

Inventory can be a perplexing number. I walked through a plant once and saw a big pile of goods with a large tarp over it. Upon asking what was under the tarp, I was told, "spare parts." I looked under the tarp and saw some rusty junk. When going over the inventory numbers I found the spare parts sitting there at full value, just waiting for the auditor to write them off.

Fixed Assets

What capital budgeting procedure is used by the company and who decides what production equipment and machinery to buy? What is the minimum acceptable return on investment used to determine which capital budget items to buy? Does the company consider leasing? Who does the analysis on lease versus purchase? What capital expenditures are budgeted for the coming years?

Liabilities

You must go through the liabilities in the same way that you walked through the asset side of the balance sheet. You need to determine the size of the accounts payable. Who they are owed to? How far back do they go? Accounts payable must be aged. You should determine if the IRS is owed payroll taxes or if any income tax bills have not been paid.

Usually this section of the analysis shows the loan from stockholders, banks, and others. Make a list of all debts and confirm each later.

BUDGETING AND CONTROL

Sound budgeting and effective controls of the company are the key to a successful operation. Although budgets may be based on a shorter time period than the projections you will analyze, you should investigate how the company budgets its funds and its day-to-day activity. How does the company control its operations? The basic question you need to ask is What are the company's budgeting procedures? That is, how often are the budgets put together and are they modified on an interim basis? How are the budgets used to manage the company?

Some other key questions are as follows: How are the budget figures derived? What supporting schedules are available for these budgets? You need to understand how the corporation sets the budget objective. Does management set goals and then translate them into numerical budgets? How is the process carried out in the company? In your analysis of the budget, find out how well the company has met its budget in the past. What discrepancy, if any, shows up in the past between its budget and its actual achievements? How often does the management measure performance in relation to budget figures? What kind of accountability is established for employees? Who is held responsible when there is a deviation from the budget and what corrective procedures are followed to make sure that future budget numbers and performance are the same?

PAST FINANCINGS

During its lifetime, each company goes through a number of financings, from banks, insurance companies, venture capitalists, individual investors, and so on. You should set down the past financings of the company chronologically and indicate how they came about and what value is placed on the company. You should establish the current status of these investments. That is, find out whether bank debts are being paid as agreed. Are individuals getting the dividends they were promised? Are past investors happy with the situation and willing to invest again? You should determine if any personal guarantees were part of these earlier financings and what assets of the company were pledged. That is, what outside assets belonging to individuals have been pledged for these financings?

I have found that past financings to be paid off by money from venture capitalists often contain onerous terms with respect to the personal signatures of entrepreneurs. In some cases, houses or other assets outside the business have even been pledged. Entrepreneurs are extremely anxious to have these types of financings paid off and it's common for an entrepreneur to push hard for venture capital financing because the business is in trouble and he is trying to save his house by getting the bank loan paid off. You should keep an eye out for this type of financing.

Also keep in mind that if the entrepreneur has guaranteed the bank financing and if the business gets in trouble in the future, the entrepreneur will be working hard to pay off the bank without regard to your investment or what is best for the business. In a workout situation, the entrepreneur will want to make sure the bank is paid off but will not care about your investment. I've lost money because of this one, so be careful.

Past Bank Financings

In reviewing the company's past bank financings you should go through all the pieces of information about each loan, including the legal documents. You should determine what collateral has been used for these loans, such as deeds of trust and life insurance, as well as specific assets on the balance sheet. Have there been personal or corporate guarantees? What are the requirements of the loan? That is, are there current ratios, working capitals, milestones, and the like? Determine what things the company must do in order to maintain the credit line with the bank.

I remember one situation in which certain bank requirements had not been met, but the bank was still willing to work with the company so that it could go forward. The day after the venture capital financing agreement was reached and the money was deposited in the bank, the bank offset its loan amount due against the money in the account to pay down its own line of credit. The bank claimed a default in the loan and demanded that all future cash payments be made to the bank. Needless to say, this left the venture capitalists in a very unhappy situation. But, since it was a winery, the venture capitalist took some solace in his plight by drinking several cases of the wine. Looking back, each case cost about $65,000. And it wasn't very good wine, as I remember it.

Entrepreneur's Investment

In reviewing past financings, you should determine how much money the entrepreneur has invested in this business and how much stock he received for it. Sometimes you will find that entrepreneurs have put very little in the company and have very little to lose if the company goes bust. This often makes me nervous because nothing keeps the entrepreneur's attention riveted on business like a substantial investment in the company. I remember one situation in which the entrepreneur had invested $200,000, but he had made $1.2 million out of his past company. He had used the money to invest in other venture capital deals and only put $200,000 in this second business. When the company got into trouble, the individual worked very hard to save it. One will never know, if the entire $1.2 million had been invested, whether he would have had the incentive to save the business. As it was, he lost his $200,000, but he was still able to walk around with a smile because he had over $1,000,000 in other situations. As a venture capitalist, you want to make sure that 100% of the entrepreneur's time is committed to the business you are investing in. A large and significant financial commitment is one of the strongest indicators of the entrepreneur's desire to make the business a success.

When entrepreneurs don't have a great deal of money, it is best to get them to guarantee part of the venture capital investment in order to ensure that, if things turn sour, they won't walk away without a substantial personal loss. The fact that entrepreneurs will hock their houses by taking out a second mortgage in order to buy stock in small businesses is one of the strongest signs of commitment that an entrepreneur can show a venture capitalist. I have heard all the other arguments – "My life and soul are wrapped up in this business" or "My reputation and prestige are on the line for this investment" – but none of these arguments carries any weight when compared with these words: "Everything that I own is invested in this company."

Entrepreneur's Ownership

Similarly, you should determine how much of the company the entrepreneur owns. No entrepreneur is going to work hard for the company if he owns little of it and has nothing to gain. I remember looking at a small company in Atlanta in which the entrepreneur had been diluted by individual outside investors to the point where he owned such a small part of the company that he was virtually a hired employee. Always make sure that the entrepreneur has a substantial stake in the company (so he can make lots of money). Otherwise, he might give the company no more attention than a hired employee would. In several financings in which we have invested, we have insisted that the entrepreneur increase his ownership, to the detriment of prior investors, in order to make sure that the entrepreneur would be motivated enough to make the company successful. I find it hard to believe that any entrepreneur would work hard for less than approximately 20% of the small business. If it is a large business, 5% may be fine. With anything less you probably won't have the entrepreneur's full time and attention. He will be out looking for another company to jump into where he can own a substantial amount of the equity.

Participation with Other Investors

Investing with other venture capital companies or other individuals is always a benefit. However, those who have invested in the past and are now watching you invest your money have a vested interest in (a) not giving up much equity and (b) making sure you put your money in so theirs will continue to be worth a great deal. The views, comments, and information gathered by a past investor who is now trying to induce you to make an investment are not nearly as valid as the analysis made by a current investor putting in new money for the first time along with you. It is interesting to talk to these past investors, but one needs ask why they invested and what profit they expect to make in the future. However, it will be practically impossible to gain unbiased information from this quarter.

In analyzing these past investments, you should determine who invested, how much they paid, and what valuation is placed on the company. This will give you a good idea of how much they are stepping up the investment from the time they invested to the time they are asking you to invest. If the new value is substantially increased from the last financing, then you need to ask: What has happened to the business since the last financing that would make the value increase so much?

USE OF PROCEEDS

It is important to establish how past financings were used. If a company raised cash in the past, it is important to know where they spent it. This will give you a good indication of how well the company has been run and how far it will be able to run on the money that you are investing.

You should review the company's use-of-proceeds statement in detail in order to determine why the company needs money for each of the items listed. Vague comments on the use of proceeds, such as "working capital," should not be accepted. You need to know exactly where the money is going before you put it in. You need to determine if the new money will make a difference in that company's future.

If a fee is to be paid to a financial broker, make sure it is listed on the use of proceeds. These fees have a way of being overlooked until the day before closing.

PROJECTIONS

Among the items that you and the entrepreneur will come back to many times are the entrepreneur's financial projections. These constitute the numerical forecast that you as an investor are buying. The entrepreneur is saying these projections are possible, and you are purchasing a part of the company on the basis of these projections. Your return on investment, the cash that you will receive back, depends on the company making these projections. Your analysis of these projections is one of the key aspects of your investigation of any business opportunity.

You will want to investigate the assumptions being made about the projections. How realistic are the margins being projected?

How realistic are the financings? Go through all of the assumptions in detail with the management team in order to determine whether the projections are based on sound assumptions.

One of the main assumptions that I always have difficulty accepting from entrepreneurs is sales growth. Entrepreneurs are extremely bullish individuals whose sales projections tend to go through the ceiling. It is not uncommon to see unrealistic entrepreneurs thinking that they will double sales every year for ten years. Sometimes sales projections are prepared in a haphazard manner. This is usually the case when a sales projection has a lot of zeros. For example, the first year might be $1,000,000 even, the second year $6,000,000, and the third year $15,000,000. These round figures are a sure tip-off that the entrepreneur's projections are being shot from the hip rather than coming from analysis.

With the aid of computer programs, it has become much easier to run sales and profits projections. However, computer programs can increase sales by whatever percentage per year the entrepreneur dictates. As a result, the computer programs cannot be taken as the strong evidence that the multizeroed financial projection is accurate, even though the computer carries out the projections with brutal numerical accuracy. For example, if sales are to increase 67% each year and sales in the first year have been $1,253,000, the computer will show sales for the following year at $2,092,510. This means that your tip-off is not zeros but numerical accuracy. You will have to do much more digging into the rationale of the projections because you will no longer have the many zeros to tip you off that the entrepreneur is shooting from the hip. With the aid of the computer program, the entrepreneur is giving you a different type of projection, but this time it is based on a flat rate that he has assumed will be constant. You need to make sure you know how the entrepreneur has arrived at the projections and what degree of work has gone into formulating the assumptions.

In addition, you should be given projections of the balance sheet, cash flow, and the profit and loss statement. Without these three figures, you will be left out in the cold. You need all of them to make a valid judgment as to where the business is going and how it is going to get there.

The projections should include a breakeven analysis, with respect to profit and loss and cash flow. That is, the entrepreneur should show you monthly projections up to the point where the company expects to break even in terms of profit and loss, meaning it is no longer losing money. However, because of growth in accounts receivable and inventory, some companies may show a profitable financial statement even when they are having negative cash flow. This is the reason that the entrepreneur should show you a cash flow breakeven analysis. You want to determine at what point the company will stop having to raise capital and be able to finance itself on bank debt and other conventional borrowings. Until the entrepreneur shows you this breakeven analysis, you will not have a good handle on the company.

Make sure you have a balance sheet before and after financing so you can see how the proposed financing will affect the company. It is necessary to trace the flow of funds into and out of the company, especially as a company transaction. Without a transition balance sheet, you will not be able to follow the flow of funds.

Quite often the funds flow statement will not include the brokerage fee that the entrepreneur must pay as part of the financing. Make sure the fee has been subtracted from the cash available to the company. In addition, look for any consulting fees to be paid going forward and make sure that these consulting fees have been deducted from the cash flow statements.

The projections should be based in part on assumptions about the stage of growth, when prototypes will be completed from the amount being spent for research and development, when the first model will be installed, when the beta test sites will be finished, and so on. You also need to know when branches in new cities will be opened with marketing staffs and when new locations will come on line. The cost of these items should be in the projections.

Almost every venture capitalist has difficulty obtaining reliable projections. Quite frankly, most entrepreneurs know little about how to make projections and usually need help from an accounting firm.

BASIC INFORMATION

Ratio Analysis of the Financial Statement

There are a number of financial ratios to consider, each of which is significant. Generally speaking, the ratios in the financial area revolve around four areas: profitability, equity, leverage, and cash management. Each of these has its own slice of the financial numbers and can give you some indication of how well the company is doing.

Profitability Ratios

Gross Margin Percentage can be calculated by dividing Gross Profit by Sales. This will measure the margin that the company is achieving on sales. Over periods of time, it may reflect transit profitability.

Profit Margin Percentage can be determined by dividing Net Income before Taxes by Net Sales. This indicates the profitability of the company on each sales dollar. Over a period of time, it measures the profit trend of the company.

Return on Equity can be determined by dividing Net Income by Total Shareholders Equity. This measures the return on invested capital and can show you how hard management is making the equity in the business work.

Return On Assets can be calculated by dividing Net Income by Average Total Assets out during the year. This indicates the return on the average dollars of assets outstanding during the year.

Liquidity Ratios

The *Current Ratio* can be calculated by dividing Current Assets by Current Liabilities. This gives you some indication of the ability of the company to pay short-term obligations.

Quick Ratio can be calculated by dividing Current Assets minus Inventories by Current Liabilities. This is also a measure of the ability of the company to pay its short-term obligations without selling off its inventory to generate cash.

To calculate the *Working Capital as a Percentage of Assets*, divide Working Capital by Total Assets. This will indicate the due date of the assets relative to the total assets of the company.

Liquidity Ratio can be calculated by dividing Total Assets by Total Liabilities in order to measure the overall liquidity of the company.

Leverage Ratios

Debt Equity Ratios can be computed by dividing Total Debts Outstanding by Total Stockholders Equity. This measures the degree the company has leveraged itself with debt.

A similar ratio which is *Total Liabilities to Stockholders Equity*. It can be computed by diving Total Liabilities by Stockholders' Equity. This will give you a feel for how much of the capital has been provided by the stockholders versus creditors.

The *Working Capital to Net Sales* ratio is also of interest. It can be computed by dividing Net Sales by Working Capital. This will measure how efficiently the company has been able to generate sales on the basis of working capital.

Debt Coverage Ratio is something bankers always compute. It is calculated by dividing Earnings before Interest and Taxes by Total Annual Debt Service. This measures the ability of the company to see its debt obligations.

Cash Flow Debt Coverage Ratio. This is more difficult to compute. Here you must calculate Earnings before Interest and Taxes plus Depreciation divided by Interest and Principal Due on all of the company's debts. This will give you a more cash-oriented measurement of whether the company can meet its debt service.

Percentage Fixed Charges of Earnings is another good calculation. Here you divide the Fixed Charges by Earnings before Interest and Taxes plus Fixed Charges. This will give you a measure of how much the earnings could decline before you would be unable to meet the fixed cost.

Cash Ratios

Cash Flow Cycle can be calculated by dividing Receivables plus Inventory by the Cost of Goods Sold. This gives a general measure of the number of days it takes to convert inventory and receivables into cash.

Calculate the *Receivables Cycles* by dividing Net Credit Sales by Average Trade Receivables. This will give you the time it takes to collect credit sales.

A similar index is the *Past Due Index.* This is calculated by dividing Total Receivables Past Due by Total Receivables. This will give you a trend in the collection activity over a time.

Calculating the *Bad Debt Expense as a Percentage of Sales* is a matter of dividing Bad Debt Expenses by Total Credit Sales. This calculation will give you a trend of the bad debts that the company is experiencing.

Inventory Turns can be calculated by dividing Cost of Goods Sold by the Average Inventory Outstanding in a year. This measures the number of times the inventory is sold and replenished during a given period of time.

Another measure of cash flow is the *Percentage of Cash Flow to Total Assets*, which can be calculated by dividing Net Cash Flow by Total Assets. This will measure the cash-generating ability of the assets over a period of time.

Financial Reports

You need to determine which financial reports the financial management team uses in carrying out its tasks. The reports they use in day-to-day operations will give you a good indication of how they are managing the company. In addition, you should ask the financial people to give you copies of the reports that they provide to top management and, of course, you should find out how top management uses these reports to analyze the financial health of the company.

Conclusions on the Financial Area

At the end of the financial analysis, it is important to evaluate this area as follows: What do you think the major problems will be over the next two or three years? Does this financial team have the wherewithal to tackle these problems? Can this team finance this company over the next two to three years? Can it manage the assets of the company in such a way that it will not have financial problems? Do you feel comfortable with this financial team negotiating bank debt and other credit lines? At the end of the day, you will have to ask yourself, Can they do the job?

Checklist

Appendix 1 contains a long list of items that you should look for in the Financial Area. It lists the documents that you should collect when you have made your analysis of the financial area. In addition, you should obtain as much information as possible about the numerical analysis of the company in order to satisfy yourself that you have all the reports that count.

CHAPTER 7

REFERENCE INFORMATION

It seems unusual that some business proposals don't contain basic information about an entrepreneur's corporation. However, entrepreneurs may be so taken up with the marketing of a new product or the firm's financial possibilities that they leave out the general information that you will need to understand the type of deal you are getting into. You will find yourself having to dig out some of this information from the business proposal because it won't all be in one place. Much of it will have to come from the entrepreneur during your questioning period.

CORPORATE IDENTIFICATION

Remember to ask the entrepreneur for the exact name, address, and telephone number of the company. You will also need to know where (the State) and when the business was incorporated and the States in which the company is qualified to do business. Usually the lawyer will pick up this information as well as some of the other items on this list.

You will need to know the location of the minute books, the bylaws and the certificates of incorporation. You will also need to know if the organization has had any predecessor. By investigating this area, you may determine that your corporation has gone through several reincarnations to arrive at its current corporate organization.

At the same time, you will probably want to determine the standard industrial classification code for the company and the employee identification number that the company used for reporting its taxes.

CORPORATE STRUCTURE

The corporate structure, with all its subsidiaries, divisions, and branches, needs to be detailed. You need to know the names and locations of these subsidiaries and what operations consist of in each location. It is quite tempting at times to lump everything into one big corporate pile, but most corporations have various operations. Even within a single location you should understand exactly how all of these parts fit together.

If the company has subsidiaries, make a list of them with the exact names of the subsidiaries, where the stock for each one is located, who holds the minute books, bylaws, and certificates of incorporation, and in which States the subsidiaries are qualified to do business. You will also want to determine if any of these subsidiaries have predecessors.

Is the corporation a Subchapter-S Corporation? Is the stock 1244 stock? Are there any differences in the corporate structure from a standard corporation?

MANAGEMENT QUESTIONS

Determine if there are any actions, lawsuits or proceedings pending or threatened against the company and any of its officers or directors. If there are any actions, list them and go over them with the corporate attorney.

Does the company or any of its officers own 10% or more of the equity of any company other than this company? If they do, you will want to make a list of their holdings. It may be that this company is doing business with the company in which an officer owns more than 10%, and thus some special deals are going on.

Determine if the company has any shareholder agreements. That is, certain shareholders will own certain amounts or certain shares cannot be traded. You should make a list of these shareholder agreements and get copies of them.

Does the company have any management contracts? If so, you will want to get a copy of them. You should at least make a list of the terms and conditions of each of these contracts so that you will know exactly what is going on with regard to management's contractual relationships with the company you are about to invest in.

Is any broker entitled to a commission on this financing? If so, determine what the fee is and who it is being paid to. Determine if the company has paid commissions in the past for financing.

Are there any restrictions on the company's common stock? Sometimes the minutes of the company will indicate whether a restriction is to be placed on the future sale of company stock and whether common stock cannot be sold to anyone outside of the company. Make sure you know the restrictions.

Determine whether any affiliated transaction exists between the company and any of its officers, directors, or relatives, and whether it has been an arms-length transaction and not a sweetheart deal. Even if the company has been getting a sweetheart deal, this should concern you, because at some point in time sweetheart deals usually go sour. This would mean that if an officer's company has been selling the company an item below or near cost, when the price comes back to normal, the company you invested in will have less profit.

Determine if the company has any patents, trademarks, copyrights, or licenses. If so, speak to the lawyer who handled the application to find out what makes these patents, trademarks, and copyrights so unique. It is quite easy to get a patent, but much harder to defend it if it isn't strictly unique.

Stock Questions

Does a voting trust agreement exist on any of the company's stock? Some entrepreneurs will agree to a financing and will place their shares in a voting trust to be voted by the financing group. You will want to make sure no such agreements exist before you come in and require voting trusts so that you can control the company should the entrepreneur make the wrong step. We discuss this point further when we look at the structure of the deal.

Do any preemptive rights exist on the company's stock? That is, does anyone have the right to buy certain stock of certain people or from the company for any reason? In addition, do these rights relate to the sale of new shares in the future? If so, what are the exact rights?

Is there an option or right outstanding of first refusal on the sale of any shares of the company's common stock? If so, you may want to have the company obtain a waiver from the person who holds this right to let you purchase the stock that you want to purchase. Without such an approval, you may go all the way to the end and find that you can't do the financing because somebody else has the right to handle the financing that you proposed and they want to take it.

At one time, we were going to buy a group of fast food restaurants. We worked very diligently along with the entrepreneur on the purchase of these restaurants and had the deal almost complete. At the last minute, the franchisor was asked to waive its right of first refusal to acquire the locations. The franchisor thought the purchase price was a bargain and bought the units. The entrepreneurs had wasted three months and a large amount of money doing due diligence only to have the right of first refusal exercised by the franchisor.

Does the company have more than one class of stock? If it does, make sure you understand the various classes and also which class the company wants to set up in. Many entrepreneurs try to raise money by selling nonvoting stock to venture capitalists. They usually do this because the entrepreneur believes that the "venture capitalist wants to take control." You will have to work through this with your entrepreneur, but purchasing non-voting stock is not the way to go.

Does the company have any stock purchase warrants, options, subscriptions, convertible instruments, or any contracts or agreements for issuing common stock to anyone? If these exist, you will need to take them into account in determining how much of the company you should own. I remember one company in which the management team had an option to buy stock at a nominal amount in order to maintain their position of 51% of the company. This meant that no matter how much money anyone put into the company, they could not be diluted beyond 51%. This certainly prevents anyone from taking control of your company. However, from a venture capitalist standpoint, you don't want to sign anything that precludes you from putting up more money and diluting all stockholders.

Determine if any puts and calls or other equity purchase or sale instruments exist. Sometimes in the sale of stock to new stockholders, an entrepreneur will agree to "buy back any shares at cost" in his fine company to prove to the unsuspecting stock buyer that there is no risk in buying shares in this company. These "puts" mean that the stockholder has the right to put the stock back to the company at any time and take cash out of the company for those shares. Make sure you know what puts exist in your company.

In addition, the company may have a call on the shares that are outstanding. This can make a deal even more attractive, for if the call is at a low price and if the company can later buy back a large amount of equity at a fixed price, this can limit the upside of some of the stockholders and give you and the entrepreneur an opportunity to buy them out and not let them make a lot of money. It is very unusual to give a call, but sometimes it happens.

Determine if the company has any treasury stock and if it does, determine why this treasury stock exists. Again, sometimes an individual will be bought out for any number of reasons and the stock will become treasury stock. When stock is bought back, make sure you understand the full reason for its having been purchased. If necessary, contact the person who sold the stock back to the company in order to find out why they sold the stock.

In one company we looked at, the individual had treasury stock. Upon investigation, we found that he had purchased this stock from three or four individuals who were early investors. After contacting these individuals, we determined that they had been "screwed out of their stock by an unscrupulous entrepreneur." Needless to say, this was enough to tell us what kind of future we might expect with this entrepreneur.

PROFESSIONAL REFERENCES

You will want to contact three groups of professionals when looking for references on this company: the bankers, the lawyers, and the accountants. Landlords should also be questioned.

Questions for Bankers

You are primarily interested in finding out what the banker knows about the company that will give you greater insight into the operation of the business. The bank will be expressing a financial viewpoint so make sure your questions are oriented toward that area, except for those about management.

How long has the company been dealing with the bank? If it has only been a short time, then you will need to contact the former bank. You will notice that companies that have an unsatisfactory relationship with their bankers move frequently. When you find this is the case, you will also probably find a banker who has an unhappy relationship with an entrepreneur. Make sure you contact former banks to find out why the relationship went wrong.

How long has this particular bank officer dealt with the company? If it has only been a short time, then you will have to contact the others within the bank who have had a longer relationship. Banks are notorious for changing bank officers and it won't be unusual for you to find a new bank loan officer servicing the credit of the company.

Determine the amount of credit the bank has with the company. That is, what is the total amount the company has ever borrowed from the bank, both the high and the low? What formulas have gone into determining what the highs and lows are for the company?

What collateral is there for the loan? Determine what collateral the bank can sell if the company does not repay the loan. Find out if the company meets its payments as agreed. That is, has it been late on interest or principal payments?

Determine if the bank has ever been in default on any of its loans to the companies. Has the bank ever called a loan in default and later reinstated the loan? What were the circumstances surrounding any defaults on the loan? Remember, if the company is in default on its loan, you can expect the same thing on your investment.

Has the company ever asked the bank for lines of credit and been denied? If so, how large was the credit line and why was it denied?

Ask the bank officer if he believes the company has operating problems. Although the company may be making its payments, it may have other operating problems that you missed.

Ask the banker if the management is good. Sometimes bankers may lend money to the management because they have collateral, even though they do not like the entrepreneur. You can determine this after a few minutes of discussion. Ask the bank whether management have any drug- or alcohol-related problems. Also find out if the banker thinks they live too high on the hog. If they are high livers now, think how high they will be living once they have your money.

Other Institutional Lenders

Sometimes other institutional lenders are lending money to the company. These include finance companies and leasing companies. You should ask each of them the same questions you have asked the banker in order to determine how they view the company. Make sure you understand who is financing the company and have asked all such lenders they really think of the company.

Accounting Firm

You will need the names, addresses, and telephone numbers of the accountants for the company. If the company has changed accountants, you will want to ask these questions of all prior accountants.

Verify the numbers in any audit or compilation. Call up the accountant and go through the numbers one by one to make sure that the accountant agrees with them. You may even want to do this with the tax return to make sure the accountant has signed off on the numbers in the return given to you by the company in order to determine if it is correct. In one situation Allied is familiar with, the entrepreneur was not satisfied with the audit that he received from a large accounting firm. He xeroxed the top of the accountant's report in order to duplicate the letterhead on some blank pages. He then constructed his own audit and opinion and in it showed his company making a considerable amount of money when in fact the auditors said it was losing money. He presented these falsified accounting statements to his board of directors and various others in order to obtain financing. Needless to say, once Allied began checking with the accountants to determine if the numbers were correct, they uncovered a tremendous fraud. The entrepreneur served three years in prison for this act.

Most accountants issue a management letter stating what they find wrong with the day-to-day operations and, specifically, the financial controls of the company. If the accountants have issued a management letter, you will want to make sure you get a copy and talk with the accountant about its content.

Ask the accountant if the books and records of the company are in good condition and easy for them to audit or whether they need substantial improvement. If the accounting records are a mess and the accountant is making hundreds of adjusting entries, it will mean the company is, in a financial sense, out of control.

Ask the accountant if there are adequate controls in place to foil any misuse of funds.

Ask the individual at the audit firm how long he or she has been handling the work of the annual audit and working with the company on its financial matters. If the individual you are talking to is a relative newcomer, then you will need to talk to those who have worked with the company over the years and ask them many of the questions you are asking this new person.

Ask if the financial officer for the company is a good one and if that person can grow with the company to manage all of the company's financial needs in the future. Ask the accountant if he thinks the management team is a good one and if so why. Sometimes they will have a unique perspective on the management team.

Ask the accountant if the company is having operating problems. If he says it is, ask him to help you to determine what they are. Many accountants are quite candid in their assessment of the financial operations of the company.

See if they have begun work on this year's audit. If they have, you should ask them whether there are any material changes from the financial statements that have been prepared by the company. I know of one public company that would show earnings for three quarters in a row, but when it came to the fourth quarter, the accountants would have to make so many adjusting entries that all of the profits for the previous three quarters were wiped out. The company overstated its profits and the stockholder would not get the sad news until the end of the year. Ask the accountant if this has ever happened with the company. It is another red flag indicating that the company doesn't know how to manage its financial business. If it doesn't know how to manage its financial business you should not invest.

Ask the accountant if there are any significant changes in the numbers set out by management. When you review his audit, look for disagreements over the inventory values or disagreements between the goodness of accounts receivable. Ask him if there was a disagreement over the work in process and the cost of goods sold. Ask if there have been any material differences between the audit and they actual financial statements.

One of the key questions to ask the accountant is whether anything in the audit would indicate that the company is having operating problems. This is usually a standard question and auditors always expect it.

Questions for Lawyers

Another professional you will want to spend some time with is the lawyer for the company. Make sure the current lawyer has been around long enough to know all of the company's secrets. If this is a new legal group, make sure you go back and talk to past lawyers and find out why they were dumped.

The basic question for the lawyer is What suits are against the company today? Ask what suits have been filed against it in the past and how were they resolved. Ask the lawyer if any potential suits are brewing against the company. Also ask the lawyer if the company has filed any suits against others that are still open. Ask the lawyer to enumerate suits that the company has filed against others during the last two years. Ask the lawyer if he knows of any suits the company plans to file against others. It is important to establish the litigation history of any company that you intend to invest in. Although it is becoming a way of life in business to solve many problems through the court system, any company that sues a great deal or has been sued a great deal is most likely to end up in a suit with you. Any company that is litigious will try to solve its relationship with you in a litigious manner at some point in time. Be careful to document all legal situations so that you understand them in detail.

Ask the lawyer about product liability suits or problems as well as any union suits or legal problems regarding the union. Has this lawyer or any other lawyer helped the company file patents or defend patents in suits? Has the company been filed against because it is infringing on others' patents?

Suit Settlement

If there have been suits and they have been settled, determine the following. First, what is the maximum settlement that has been assessed in each case? What is the most likely settlement for any suits that are outstanding now and when will they be settled? What is the nature of any suit that is outstanding? Does the suit have merit? Why does the suit have merit? Again, make sure you understand the litigation history of the company.

I usually end my conversation with a lawyer with the following question: "Are there any legal problems with this company whatsoever?" Sometimes a lawyer will hem and haw in response. If they aren't being straightforward, ask them point-blank, "Why are you being so hesitant about saying there are no legal problems with the company?" Again, if you find them reticent, you may want to visit the law firm and go through the complete file, with the permission of the company of course.

You should ask the lawyers to give you their appraisal of management. Also, ask them if they know of any nonlegal problems. All of these should be open-ended questions so that you can get the maximum information out of the lawyers.

You should ask the lawyers if they know of any suits against the management team or any of the individual employees of the company. Have any suits been filed by trade creditors or customers? This will also give you a flavor for how the company treats its customers.

Questions for Insurance Agents

Interestingly enough, the insurance agent can be a bonanza of information about the situation at the company, especially in the areas of product liability and life insurance. You should ask the insurance agent to explain the company's fire and casualty insurance, the product and general liability insurance, and fidelity bonds along with life insurance on the entrepreneur.

Ask the insurance agent how many claims the company has made. Ask the insurance agent if the company has been dropped from any insurance in the past. Ask the insurance agent if the premium being paid by the company is standard for the industry or if premium is based on a poor record.

Ask if the company or the entrepreneur has been turned down for insurance. If so, why?

If the insurance agent hasn't had a long relationship with the company, then you will want to find the insurance company that is no longer the carrier and determine why the association was terminated.

Questions for Landlords

Where the company rents space from landlords, you will want to ask what they think of the company. You will want to document the company name of the landlord, the telephone number, and the person you talked to, because usually you will not have access to the investor/owner of the real estate, but will talk with the real estate agent who handles the situation. The following questions are appropriate.

How long have you been renting to the company? How many square feet do you rent to them? Sometimes this differs from what the company has told you and you will want to determine why.

Nail down where the rental property is located. If the company has given you the name and address of two properties but the rental agent only knows of one, you may have a bamboozling entrepreneur on your hands.

What is the monthly rental on the property? How timely have their payments been? Have you ever had to contact them for failure to pay rent? Have you ever had to threaten to evict them in order to collect rent?

Do they keep the property up? Do they make sure the property is in good working order at all times? Do they constantly ask you for changes in the lease and assistance in maintaining the property?

Would you rent to them again? This is a key question that you should always ask.

Finally, you should probably ask for any general comments about the company or its management team.

Questions for Manufacturers' Representatives

Ask the representative what products he represents for the company. It is important to know precisely which products the representative handles. Sometimes a representative will only handle one of the company's products.

How long has this person been the company's representative? Remember that representatives come and go in most industries. Nevertheless, it's important to know why a representative is no longer representing a product, or why an existing representative continues to represent the product.

What products *not* made by the company does this person represent? With this question you'll begin to get a feel for the representative and be able to determine whether this is an important product for him, or just a sideline. What percentage of his sales does this product account for? Is this an important product for him?

Be sure to ask the manufacturer's representative how many of the company's products he has sold during the last twelve months and what dollar volume that amounted to. This might not jibe with the numbers being given to you by the company. At any rate, it's a good check.

Ask the representative how many units he thinks he can sell in the next twelve months, and what the future holds in the next five years for this product. These projections will help you substantiate the projections being made by the company.

Ask the representative if the quality of the product is good and how it compares with competitors' products. Ask him if his customers like the product. How does he feel about it?

Does the representative receive many complaints about the product? If so, what kind of complaints? Is the company quick to respond to problems with the product? Does it "make good" to the customer if there are problems?

Ask the manufacturer's representative to compare and contrast the company's product with those of competitors in the same market. Is the quality better? Is the delivery better? Is there a perceived name for this product? Is there good name recognition? These are all important questions for the manufacturer's representative.

The final question I usually ask is about price. Is the price right? Too high or too low? How does it compare with the competition? What price does the representative think the product should sell for? Pricing is one of the most revealing topics you can discuss with customers or manufacturers' representatives.

Questions for the Advertising People

When you talk to the people at the company's advertising or public relations agency, you will want to ask some specific questions. First, find out how long the agency has been advertising for the company. If it's only been a short time, then you must find out the name of the previous agency and why a switch was made.

In addition, you should determine how often the company advertises. Perhaps its advertising has been rather spotty. The advertising people may be able to explain why that is a good approach. Ask about the average size of the company's printed ads to get a feel for whether they are adequate. Does the advertising agency have a standing order to place certain ads in certain publications? If so, find out how much and why the company will continue to advertise in that specific periodical. What is the cost of advertising and what is the average amount the company is spending? How does this compare with other companies in the field?

Is the advertising agency always paid on time? Has it ever had to contact the company for failure to pay? Remember, if the company is not paying the advertising people and this a persistent trait of the existing management team, you may never be paid either.

Will the advertising agency continue to run the ads for this company? Does it feel the company is making the right moves in its marketplace? Who is the agency's contact person at the company? If the agency deals with someone different from the person you've been talking to in marketing, you will want to talk to the agency's primary contact to see why they feel the agency is good. In addition, you should solicit any general comments from the agency regarding the company. How would they change the ads to make them better? What could the company do to capture more market share? These kinds of general questions can prod the advertising agency into giving you more information about the industry, the competition, and the company you're analyzing.

Questions for Suppliers

The leading question is What does the supplier supply to the company? What is the annual dollar volume that the company supplies? What credit limit do you have for the company?

Do you anticipate any shortage of any items you supply to the company? How promptly are you paid by the company? Has there ever been a problem with payment? Have you ever shipped to the company on a COD basis only?

What do you like about the company? How would you describe your relationship with the company? Are you treated as a good supplier?

Will you continue to supply the company in the future? Have you met the management team? What do you think of them?

Questions for Customers

What products have you purchased from the company during the last two years? How long have you been buying from the company? Here you are trying to establish how long the relationship has lasted with the company.

How long ago did you purchase the product from the company? Has it served you well? What are the current outstanding orders that you have with the company? Are you a repeat user, or is this your first time? What do you like about the product?

Has the company's product lived up to the quality that you originally perceived? Does the company's product perform as well as you expected?

Have you ever been shipped faulty goods? If so, what happened? Did the company make good on them or was there a fight?

Has the company lived up to the service representations it made to you before you bought the product? Has it been responsive?

Did you find the product overpriced? Or, was it a bargain? Would you pay more for the product?

Do you think that the product has brand name recognition? Is it strong brand recognition, or weak?

Have you purchased products from the competitors of this company or from other manufactured brand names similar to the one the company produces? How would you compare them to the company's product? When you compare the company's product to others, how does it rate on quality, price, and the service?

Do you intend to buy from the company again? Could you estimate how much you will purchase from the company during the next twelve months?

What change would you like to see in the company? What changes would you like to see the company make in the product? What do you think of the people you have had contact with in the company? Have you met any of the management team? What do you think of them?

Questions for Competitors

It is very difficult to call a competitor directly for information. However, under certain circumstances you may be able to develop information on the competition. Certainly credit reports and information surveys abound on industries and certain companies. It is also possible to hire an investigator to call the company's competitors and get information in this way. You will want to make sure that you cover the competition in detail in order to satisfy yourself that you know where your company stands in relationship to those competitors.

Questions for Subcontractors

Some of the questions that you will need to ask the subcontractor are as follows:

How long have you been doing contract work for the company? What is the annual volume that you produce for the company? Do you provide subcontracting to others in the industry? What is the annual volume of subcontracting work you do for all others?

Is the business with the company an important contract to you? If you lost this contract, would it be detrimental to your business? Have you had any disagreements with the company over production? Has the company ever refused to pay you for products that you have produced? Has it returned products to you, and if so, what happened?

What kind of investigation of your production facility did the company perform before it chose you as a subcontractor? Do you plan to continue to do work for the company? Do you like working for the company? Is there any possibility that your company will be shut down by strike or other problems at your plant in the next twelve months? If your plant burned down, would there be another subcontractor that the company could go to for the same merchandise?

CREDIT INFORMATION

Information on various aspects of a company can be obtained from basic credit reporting agencies. Certainly Dun and Bradstreet Reports provide such information, but information about the individuals will be available from credit reporting agencies. You should run the reports on the company as a standard procedure in order to make sure that the company does not have a bad credit history.

There are a number of major investigatory agencies that can help you find information about the company. You may want to hire one of these in order to gain more detailed information about the company.

DOCUMENTATION

In this section you will have developed a tremendous amount of information from the questions that you have asked of the many who deal with the company. You will also have collected data from numerous trade journals. Remember that investigation is a long and arduous process, during which you need must leave no stone unturned.

CHAPTER 8

NEGOTIATING THE DEAL AND COMMITMENT

In this chapter we discuss how to calculate your risk and return, how to structure deals, and what to put in the commitment letter. You need to know what risk you are taking and what the expected return will be. It's important to structure a deal to your advantage and to spell it out in business terms so that the lawyer can put it in legal terms.

PRICING THE DEAL

Pricing a deal is one of the investor's most difficult tasks. There are dozens of different critical aspects to pricing and this chapter touches on some of them.

Risk/Reward

The greater the risk, the greater the reward. Supposedly. But how do you identify and define risk? And how do you quantify risk? What is the probability that an enterprise will succeed? There are just so many variables in every investment we review that it becomes extremely difficult to quantify risk in most business situations. This is why experience is so important. From experience one can get a "feel" for the situation and judge the likelihood of success.

At the same time, we can rely on some obvious factors to judge the risk involved in a business. For example, a large business with a large amount of gross sales usually has less chance of going out of business than a smaller company. An existing business that has existing cash flow will be less risky than a new business. A business in a stable industry will be less likely to fail than one in a new industry. And a company with a management team that has been around for several years will have greater likelihood of success than one with a new management team. One could continue the list, but it will give a general idea only of the risk. Good hard work during the due diligence process will reveal the strengths and weaknesses of a business and its management team. From the results of our due diligence we can determine the risk.

Removing Risk by Structure

An investor can use the structure of the deal to reduce risk. The investor will have to give up something, but it may be worth it. For example, the investor can set the investment up as a debt instrument rather than as common stock and secure the debt instrument as much as possible. Where possible, he can take collateral and in as many cases as possible file UCC-1s in order to move from being a general creditor to being a secured creditor. As an investor you may want to avoid high-risk common stock and preferred stock, both of which provide a disaster scenario when a company gets into trouble.

Within the bounds of debt you can refine the structure to an art form. You may prefer a loan with warrants rather than a convertible debenture because the loan can be repaid in a deal that doesn't make a great deal of money in the early years. As time passes, you will have your stock options, which cost little or nothing to purchase and which may be worth something someday. You can hold the warrants for a long time and have no great reduction in your return if you didn't pay much for them. Also, on options, you should ask for less of a company's equity for a *low price* rather than more of a company for a high price. For example, would you rather own 20% of a company for no cost or 30% for a $500,000 exercise price on the warrant? You may want to do this because if the option runs out you can afford to exercise the option at a low exercise price, and it doesn't cost a lot to carry the resulting stock. You can hold onto low-cost stock forever and hope that someday it will be worth something. These structural approaches lower the risk.

While you are structuring the deal and assessing the risk on a nonquantitative basis, it's time to start thinking about return on investment.

Return on Investment

As a backdrop, remember that venture capitalists have *averaged* 25% return on investment for the last ten years. Obviously, you want to achieve this strong return on investment (ROI). From another perspective, if you get five times your money back in five years, it's a 38% compounded return on investment. In fact, a rule of thumb is if you can get one times your money back for each year you are in the deal it's an excellent investment.

If you looked at every one of your investments and thought that you could get, on the upside, a 25% return on investment, including interest, if everything worked right, then you would be very lucky to exceed a 15% ROI. This is because some of the deals will return more than you expect them to; however, most will give you less than you expect. On the average, you would probably have less than a 25% return. So the return on each deal must be higher than the average you want on all your investments.

Sometimes you may be tempted to go into a deal that has been referred to as a "safe deal," "no-brainer," "good collateral," and "no real downside." Every venture capitalist has heard these buzz words and been tempted to take a 20% return on investment. But before you jump into deals like this, or any deal for that matter, you need to know what kind of investment you're really getting into. The fact is that deals fall into several in categories.

Types of Deals

In general, deals can be divided into six basic groups as, outlined below.

1. *Big Winners.* Here we are talking about a big winner for you, not whether the company is a big winner, although the two usually go together. In this situation you get three or four times the money you expected to get, or about a 90% or 100% return on investment. These are outstanding deals. These are the exception to the rule. Normally you are looking for a 50% ROI and are surprised when the company gives you the big upside.

2. *Winners.* In this situation you get what you expected, a solid 30% to 35% return on investment and everybody is quite happy. Unfortunately, there are not as many of these deals as we would all like to see.

3. *Sideways.* A sideways deal is one in which you get the principal and interest back, plus a little on your equity for about a 10% or 15% ROI.

4. *Workouts*. You will have your share of workouts. In these situations you normally get your principal back with little or nothing else.

5. *Losers*. Losers usually consist of a 50% hit. That is, you might put in $200,000 and get $100,000 back. You should pray that you have few losers.

6. *Wipeouts*. Although venture capitalists rarely have wipeouts, they do occur now and then. This is where the investor loses all or practically all of the investment. You must avoid wipeouts at all costs.

Using Probability

So what have you learned? Invest in more winners and less losers. Obviously! In order to quantify your risk/reward and help you price a deal, you should categorize your new investment opportunities by the six categories discussed above. The deal you are considering will be in one of the following categories:

Category	ROI (%)	Probability Deal Will Hit (%)	Weighted Average (ROI x Probability) (%)
Big Winner	100	10	10
Winner	30	50	15
Sideways	10	20	2
Workout	0	10	0
Loser	(50)	5	(2.5)
Wipeout	(100)	5	(5)
TOTAL ALWAYS		100	19.5

The weighted average of the investment is computed by multiplying the probability times the return and adding the columns. In the case above it adds up to 19.5%. If your ROI objective is 30% and if the weighted average is not in excess of 30%, then you shouldn't complete the deal!

Here's an example of two companies that Allied Capital invested in.

142

	Company #1 (%)	Company #2 (%)
Big Winner	10	10
Winner	70	50
Sideways	10	20
Workout	5	5
Loser	5	5
Wipeout	0	0
Average ROI	34.5	28.5

Probabilities and Deviation

When you set the probabilities in the return column you are also establishing the *risk* of receiving it. You have established a standard deviation curve for the expected return. For example, compare the two deals set out below:

	Deal A's Chances (%)	Deal B's Chances (%)
Big Winner	20	70
Winner	30	0
Sideways	50	0
Workout	0	0
Loser	0	0
Wipeout	0	(30)
	34	40

Look at the difference between these two investments. Is Deal B a better opportunity? Deal B is more of a crap shoot, a big winner or a wipeout, whereas Deal A has a greater chance of making some money. Given the expected return, one would want both deals, but given an investor's bias toward lower risk, deal B's return may not be high enough because it is such a high risk. So how do you judge deals that are so far apart in risk? The answer is to look at the return. Is a 40% weighted average return enough to take the risk implied in Deal B? Is 34% enough return to take the lower risk implied in Deal A? This is the type of judgment you will have to make as an investor.

Return

Another point we need to cover concerns the term return. In the investment business, we have too many ways of defining return. We talk about return on investment (ROI), the internal rate of return (IRR), and how many times our money an investment. We do it before interest and with interest. We do optimistic, average, and pessimistic projections. This is a fine exercise, but when it's over, there should be only one scenario, and the return to the investor should be computed on only one scenario - the most likely scenario. As an investor, you should set up the situation as demonstrated below:

The ABC Corp. (in thousands)

	1st Yr.	2nd Yr.	3rd Yr.	4th Yr.	5th Yr.	6th Yr.	7th Yr.
Investment	($1,000)						
Return of Capital				250	250	250	250
Interest	75	100	100	100	75	50	25
Net Gain							10,000
Cash flow to investor	($ 925)	$100	$100	$350	$325	$300	$10,275

By using this type of projected cash flow to the investor, you can call upon various techniques to analyze the return. You should always set up investment projections like this so you can understand them more easily.

Return to Investor

Hundreds of techniques can be used to measure return on investment. Simple return on investment (ROI) is the amount of money invested divided into the amount returned. For example, a deal that pays interest of $15,000 per year on a $100,000 investment has a ROI of 15% ($15,000/$100,000). When there are multiple years you can adjust the ROI for multiple years by dividing the ROI by the number of years. So a deal that paid $15,000 in year one and $30,000 in year two would have an annualized ROI of 22.5% [($15,000 + $30,000)/$100,000/2].

However, this simple annualized ROI lacks the added dimension of time. ROI doesn't take into account the time value of money. We all know that a dollar you receive today is worth more than a dollar you receive tomorrow. Why? Because you can reinvest the dollar you receive today and make even more money and because the dollar you receive on the future will have less buying power because of inflation. The technique of adjusting for the time value of money is called present value.

Present Value

The term *present value* has been used to define the present value of a dollar that is to be received in the future. Present value achieves this by discounting future dollars to be received by a certain interest rate. Often the rate is the alternate rate at which one could invest the money. This alternate rate is referred to as the discount rate. For example, if you could leave your cash in a bank at 8%, then a discount of 8% would be used to discount the receipt of future cash flows. Under your 8% discount rate, $1 to be received in one year is worth only about $0.92 in present value. This discounting of future income can become complicated when multiple years are involved and the discounting is compounded each year. This complex approach is embodied in a technique of analyzing investments called the Internal Rate of Return.

Internal Rate of Return

IRR can add the time dimension. It is the interest rate that equals the present value of the expected future receipts. Theoretically, by computing IRR one finds the interest rate at which one would have to invest the money to equal the cash flows generated by the proposed investment. If a proposed investment had an IRR of 20% computed on the cash flow to us, we can say if we invested our money in a bank at 20% it would give us the same return as the proposed investment. The present values are the same.

There is one flaw in using IRR. It assumes you **reinvest** the money received in the early years at the same rate as the overall deal. So interest received in the early years is reinvested at the same rate. For example, if the IRR on a deal is 35%, the calculation assumes that interest received from the investment in the early years is reinvested at 35%! This is not true in most investment situations. Although this is a distortion of the basic situation, but it is one that most analysts accept. There is one technique that lowers this reinvestment rate. It is called Net Present Value (NPV).

Net Present Value

Net Present Value can correct this flaw in IRR. NPV assumes that the money received in the early years in reinvested at the discount rate used in calculating NPV. So if we used a discount rate of 8%, that same rate would be used for reinvesting the interest received in the early years. This is a more conservative approach to calculating return.

145

Investor's Standard

There is no clear consensus in the investment community on which type of return calculation should be used. As far as analysis goes, you should use either IRR or NPV, and be specific when stating which technique has been used.

The more difficult question is, what is the minimum IRR or NPV you are willing to accept? Here are some suggestions on IRR from the venture capital industry by type of investment.

	Percent
Seed capital	100
Start-up	50
Second round	40
Third round	30
Bridge, before public offering	25
Turnaround	50
Leveraged buyout	35

COMMITMENT LETTERS

Every investor and venture capital company has a very different way of making a commitment to an entrepreneur. Some venture capital companies will not issue commitment letters. They have an oral agreement with a small business person and then they begin to draw up the legal documents and attempt to close on the investment on the basis of the oral understanding.

Other venture capital funds use a one-page "term sheet" that spells out the high points of the deal, that is, those items that are most critical, such as amount of equity owned and type of investment. A term sheet does give the lawyer something to start with.

I prefer more detailed commitment letters. It has always seemed to me that there should be an intermediate step between the oral understanding and the legal documents. Although this means outlining in a commitment letter the bargain struck on each side, it lets two business people state in business language what they believe the deal may be.

Some banks use very short commitment letters to identify the terms and conditions of a bank loan. These are more akin to term sheets than the type of commitment letter that most venture capitalists use.

In the commitment letter it will be important to specify why each item discussed is necessary in an investment. Every commitment letter should cover five basic points: (1) the terms on which the loan is being made to the company and the equity options

146

(this is the fundamental point of any deal); (2) the collateral for any loan or any external aspects to the loan that will be picked up by the investor; (3) the conditions of the investment, both negative and positive; (4) the representations made by the entrepreneur to induce the investor to invest in his company; and (5) the conditions on which the commitment was made to the entrepreneur. Each of these points is now discussed in turn.

1. Terms of the Investment

In the section of the letter dealing with this point, the investor needs to state clearly the terms and conditions on which the investment is being made.

> 1.01   The venture capital company will make a loan of $500,000 for eight years at an interest rate of 12% per annum paid monthly on the first of each month.

This sentence is self-explanatory. In essence, the company has a $500,000 infusion at 12%.

> 1.02   The loan shall have payments of interest only for the first thirty-six months, and beginning with the thirty-seventh month you will pay principal and interest sufficient to fully amortize the loan over the remaining sixty months. All principal and interest outstanding at the end of eight years shall be due and payable in full.

The investor is abating principal repayment during the first thirty-six months and after that period the investor expects the loan to be amortized over the next sixty months.

> 1.03   The loan may be prepaid in whole or in part, at any time with no prepayment penalty.

Here the investor is allowing the small business to repay the loan. In some situations where the interest rate is high, you should add that the company cannot prepay the loan at any time. Otherwise at some strong moment the company will prepay the loan and cut down the return on investment you were counting on with the high interest rate. On the other hand, if you have a large equity ownership in the company resulting from the loan, you will want to encourage the entrepreneur to prepay the loan.

> 1.04   Disbursement and takedown of the loan shall be 100% of the loan at closing.

Here the investor has invested the entire amount of money at one fell swoop into the company. It is much more common for the investor to require the entrepreneur to jump certain hurdles in order to draw down the money. For example, disbursement at closing might only be 25% of the amount being invested, with the rest coming in when the company has achieved certain milestones such as sales of a certain amount or completion of a research and development project.

1.05   In connection with this financing, the venture capital firm shall receive at the closing separate stock options to purchase stock in the company. The cost of the options to the venture capital firm will be $100. These options when exercised will provide stock ownership in the company of 20% at the time of exercise. The exercise price will be $20,000. The options will expire ten years from closing. The venture capital firm will share pro rata in any redemption of stock by the company in order to expand its pro rata ownership.

In this situation, the venture capital firm is receiving a large amount of cheap options in the company. Once this piece of paper is signed, even if the loan is repaid, the investor has an option to buy the stock in the company for a significant amount of time. If you are the type of investor who likes to invest in a company and receive warrants, your basic objective is to run your money through the company as quickly as possible in order to pick up as many pieces of options as possible. Sometimes, rather than using a percentage of ownership, it will actually state the number of shares and the price per share. If so, there will also be an antidilution clause stating that if the company sells additional stock and it is below a certain price, then the venture capitalist will be issued additional shares so as to maintain the equity ownership. This is standard in most deals.

1.06   There shall be an "unlocking" provision whereby if there is a bona fide offer to purchase the company and the venture capitalist wishes to accept the offer whereas the company does not, then the company is required to purchase the venture capitalists's interest on the same terms and conditions as the bona fide offer. If you do not buy out the venture capitalist, then you must sell the company according to the terms of the bona fide offer.

148

The "unlocking" provision gives the venture capitalist an opportunity to exit from the company if there is a bona fide offer to purchase the company. In essence, it says that if someone offers to buy the company and the venture capitalist thinks it should be sold for that price and the entrepreneur has agreed, they will either (a) buy the venture capitalist out at the price per share indicated by the offer; or (b) sell the company on the terms and conditions made by the bona fide offer.

1.07   There shall be a "put" provision whereby anytime after five years the venture capital firm may require the company to purchase its stock options or the resulting stock from the options at the higher of the following:

1. $50,000 cash;
2.   120% of book value times 20% ownership;
3.   five times net pretax earnings for the year just ended times 20% ownership;
4.   ten percent of sales for the year just ended times 20% ownership;
5.   ten times cash flow times 20% ownership; or
6.   appraised value times 20% ownership.

Most entrepreneurs will not agree to a "put" position, especially if it is at a reasonable price. As a negotiator, you will probably have to convince the entrepreneur that a "put" is in your best interest and he should give it to you because if for some reason the company does not do what the entrepreneur says it will do, you as an investor want some way of cashing in and going on to the next deal. Usually at this point the argument revolves around the price of the "put." In most instances, an entrepreneur will give in if the "put" is at a low price that just gets the venture capitalist out but not at any big return on investment.

1.08   There shall be a "call" provision for a period of three years whereby after five years from closing and after the venture capitalist's loan has been paid in full, the company can purchase the stock options or resulting stock from the options on the same terms and conditions as 1.07 above.

As an investor, you should avoid "call" provisions if at all possible, even at astronomically high rates, because the only time the entrepreneur is going to exercise the "call" provision is when the company has made tremendous strides and all you're doing is capping your return on investment. Certainly if a 40% return on investment is built into the "call" provision, it's nice to have, but you're only going to be called out and capped in your return on investment when the company is doing very well. You should, as an investor, avoid "call" provisions.

> 1.09   Anytime after five years from closing the venture capitalist may require a registration and public offering of the shares owned by the venture capitalist at the company's expense.

Demand registrations, as they are known in the business, are standard procedures for people investing in small companies. It is rare that a venture capitalist will require a small business to register, but most often the venture capitalist and the entrepreneur are ecstatic with the idea that they can register the shares and make some money for them and for the company. However, it is standard procedure for the investor to ask for a demand registration clause and entrepreneurs, while usually not keen on giving this provision, usually give it reluctantly.

> 1.10   The venture capitalist shall have full "piggyback" rights to register his shares whenever the company or its management is registering shares for sale, and such registration of the venture capitalist's shares shall be paid for by the company.

This paragraph enables you as an investor to ride on the coattails of any registration that goes on for public sale of the company. It means that when the stockbroker is going to take the company out for public offering, you as an investor have the right to offer and sell some of your shares in the public offering. Generally speaking, the brokerage house will not permit inside investors to sell more than 10% or 20% of their holdings in the public offering, but it's nice to have this opportunity so that you can sell some of your stock in any public offering. This "piggyback" right is a standard paragraph for investors in the venture capital situation.

2. Collateral and Security

In this section of the commitment letter you as an investor must set out what is collateralizing the loan that you are making to the company. Which assets of the corporation will be yours in case the company has problems? What personal assets will the entrepreneur pledge? You must enumerate these in detail.

150

2.01   The venture capitalist will have a second deed of trust on land and building of the business subordinated as to collateral to a first mortgage of $200,000 from a bank on terms acceptable to the venture capitalist.

According to this paragraph, the venture capitalist will have a second deed of trust on the land and building owned by the company and it will be subordinated to a $200,000 first mortgage by the bank. There may be no equity left in the land and building at this time, but as time goes on it's amazing how the equity in the land and building, and other assets will build up. As an investor, you need a secured position on assets whenever you can.

2.02   The venture capitalist will have a second secured interest in all the tangible and intangible assets of the company, including but not limited to inventory, machinery, equipment, furniture, fixtures, and accounts receivable subordinated as to collateral to a first secured bank loan of $100,000 on terms acceptable to the venture capitalist.

In this situation, the investor has a second secured interest in all the tangible and intangible assets of the company and is subordinated to a secured interest of a term loan from a bank of $100,000. A venture capitalist will frequently try to secure his loans in order to remove himself as a general creditor of a company. This gives him some protection in case the company falters and goes into bankruptcy. It's not a sure-fire thing because many times the equity built up in secondary collateral is not very much. However, a second or third secured interest in the assets of the company is better than being among the general creditors; sometimes this can help out an investor.

2.03   The company will pledge and assign all the stock of the company and assign any and all leases of the company to the venture capitalist.

In this situation, you ask the entrepreneur to pledge his stock or the stock of his investor group as collateral for your investment. This will give you the ability to foreclose on the stock of the company and then own it should trouble come along. It is unlikely that you would ever do this, and it's probably more of a psychological thing to have the entrepreneur pledge his stock to you than will be meaningful in a workout situation. Imagine a company having a great many problems and you are foreclosing and own the

151

stock of this company. Now, suddenly you can replace management but still have all the problems the previous management created.

2.04   The entrepreneur will give her personal signature and guarantee (and that of her spouse) to the loan.

Most venture capitalists ask for and receive the personal guarantee of a small business person on a loan to the company. It is not quite as common on later stage investments or leveraged buyouts. Sometimes the personal guarantee is used to make up for the entrepreneur's having little or no money to invest. It makes the entrepreneur think twice about doing something if she knows that personally she will be wiped out if the company is liquidated.

2.05   The venture capitalist will obtain a life insurance policy on his life for the amount of the loan outstanding with the venture capitalist listed as the loss payee to the extent of his loan.

It is becoming standard practice in the venture capital business to require a life insurance policy on the life of a key entrepreneur or on several members of the management team. If the key entrepreneur dies, the policy will pay back the venture capitalist some or all of the money he has invested in the company and cancel any debts due from the company to the venture capitalist. This helps both the venture capitalist and the entrepreneur since the entrepreneur's estate will be the major benefactor of the company, which is practically debt-free.

2.06   The company will obtain adequate hazard and business insurance, which shall include flood insurance if the business is located in a designated federal flood area. All such insurance shall be assigned to the venture capital firm, which shall be listed as the loss payee to the extent of its interest. In this regard, the company will supply the venture capital firm with a list of all business insurance, and such insurance and coverage shall be acceptable to the venture capital firm.

Business insurance is an absolute requirement of any venture investment in a company. In today's litigious society with huge awards being given to people for very routine suits, it has become absolutely necessary to protect the assets of the business by having a large insurance policy.

3. Conditions of the Loan

In this section of the commitment letter the investor should enumerate all the conditions of the loan. This will let the entrepreneur know up front what he is expected to do in order to stay in the investor's good graces.

> 3.01 The company will provide the venture capitalist with internally prepared, monthly year-to-date financial statements, in accordance with generally accepted accounting standards (including a profit-and-loss statement and balance sheet) within thirty days of the end of each month.

This section is fairly self-explanatory, but it means that the investor will be kept apprised of the financial status of the company through monthly financial statements.

> 3.02 The company will provide the venture capitalist with a monthly one- or two-page summary of operations, to be submitted with the financial reports detailed in 3.01 above.

Every investor needs to know what is going on with the company beyond the numbers covered in 3.01 above. Most investors will require that the company prepare a one- or two- or three-page summary of the major things that have happened to the company during the preceding month. This will accompany the financial statements as they go out to the investor. Sure, the investor should be in touch with the company frequently and he should know what's going on, but it's also good to have management record on paper exactly what's happened in the last thirty days.

> 3.03 Within ninety days after the year end the company will provide the venture capitalist with an annual certified audit from an independent certified public accounting firm acceptable to the venture capital company.

A certified audit from an independent certified public accountant is absolutely mandatory in these days of complex financial statements. As an investor you should require every company that you invest in to give you certified financial statements. If a company can't do that, it is normally in deep trouble, and without audited certified financial statements it will be impossible to sell that company to someone who thinks that they can turn it around and fix it or attract good management to replace the existing management. Always insist on having certified financial statements.

> 3.04 Within thirty days of the year end, the company will provide the venture capitalist with projections for the next fiscal year in the same format as the financial statements.

Projections that you receive now while you're making your investment will go stale within a few months, and certainly within a year they will be worthless. It is important to have the entrepreneur prepare new financial statements each time the company goes through a big change and to receive new projections at least once a year.

> 3.05 Within thirty days after they are filed, the company will provide the venture capitalist with a copy of all material documents filed with government agencies such as the Internal Revenue Service, the Environmental Protection Agency, and the Securities and Exchange Commission.

An entrepreneur can easily provide information about the company by xeroxing copies of filings before government agencies and sending them to you. This is not a great hardship for the small business person, and these documents will enable you to get a better view of how the company is doing. Tax returns in particular contain a wealth of information.

> 3.06 The president of the company will provide the venture capital company with a certificate each quarter stating that no default has occurred in the terms and conditions of this loan.

It's also good to have an entrepreneur submit a monthly progress report indicating that all of the things you asked him to do in the legal documents are being done. This is something of a positive statement that everything is going well and it can be presented simply. Entrepreneurs don't usually argue about this.

> 3.07 On a quarterly basis and within thirty days of the end of the quarter, the company will provide the venture capital firm with a list of inventory, accounts receivable, and other collateral to be compared with certain ratios.

The venture capital firm will often ask for certain levels in the business to be maintained, the reason being that if the company falls below these certain levels the business will be worth much less. It's important to include such items in a commitment to a small business.

3.08   In accordance with generally accepted accounting principles, the company will maintain:

1.   A current ratio of one to one;
2.   Accounts receivable to loan balance of one to one;
3.   Inventory to loan balance of ___%;
4.   Sales of $1 million per year;
5.   Net worth of $300,000.

In this section you have dreamed up some ratios in which you want the entrepreneur to live up to. These things make the agreement more like a bank loan, but usually you only put them in for certain critical items. For example, in the radio business, radio stations sell at a multiple of sales. It's not uncommon for the legal documents for a radio financing to specify that the loan will be in default if the radio station falls below a certain amount of gross sales per month, per quarter, or per year.

3.09   There will be no change in control or ownership of the company without the venture capital firm's express written approval.

Under the terms of this section, you as the venture capitalist will not permit any change in control of the company. To the small business person this means that you have debt on this person and you do not want horses to be changed in mid-stream without your permission. Most entrepreneurs do not have a problem with this as they think they will be in control forever.

3.10   Management will not sell, assign, or transfer any shares it owns in the company without written approval of the venture capital firm.

Here again the venture capitalist, as an investor, is trying to make sure that the small business person will not sell, assign, or transfer his shares in the company without the investor's approval. You want to make sure that the person you have bet on stays with the company and continues to work for it and reaps no benefit if he decides to leave. Again, most entrepreneurs don't have a problem with this section because they are intent on making their fame and fortune in this situation.

> 3.11 The company will have board meetings at least once each quarter at the company's business offices. Although the venture capital firm's representative will not serve on the board, its representative will have the right to attend each meeting at the company's expense and the venture capital firm shall be notified of each meeting at least two weeks before it is to occur.

By setting up a paragraph such as this you have given yourself as an investor an opportunity to come in and see how the company is run, not at the management level but at the board level. You may even want to consider taking a seat on the board of directors; however, being a board member of a small company carries with it a tremendous amount of liability. Only those who can stand the liability of suits from IRS for nonpayment of payroll taxes, and other suits from suppliers and disgruntled investors should sit on the board of directors. You can gain just as much information by attending board meetings without being on the board.

> 3.12 The company will pay no cash dividends and the company will not sell any assets of the business that are not part of the regular course of business without the venture capital firm's approval.

The venture capital company is usually very intent on making sure that a small business does not waste its assets. As an investor you want to make sure they don't pay them out in dividends, but rather reinvest them in the business that you've invested in and that the company goes forward and prospers. You also want to make sure they don't sell off pieces of the company in order to keep it afloat, especially if those pieces are needed to make the company run the way it was originally envisioned. This paragraph is a standard requirement and one that most small businesses don't have a problem with.

> 3.13 The company will not expend funds in excess of $10,000 per year for capital improvements without written approval of the venture capital firm.

This is a general restriction on the amount of money that will be spent for capital improvements. You'll have a lot of fistfights with entrepreneurs over what the amount will be, and some will even say, "If you don't like the way I'm running things, then you should vote me out as management rather than restricting each and every item that I might make a decision on." But in this area of capital improvements it is important to make sure you have some restrictions over management. If you don't, you'll build a palace with no income. This is one way to keep restrictions on an entrepreneur who wants to build a palace to himself.

> 3.14 The management team, including you, will live in the metropolitan area where the business is located. The business will not be relocated without the express written permission of the venture capital firm.

Most investors want to make sure that the management team remains with the company and continues to live and work in the same area. It is practically impossible to run a small business from a distance, so restricting an entrepreneur to a geographic region should not cramp his style. It also keeps you from having to chase an entrepreneur who has moved out of town, because if he does so he will be in default on the agreement and you can foreclose and take over the business.

> 3.15 The company will not pay any employee nor will it loan nor advance to any employee money that in total exceeds $50,000 per year without the written approval of the venture capital firm. If the company is in default for nonpayment on its loan to the venture capital firm or in default on any senior lien, or if the company is not profitable for any calendar quarter, then the company will not pay any employee nor will it loan nor advance to any employee money that in total exceeds $30,000 without written permission of the venture capital firm.

Every venture capitalist will want a ceiling on the salary of the entrepreneur, and you should be no exception. It is not hard to understand and to make the entrepreneur understand that you don't want to invest your money if it is going to be drawn out as salary by the entrepreneur. If you put $500,000 in and the entrepreneur takes a salary of $500,000 out, what have you done except finance his salary for the first year? Although arguments over the amount of salary will be long and heated, it is of paramount importance that you have some kind of provision preventing the entrepreneur from taking a great deal of money out of the company.

> 3.16 The company will not pay any brokerage fees, legal

fees, or consulting fees in excess of $10,000 per year without written approval of the venture capitalist.

This paragraph is meant to prevent the entrepreneur from hiring a bunch of hangers-on who are not necessary to the business. It gives you some control over how many people outside the company are going to be paid. It is not a very big provision, and you may want to trade it for something else when bargaining.

3.17   You will pay all closing costs and recording fees, which include all attorney's fees, even those of the venture capitalist's attorney. You may use any attorney to draw up the legal documents; however, the documents must be reviewed and approved by the venture capitalist's counsel. A simple review by the venture capital company's counsel will not incur a legal fee; however, if the work done by the venture capitalist's counsel is beyond a simple review, a fee will be charged and the fee will be paid by you.

One of the conditions in almost every deal is that the entrepreneur's company pay for all of the legal and closing costs. This is becoming a standard practice in the investment world. Just make sure that you have a professional drawing up the documents so the entrepreneur cannot complain about legal costs.

4. Representations

In this section of the letter you will state the representations made by the entrepreneur that induced you to invest in his company. If any of these representations are not true and the entrepreneur signs this agreement and takes your money, you have the prerogative to declare the investment violated and demand your money back. It may also give you leave to sue the entrepreneur for fraud.

4.01   The company is a corporation in good standing in _____ (your State). You will provide the venture capital firm with a certificate of good standing, and a copy of the charter, the bylaws, and the organizing minutes of the company.

This is a standard certificate the company will have to provide; usually the company's attorney can do it.

4.02   The company is primarily engaged in the business of _____ (type of business).

Here you want to state exactly what business the company is in so that if it gets off the straight and narrow and tries to get into another business, you will be able to invoke one of the representations the company has made, namely, that it is in a certain business, and one of the conditions of the loan is that it won't change the business it is in.

    4.03   There are no lawsuits against the company, its directors, or its officer, nor do you know of any that may be contemplated. If there are any suits outstanding or contemplated, your attorney will provide the venture capital firm with a letter stating the nature of such suits and a copy of such suits at least thirty days prior to closing. You will provide the venture capital firm with a copy of all lawsuits you have filed against others.

This is a fairly standard representation made by every small business and you should make sure it is correct through your due diligence, but here you are also requiring the entrepreneur to state that it is true.

    4.04   The company is current on all taxes owed; in this regard you will provide the venture capital firm with a copy of the last three years' tax returns plus a copy of the receipts for payment of the last four quarters of payroll taxes.

Again in this section, you should have verified that the company is current on these kinds of things, but as final evidence that everything is all right you are asking the entrepreneur to state something that he has already told you.

    4.05   You have presented financial information, business information, and a business proposal that you represent to be true and correct.

This is a more difficult paragraph to get the entrepreneur to sign. What you are trying to do is get him to say that the prospectus he has given you is true and correct. This means that if any of the information presented to you during the first year is found to be incorrect, under securities law you will be able to ask the company to rescind the financing and give you your money back.

    4.06   Your personal financial statement showed that you have a net worth of $500,000.

In this paragraph you make the entrepreneur represent his personal net worth, but only if he is a guarantor of your loan.

> 4.07   You will invest an additional $50,000 of cash in the company as equity on or before the closing on this loan on terms acceptable to the venture capital firm. You will provide the venture capital firm with written information on the terms of this investment.

If the entrepreneur is going to invest additional money, it needs to be covered here.

> 4.08   A group of investors will invest $150,000 in the business as equity on terms acceptable to the venture capital firm. You will provide the venture capital firm with written information on these investments.

If a group of investors is going to invest additional money, that too needs to be placed in the commitment letter.

> 4.09   The money borrowed will be used as follows:
>
>   1.   Pay accounts payable, $100,000;
>   2.   Pay bank debt, $300,000; and
>   3.   Provide working capital, $100,000.

In this section you cover in more detail the company's use of the proceeds. Don't be surprised to see changes made at the last minute here.

> 4.10   Upon closing of the investor's loan, you will have approximately the following assets:
>
>   1.   Cash, $300,000;
>   2.   Inventory, $700,000;
>   3.   Accounts receivable, $1,000,000;
>   4.   Machinery and equipment, $500,000;
>   5.   Land and building, $300,000; and
>   6.   Other assets, $20,000.

A venture capitalist will look for representations made by the company and if there have been no audited financial statements the venture firm will select items that the company has represented that are critical to the operation of the company in order to make a specific representation about some aspect of the company.

4.11   With regard to all material leases, the company will provide the venture capital firm with a copy of each lease.

Here the venture capitalist will want copies of leases and other items that the entrepreneur has represented that as being in his ownership.

4.12   The company will pay no brokerage fees, legal fees, or other fees in connection with this loan without the venture capital firm's written approval; and, in addition, will indemnify the venture capital firm against all such fees.

Here the venture capitalist, like the entrepreneur, wants to make sure that he doesn't have to pay any brokerage fees. If certain fees are due, he wants to make sure they are due to the company and not to the venture capital firm. Almost everybody who's been in the investment business realizes that a broker pops his head out of the woodwork somewhere near the end of the deal asking for a fee. A representation by the company early on will prevent this from happening.

4.13   During the past ten years none of the directors, officers, or management has been arrested or convicted of a material crime or a material matter.

Every investor needs to know that there are no crooks in the company and this type of representation is standard.

4.14   The company has a commitment from a bank or other financial institution to borrow $200,000 on terms acceptable to the venture capital firm. With regard to this commitment, you will provide the venture capital firm with a copy of your commitment and closing documents.

If the company has a commitment from a bank, make sure you put it into the commitment letter and certainly in the legal documents in order to assure yourself that the commitment from the bank is there. You should have already developed this during the due diligence process, but it is just another way of making sure the representation is carried forward in the legal documents.

5. Conditions of the Commitment Letter

A number of conditions will not be embodied in the legal documents. These are the conditions of the commitment letter. If any of these conditions don't go forward, then the commitment letter is rendered void.

> 5.01 In connection with this financing, the venture capital firm will receive a 2% ($10,000) fee. Upon acceptance of this commitment letter, you will pay the venture capital firm $5,000 of the fee and the remainder at closing. Should closing not take place through the fault of the venture capital firm, then the fee in total would be returned. Otherwise the paid portion of the fee would be forfeited and the unpaid portion of the fee would be due and payable immediately. Acceptance by you of this commitment letter and the return of one copy of this letter to the venture capital firm fully executed by you with the fee must be received before _____ (date).

It is becoming more common for investors to receive one or two percentage points when the deal closes. This usually covers some of the out-of-pocket expenses involved in due diligence and investigating companies. Although most entrepreneurs hate to pay fees up front, reputable venture capital firms are not in the business of making money from taking fees up front, and the more an individual can hold himself out as a good institution the more likely an entrepreneur is to pay a fee up front.

> 5.02 Closing must take place on this investment before _____ (date).

Every investor needs to have a date by which the commitment is rendered null and void if the investment hasn't been closed with the legal documents.

> 5.03 All legal documents must be acceptable to the venture capital firm.

As an investor, you need to know that the legal documents will be acceptable to you. It is conceivable that a lawyer might draft up legal documents that didn't follow the document precisely. That would not be acceptable to you. In this area, you protect yourself by inserting this paragraph.

5.04   Allied must complete a "due diligence" report reflecting favorably on the company, its management, and its industry. This will include a favorable credit check of the management and the business, and no adverse material occurrences before closing.

Every investor should run good credit checks and other reference checks on entrepreneurs. Many times the commitment letter is signed before all this is finished. This paragraph will protect the investor from bad news that could be uncovered after the commitment letter is signed.

5.05   A favorable visit to your business operation by the venture capitalist must take place.

Sometimes the commitment letter is signed before a visit is made to the firm. In this case, again, the proviso that the investor likes the company when he visits it is in order.

5.06   The entire funds set forth in this commitment letter must be raised. Allied will invest only $_____ of the amount set out in this commitment letter and will use its best efforts to assist you in raising the remaining funds.

Often the commitment letter will be for less than the amount needed by the company and in this case an escape clause should be added for an investor who has committed early to drop out in case the full amount is not received. This section will protect you from that.

AN INVESTMENT MEMORANDUM

Equity investments often go under the terms of investment memoranda and term sheets rather than commitment letters. Almost all of the terms in an investment memorandum or term sheet are the same as those set out above; however, let's discuss the equity section of this item so that you can see what a typical commitment looks like if you are involved in an equity investment.

1. Terms of the Investment

In this section of the memorandum, you are trying to state exactly what you intend to do with this investment.

1.01   The venture capital firm will purchase 100,000 shares of common stock in the company at $3 per share.

1.02   All shares will be purchased at closing.

1.03   If any stock of the company is sold by the company
        for less than $3 per share at any time within five
        years from this sale, there shall be antidilution for the
        ownership of these 100,000 shares.

1.04   If the company has not had a public offering of its
        stock within five years from the closing date, then the
        venture capital firm will have a "put" provision
        whereby the venture capital firm can require the
        company to redeem the shares resulting from this
        purchase at the higher of the following:

        1.   Book value per share;
        2.   Earnings per share times ten; or
        3. $6 per share, fixed price.

1.05   At anytime after five years from closing the venture
        capital firm may require a registration and public
        offering of the shares owned by the venture capital
        firm at the company's expense.

1.06   The venture capital firm will have full "piggyback"
        rights to register shares any time the company or its
        management is registering shares for sale, and such
        registration of the venture capital firm's shares shall
        be paid for by your company.

2. Collateral and Security

Usually there is very little collateral or security except life
insurance or the hazard insurance on the business, but sometimes a
venture firm will put in a liquidation preference, especially if it's
preferred stock or common stock and he wants to make sure that
the investor gets out first if the company is liquidated.   The
paragraph dealing with this point looks like the following one.

2.01   Should the company be liquidated, it is agreed that the
        shares being issued to the venture capital firm shall
        have priority in liquidation to the shares owned by
        anyone else.   This means that any funds remaining
        after all creditors have been paid will first be paid to
        the venture capital firm to the extent of its
        investment of $300,000, and the remainder shall go to
        other stockholders, who are assumed to be

management, until the cost of the shares is repaid. If any funds remain, they shall be divided pro rata.

3. Conditions of the Investment

Almost all of the conditions of the investment are the same as those for a commitment letter and don't need to be repeated here.

4. Representations

Again, representations for an equity investment are very similar to those of a debt investment and therefore don't need to be outlined here.

5. Conditions of the Commitment

Almost all of these are the same as in a commitment for debt money and don't need to be repeated here.

Different Items

A number of items emerge from an equity investment. One of these is a consulting agreement. In order to get income, an investor may set up a consulting arrangement, whereby he buys stock so that he can obtain funds, rather than setting it up as a debt. This is better for the entrepreneur because the equity doesn't have to be repaid. Moreover, if the company gets in trouble, the consulting arrangement can be stopped because it has no collateral security in the company. A typical consulting arrangement will be stated as follows.

> 1.11 The company will enter into a consulting arrangement with the venture capital firm whereby the venture capital firm will provide consulting services to the business for $2,000 per month. This consulting agreement will be in effect for the first twelve months subsequent to closing on the investment.

Another item connected with equity investments is the voting trust. This means that the entrepreneur will place all of his shares in a voting trust to be voted by the venture capitalist. Therefore if the company misses its projections or somehow gets in trouble, the venture capitalist will be able to vote the shares owned by the entrepreneur and elect a new management team. This can be put into your commitment letter is as follows.

1.12   All shares of the company will be placed in a voting trust. The trustee shall be an officer of a bank acceptable to both you and the venture capital firm. If the company's sales are less than $50,000 in any month, then the venture capital firm may name two additional trustees to the trust. A majority vote of the three trustees may vote the shares placed in the voting trust.

NONLEGAL COMMITMENT LETTER

Both you and the entrepreneur should remember that the commitment letter is not a legal document. Its main purpose is to define in writing the *business deal* and the terms of the agreement between the venture capital firm and the entrepreneur's company. It has been my experience that when you ask a lawyer to help you go through a commitment letter, it turns into a very long legal document. You will probably end up paying a very substantial legal fee and not achieve the objective that you are seeking, which is a good business letter.

Good business judgment on your part is probably worth more than a legal review of the commitment letter, although if you are a novice at the business, then it is wise to have a corporate lawyer go through the commitment letter with you and point out items that may give you some problem. However, you should remember that you have one more shot at formulating the business structure when your lawyer and the lawyer for the entrepreneur draw up the legal documents. The legal document will take each paragraph of the commitment letter and expand and clarify parts of it. However, if you do not understand the clarification proposed by your lawyers, you should help them understand the true business meaning of the commitment letter.

It is vitally important that the commitment letter spell out the business deal and not the legal deal between the entrepreneur and the investor. If it doesn't clearly state the business deal, then you should revise it until it does. Once a commitment letter is signed, it is ready to be given to the lawyers so that they can draw up the legal documents.

CHAPTER 9

THE LEGAL CLOSING

After you finish all of your due diligence and you and the entrepreneur have agreed on a deal, you will be in a position to sign a commitment letter. Once the commitment letter is signed, you will want to bring in the lawyers. This may be the entrepreneur's first exposure to a closing so that some "hand-holding" may be needed along the way. The lawyers for both sides should be competent in venture capital transactions. One of the most painful processes is to try to the educate a new lawyer in venture capital financing. Avoid amateurs if at all possible.

As an investor, you will want your lawyer to draw up the legal documents for closing. They should follow very closely the commitment letter. When they are completed, copies for review should be forwarded to you, to the entrepreneur's attorney, and to the entrepreneur. As an investor, you should read the legal document to determine if it agrees with the business deal. The legal document should contain standard paragraphs, sometimes called "boilerplate" paragraphs, that lawyers need to put into these kinds of legal documents and that are not part of the commitment letter. Make sure the lawyer for the entrepreneur explains these boilerplate paragraphs so that the entrepreneur doesn't think you are trying to pull something over on him. An example of legal documents with these boilerplate paragraphs is provided in Appendix 2.

In this chapter we discuss two types of closings: a loan with an option to own stock (warrants), and an agreement to purchase common stock.

FIRST TYPE OF CLOSING: LOAN WITH OPTIONS

It would be truly be wonderful if an entrepreneur could simply sign an IOU to an investor and get his money. Unfortunately, neither party would be well served by such an approach to this type of investment. There must be adequate legal documentation before any investment can be closed and the proceeds disbursed. Any investor who puts up money before the legal documents accurately reflecting the deal are complete and signed by all parties has made a big mistake. Three fundamental legal documents are involved in a loan with an option to buy stock: (1) the loan agreement, (2) a note, and (3) the stock purchase option. Each document has specific objectives and each covers separate ground.

It is important for every investor to realize that these documents will govern the legal relationship between the entrepreneur and the investor. As the investor, read the legal documents carefully. There is nothing frightening about legal documents. They are written in English and not a foreign language. As you read them, make sure they say precisely what you and the entrepreneur had in mind. There can only be two reasons why they may not. Either the entrepreneur has changed his mind and has instructed his lawyer to make changes in the documents, or there has been a mistake. In either event, you should discuss the changes with the entrepreneur and make sure that he is not trying to back out of the deal. This will head off an expensive argument between your lawyer and the entrepreneur's lawyer. Now let's review the three basic legal documents of our first closing.

Document One: The Loan Agreement

By far the largest document in this trio will be the loan agreement. It will contain fifteen to fifty pages, and possibly more if the investment is a complicated one. To some extent, the loan agreement will include the items in the commitment letter plus items standard for such loan agreements. A loan agreement contains ten sections, each of which is discussed below.

1.   Purchase and Sale

In this section the lawyer will use specific language to describe the loan with all its terms and conditions. He will describe the equity option will all its terms and conditions. This section will describe in detail the securities to be purchased and will specify the following:

- The interest rate per annum
- When repayment of principal will begin and over what period it will be repaid
- Dates on which payments are to be made, such as the first day of each month
- Delivery date of the funds by the venture capitalist to you
- Description of the venture capitalist's stock option
- Ownership in the company by the venture capitalist
- Cost of ownership.

Also, this section will establish that the company has authorized and empowered its management to enter into the sale. It will discuss any other venture capital participants and the amount that they will be purchasing in your company.

2. Collateral Security and Subordination

This section will describe the collateral for the loan in great detail and it will refer to a collateral security agreement that will be an exhibit to this agreement. Normally, the lawyer will describe each piece of collateral as set forth below:

- A second mortgage on specific land and building
- A third secured interest in machinery and equipment of the company
- Personal guarantees of certain individuals
- Assignment of certain leases
- Assignment of life and casualty insurance.

3. Affirmative Covenants

This section covers all the items the entrepreneur agreed he would do as long as this loan or option to own stock is outstanding. The company will do the following:

- Provide the investor with detailed financial and operating information on a monthly basis.
- Provide the investor with any documents filed with the Securities and Exchange Commission or other government agencies.
- Provide an annual budget by a specific date each year.
- Advise the investors of any adverse changes in the company's status.
- Maintain certain current ratios, working capital amounts, or net worth amounts.

- Maintain life insurance on certain executives of the company.
- Maintain property and liability insurance in sufficient amounts.
- Notify the representative of the venture capital company when board meetings will occur so that the venture capital representative may attend the meetings.
- Provide access for the venture capitalist to the premises and to the books and records of the company.
- Keep all equipment and property in good repair and in working order.
- Comply with all applicable laws and regulations
- Pay all taxes and other levies of taxes against the company.
- Maintain its corporate existence and other business existences.
- Give the venture capital firm the right of first refusal on new financings in the future.
- Maintain a standard system of accounting in accordance with generally accepted accounting standards.
- Notify the venture capitalist if it is in default on any loans or leases.

The items above will be spelled out in separate paragraphs in the affirmative covenants section of the loan agreement. Be sure you understand each covenant because once you sign the agreement this will be the only thing the entrepreneur must do to keep the loan out of default. If a new covenant is brought up as a "standard" covenant, discuss it with the entrepreneur, not the entrepreneur's lawyer.

4. Negative Covenants

As you can imagine, this section specifies what the entrepreneur does not agree to do. Some typical negative covenants are as follows:

- There will be no change in control of the company.
- Management will not sell, assign, or transfer its shares.
- The company will not change the basic business it is in.
- The company will not change its current business format, that is, change from being a corporation to a partnership.
- The company will not invest in other companies or unrelated activities.
- The company will pay no cash or stock dividends.

- The company will not expend funds for capital improvements in excess of certain amounts.
- The company will not pay nor loan to any employee money in excess of a certain amount per year.
- The company will pay no brokerage fees and the like in excess of a certain amount.
- The company will not transact any business with members of the board of directors or management or its officers or affiliated individuals.
- The company will not dissolve, merge, or dispose of its assets.
- The company will not change its place of business.
- The company will sell no additional common stock, convertible debt, or preferred stock.

Each item above will be covered by a short paragraph in the legal documents. Violation of any of the above items will be considered a default, as set out below. Each item should have been discussed with the entrepreneur. If a new item appears, you need to discuss it with the entrepreneur because it will have an impact on the way you conduct business. If substantial new covenants appear in this section, you may have to meet with the entrepreneur to negotiate the terms in the legal documents.

5. Events of Default

This section describes items that will cause a default of the loan. A default may mean the company will have to repay the loan in full on the day of default. A default is usually called on any of the following items:

- If the company does not carry out the affirmative covenants
- If the company violates any of the negative covenants
- If the representations and warranties made in the legal documents are not true
- If the company does not make the loan payments on time
- If the company does not pay other debts as they come due
- If the company has any other loan called in default
- If the company has any lease called in default
- If a final judgment is rendered against the company by a creditor
- If bankruptcy or reorganization of the company should occur.

In this section the lawyer will also specify what remedies are necessary to remove the default. As an example, suppose a default is called because the company has not made a payment; making the payment within ten days of written notice of the default may be the solution to remove the default. Some defaults can happen easily, as in the case of a payment that is not made on the due date. If the company misses the payment date by only one day, the investor can call the loan in default. A grace period should be provided in the legal documents. This refers to the amount of time the company has to correct a default once notified. In granting grace periods, remember that the longer they are, the worse it is for the investor.

6. Equity Rights

Here the agreement may cover a wide range of items relating to the equity of the company, the equity of the investor or venture capitalist, or option to own equity held by the investor of venture capitalist. These items include:

- The right of the venture capitalist to force the company to register the venture capitalist's shares in a public offering, free of charge
- The right of the venture capitalist to include his shares in any registration of the company's shares, free of charge
- Any restriction on the transfer of the shares being received by the venture capitalist
- A section referring to certain Securities and Exchange Commission regulations to which everyone must conform
- An indemnification of the venture capital company against any violations on your issuing the stock
- Representations on your part about the number of shares and options outstanding
- Any rights the venture capitalist may have to require you to repurchase the shares held by him (this is the put)
- Any rights you have to repurchase the shares at a later date (this is the call).

This section covers all the equity rights that the investor will have. This part of the document should cover all matters that you and the entrepreneur have agreed upon with regard to the equity rights in your company. These equity rights are the mechanism whereby the venture capitalist will someday realize a profit on the equity position. It is the investor's exit. Be sure you understand how you will realize a profit on this equity. This section is particularly critical to you. You want to exit from your deal someday and these equity rights will be the mechanism for doing so.

172

7. Representations and Warranties

This section constitutes a warranty from the company that the representations in the legal documents are true.

- The corporation is in good standing.
- The company is in compliance with all laws.
- There is certain capitalization of your company.
- There are no subsidiaries.
- The financial statements are correct.
- There have been no material adverse changes since the last financial statements.
- There is no litigation going on, or if there is, a description of it is attached as an exhibit.
- The company is in compliance with all government regulations.
- There are no defaults on current borrowings.
- The company is current on all taxes.
- The company has rights to any patents that the entrepreneur owns.

Paragraph after paragraph of these types of representations and warranties can be expected in the legal documents. Each one has a specific focus and meaning. Your lawyer should be able to substantiate most of the claims. Read each one and be sure that on the closing date all representations made by the company are the ones you expected.

8. Fees and Expenses

This section will explain who pays the lawyers for drawing up the documents, who pays for filing any legal documents at local courthouses, who gets notices, and so on. Normally, the entrepreneur's company will pay all the lawyers' fees and closing costs.

9. Definitions

In this section the lawyers will define every technical or legal term appearing in the document. You should understand the definitions because they are an integral part of the entire document.

10. Conditions of Closing and Miscellaneous

This last section includes items such as indemnification, waivers, notices, and addresses. In this section, too, the lawyer will list all the conditions for closing. Condition-of-closing items are things such as

- Certificate of incorporation
- Copy of bylaws
- Certificate of incumbency
- Opinion of entrepreneur's lawyers
- Certified audit
- Certificates from secretary of state
- Copies of all corporate action taken by the company to authorize its execution of these documents
- Copy of letter from senior lender consenting to this transaction.

There will also be a final page for your signature, the entrepreneur's signature, and the signatures of any guarantors.

This is a general overview of the loan agreement. You should find that the loan agreement follows closely the terms and conditions set forth in the commitment letter. If it does not, something is wrong.

Document Two: The Note

Usually the note will be written on one to five pages. The note will be an in-depth, detailed statement of the terms of the loan. It will specify:

- How much money is being loaned
- When it is to be repaid
- The interest rate
- What day of the month it is to be paid
- Guarantors
- Conditions of prepayment of the loan
- Collateral for the loan
- Subordination of the loan to other loans
- References to covenants in the loan agreement
- A complete list of defaults
- Waivers and amendments.

It will be signed by the president and usually the secretary of the corporation, plus any guarantors of the note. The corporate seal will usually be affixed to the last page.

Document Three: The Stock Purchase Option

Finally, you can expect a four- to ten-page document describing the stock options to purchase stock in the company. It will provide details such as the following:

- Duration of the stock option
- Any covenants of the company during ownership of the stock option
- The mechanism for surrendering the option in exchange for stock
- The exact price that must be paid when the option is exercised
- Adjustments to the exercise price (that is, the formula that will be used in case shares are sold at a low price or additional shares are issued by the company)
- The availability of shares owned by the company to be issued if the option is exercised
- Any written notices that must be given
- A definition of common stock
- Expiration date of the stock option
- Transferability of the option.

Normally this option will be signed by the president and the secretary of the company on the final page of the stock purchase option.

Other Documents: Exhibits

As few as five, but usually about ten, exhibits will be attached to every financial agreement. Most of these were listed in our discussion of the sections of the loan agreement. Be sure you understand what each exhibit states because you will be agreeing that it is true and correct. Some typical exhibits listed for a closing are

1. Security agreement describing the collateral security for the loan (be sure the collateral agreed upon has been given)
2. Financing statement that includes UCC-1 forms that will be filed in the records of the courthouse (this statement will let all creditors know who has a claim on assets of the company)
3. Opinion of the company's counsel on the validity of the transaction

4. Copy of all corporate actions taken by stockholders to effect the transaction
5. Copy of certificate of incorporation
6. Copy of the bylaws of the company
7. Certificate from the secretary of state evidencing good standing
8. Copy of a certified audit from accounting firm for the company
9. Any forms necessary for government-related financing.

The description above is a simple overview of the documents and exhibits. Appendix 2 contains a set of documents from an investment made by a venture capital company. When you receive the real documents, you should read each one in detail to make sure you understand what you are signing. Investors rarely read the legal documents. Some investors ask their lawyers if everything is all right, and if the lawyer nods yes, the investor signs it without reading the legal documents. The lawyer's nod only means legal documents are fine. It does not mean the that the business deal is correctly presented in the documents. Only you can determine that. Some entrepreneurs do not read the legal documents. That is their mistake. Be smart; read your legal documents. Ask questions if you do not understand the legal descriptions.

Simple Is Good

The complexity of legal documentation has baffled American businessmen for decades. The simpler the legal documents are, the better it is for all parties. If there is a simple way to say something in a legal document so that everyone will understand it, that should definitely be the order of the day. Some lawyers are carried away with a great deal of verbiage. You should ask them to refrain from following this practice. In legal documents, simple equals good.

The best legal documents are those that you never refer to after the closing. If, during your relationship with the entrepreneur, you never have to look at the legal documents, then the deal has worked well. If you or the entrepreneur are constantly referring to the legal documents and questioning the meaning of every word, then something is wrong. You and the venture capitalist have a problem.

SECOND TYPE OF CLOSING: LEGAL DOCUMENTS FOR THE PURCHASE OF STOCK

You would think that the purchase of stock would be a simple transaction – that an investor could write a check and would issue him some stock certificates. As it turns out, that is far from the truth.   There will not be a stock option (unless options are an additional part of the stock purchase), but there will be a fairly lengthy stock purchase agreement. An example of a stock purchase agreement is given in Appendix 2.   The stock purchase agreement will be similar to the loan agreement described above, but let us discuss the points again from the perspective of a stock purchase.

Stock Purchase Agreement

The stock purchase agreement has ten to twelve sections. Many of the sections will be similar to the ones covered below.

1.   Purchase and Sale

In this initial section the lawyer will describe the sale of stock and the price being paid, as in the corresponding section of the loan agreement above.

2.   Affirmative Covenants

Many of the affirmative covenants that were covered above in the loan agreement will be set forward in this section.

3.   Negative Covenants

Again, many of the same negative covenants will appear in this section for the sale of stock.

4.   Equity Rights

In this section the lawyer will carve out the liquidation rights of the stock: Are the shares being sold to the investor on the same basis or do the shares get preference in liquidation? What dividends do they receive? What rights do they have to elect directors? As an investor, you may want to do what venture capitalists do. It is typical for the venture capitalist to have the right to elect one to three directors, as long as he does not elect a majority.   Although the venture capitalist may have the right to elect as many as three directors, he often elects only one. This single director will follow the company, attend the board meetings, and if things become critical, will ask the company to elect two additional directors who will then have more to say about the operation of the business.

Covered in this section are the many equity rights of the venture capitalist, including the right to register his shares in any public offerings and the right to require registration of shares free of charge. These equity rights are the primary exit for the venture capitalist. Be reluctant to change any of these equity rights.

5.   Representations and Warranties

A full set of representations and warranties similar to the ones in the loan agreement will appear here.

6.   Fees and Expenses

Again, this section explains who will pay all the legal fees; usually it is the seller of the stock.

7.   Definitions

There may be a short section on definitions, but usually there is none.

8.   Restrictions

Some restrictions may be placed on the entrepreneur's operation of the company. He may have to operate under certain guidelines as long as the venture capitalist owns his shares. This section will describe any operating restrictions.

9.   Voting Trust

A voting trust may be involved in a sale of stock. If so, this section will discuss the voting trust in detail. Here is how a voting trust works. Usually a trust is set up at a bank trust department with a bank trust officer as trustee. Shares of the entrepreneur and the shares of others are put in the trust. The venture capital firm controls the voting trust, but only under certain conditions can the venture capital firm vote the shares in the trust. This section will give the precise details on the voting trust.

10.   Employment Agreement

Many times the venture capital firm will want to ensure that key employees continue to work for the company, at least for a specific period of time. The venture capitalist may therefore ask key employees to sign one-way employment contracts ensuring that the key people will be with the company as long as the venture capitalist is an investor. As part of the agreement, the employee may be asked not to reveal confidential company information if he is permitted to leave the company.

The employment agreement can be turned around, of course, to the advantage of the entrepreneur. It can ensure that his job is secure during a period in which the venture capitalist firm may have an opportunity to take over the company. Usually this security is overshadowed by the one-sided nature of the contract. A venture capitalist told me of three young M.B.A.'s who signed employment contracts. The contracts provided that these gentle souls be paid a reasonable sum despite their brief experience in the business world. However, the contracts were for five years. As fate would have it, the business failed. Among the "assets" of the business were the three employment contracts. The institutional investor who had invested the funds foreclosed on all the assets of the business and picked up the employment contracts of the three M.B.A.'s. For the remaining four years of their contract, these men were virtually the slaves of this corporate giant.

11. Consulting Contract

Many venture capital firms play an active role in the management of the company in which they invest. They may help the company to establish marketing or financial controls or to address any number of problems that may arise in a new or small, growing company. They want compensation for the time and attention their consultants take to help the new business get off the ground. Compensation is usually arranged through a contract with the venture capital firm for management consulting services. This agreement will describe the services to be rendered, and the terms and the amount of payment that will be made to the venture capital firm for these services.

12. Conditions to Closing

Again, there will be a section on indemnification, waivers, and notices. There will be a list of items that must be completed before closing can occur. At the end there will be a page for you, the venture capitalist, and other parties to the agreement, to sign.

LAWYERS AS BUSINESSMEN

Many lawyers will take it upon themselves to tell a client not to enter into a business arrangement because it is a bad business deal.

179

All clients want to know if something is wrong from a legal perspective, but most business people become upset by lawyers who jump into the business fray in order to "save" their client from signing a bad business deal. Some good lawyers are certainly good businessmen. However, very few *practicing* lawyers are good entrepreneurs or venture capitalists. It's difficult for anyone to carry on two professions successfully. Every venture capitalist can tell you about a lawyer who killed a business deal because he felt his client was not getting a good deal. If lawyers would stay in the legal profession and leave the businessmen to the business profession, the world would be a better place.

You should encourage your lawyer to refrain from trying to renegotiate the deal for you. If you lawyer tries to renegotiate the deal, the entrepreneur will assume that you have directed him to do so. He will believe you are trying to change the deal, or find a way to get out of it. Needless to say, this will take his attention away from closing the deal. Be very careful before you instruct your lawyer to openly negotiate with the entrepreneur. If there is something you do not like about the legal documents, go to the entrepreneur and negotiate for yourself. Do not use a surrogate who is not familiar with the business deal.

EXPERIENCED LAWYERS ARE BEST

A lawyer experienced in drawing up legal documents for venture capital investments is worth his weight in gold. A lawyer trying to bluff his way through this type of investment agreement will destroy your chances of a quick and successful closing. Usually, you will be better off having your lawyer complete the first draft of the proposed legal documents and then having the entrepreneur's lawyer review them. If you start with your lawyer, the document will have all the things you need in it and you will not have to argue with the entrepreneur's counsel to put language in the agreement. This can save significant time and expense. Be economical in your use of lawyers; they are expensive.

One of the main factors to slow down the legal process is the lack of time that lawyers have to work on legal closings. Legal documents sent by a venture capitalist's attorney to the entrepreneur's attorney can sit on the desk of the entrepreneur's lawyer for weeks before he gets around to reviewing them. You should remind your entrepreneur that he should remind his lawyer daily, if necessary, that he cannot close until the lawyer reviews the documents. Do not let the entrepreneur put you in charge of riding herd over his lawyer.

You may not realize it, but your lawyer may have incurred a liability if he doesn't perform quickly and reasonably. Any lawyer who does not close a deal that should have closed could be held liable for whatever damages are caused. Certainly a lawyer who does not act on legal documents sent to him for review within five days is courting disaster.

PROCEDURE FOR REVIEWING DOCUMENTS

When you get the first draft of the legal documents, *read them.* Too many people do not read the legal documents. Read the legal agreement for the basics of the deal, not the meaning of every word. Compare your commitment letter with the legal documents. Make sure each point in the letter is covered in the legal document. Lawyers sometimes make mistakes.

LEGAL FEES KEEP GOING UP

Legal fees are rarely low. In fact, of all the fees that businessmen complain about, legal fees probably top the list. The question is not whether legal fees are too high, but whether a specific legal fee is fair, in view of the work that has been performed by the lawyer. Some attorneys are unethical in their billing practices. They think nothing of padding a legal bill with ten or twenty hours of work and then mail the bill to the client without a great deal of explanation. Most legal bills consist of a single line, "for services rendered," followed by a dollar amount.

Because legal bills have become such a large part of business life, most businessmen are attempting to manage the fees. The most common method of managing legal fees was introduced by large corporations, many of which now require a detailed legal bill. The bill must include hours worked, the specific project on which the time was carried out, the billing rate of the individual working on it, and the name of the individual authorizing work on the project. In addition to these detailed bills, many smaller businesses are requiring the law firms to give them advance estimates of the time it will take to complete a project. They ask the lawyer to call them once he reaches a certain amount of time expended. By doing this, the small business keeps track of the law firm's hours and does not let it run up a big bill.

If the small business has agreed to pay the legal fees for both your lawyer and for their lawyer, it is incumbent upon you to help the small business manage the legal fees. This means contacting your lawyer and discussing fees. You must discuss the procedure for working on your deal and how the bill will be rendered. Do not let yourself in for a surprise when you arrive at the closing table and see the legal bill. If you are surprised by the amount of the legal bill, then you have not been managing your lawyers very well. All too often, entrepreneurs receive a shock at the closing table. As an investor you may be in a poor position to help the small business negotiate fees. If the lawyer for you is a close friend, you will have a hard time questioning him about legal fees, even if they seem too high. Although an investor cannot be expected to manage the small business legal fees, it is important that you manage all your own legal fees so you are satisfied with the amount that is being charged at the closing table.

HOW LAWYERS RUN UP YOUR LEGAL BILL

Beside the unethical padding mentioned above, watch for the many methods employed either intentionally or unintentionally to run up your legal fee. Listed below are five of them.

Disagree on Legal Points

Your lawyer or perhaps even the small business lawyer will often disagree on many points. This means that they will have to spend innumerable hours discussing these points and working each one out to their satisfaction. Remember that when these two lawyers disagree, you are paying the bill on both sides of the table, even as they argue about minuscule points. There is a fairly simple way to cure this problem. When your lawyer has reviewed the papers drafted by the small business lawyer, tell him to mark each item in the documents that he sees as problem. Before he discusses these points with the small business's lawyer, ask him to discuss each one of them with you. Many of them may have no material business significance and therefore you will be willing to let the small business lawyer put them into the agreement. Each time you knock out one of these small points for discussion, you save legal fees.

Rewrite Sections

Some lawyers increase their fees by rewriting sections of the documents over and over again. Suppose the small business's lawyer presents his written version of the document. Your lawyer may rewrite the documents completely. He will run up secretarial time and drafting time in order to redo entire sections. You should instruct him, from the beginning, that there is to be one writer of the documents and one commentator on the documents. Your lawyer should be the writer and his lawyer should be the commentator. This arrangement will reduce legal fees.

Research Points of Law

Often lawyers will disagree violently over points of law. The disagreement will send them scurrying to the library or to other research sources in order to clarify various points of law. This research can burn up many hours of time. Each lawyer is trying to show which one is the best legal scholar. You should instruct both lawyers that you do not wish them to research various points of the law without your permission, and that you will not pay for such research.

Legal Style

Lawyers will correct each other on usage, style, grammar, and even spelling. They will use up your time for the purpose of "clarifying the language." Tell the lawyers that you are not interested in matters of style. Stress that you want a clear document and that is all.

Arguments

Most lawyers are by nature argumentative. They spend three years in law school arguing points back and forth. Once they enter the real world, they continue to argue with one another. You should remember that you are paying for all of these arguments. If you have two lawyers arguing with each other, and they are each billing you at the rate of $150 an hour, you are paying $5 per minute to hear them eloquently debate the merits of a legal point. Act as a moderator and get to the heart of the argument. Ask your lawyer what the consequences will be if you agree to the words being proposed by the lawyer. If these consequences are quite modest, or if the consequences are extremely unlikely, you may wish merely to sign the document rather than fight to remove the words. On the other hand, if the consequences appear to be drastic, you must adjourn the legal meeting and call a business meeting with your entrepreneur partner to iron out the problem.

SYNDICATIONS AND LAWYERS

When you are dealing with a syndication of investors, each investor's lawyer may want an opportunity to review legal documents. There should be only one fee, for the lead investor's lawyer, not for each participant's lawyer who wants to look at the documents. If the small business agrees to pay for all the lawyers, and if four or five investors' lawyers look at the documents, the small businesses are opening up the cash register. When you let the lawyers take out what they need to cover their time and effort in reviewing the documents, the "review" may go on indefinitely.

Many lawyers tell an interesting story about the young lawyer who began working in his father's law firm. His father took a much needed vacation to Europe and left his son behind to continue the legal practice. The first case the young lawyer worked on was a railway right-of-way case. The young lawyer noted that his father had been working on the case for almost twenty years. In several days, the young lawyer assembled the parties in a room and negotiated a settlement. The case was closed. When the young lawyer's father returned from his vacation, the young lawyer explained with glee that he had settled that long outstanding railway right-of-way case. Needless to say, the father was extremely upset as he explained to his son that the railway case sent all of the young lawyer's brothers and sisters to college, and the annual fees from the case had even sent the young lawyer to law school. Remember, lawyers receive fees while cases are open. They do not receive fees from cases that are closed.

Another factor to watch for in syndications is the tardiness with which other investor's lawyers may review the documents. Invariably one of the lawyers will be slow and not get around to the documents for days. You must obtain the names of all the lawyers and constantly put pressure on each lawyer to submit his comments so that closing can take place. You can help manage this process. The lead investor needs to lead the lawyers to a closing.

THE CLOSING: A MOMENT OF TRUTH

Once the lawyers have drawn up and examined the documents and once the businessmen have ironed out the business problems, a big pile of legal documents will be ready for signing. Normally, three to ten copies of each document will have to be signed. The closing usually takes place in a conference room. Every closing seems to have its crisis. Usually the entrepreneur's lawyer will bring documents, such as incorporation papers or life insurance, that are not in the proper form. If all the documents required are not present at closing, your lawyer will not be able to close the investment. In large deals the lawyers will get together the day before the closing date to see if all the papers are in order and if it is possible to close the investment. An inexperienced lawyer for the entrepreneur or venture capitalist may try to have a closing without reviewing all the documents beforehand. To just pick a date and show up for a closing is almost a sure way to abort the closing.

A closing is an extremely exciting moment because it is the moment when the venture capitalist parts with his money and the entrepreneur's business gets an injection of capital. The physical process can take hours and be extremely boring. Documents are signed, shuffled around the table, looked at by lawyers, and verified by lawyers. It is, to say it most simply, a lawyers' environment.

LAST-MINUTE CHANGES

You can always expect last-minute changes. Generally these are minor items, but occasionally they are material. My recommendation to you as an investor is not to waive any major items. This is the only time the entrepreneur will be fully motivated to get everything done. Once it is closed and you have invested your money, the items you needed at the closing are less urgent. The entrepreneur will then have more pressing things to do. On one occasion I waived the life insurance requirement at a closing. The entrepreneur seemed to be in no rush to get the policy. Four weeks after I invested, he had a heart attack, but there was no insurance policy. Be tough at a closing. Do not waive material items.

CLOSING FEES

Lawyers can spend considerable time on the actual closing itself. Many hold a preclosing the day before the actual closing. This dress rehearsal, as well as the actual event, can be costly. Envision the lead venture capitalist's lawyer, the lawyer of the bank giving a loan, as well as the lawyer for the small business. These three lawyers may charge as much as $150 per hour each. On top of these fees are those of the junior attorneys, paralegals, and secretaries, which can run from to $30 to $80 per hour. All in all, the deal is probably being billed at the rate of $800 to $1,000 per hour. If the deal is extremely large and complicated and involves additional people, that figure can be multiplied by two or three. But for the moment, assume the minimum is $800 per hour. Assume the lawyers spend five hours in preclosing and seven hours in the actual closing, for a total of twelve hours. Twelve times $800 is $9,600, or almost $10,000, just for the closing, quite apart from what you will pay for the drafting, research time, and other document gathering.

There is only one way around the expense of closing, and that is to be absolutely ready when a closing date is set. Your lawyer should have reviewed all the documents in detail with the small business lawyer to assure himself that when closing occurs and everyone is sitting around the table, everything that is needed to close will be at the table. There will be no last-minute scurrying for any documents and there will by no last-minute changes. If you can impress upon your lawyer that you do not want the closing set until everyone is absolutely ready, then you will be doing yourself a big favor. Do not go the closing table prematurely. It will cost a lot of money if you do. What is worse, you will have to do it over again if the investment does not close.

WHAT TO REMEMBER ABOUT LAWYERS

You should remember that lawyers are merely specialists in a specific area and have knowledge of an area in which you do not, namely, the laws that govern business activities. Remember, too, that they are providing a service and that you hire them just as you hire any other employee or advisor. Tell them what you want them to do and you will have a satisfactory relationship with your attorneys.

Also remember that lawyers make money by charging for time and that they are disposed to spend a great deal of time working on something. Most of the problems lawyers work on are not legal problems. They are simply problems that businessmen have left to them to solve. Many business problems turned over to lawyers can easily be solved by two businessmen in a head-to-head discussion. Before you try to solve a problem from a legal standpoint, be sure you have exhausted all other remedies. Legal solutions are expensive. In one case in New York City, a venture capitalist lost $50,000 when the lawyer, who was a member of one of the large prestigious law firms in New York, had been negligent in his closing of the loan and clearly was open to suit. When the venture capital firm looked into suing this lawyer, it found that it would probably have to pay at least $50,000 to do so. The venture capitalist was told that he would be lucky if he recouped any of his legal fees, much less the $50,000 that the lawyer had lost for the venture capital firm.

Also remember that the number of lawyers in the United States is higher than ever before. By many counts there is a surplus of lawyers. If you do not like the lawyer you are working with, find a new one. There are hundreds of good lawyers seeking work with a growing company.

DOCUMENTATION

The lawyer should supply you with a complete original of all the documents collected at closing. They should be packaged by the lawyer into an indexed file that will become the basis for your legal relationship with the company. Make sure your lawyer delivers the package.

CHAPTER 10

MONITORING THE INVESTMENT

Investing in a small business has been compared to getting married, and closing the deal is said to be the wedding ceremony. To carry the analogy even further, after the honeymoon is over, the investor and the entrepreneur will have to make a life together. For the next three to ten years these two individuals will be working together – working together not so much on a day-to-day basis, but indirectly, and the relationship will be one of investor and entrepreneur rather than husband and wife.

INVOLVEMENT

Before you make the investment, you will have to determine how much you intend to be involved in the small business. Most venture capital investment firms are not completely passive. A few large venture firms are extremely active in the management of companies and have a consulting staff to perform this task. These consultants may supply marketing expertise to help improve the small business's marketing effort. The venture capitalist might also supply production expertise to help with problems in the production area or financial expertise to help with financial matters. Furthermore, the consultants can help with the overall management of the company.

However, most venture capital firms are not staffed with consultants. Many will not invest in the company unless it has a full management team to run the company on a day-to-day basis. By and large, venture capital firms do not have expertise in marketing, production, or administrative matters. Most managers of venture capital companies are heavyweights in the area of finance.

If they have been in business for an extended period of time, they may possess considerable knowledge of small business practices. As an investor, you will need to determine what role you will play in the small business. If you want a very small role, be sure the management team is complete so that they will not have to depend on you.

MAJOR POLICY DECISIONS

All major policy decisions about the company should be discussed with the investor and the entrepreneur. Both of you have a vested interest and any major changes should be discussed by both. It is very helpful if the entrepreneur describes any major decisions that need to be made in a memo. This memo should be the basis on which the two of you get together and discuss the situation. I have always found that when entrepreneurs put "major problems" down on paper, they seem to be reduced considerably.

Monthly Reports

Monthly financial statements are usually required by venture capital firms when they invest in the company and this is the minimum any investor should require. The importance of timely monthly financial statements is second only to that of timely monthly payments on debts owed to investors. If you are not receiving timely monthly financial statements and a report on the company, you need to visit the company and find out why. It is usually a sign that the company is having more than reporting problems. I believe I have heard practically every excuse for not preparing a monthly financial statement. To date, none are worth the breath is takes to utter them. Simply stated, no firm can be managed without accurate, timely monthly financial statements. Any entrepreneur who begins to tell you that he doesn't need them should be replaced. Without regular financial statements, there is no way that an investor can make reasonable decisions about the situation the business is in. Tardy monthly financial statements are a big red flag to every venture capitalist.

Not only should these statements be prepared monthly, but they should also be accurate. Every venture capitalist has been in an investment in which he had quite a surprise at year end after the auditors have come in and adjusted the financial statements. There are various types of surprises, but the most common one is lower earnings. Typically, a company will show profits for eleven months and a huge loss for the year, after the accountant adjusts all the sales and expense numbers. The usual reason given for these surprises is inaccurate accounting records for accounts payable and inventory. Some entrepreneurs blame the problem on standard costing system as a reason for having a year-end write-down. No investor should be surprised at year-end financial statements. If they are, then it is time to change entrepreneurs. Few financial statements aren't adjusted at year end. It is the magnitude of the adjustment that we are talking about. The reason for any large change in financial statements at year end needs to be explained fully. Any entrepreneur who gives you a big surprise at year end has destroyed much of his credibility for the future years where monthly financial statements are concerned. When credibility is gone, your investment is definitely in trouble.

Monthly Written Report

A monthly written report in letter form or memo form stating exactly what is going on at the business is required by almost every venture capital firm. An example of such a monthly report follows:

MEMORANDUM

TO: A. V. Capitalist
FROM: O.K. Entrepreneur
SUBJECT: Monthly Report for October

Attached are the monthly financial statements for the nine-month period ending September 30. The profit-and-loss statement is understated in that our company will probably not pay taxes at the rate of 50% this year because of our net operating loss carried forward from last year. This should put approximately 95% of the pre-tax dollars to the bottom line.

As we near year end, it is evident that the next year will be an extremely busy year. Our backlog has increased fivefold over last year. You should also note that inventories have increased approximately 40% more than our forecast. This is due to three very large orders that are now working their way through our production line. We have had to add people to the second shift to make sure that the items come through on schedule. None of these three orders will be completed and shipped by our year end, and therefore we will start out the year with an extraordinary amount of sales in the first several months.

We have talked to four people since we began looking for a controller to relieve some of the duties of our vice-president of finance. However, as of today we have not found a suitable candidate, but may be able to find one within the next ten to twenty days.

Finally, I am happy to say that the second generation of our product has now been completely designed and developed, and should be ready for introduction into the marketplace within six months at the national convention/trade fair. It will be an important milestone for our company; we introduced our first prototype only two years ago and have since built many of these products. At our next board meeting we may be able to see a second-generation unit.

The monthly report above mentioned several key items, each of which has bearing on the future of the company. It also included a brief discussion of the financial statements, which are fairly self-explanatory. The discussion of the financial statements brought out a point that probably was not obvious to the venture capitalist reviewing the financial statement for ten minutes. It is incumbent upon you to highlight in the monthly report any negative, or in this case, positive developments.

Board Meetings/Investor Meetings

The company should have regular board or investor meetings so that the investor can hear an oral report and ask questions of the management. You can keep fairly well informed through financial statements and memos, but a face-to-face meeting four times a year, or possibly only two times a year, is a necessity if you are to keep up with the deal. It is important that the small business prepare for these meetings. Management should have an agenda and go through it as if they were holding a formal meeting with their board of directors and stockholders.

The first thing on the agenda should be the financial statements. Every management team should be required to review the financial statements against statements of past periods and projections. If management is presenting a new set of projections, a detailed explanation is in order. In general, the entire meeting should have a financial orientation rather than a marketing or production orientation. As an investor, you are looking at the numbers and the numbers speak louder than words. The entrepreneur should tell you how much cash the company has on hand, and how much credit in the bank lines.

As part of the meeting, the investor should be taken on an abbreviated plant tour and shown any new improvements that are being made in the company. Other members of the management team should be present at these meetings and should participate in the discussions. An investor should have easy access to all of the individuals on the management team and each should be questioned during these sessions.

In the early stages of the investment, the entrepreneur should be able to produce a cash reconciliation showing exactly where the money invested by the venture capital group was spent.

Other Discussion Items

If the entrepreneur has completed any market research or customer surveys, he should share the results with the investor, especially if there is a significant change from the company's original perception. If the entrepreneur has news about the competition and their activities, it should also be passed along. If suppliers have changed policies or if the entrepreneurs have found new suppliers, then the investors are normally told of these changes at this time. And if the entrepreneur fails to do so, you should ask your own questions about such items. You may want to ask if any industry studies or articles about the company or industry in general have appeared in any trade journals and whether you can get copies of them for background information. You will want to ask if the company has hired any key people or if it has fired some of the people that you have met before. Hiring a new director of marketing or changing a controller is a material action and you should look for these changes. You should ask what changes in overhead have transpired, what additions or subtractions, and ask for an explanation. If the company is opening additional offices, find out how it justifies this move.

Make sure to find out what kind of capital expenditures have been made since the last time you met. Any material changes in the backlog, either up or down, should be highlighted in the entrepreneur's discussion. When audit time comes around, make sure you determine when the audit is going to be out; if it is going to be late, find out why. If research and development is going on, as for completion dates. As an investor, you should make sure the company meets those completion dates. If there is a target date for introducing a product into the marketplace, you should see if the company makes it. As an investor, you will always be seeking material information about the company you have invested in. You don't want to be inundated with a huge amount of statistical information, but you need to keep up to date on any material changes in the business or the industry that the company is in.

I find it helpful to subscribe to the magazines and newspapers in any industry that I am investing in. This way, at least once a month or sometimes every week, in the case of a newspaper, I gather information about the industry in which my company is competing. It keeps me up to date. The more you keep up to date on the business and industry, the more successful your investments will be.

MAINTAINING GOOD RECORDS

Maintaining records of your investment will be the key to keeping up and understanding the investments you have made in a company. It is imperative that the following records be kept accurately.

Legal Records

The legal documents are your bible for every investment that you are in. You should have complete files containing accurate statements of all amendments, extensions, conversions, sales, exercise of warrants, and the like. The items in your files should be executed copies of the purchase agreement, with all modifications. Any supporting agreements should also be enclosed. In addition, you should have conformed copies of all the securities, corporate charter documents and bylaws, specific documents to which the SBIC is a party, and copies of pledges, voting trust, escrow agreements, and mortgages. Any options or employment benefit plans and any franchises or patents as well as any legal opinions and other miscellaneous items should also be included. All of these should be bound and indexed in a strong file that can easily be referenced in case one needs to consult them and determine what rights an investor has. If you have not organized your legal file correctly, you are in big trouble.

Correspondence File

You should maintain a general file of correspondence between you and the company. The contents of this file should be arranged in chronological order but do not need to be indexed to specific sections. Instead tabs can be placed on specific correspondence with meaningful data in it.

The general correspondence file should also include any memos that you dictate to the file to record conversations with the management team. It is extremely helpful to put these notes in the file because they will jog your memory about things that have occurred in the business and that you may need to remember in order to follow a company accurately. The memo need not be typed up each time you talk to the entrepreneur. But, if you take notes constantly, as I do, you will want to record the highlights of the conversation. At the top of the page, write the name of the investment and make sure that you put it in the general correspondence file. This will let you refer back to conversations that you have had with the company and will put you in a better position to judge the progress of the company.

Financial Recording File

In addition to the legal file and the general correspondence file, you should keep a file of the monthly financial statements as well as any annual audits. Other financial information such as tax returns or flash reports on sales, for example, should also go in the file. In addition, there should be projections in this file and they may be segregated on one side versus the actuals on the other. This will help you continue to monitor the situation in which you are an investor. In addition, you may want to file in this section the one- or two-page reports supplied by the company as to the financial operations of the business. It may be easier to keep them with the financial information so that you can follow the company's progress without waiting for a lot of correspondence.

Board Meeting Files

If you have been elected to the board of directors or if you are a visiting member of the board of directors on a regular basis, you may want to set up a file that includes all the information that you have been given at board meetings, except for the financial information that you will put in the financial file. This will give you an ongoing file that will help you follow the progress of the company from the standpoint of the board of directors. It may be critical for you to review certain events at the board level in order to determine if the company is going in the right direction. For the above reasons, you may need a separate board file. If you are on the board of directors, this separate file will also help you remember what has happened at prior meetings when you go to the board.

Tracking File

A great number of venture capital funds track the financial progress of their investments by setting up tracking files. These are nothing more than spread sheets that contain past key information as well as budget and projected information so that when new information comes in, the venture capitalist can compare historical information with current information to evaluate the progress of the company and compare budgeted information with actual information to see if the company is on budget. These tracking files often contain all the ratios in full so that a venture capitalist can quickly see if the company is having financial operating problems.

Because computers have become so prevalent, most of the tracking files are kept on the computer and are printed out at regular intervals for people to review, or the files may be in the computer in institutions where the venture capitalist has easy access to the monitor and can obtain the information they contain.

When financial information is received, it is put into the computer or into the spread sheet and a tracking file; this information is then used to compute all the ratios you are interested in and to compare them with past results or projected results. This type of detailed financial information can be extremely useful in monitoring a company and will indicate how strong that company really is.

WARNING SIGNALS OF PROBLEMS

Generally speaking, entrepreneurs are unrealistic in evaluating problems. They often fail to recognize the early stages of their failure. Entrepreneurs are by nature optimistic. They will cling to their dreams until the doors to their business are locked tight and the auctioneers have sold off the last piece of equipment.

In all probability, you will have to be the first to react to the warning signals you receive about the business. This is not a difficult task. These signals of problems are commonly called red flags. Normally, investors are the first to point out problems and burst the dream bubble of the entrepreneur. As such, you are apt to incur the anger of your entrepreneur. It is in your interest to seek cooperation from your entrepreneur, but at the same time, you should not let an obvious point go by. If you see the problem and your entrepreneur doesn't, then you are doomed to have a problem business. Listed below are a number of red flags that venture capitalists often see.

Late Payments

If the entrepreneur is late in making payments on a convertible debenture or debts to the bank, the investor will see this tardiness as a very tight cash flow. Some entrepreneurs think it is acceptable not to make payments on investor's debt so that they can use the money as working capital. If the entrepreneur's business is not making payments to you, it is probably not paying other folks, including the IRS, payroll taxes, and suppliers. It is only a matter of time before the day of reckoning will arrive. When you find these early warning signals, make sure you try to become involved in the business early enough to head off any potential problems.

194

Losses of Profits

If the monthly financial statements start showing losses, you should become concerned. Losses can be a temporary aberration, but you need to determine this very quickly. Don't listen to the entrepreneur who says he'll be out of it in a short while. Make sure you go into the details of the problem with the entrepreneur to determine exactly why he thinks the company is going to turn around. Go in and do your own due diligence on the numbers, if possible, so you can better understand problem.

Late Financial Reports

Tardiness in sending out financial reports and other items to the investor is a clear sign that the business is not operating well. Usually financial statements are late because they are bad news. Every investor should know that when the statements are late he is likely to get a financial surprise. If financials are late, make sure you contact the person responsible in the firm and find out why. No one can run a business without timely financial statements.

Poorly Prepared Financial Reports

Sometimes the entrepreneur prepares financial reports quickly, but not accurately. Poor reports are unreliable indicators of how the company is doing. They are definitely a red flag to anyone investing in a company. Once an entrepreneur sent me financial statements that showed the company to be marginally profitable. This was good news, since the business had been losing money. Then I discovered that several line items, such things as rent and interest payments, had been excluded from the statement. What was worse, when we added up the expense column, we found an error, which understated expenses by 20%. The entrepreneur said these were merely minor mistakes, but within six months the company was liquidated.

Large Changes in Balance Sheet Items

If accounts payable have increased rapidly, you should suspect that the company is not paying its bills. You need to find out why as soon as possible. If inventory has become very large, you should also become suspicious. It means that sales are not keeping pace with production and the items are ending up in inventory. Similarly, ballooning accounts receivable may mean that the company is unable to collect some of the receivables that have been booked as sales but perhaps weren't sales at all, merely products put out on consignment that will come back at a later date. Certainly, this is a red flag.

Unavailable Entrepreneur

When your telephone calls to entrepreneurs are consistently not returned, this is a sign of problems. The entrepreneur may be afraid that you will ask questions about the business and find out it is in deep trouble. Another bad sign is the entrepreneur's failure to schedule regular board meetings. This is a clear warning signal to the investor.

Large Thefts

Unexplained large thefts of inventory may be an indication that the entrepreneur himself is stealing from the company and covering it up by reported theft. More revealing is a theft that the insurance company does not cover. This normally means that the entrepreneur is unwilling to pursue the case with the insurance company because he does not welcome the insurance company's investigation. An unexplained fire falls in the same category. Entrepreneurs in trouble often try to cover up their problems with fire. In the South, a large fire that destroys a business inventory has been called "selling out to a Northern concern." As the story goes, the good old boys will insure their assets through a Northern insurance company, then a mysterious fire will wipe out all of their inventory, and they will collect from the company.

Major Adjustments in Figures

As discussed before, large year-end adjustments of numbers indicate that management is not running the company well. If the company has to write off a large part of the inventory or if the accounting firm is not willing to capitalize some expenses, then the run-through impact on the profit-and-loss statement will be disastrous and a sure indication that management is not running the company well. This is a very large red flag.

Significant Changes in Management

Because the decision-making process is handled by so few people in a small company, when one of these decisionmakers leaves, it is a sure sign of trouble. Continuity of management is essential in business, and the lack of it throws a warning signal not only to the investor, but also to employees, customers, and other creditors.

You must determine whether an employee has been fired for good cause, or whether the departing employee "jumped ship" because it will soon be sinking. If possible, talk to the employee and find out why he has left.

Major Changes in Sales and Order Backlogs

As an investor, you are probably following the backlog and sales of the company in more detail than the actual financial statement. When you see the backlog declining, this is a sure indication that the company is going to have problems in the future. Increasing backlog may indicate a problem in production or shipping. Decreasing backlog may indicate that the company is having severe problems in the marketplace. Any rapid change in the backlog needs to be explained.

At times, backlog builds up because the price of the product has been cut and now the company will have a tremendous problem in meeting the new pricing structure. A big change in gross profit margin can keep sales increasing, but profits will eventually be eroded. Keep your eye on the backlog, as it may mean that the company will have to revise its lead times in order to meet customer demands. This backlog could ultimately affect sales. It also may mean that the company will have to expand its production capacity in order to meet the demands of its customers.

Inventory Changes

Inventory figures can give you a clue as to what is going on in the company. Inventory turnover that is low in comparison with the rest of the industry may indicate that the company's product is not being accepted in the marketplace and that too much money is tied up in inventory.

Out of stock items especially on fast-moving items can be a sure indication of problems on the production side of the business.

Any inaccuracies in inventory are a sure sign that the company is not being run well. Large changes in the records so they match physical inventory may indicate the production process and inventory are both being poorly managed. Eventually these changes in inventory will have to hit the profit-and-loss statement and will harm the company.

A properly managed and documented system is the backbone of a good company.

Lack of Planning

Every company needs to budget and plan. A company that does this poorly will surely not survive. A company with a sound planning system will be able to tell where the company is going. When a budget is missed month after month, you should determine the reason. In addition, you should become concerned if you find that the company has failed to meet the goals of its long-range plan. It cannot succeed in the marketplace if it continues on such a course. As a business grows from being an entrepreneurial one, the preparation of financial and operating projections become more important to the decisionmaking process. Thus the business cannot continue to prosper without timely and accurate data.

Changes in Accounting Methods

At times it is necessary for a company to change its accounting methods, but at other times such changes are adopted so that creditors and potential lenders will not detect the problems that are brewing. The key signs to look for here are changes in the depreciation or useful life of units, changes in the method of recognizing income (such as recognizing revenue before the company has had all the performance criteria), and changes in the method of valuing inventory such as LIFO to FIFO for overhead rate or the amount of scrap rates. Eventually they all show up on the profit-and-loss statement.

Loss of a Major Customer, Supplier, or Lender

One of the easiest warning signals to pick up is the loss of a major customer. This is a sure sign that the company is not doing something right and that it may eventually lose additional customers.

The same is true for suppliers and lenders. When a supplier drops a company or a lender refuses to lend, something is wrong with the company, and it should be a quick tip-off to you that the company is having problems.

Labor Problems

It is the duty of management to get along with labor. An entrepreneur should instill in his employees the same kind of fervor that he feels for the industry and the business. Whenever employees grow dissatisfied or go on strike, management is not doing its job right. Problems in the work force are a sure tip-off that the company is in hot water. Keep your eyes out for labor problems, which are indicated by either a wildcat strike or a loss of employees.

Changes in Prices and Market Share

Declining sales in a booming industry are an obvious sign of problems, but sometimes the clues are more subtle. Sales may be expanding but the company's share of the market may be shrinking. If it is getting less than its fair share in a growing industry, then it is having a problem in the marketplace.

Also, if the company drops its price quickly, this probably means that the product is not being received well. Perhaps the product itself is at fault or perhaps it isn't suitable for the customer that it is oriented to.

External Warning Signs

Signs outside the business can also signal trouble. Here are some of the common ones to look for.

Technical Change

New developments and processes may change the way companies compete in the industry. An entrepreneur must be aware of all such changes to determine how they will affect the way that the company does business in the industry. You must determine if the company has the flexibility to respond to these changes and stay in the market. Each time there is a technological change the entrepreneur and the investor must determine what they need to do in order to meet this new challenge.

General Industry Decline

At times the industry itself may go into a slump because the major consumer of the product is no longer demanding the number of units it asked for in the past. These general slumps come and go in almost every industry and you need to determine why the slump has occurred, how long it will last, and what can be done to reorient the company's products so as to take advantage of some other market that may be developing.

Government Changes

Many industries are regulated heavily, whereas others are not. Whatever the case, every industry is subject to some regulation. Each time the regulations change, industry is affected. Government has been known to regulate a company right out of business. This has happened several times in U.S. history. You need to keep your eyes open for new regulations.

Ratio Analysis as a Warning Indicator

A host of early warning signals can emerge from the analysis of key ratios in a company. These include not only current ratios and the ratios of stockholders to total assets, but also ratios of working capital turnover in debt to equity. All of these factors will give you a clear picture of what is going on with the company.

If receivables turnover (net credit sales divided by the average net traded receivables) begins to change rapidly, you'd better find out why. If daily sales and receivables continues to change, you also need to find out why. Any number of profitability and productivity ratios and market ratios can be found in a standard textbook on business ratios. Each one of these will give you an indication of what is going on. The sooner you begin analyzing the company in terms of these ratios, the better you will be able to determine what problems a company is having.

My Personal Early Warning Signals

Here are a number of things that you may not pick up unless you have had years of experience watching for telltale signs.

1. An entrepreneur once told me that he had decided to move from Massachusetts to Florida because the weather was much warmer and thought that he could run the business just as well from Florida. Even the most casual observer will recognize that you cannot run a business from a great distance. Most small businesses needs hands-on management. So, when an entrepreneur says he is going to move to a different town, you'd better make sure that he is going to move the business with him or you will have some problems. If at all possible, you should keep the entrepreneur from moving.

2. Moving the business is perhaps the most dangerous thing anyone can do with a small business. The physical disruption alone can affect almost every aspect of the business. Not only do you lose a lot of people, but it often takes six months to a year to resume operations fully in the new location. I no longer finance companies that are about to move. It is just too traumatic, and I always end up losing money on businesses that move.

3. Sometimes an entrepreneur will come in and tell you about an investment that he is going into personally. This is always a big red flag. Whenever an entrepreneur puts his full time and attention into anything else, you can be sure that the business you invested in will suffer. No entrepreneur can run two businesses. You might as well settle down to the fact that if your entrepreneur is going into another business, your business is not going to do as well. Use all your persuasive powers to convince your entrepreneur to ditch the idea. Try to tell him that he can make all the money he ever wants to make in this world by sticking to one business and doing his best there. Every time an entrepreneur changes investment objectives, the investor suffers.

4. All too often an entrepreneur will come into your office one day and suddenly announce, "I am out of money and I cannot meet Friday's payroll." Invariably, the entrepreneur's cash flow projections showed that he had enough money to get along for another year. Somehow he has gone through all of the money that you and other investors have given him. The man is out of money. What is worse, the entrepreneur always comes in at the last minute and expects the investor to bail him out. Resist doing this at all costs and make the entrepreneur get through his crisis by himself. If you make it easy for him to get out of his situation, he will do it to you again and again in the future. The second thing to do when you find that the entrepreneur has led you to the brink of disaster is to look for a way out of the investment. Your other option is to fire the entrepreneur and get someone in that is responsible.

5. Entrepreneurs who are in love with technology and engineering often create problems. They no sooner finish a prototype product than they are ready to develop the next product, even before they have run any profits out of the first one. This will show you that your development people are not marketing people and that you have just invested in the wrong kind of company, a development company. You should always invest in marketing companies. Whenever you find yourself in a development company, try to get out as soon as you can. Development companies are rat holes in which investors dump millions and millions of dollars, never to see a cent of it return.

6. An inventor entrepreneur will develop some great products for you. However, the same entrepreneur will also invent products that are unrelated to the business that you have invested in.

If you have invested in a company involved with biotechnology, you may find your entrepreneur hot on the trail of the next great solar energy product. Every entrepreneur believes that each product he is working on will launch the next great technological revolution. They want to put money into all of these products. This is the wrong type of management team to invest in. Get out of the business or you will lose every nickel you have put in.

This is a personal sample of some of the nutty things that I have run into as an investor. Whenever you see these, start working on a way to get out of the deal.

WHY ENTREPRENEURS HAVE FINANCIAL PROBLEMS

When you ask a venture capitalist, "What makes a good company?" he will always say, "Good management." But, in a sense, that goes without saying. If the company shows strong growth and the venture capitalist makes money, then it had good management. If the company gets in trouble and loses money for the venture capitalist, then the company had poor management. So what did the venture capitalist mean by "good management"? He meant that management knows that the problems a small business fears most are (1) lack of financial monitoring and control and (2) undercapitalization.

The Financial Control Problem

Most entrepreneurs can put together a good business plan and solid projections, and can understand the cost of the required capital from banks and venture capitalist. However, only a few will set up a system to monitor progress and analyze the information they are receiving. As an entrepreneur, you should want to know the weekly sales figures. Some in retail operations even want to know the daily figures. Every entrepreneur should be watching the figures closely. When cost figures do not coincide with those projected, find out why. When sales do not match projected figures, find out why. When the projections do not work out precisely, revise the future projections in order to determine how much capital you are going to need to go where you want to.

The most successful entrepreneurs have been "cash flow freaks." These are people who know exactly what is going on in their company from a numerical standpoint. They know when they will run out of cash, the so-called "drop dead date." They know what they have to do in order to increase cash flow. When things get rough, they know how much money they need to carry them

202

through the next stage. They know precisely what they are doing in allocating their scarce resources properly. A monthly profit-and-loss statement is almost an afterthought for them. They ride herd on the company's cash on a weekly and sometimes daily basis.

The Undercapitalization Problem

Undercapitalization has always been a serious problem for small businesses. Too often the entrepreneur will fail to raise the amount of money he needs. He will raise $200,000 when he really needs $500,000. He does this so he won't have to give up as much equity to the venture capitalist. This approach is shortsighted. Most businesses need more money than originally projected in order to reach profitability. When the entrepreneur needs the extra money, the venture capitalist may charge a high price. Always raise enough money.

Smart management recognizes the need to have sufficient capital in the company. It does not tie up excess capital in accounts receivable or inventory. It seeks ways to increase the capital in the company. When the company grows, management knows the company must increase its capitalization. Be a good manager and maintain adequate capital for your company.

WHY ENTREPRENEURS HAVE PEOPLE PROBLEMS

Many an entrepreneur can run a company well when it consists of a small intimate group, but cannot manage the business when it begins growing into a larger company. This failure often relates to the selection and management of people. As can be expected, no business can grow and remain a one-person operation, nor can an entrepreneur remain a chief with many Indians. In order for a company to grow, the business must attract top-notch middle management to the team. There are five basic reasons that many small businesses fail to build a strong middle management team.

Poor Job Definition

Senior management often fails to understand precisely what jobs need to be filled. Entrepreneurs are accustomed to dealing with undefined job responsibilities. They expect the team to join in and work. However, as a company grows, specialization becomes important. Certain jobs must be segregated and defined so that suitable individuals can be hired to do those specific jobs. As manager of the company, you must define jobs.

Poor Selection Process

Once the job has been defined, top management may use a poor selection process. It is easy, for example, to let "good ole" Joe continue to be controller of the company since he has been the bookkeeper from the beginning, or to hire a relative out of loyalty rather than because of his ability to manage the job that needs to be done. These practices do not ensure strong middle management.

Poor Incentives to Management

In order to attract middle management to your company, you need an effective incentive plan. The members of the entrepreneurial team have a high incentive because they own a large share of the company. Their egos are submerged in the business and they want to make it a success. New members of the management team won't have the same rewards. In order to motivate them, top management should consider the various traditional methods of compensating top-notch middle management. These include stock options, stock performance rights, good pension and profit-sharing plans, bonuses based on formulas of sales or accomplishments, and the like. If you do not set up a proper reward system for your middle management people, they will not perform.

Poor Review Program

Because middle managers do not get the same satisfaction out of the growth of the company as entrepreneurs, they need to be rewarded through traditional review programs that let them know when they are succeeding and when they are failing. A good review program will give you an early warning of any problems with middle managers. If will also give you an opportunity to correct the problem. You must have a review system that is in concert with your incentive system.

Poor Development Program

Sometimes a company outgrows the abilities of the initial middle management team simply because the managers are not given a chance to develop their skills through seminars and other educational methods. This situation can be avoided by having all the members of the middle-management team come together to share their ideas and discuss the problems they are having within the company. This interaction permits marketing to become acquainted with what is happening in production, and allows finance to better understand the problems of marketing, as well as other aspects of your business. This kind of internal professional development program is necessary for any growing company, and should supplement a regular development program.

WHAT TO DO WITH PROBLEMS

When a company has a severe operating problem, as an investor you will be trying to make one basic decision. Should you try to remove the current management and find a new group to run the company? If you have lost confidence in the management team and this has turned into a crisis situation, removing management might be the best thing you can do for the company. In general, there is a rule in the venture capital community that an entrepreneur only gets one chance. This means that if the entrepreneur screws up and brings the company to a very difficult situation, then the venture capitalist will try to exercise his rights and force out the entrepreneur or sell the business.

In analyzing this situation you will want to determine the best method of getting back all of your money. You need to minimize your losses. First analyze the earning capacity of the company. Can the problem at hand be solved and how quickly can it be solved? How much will it cost to carry the company while the problem is being solved? If the problem is solved, will the company be sellable? Before you invest any additional money in the company, you need to analyze the company in the same way you did when you made the initial investment. Each new dollar that you invest is like a new investment. You must ask, "What will be my return on investment?" Throwing good money after bad money is one of the greatest mistakes investors make. Meeting another payroll just to keep the company alive so you don't have to write off an investment is the easiest way to end up with a lot of money in a bad deal.

Second, after looking at the earnings power, you will have to examine the "bricks and mortar." This means that you must look at the assets of the company to try to see what it would be worth in liquidation. If you move in, liquidate the company, pay off the bank, and have the remaining amount coming to you and other investors, what will you end up with? In doing this analysis, you should look at suppliers who might offset against the inventory, any mechanic's liens that are in place from work that has been done for the company, taxes that could conceivably jump in front of everybody else, and any other creditors that may come out of the woodwork and put a claim on the assets. Once you have had a chance to review this situation in detail, you will have to choose the "earnings power approach" or the "bricks and mortar approach."

When you have decided which road to follow, you will need to stick with it for a while.

What Is Your Next Step?

Whenever I have had to analyze a company in crisis, the outcome has been less than satisfactory. In fact, most analyses of companies in trouble are inconclusive. Nonetheless, as an investor you will have to make a decision concerning the company in trouble. There are five basic options open to you as an investor.

1. Fix the Problem

In order to fix a problem, whatever it may be, you are going to have to invest more money in the business to keep it going. You may have to hire additional people or do whatever else is necessary to solve this specific problem and save the company. Most entrepreneurs will plead with an investor to put more money in and go forward with the company, that the end of the rainbow is just around the corner.

I remember in one venture capital situation, the company was in the cement business, which is a very cyclical business based on the demand for housing. In the early 1980s when the housing industry was in shambles, some new projections suggested that a turnaround was about to take place. The entrepreneur and the venture group bought the cement company in the fall and used the capital during the winter to carry the company. By spring it needed an additional injection of capital, and the equity partners put in additional capital. By the end of the summer, the housing industry had not come forward and the equity partners were called upon once again to place additional equity in the company to carry it through the winter. Only a few of them put up additional money. By this time, the partners owned approximately 75% of the company and the entrepreneur 25%. When spring came and another capital infusion was needed to carry the company through the summer, the venture partners put up more money and diluted the entrepreneur down again. The expansion of housing starts never took place, and this time the venture firm sold the company for a pittance, took a few bucks, and left town.

The important thing to remember here is that each new investment opportunity that you are offered should be treated as if you had never had an investment in the company. Don't think about the money you have sunk into the company. If your feelings about a new investment in this company are negative, you should tuck your tail between your legs and walk away like a wounded dog.

You should not continue to invest good money in bad deals. You should select one of the other alternatives set out below.

2.   Sell the Business

Many venture capitalists have gotten out of bad deals by merging them with other businesses. Invariably it seems that every business is worth more as an operating entity than one that is shut down. This is certainly true of every service-oriented company. Merging the company in which you have an investment with a larger entity that can bring in money and management to build the company you have invested in may be the only way to get your money back.

There was one venture capital situation involving a retail tire store where the alternatives were to inject additional money into the company or sell it. Since the venture capitalist had lost faith in the entrepreneur, the only thing to do was to sell the business quickly. As you can imagine, the tire business is made up of leased locations, inventory, and people. Without these three ingredients you have nothing of value. It was necessary to move quickly and find another tire retailer who wanted to enter the marketplace in which this tire company was located. It was the only way to save the investment.

You will be faced with quite a few situations in which you will want to find a buyer for the company. Before they even go in, some venture capital firms work out a scenario in which they identify companies that would be potential buyers should the company get in trouble. You may want to do this.

3.   Foreclosing on Assets

It you were smart enough to make your venture capital investment in this problem company as a loan with an option to buy stock or convertible debenture, then you are a creditor in this company rather than an investor and you can foreclose against the assets of the company. If the company is not paying you principal and interest as agreed, your loan can be called in default and you can begin to seize the assets and try to operate the business or sell the assets in a general auction in order to get your money back. This is a very difficult method of operation and most venture capitalists do not achieve it successfully.

If you were able to get a secured position on the assets through a UCC-1, you are a secured creditor, and as such you have the option of moving in and foreclosing on the assets. In one venture capital situation, the investment group had to foreclose on the assets of a large radio station and they took over the assets of the company and began operating it because the previous owner just couldn't get any ads to be played on the station. In operating the radio station, the investors would listen to the radio as they drove to meet the payroll. One day as they were driving along they heard many classy ads being broadcast, and when they arrived they asked the radio disk jockey how he had been able to sell so many good ads. The disk jockey coyly replied, "Oh, I didn't sell any ads, I just like to listen to the ads on the air so I put them on free." Venture capitalists are usually not good operators. As an investor, you may not have the time or the inclination to run the business. On the other hand, you still have the option of holding a foreclosure sale and selling the assets at auction and taking what money you can get out of that and applying it to the money owed you.

4. Bankruptcy

Some investors now look at bankruptcy as less of a bad place to be, especially if the company has large debts from banks. When the bank begins to move on the assets and foreclose, the only way to salvage anything for the stockholders is to take the company into bankruptcy. The new bankruptcy code is quite lenient toward business owners. It allows the creditors to take the company and work with it for a number of months in order to try to restructure its liabilities and pay them off over an extended period of time. In one situation that we are familiar with, bankruptcy was used to hold off the senior creditor for three years while the company operated as "debtor in possession." This meant that the management team continued to stay in place and run the company and held the bank at bay. The senior creditor was unable to foreclose on the assets and the company continued to show improvements, and in a short time came out of bankruptcy and was able to pay back its debt. This is easily one of the few times this has happened for small businesses in bankruptcy. Usually they get liquidated.

5. Liquidation

Liquidation has been mentioned along the way, but it is the least desirable of all of the alternatives simply because it usually doesn't pay off. Sometimes a business that is asset heavy may be worth more "dead" (liquidated) than it would be as an operating entity. As an operating entity, it is going to continue to lose money. If an investor is placed in this position, he definitely needs to seek liquidation of the company's assets in order to recover as much money as possible. None of these choices are easy. As an investor, your principal concern is to find a way to salvage your investment.

SECRET OF A SUCCESSFUL RELATIONSHIP

Every relationship is based on trust. If you have entered into a financial deal with a company that you do not trust, you have made a grave mistake. You are sure to have some doubts about the firm in the initial months, but if your checking has been accurate, then the firm should prove trustworthy. Assuming you both trust each other, there must also be a desire to help each other. The company wants to make money, and you want to make money. You both have a common objective. One should not be making money at the other's expense. You should be on the same level, and therefore, should have a desire to help each other. From time to time, you may be asked to help with various problems encountered by the company. Remember, you are partners.

More than anything, the secret to a successful relationship is the ability to talk to each other, and to communicate both the good and the bad news to one another. If two individuals can openly discuss the things they like and dislike about a relationship, as well as tell one another what things are good and what things are bad in a constructive critical approach, then the relationship will most likely be a successful one. In turn, the business will probably prosper.

I remember an entrepreneur who was highly motivated, well-trained, and an achiever of the first order, but who was unable to admit failure. This flaw dominated his personality to such a degree that not only did he refuse to admit small errors, but he would not accept the fact that his company had lost $175,000 at the end of its second year. When he received the audit from a large accounting firm, he would not accept it. He made the accounting firm restate the figures, but give him a qualified opinion. The financials showed the company had made a profit and was in good financial condition. The accountants' opinion had a section which said the financials were correct, subject to the adjustments made by the entrepreneur. The entrepreneur presented these financial statements to his board of directors, to his bank, and to his investors. He seemed to think that if he could somehow get through the year without anyone except the accountant knowing his true condition, then he would have time to turn the company around and cover up past mistakes.

This entrepreneur was unsuccessful in his cover-up. The company was liquidated. Many people lost a great deal of money. In relationships with investors, boards of directors, and employees, the players should be open. Save all the connivings and devious actions for the competition, as long as the actions are legal and acceptable in the marketplace where the products are sold.

DEGREE OF INVOLVEMENT BY THE VENTURE CAPITALIST

The amount of time you as a venture capital investor want to spend with the company will depend on a number of factors.

Amount Invested

The amount the venture capitalist has invested in the company, compared to other investments, will determine how much time you spend with the company. If you have invested $50,000 in an early stage, you may not spend nearly as much time as if you have had invested several million dollars. The larger the amount invested, the more upset you will be if you lose it. The more the invested funds mean to you, the more attention you will give.

Need for Assistance

If the company has a management team and does not need assistance, then you do not need to spend time with the company. If the company needs a financial adviser or someone to discuss marketing, then you may perform that function. The more help the company needs, the more you should be concerned, and the more time you will need to give to the company.

Management's Willingness to Accept Advice

If management is willing to accept advice, most investors are willing to give it. If management resists every suggestion, obviously a venture capitalist will not waste his time making suggestions to management. There is a fine line to walk here. Entrepreneurs should be hungry for advice on major decisions, but not on day-to-day operations.

Experience in Certain Areas

If you are not experienced in a certain area where the company has a problem, you will not try to advise the company on the matter. If the entrepreneur has good financial information and is a financial whiz, the venture capitalist may not try to help with financial decisions.

Lead Investor

If the venture capitalist is the lead investor, he will probably spend more time with the company than if he were the sole investor. This arises from his feeling of responsibility to the other venture capital investors. While he is under no legal obligation to ensure that they make money, his reputation is on the line with his friends. He wants the company to succeed so he will probably spend more time with the company.

Distress of Company

If the company is in distress, then the venture capitalist will try to play an active role. Every venture capitalist spends most of his time working out problems rather than reviewing new deals. In fact, many venture capitalists say they are not in the venture capital business at all, but rather are in the business of working out bad deals. They are always trying to avoid losing their money. It seems that the good companies take care of themselves.

Relationship with the Entrepreneur

Often a strong bond will develop between the entrepreneur and venture capitalist. A certain chemistry that exists among people in venture situations draws them together. Great friendships have arisen from these relationships, even in dire circumstances.

Time Availability

As you know, investing in small companies is very time-consuming. You need to work on the most pressing problems first. If the new investment is a small problem or if it is operating well, you can invest most of your time in solving more serious problems. Make sure the entrepreneur does not interpret your lack of attention as a lack of interest in the company. The amount of time spent on an investment is usually inversely proportionate to the success of the investment. In general, you cannot make a company successful, but you can often save his investment when there is trouble.

Tips on Monitoring

There are some basic things that you should try to do as an investor in the company if you want to monitor the company. It is extremely important that you follow some of these suggestions to save yourself from waking up one morning with a serious problem on your hands.

1. **Set the Tone on the Way In**

    When you make your investment, make sure that your entrepreneur understands your objectives and understands that you believe that this is a partnership in which you both share a great deal of information about the business. Make sure you set the right tone on the way; explain that you expect him to give you information on a regular basis so that you can keep up with the business. Exhibit a great deal of interest and enthusiasm for the business and you will find that the entrepreneur will understand your interest and supply you with plenty of information.

2. **Understand the Business and the Products**

Make sure you understand what business you are in and what products the company produces so that you do not come across as a complete fool when you are talking to the entrepreneur about his business. He does not expect you to be an expert in the business, but if you do not know one product from the other or continually show little knowledge of the industry, he will conclude you do not have as much interest in the industry as he does, and, therefore, will stop giving you information about it. Stay on top of the business and its products so that you can talk knowledgeably with the entrepreneur.

3. **Keep Up with the Industry and the Competition**

It is also important that you know who the competition is and that you continue to seek information about them. Every time you see information about the competition, clip that piece out and send it to the entrepreneur and show him that you are keeping up with what is going on in his business. If there is a study coming out on the industry, try to read it and share your thoughts about the industry with the entrepreneur. By being an informed investor, you will be sure to gain additional information from the entrepreneur. He will seek you out as a knowledgeable person with whom he can discuss the problems of his business and the industry.

4. **Join the Trade Association**

You may not need to join a local trade association in order to gather the information about the industry, but you will definitely want to subscribe to industry magazines. They may be boring reading from time to time, but one or two articles will come along that will let you know more about the industry than you did before and also be a source of information to discuss with the entrepreneur running the business. Because it is important to keep up with the industry, a subscription to the industrial magazines is a must; joining the trade association is an option.

5. **Know the People in the Business**

You need to know all of the people in the business that you have invested in. Know the top five or six people; get to know the secretary to president. Let them become part of your group. At a minimum, write down all of their names, so that when it comes time to meet them again you will have their names on the tip of your tongue. Do not walk up and say "Hello"; say, "Hello Joe, it's been a long time since I have seen you." Make sure you know the people in the industry and keep talking to them. If on that one occasion, you are unable to reach the president of the company, call the marketing vice-president and ask him the question, if it is a marketing question. This will let the management team know that you are out there and that you are part of the team. You do not want to be a pest, but you do want to be part of the team

6. **Spend Time with the CEO**

The greatest way to obtain information about the company is to spend time with the chief executive officer. It is an unwritten law that the people who do not spend time with the president are not going to know much about the company. The CEO is at the center of all that is going on in the company. If you do not spend time with that person, you are not going to learn much about the company. It is essential that you and the entrepreneur become close friends and go forward and try to make money together.

It is also essential in the care and feeding of the CEOs that you continue to communicate with them. You need to praise them when they do things right and criticize when they miss the mark. Help them build a team by keeping praise on when they do a good job. Make specific observations, but always qualify them with "I am not an expert in the business, but . . ." This will let them know that you are not trying to present yourself as a manager or leading authority in the industry, but rather as a person who is greatly concerned about the company and one who is offering friendly advice.

7. **Track Performers**

Do not ever let up on tracking the performance of a company. It is imperative to keep up with sales and earnings of the company as well as all of the financial ratios. If you let down your guard in this area, you are apt to wake up with a big surprise one morning, even though you are the best of friends with the CEO. Tracking performance is one of the critical aspects in watching the company grow.

Pitfalls of Monitoring

The quickest way to blow it as a monitor of a company is to do one of the following items:

1. **Appear Only When There Is Trouble**

   If you appear at the company only when it is having problems, you will be considered an enemy and not a friend. Enemies (vultures) only appear when a company is having problems. This is the most often heard criticism of bankers among small business people. Bankers are never available until a problem occurs, then you cannot get rid of them. Although a banker may be satisfied with this kind of relationship, you as an investor cannot.

2. **React to Problems**

   It is very easy to react to every problem that the company has rather than being part of the planning process. If you do react each time, you will again be considered an outsider. Be part of the planning process and understand what the company is trying to achieve. When it misses the mark, come down on the company in terms of negative feedback, but do not react emotionally.

3. **Second-Guess Management**

   Being a Monday-morning quarterback is an easy skill. It is easy to second-guess a management team. However, it is hard to dish out a negative feedback without looking as though are second-guessing them. Be sure you do not say, "If I had been in your shoes, I would not have done that." If you are part of the planning team, you were there when the decisions were made. Try to work your way out of problems and not compound them by discouraging management.

4. **Pain Factor**

Everybody wants the company to make money. You do not want to be so involved in the company that you become a pain to the management. You want to be a plus to the management team rather than a thorn in its side. As long as management if following the best path for the company you should try to be part of the team. In times of trouble, praise works better than pain.

VENTURE CAPITALIST'S OBJECTIVES

During the period of time you are working together, you will have one objective: growth. You want to see the company grow as fast as possible and to see it become as large as possible. You want to see sales go up, and you want to see profits go up. Those are your basic objectives in investing in the company.

If the company has grown sharply and is now becoming large, you will be looking toward liquidity. You want to be able to sell part of the investment when the time is right. You receive no bonuses because of the company's growth and success. You receive your rewards when you are able to sell part or all of your investment and make a large profit.

CHAPTER 11

THE EXIT

There has always been a love-hate relationship between the venture capitalist and the entrepreneur. Most venture capital investors are frustrated entrepreneurs and think that if they could only run the business, they could do it better than the entrepreneur they have backed. On the other hand, most entrepreneurs love their investor on the day they receive an investment from him, but as the years wear on, they feel they have done all the work and the investor has done nothing to earn the money that he has received. The relationship between the venture capitalist and the entrepreneur becomes more strained when the company is operating poorly. At such times, you must step in to try to save your investment, and this usually causes great friction. Whether it is a successful endeavor or one with a great many problems, there will come a day when you will want to exchange your ownership in the company for cash. "Cashing out," as it is called, is a normal end to any investment.

As an investor in a small business, you should make the entrepreneur know that your stock ownership in the company is for sale at any time; it is just a question of price. Every investor should let the entrepreneur know that someday the investor will want to cash out on his equity ownership, and that will be as soon as the price meets with the investor's expectations for the return on his money.

There are six basic approaches to cashing out of an investment. All of these involve various types of companies in various stages of development or trouble. The items discussed below are the public offering, selling the company, selling the investor's shares back to the company, selling the investor's shares to a new investor, reorganization, and liquidation. All of these have a way for the investor to "cash out." They may not always be at the price one wants in order to get out, but each provides a unique avenue for an investor to exit from a deal.

EXIT ONE: GOING PUBLIC

One of the greatest methods for cashing out of your investment is to have the company you have invested in go public. In cold hard terms, the public pays more for a company than almost any other source. Therefore, the public market is the one you are aiming for. As an investor in a public company, you will have the opportunity to cash in some of your chips by selling some of your shares to the public, and eventually you may be able to sell them all.

When to Go Public

Many brokerage houses in this world can take a company public, but only a handful specialize in public offerings of small and growing companies. Each of these investment banking houses will have its own criteria for taking a company public. The large national companies will not take a company public unless it needs at least $20,000,000. Small houses will take a company public for as little as several million dollars. Most of the discussions with the brokerage house will center around the earnings of the company for past periods and projected future years. If the company has good growth in earnings and is projecting good growth and if it meets the minimum standards of the brokerage houses, then it will be a likely candidate for a public offering. If one brokerage house says that it can't take the company public, the entrepreneur and the investor should scout around until they find one that will do so.

Every investor would like to sell some of his shares in the public offering. It is nice to cash in a few dollars when the company has its initial public offering. However, the number of shares that can be sold in the initial public offering will be determined by the underwriter. Sometimes the underwriter will not permit any, and at other times the underwriter will permit up to 20% of the offering to be sold by insiders. Needless to say, if it is a good public offering, the underwriter will come back to some of the investors and ask if they can buy the shares to be sold in the secondary market or have a secondary offering.

Every investor has to review his portfolio of investments in order to determine if there are business opportunities greater than the investment in the company where he has his money parked. If there are, then obviously the investor should cash in some of his stock and get cash for it and invest it in the higher return investment opportunity.

There is also the question of good portfolio management. If you have a number of investments, but one business opportunity now makes up a great deal of your personal net worth, you should definitely cash in some of your stock in the initial offering whenever the opportunity presents itself. You should never have too much money in any one investment. Diversity is the best thing possible in an investment portfolio. When your time comes, don't forget to review your situation, and make sure you cash in some stock because that is the best thing for you to do.

Underwriter's Fees in the Public Offering

A stockbroker will charge a fee for acting as the underwriter on any stock offering. Part of the fees will go to the other stockbrokers who joined in the group selling the stock, but most of the fee will go to the firm you choose to be the underwriter. Underwriter's fees range from 5% to 10%; 8% seems to be standard. The higher the risk, the higher the fee. It is possible to reduce the underwriter's fee by giving the underwriter some options to buy stock. All in all, it is very difficult to get the fee below 5%.

On top of the underwriter's fee will be legal fees, printing costs, auditing fees, and a number of fees for writing the prospectus. The point of all of this is that if you have not negotiated to have all fees included with the expenses borne by the company in any public offering, then as a selling stockholder you will have to bear your pro rata share of the fees. This means that if you sell $100,000 worth of your stock, you may only end up with $85,000. So, the underwriter's fees become an immediate concern of any major investor as well as anybody selling stock in the offering.

Selection of a Brokerage House for a Public Offering

As you begin to talk with various brokerage firms as well as friends, accountants, and bankers, the names of some local and regional brokerage houses will come to mind as possible underwriters for the new issue that you are talking about. As you continue your research, two or three names will keep coming up and you will eventually start to interview brokerage companies in order to determine which one should be selected to take the company public.

In selecting a brokerage, you will want one of the most reputable firms. You should look for experienced underwriters in the new issue area. You should look to a brokerage house that has the financial strength to distribute the shares to its clients. You should also determine if the brokerage firm has good market-making ability. That is, once it sells the stock, someone will have to make a market in the shares. If the company you are considering is not good in this second area, then the stock will surely fall in price after the initial offering.

EXIT TWO: SALE TO ANOTHER COMPANY

The second method of exiting from a venture capital investment is to sell the entire company to a third party or another company. This is a very good way of realizing on your investment. By selling the entire company, a buyer will be willing to pay more for the company when its all of the stock rather than a minority interest only part of the stock. When someone is buying a company, control of that company is a valuable asset to acquire. Trying to sell a minority interest in a company is much more difficult than selling the entire company.

When you sell the entire company, you can be paid for your stock or the assets of the company in several ways. Basically, there are six ways that a company can be sold. You should understand each of these so that you will be able to negotiate with the buyer of the company in order to maximize the cash that you will ultimately will receive.

Sell the Stock in the Company for Cash

This is the simplest of all mechanisms and it triggers a capital gain to you and also a capital gain tax. The method needs no further discussion.

Selling Stocks for Notes

Rather than take cash for your stock you may wish to take a note from the buyer. That is, the buying company may buy the stock you own in your company by giving you a note that will pay off over time. It will pay you cash over a certain period of time, for example, five years. In the buying or selling of the business world these notes are called paper. So when buyers ask if you will "take back paper," they mean that they want to give you a note in the place of cash. Although cash is certainly made out of paper, only notes are called paper. Maybe the word paper is used here because it suggests something that is worthless. There are certainly many people who have sold their companies and have taken notes in place of cash, and those notes have later become worthless because the buyer ruined the business that was to pay off the notes.

It is common to give notes in order to establish a deferred purchase and thus give you, the seller, a tax advantage. From a tax viewpoint, you can recognize the income from the sale of the stock as you receive payments on the notes. Most sales are expected to pay some deferred payments for their stock. When it comes time to sell your company for deferred purchase notes, make sure that you know how well secured the notes are. Be sure you understand what you are receiving for your stock or you may end up with a lot of worthless paper.

Selling Stock for Stock

There may be certain circumstances in which you would rather take stock in a very large conglomerate or a large publicly traded company for the stock that you own. This will give you a definite advantage in that you do not have to pay taxes until you sell the stock that you received from the public company. Most of these "stock-for-stock" transactions are tax-free exchanges. You do not have to pay taxes until you sell the shares of the large public company. Of course, it is more dangerous to take stock in a smaller company. It might even be considered insane for you to swap the stock you hold in your company for the stock of another private company since you have neither equity nor income from the stock you received. Certainly when you are dealing with large companies you should try to obtain registered shares so that you will be free to sell the stock whenever you wish, rather than having to wait for a period of time (usually two years) before you can sell any of the stock.

Another possibility is to take a dividend-paying preferred stock from a large conglomerate that is convertible into the current conglomerate's common stock. This way you will have income while you are trying to you decide whether to convert your shares into common stock and sell them. This could be the best of both worlds.

Selling Assets for Cash

With the recent changes in the tax law, the situation in which the company sells all of its assets to a new buyer and then liquidates the company can now only be done with great care. Now when you sell the company's assets you trigger a taxable event whereby the company must pay taxes on the gain on those assets before it makes a liquidating distribution to you. In turn, you must pay taxes on the gains that you received from the company.

Because of the new tax law, it is very difficult to sell assets for cash and then liquidate the company that distributed the cash. However, in certain circumstances where the assets are being sold at book value or perhaps even below book value, you can still use the sale of assets for a cash and liquidation scheme. Since you are selling the assets below book value, there is no tax, and the tax comes only when the individuals receive the cash and the liquidations of the company.

Selling Assets for Notes

Sometimes the acquiring company may not have the cash to pay for the assets it is buying from the company you are selling. In this situation, your company may have to take notes secured by the assets being sold as payments. The assets have been sold for notes. These notes will have to be collected. Again you will have to be careful about the type of notes that you are taking for assets. If the notes are paid as agreed, the company may not recognize a gain on the sale of the assets until it actually receives the cash from the notes. Because of the new tax law, if the company decides to liquidate and distribute the notes to the stockholders, it could be considered a taxable event and taxes could be due on the amount of the gain that is the difference between the note price and the cost basis you had in the stock. You will want to have a tax lawyer examine any situation in which you are taking notes for assets.

Selling Assets for Stock

In some circumstances you might sell the assets of the company for stock in the buying company entity, such as a publicly traded company. Then you could liquidate the company and distribute the stock to the stockholders of the selling company. Because of the new tax law, this could trigger two taxable events: (1) on the sale of stock, or (2) when the stock is distributed to stockholders. You could end up with a double tax on an illiquid company, which would not be good tax planning. There seems to be a scenario in which it would make a great deal of sense for you to swap stock for assets when stock was in excess of the depreciated value of the assets. However, if you are selling assets at below book value, you could take advantage of this situation.

Other Forms of Payment

Many other forms of payment are used in concert with the above six basic structures. One common structure is called an "earn out." An earn out means paying sellers an additional amount for the company they have purchased if that company earns more than they had expected it to. In such a situation, the managers of the business would continue to operate it as a division or a wholly owned subsidiary of the buying company. To the extent that the management of the division could increase earnings above the amount projected by the buying company, the selling stockholders would receive additional payments based on the percentage of that excess. As an example, the company that purchased your entrepreneurial company might agree to pay stockholders an additional amount (the earn out) equal to 25% of the pre-tax income in excess of $2,000,000 for each of the next five years. This would mean that you and the other stockholders would get your prorated share of the cash distributed based on the above formula. Many buyers like to have earn outs because it gives the buying company the undivided attention of the entrepreneur, who wants to make additional money by getting the earnings of the company higher, even though the entrepreneur is no longer a stockholder.

As a nonoperating partner in a venture capital company, you will have to watch for entrepreneurs who sell their companies and then get significant compensations in the form of consulting contracts or noncompete agreements. I have been in a situation in which a company was willing to buy one that we were investing in, but at a significantly lower price than we felt it was worth. To our surprise, we found that in addition to negotiating a low sales price the entrepreneur had wangled an agreement for an enormous consulting contract for the next five years. In essence, the buying company was paying for the purchase of the stock by agreeing to take on this entrepreneur-turned-consultant for the next five years. The entrepreneur was trying to dip into our share of the real value of the business by taking a large portion of it in the form of a consulting contract. Our commitment letter and our legal documents now contain a provision that would prevent the entrepreneur from doing this. You should pay particular attention to this item and make sure it is in the agreement for the sale of the company you invested in.

EXIT THREE: SALE BACK TO THE COMPANY

The tactic discussed in this section is not used frequently in the venture capital community, although Allied Capital Corporation has used it in a large number of its exits. As a investor, you are prepared to sell everything that you own and in essence everything that you have is for sale. Letting the entrepreneur know this can trigger an opportunity for you and the entrepreneur to negotiate a purchase of your equity in the company by the entrepreneur or by the company itself. This can occur when the company has cash or when it can borrow the money from the bank. The entrepreneur will buy your stock by borrowing the money from the bank and purchasing it from you. After repurchasing your share, the entrepreneur and any other stockholders will own 100% of the company, but the company will have increased its liability in the

223

form of a bank loan. In some circumstances where the company has good cash flow but cannot convince the bank to allow it to borrow additional funds to buy out the investor, it may be necessary for you to sell your equity back to the company through a short-term or medium-term note. Here the investor more or less finances his own buyout. Remember that in this situation you are taking paper in a small company and you want to make sure that the loan you have made to the company is a secure one. At a minimum, you should take collateral in the stock that you selling to the company so that if the company defaults on its note, at least you will have the stock that you started out with. You will be in no worse a position than you were in just before you sold your stock back to the company.

There are other variations on this idea, whereby you sell the stock back to the company for another of its assets that you would rather have. For example, you might sell your stock back to the company for the land and building that the company owns. The company would then lease that land and building from you. You could probably dream up a number of swaps but they are relatively uncommon in the venture capital world. Most venture capitalists want cash.

Purchase by Employee Stock Ownership Trust

The vehicle that some entrepreneurial companies use to purchase an investor's stock is an Employee Stock Ownership Trust (ESOT). In this situation the company sets up an ESOT and each year has the company make a contribution to that trust based on the employees' payroll. The ESOT takes the place of a pension plan and in some cases a profit-sharing plan. This different type of pension plan must buy stock in the company and since the company is not selling the stock, it will buy from the investor. The ESOT obtains money through company contributions and therefore builds up cash. Since the contributions consist of pre-tax dollars, the company is retiring your equity position with pre-tax dollars that are contributed to the ESOT, which in turn purchases your shares. For a quicker transaction, the ESOT can borrow from the bank and then use that money to purchase your stock. The contribution made to the ESOT would retire the debt in the ESOT plan. Because the ESOT receipts are tax deductible to the company, this is a relatively painless way for the company to buy out an investor. However, ESOTs are complicated animals and must be approved by the Department of Labor as well as tax experts. Anyone contemplating this method of exiting should contact an expert in the field of employee ownership trusts and get good tax advice.

Exit by Puts and Calls

When you negotiated the investment in the entrepreneurial company, you may have set up a formal arrangement that provides for an exit by the investor. These are usually in one of two forms: a put or call. As we noted earlier, a put is the right given to an investor to require the company to purchase the investor's ownership in the company at a predetermined price or a predetermined formula. The call provision gives the company the right to purchase the investor's ownership on the same basis.

There are probably as many different put and call formulas as there are minds thinking about how to structure deals. However, there are seven popular ones for you to consider:

1. **Price-Earnings Ratio (PE).** Probably the most popular is a price-earnings ratio formula that values a company's stock in the same way as the stocks traded on national stock exchanges. The earnings per share are figured for the shares owned by the venture capitalist. A popular price-earnings ratio is selected from public stocks in the same industry. That PE ratio is multiplied by the earnings per share to come up with a price per share that the company will pay the venture capitalist for the stock he owns.

2. **Book Value.** A less common formula is based on the book value of the company. It is simple to compute the book value per share for stock owned by the venture capitalist. That would be the price the company would pay for the shares owned by the venture capital company. Book value per share is seldom used because in the early years of a company's development the company usually has a small book value. It is only in older companies that have been around long enough to establish a realistic book value that this becomes the method of valuing the venture capitalist's equity position.

3. **Percentage of Sales.** Sometimes it is inappropriate to use the earnings of the company in a price-earnings formula because in the early years of development, particularly in a start-up company, the earnings may be low owing to heavy depreciation or research and development expenses. It may take several years for the company to become profitable. Using pre-tax earnings may seem to be more appropriate. However, pre-tax earnings are often held low because of heavy salaries or heavy expenditures for promotion. In such a case, it may be easier for you to take the normal profit before tax as a percentage of sales typical for the industry. You will find statistics on the

225

industry in publications on business statistics. You may find that most companies similar to this one have a pre-tax earnings of 10% of sales. It would be simple then to take 10% of the company's sales and pretend that number is the profit before taxes. By using this method you would have determined earnings per share by using the hypothetical profit before taxes. Using the industry price-earnings ratio, one could easily determine what the value of the stock owned by the venture capital company would be worth if the hypothetical earnings existed. This can be the method used for buying back the shares.

Using the percentage of sales formula to value and buy back the shares can be very expensive. If sales are pumped up because advertising has been increased to push sales and market share up, the formula for repurchasing shares will be high. On the other hand, if the formula is based on earnings, the entrepreneur can control the amount of earnings. For example, the entrepreneur might increase advertising in order to reduce earnings and build a name for the company in the future. By using the earnings formula, the entrepreneur will be reducing the value of the shares. The entrepreneur cannot tamper with sales as easily, and therefore sales become a good indicator of the value of the company.

4. **Multiple of Cash Flow.** In some industries cash flow is a more accurate barometer of how the business is doing than are profit-and-loss statements. Using an eight-to-ten-times cash flow formula, one can value a company, and it is simple to compute the value of the percentage of the company owned by the venture capitalist. The entrepreneur can use this as the method for establishing a price for the stock.

The cash flow formula may work quite well for a stable company, but could be extremely expensive in an asset-heavy, leveraged buy-out situation. For example, in a leverage buy-out the company may have inflated the value of the assets in order to shelter income. However, when heavy depreciation is added back in the calculation of cash flow, the cash flow number will be much higher than the profit-before-tax figure. Therefore the price you receive for your equity can be high if it is based on cash flow.

5. **Multiple of Sales.** The value of some companies in certain industries is based on a multiple of sales. Radio stations traditionally sell at two to three times gross sales. If you determine the value of a company to be two and a half times gross sales, it would then be simple to compute the value of

the investor's percentage of equity ownership. As in the percentage-of-sales calculation above, the multiple-of-sales valuation also means the entrepreneur will be trying to buy back stock in a company that may or may not have earnings. Many investors in the radio business buy a poorly run station on a multiple-of-sale calculation knowing full well that the station's earnings cannot possibly pay back the investment. The investor who is buying the station must put in enough money to carry the station until its sales and earnings can be increased.

6. **Appraised Value.** It is often easy to find a business expert or a stock brokerage firm to appraise the value of the equity ownership held by the investor. The appraisal will probably be based on a combination of some of the items above. Appraisals are usually computed by two methods. First, the value of the company is determined by its earning power, both past and future. This formula is similar to the price-earnings ratio used above. Second, the value of the assets (bricks and mortar) is determined as if they were to be sold at auction as part of an orderly liquidation. From this liquidation the appraiser subtracts all debts outstanding, and the remaining value is the appraised value. The bricks-and-mortar formula is similar to the book-value calculations, except the liquidation approach includes an appraisal of the assets and a restated new book value based on their appraised value. When these two figures (liquidation vs. earnings valuation) do not agree, the appraiser usually selects something close to the higher of the two. The appraiser would assume that the highest and best use of the company was to sell all of its assets or operate it as a going concern.

7. **Prearranged Cash Amount.** Of course, a simple formula would be to base a put-and-call option on a single cash amount. That is, at the end of three years the venture capital firm would have the right to require the company to buy its equity ownership position for a certain amount, say, $200,000. Although this method saves a great deal of negotiating and appraising at the end of three years, people find it difficult to agree on a value at the beginning of the investment period.

EXIT FOUR: SALE TO AN INVESTOR

Sometimes it is possible to find a new investor who will buy your ownership in the company at an attractive price. There may be a circumstance in which the entrepreneur would like to have a

227

working partner and you could sell your position to someone who would like to become a working partner of the company. In another situation, the entrepreneur might have a close personal friend who has enough money to purchase the position held by you. All of these are rare; it is not often that you will find a passive investor who wants to be a long-term investor in a small company and who is willing to buy the position held by another investor.

Corporate Partner

Sometimes when the company has made substantial progress and has a new idea, usually technological, you can find a corporation that would like to be a corporate partner to the small business. This gives you, the investor, an opportunity to sell to the new corporation that wants to be a partner with a small business. The corporate partner's objective may be to own all of the company sometime in the future and therefore it makes good sense for them to purchase a small position in the company. In addition, the corporate partner may make a better partner in a small business than you, the investor, because the corporate partner will know more about the marketplace and how to produce the product. As an example, we once invested in a small company and later brought in a corporate partner that happened to be a large international telecommunications conglomerate. As the small company started to grow, the conglomerate decided it wanted to buy the company. However, the venture capital position was the only one that was for sale, so a bargain was struck and it was purchased. This gave the corporation an opportunity to see what was going on in the company and it was later able to convince the entrepreneur to sell out completely.

New Venture Capital Partner

In certain circumstances it is possible to find another venture capitalist or another investor to purchase a position held by an investor. For example, the first venture capital partner may be an equity-oriented venture capital fund that invests in early stage companies. The second investor group may be one that purchases equity in later-stage companies. Although it is unusual, you may be able to sell your stock to a later-stage venture capital company.

At one time, Allied Capital Corporation was an investor in a small advertising company that was having operating problems and not growing at all. The entrepreneur was able to find another venture capital fund that still believed in the new method of advertising. That venture capital fund invested enough money in the small business to buy out Allied Capital Corporation. When the company continued to show poor results, a third venture capital fund came in and bought out the second venture capitalists, who had become quite disillusioned. The third venture capital fund was able to attract several more rounds of venture financing. Eventually, this became one of the most profitable public companies backed by venture capital in recent times. As Allied Capital Corporation looked back at its inability to ride out the rough storm with the entrepreneur, it could only shed a few tears for not staying with it all the way.

EXIT FIVE: REORGANIZING THE COMPANY

Among venture capitalists and investors, the word *reorganization*, or its more grissly name, "Chapter 11," has appeared all too often in the venture capital world. Reorganization is a long word for bankruptcy. Reorganization has been used by many small businesses to remove creditors as well as investors. By using Chapter 11 of the bankruptcy code, small businesses can compromise debts and squeeze out stockholders. It is one of the most depressing circumstances an investor can be in. Without question, you are at the mercy of the legal tribunal known as bankruptcy court, which has ultimate authority. A judge can confirm a plan that actually removes the investor as a material stockholder in the company. A bankruptcy judge can "cram down" debt holders into equity positions to the extent that the original equity owner is diluted down to nothing and the new equity holders "who are the original debt holders" become the owners of the company. A bankruptcy judge has the power to determine that secure debt is really unsecured and that unsecured debt should be "compensated" by stock in the new company.

Allied Capital Corporation has been to bankruptcy court more times than it cares to remember, but on the whole we have not lost an enormous amount of money through the bankruptcy code. This has not been because we were treated well in bankruptcy court, but because we have not been in bankruptcy court as much as we should have been according to the percentages of venture capital financings that go bankrupt.

From an investor's viewpoint, bankruptcy is virtually the end of the world. When a company goes into bankruptcy, you can be sure that what you will receive for the real money you invested into the company will be a small pittance compared to what you originally put into the company.

It is unwise for any investor to attempt to use the bankruptcy court as a means of salvaging an investment. Almost everyone who has tried to do it has ended up paying enormous legal bills and has received much less than they have ever expected by going into bankruptcy. One of the iron rules of investing is to stay away from bankruptcy.

EXIT SIX: LIQUIDATION

More venture capitalists than you can imagine have made their exit by liquidating the company. If all else does not work and the business performs poorly, this may be the easiest way out. One can sell those assets that have some value and take the remaining cash to dissolve one's investment in the company. Any number of companies have grown to a certain stage and then have found themselves worth more "dead" (which means liquidated), than alive. It is conceivable that the land, building, machinery, equipment, and other assets of the company are worth more in liquidation than the company can possibly earn with those assets.

This can be seen in industries that go through very difficult periods. They may be good solid businesses for a number of years and have built up assets that were not strictly needed by the business such as land, building, and certain other nonperishable assets. Then the industry goes through a severe reversal and the profitability drops substantially. At such a moment, the assets, if sold and invested in a passbook savings account, could be worth more than the business. This is particularly true of companies that experience severe competition from foreign companies. A recent example is the chain-making industry in the United States. Making common-length chains has become a commodity business and many developing countries have developed a chain-making capability. Since their labor content is substantially lower than that of industrialized nations, these countries are able to sell chains in the U.S. market at substantially lower prices than the U.S. companies can. This lowers the profitability of chain-making companies considerably and has made some of them worth more in liquidation than as a going concern.

For the investor, if all else fails liquidation may be your most logical answer. At the moment of liquidation you will be much happier if your investment is in the form of a loan or a debenture than in straight stock because as a creditor you may get more money than a stockholder. You may be forced into liquidating a company and getting the cash from the liquidation (you hope).

Allied Capital Corporation has used liquidation on a number of occasions very successfully. However, success is based on picking a good auctioneer who can auction off the asset in a very competitive manner. Some auctioneers can skillfully work up the audience to the point where a reluctant bidder will step forward and make a cash bid for the business asset. It is quite an exciting moment when you, as an investor, have a good auction and the cash price of the asset will get most of your money back. Be very careful about the auctioneer and the auctioneer organization you choose to liquidate your company; it will mean the difference between getting out and a big loss.

WHEN YOU ARE IN A WORKOUT

Sometime during the monitoring process you will realize that something has gone wrong. It is easier to recognize a winner than a loser. This has something to do with the fact that you and the entrepreneur have your personalities entwined in the business and its success, so that when problems begin to develop, you may not be able to see them. Somewhere along the way you will recognize there is a problem. Being the first to burst the dreams of the entrepreneur and declare the investment in trouble can be dangerous because you may alarm the entrepreneur. By classifying the investment as a workout, it may cause the entrepreneur to overreact.

Workouts don't develop overnight. They develop slowly, and you must recognize the telltale signs. Although a bad loan may take time to develop, you need to treat it as though it were an on or off switch. The investment is either a problem or not a problem, and if it is a problem, then you need to take appropriate action.

Don't believe that things will get better. Always assume that things are going to get worse and make sure you understand what will happen then. Also know that money is not a cure for all problems. Many an investor has been lulled into putting in small amounts of capital and nursing a losing situation for months and years. The cumulative effect comes in one horrendous write-off when the company is finally liquidated.

Also know that there are no quick fixes in this type of investment business. Meeting the payroll will not fix the company. Saying you are going to sell the company will not let it happen overnight. There is no way to make a company turn around, get sold, or be cured in a short time. It is a long and arduous task to bring an ailing company back to profitability or get it sold to someone who can.

Your personality and that of the entrepreneur will be wrapped up in the business. It will be hard for either of you to admit that this is a bad investment, and when you do finally recognize it as a bad investment, you may be so upset that you can't think clearly. This is a time when you need to remain calm and think things through. You need to begin immediately.

Quick Study

As a first step, you need to have a damage estimate. You need to determine what, under worst-case assumptions, will happen over the next twelve months. Management of the company is rarely clear-headed enough to understand the problem and make the damage assessment. You need to spend the time to come up with that report.

As part of this quick study you need to ask yourself several questions. Why have sales projections been missed? Do any executive salesmen or other employees seem to be making less than their full contribution? Is there excessive spending that could be trimmed away? Is there a real demand for the company's product or services? Does the management have a true understanding of the cash flow? You may want to have your accountant come in to prepare adequate cash flow projections so that a true estimate of the damage can be computed. Can you pinpoint the root cause of the problem? Once you have completed that quick study, you need to move on to other aspects.

The Business Plan

In the same way that you prepared your original business plan, you need to develop a business plan for the workout. You need to review the business from stem to stern and try to come up with an aggregate business plan that will allow you to move the company from its problem situation to positive cash flow. This business plan should be completed as quickly as possible.

Liquidation Analysis

When you prepare your business plan, you also need to prepare a liquidation analysis. That is, under an orderly liquidation whereby you sell the assets of the business and pay off creditors, what would the company be worth? To do this you need to make a reasonable assessment of the assets. Go through all of the items on the balance sheet as well as assets off the balance sheet and determine if they have significant value beyond that listed on the balance sheet or perhaps a lesser value under the liquidation scenario.

You may want to consider putting the company in Chapter 11 if that is the only way to stave off creditors who are making demands on the company.

SAVE YOUR INVESTMENT

During the workout period, you must not be swayed from your main goal: to save the money that you have invested in the company. Sometimes in a workout situation you can get caught up in saving the jobs of the people employed there, saving the company that you once believed in, or not destroying the hopes and dreams of the entrepreneur. All of these are worthwhile goals, but your first priority is to save your own investment. In this situation you need to look out for number one only.

CHAPTER 12

FINDING GOOD INVESTMENTS

As chronological sequences go, this chapter should be Chapter 1. However, it seemed important that you be able to recognize a good investment before you go searching for one. So, we began this book with the due diligence process and learning how to look at investments. We now discuss where to look for good investments.

DEVELOPING AN INVESTMENT OBJECTIVE

Before you can establish a marketing approach to finding good investments, you need to develop your own investment objectives. It is not as easy at it sounds. Making money is a very general objective, and although everybody says that they are out to make money, there are thousands of ways to do it. You must make some basic choices or you'll be pulled in a thousand different directions. Here are some important areas to review in establishing your objectives.

Purpose of Investing

Every time you ask a venture capitalist why he is investing, he usually says to make money, but money is a very general term. Venture capitalists have other desires as well. For example, some major corporations invest in small businesses in order to have a "window on technology." That is, they want to see what small companies are doing in a certain area of technology. So, they invest not only to make money, but also to learn about new technologies.

Other large companies invest in small companies in order to develop information on an industry so that they can acquire companies in that industry. They also may invest as a prelude to acquisitions, like a shark taking its first bite before it swallows the whole fish. Some large companies invest for public relations purposes. That is, they try to generate goodwill in the marketplace by investing in some small community-based companies.

Some people invest to "save the world." They feel that by investing in a small company with a great technology, they will by able to help the world. It may be a new medical product. It may be a new solar generator that is going to wrest power from the hands of the oil cartel.

When you are looking around for partners to coinvest with, make sure you understand your proposed partner's purpose for investing. If it is not consistent with your own, then you should not coinvest with them. In all likelihood, you will end up at odds in trying to decide where the company should go.

The Type of Money You Have to Invest

Some investors have plenty of equity money to invest in small businesses and as a result they can invest in common stock or preferred stock or can buy debt in the company. If the investor has equity-type money and plenty of it, then the type of investment alternative will be fairly open to the investor. On the other hand, if the investor has a strong net worth but not much cash, he may be willing to guarantee a debt from a bank to a small business in return for an equity stake in the company. By doing this, the small business gets the money it wants, but it receives the money in the form of a loan and it has to pay interest on the loan as well as give some equity to the guarantor.

In another scheme, the investor may have great credit lines with the bank so that the investor can borrow the money and lend it to the small business. In this situation the investor has debt-type money and needs a debt instrument for his investment in the small business.

The type of money you have to invest will play a big role in determining what type of investment you are looking for and how you can make money.

Stage of Development

Some investors prefer to be involved in a particular stage of a company's growth. There is the start-up stage, in which the company is just beginning to produce its product. There are later stages such as second- and third-round financings. These later stages have relatively lower risk, but don't give one the great feeling of accomplishment that the investor was there at the inception.

In addition, there are such varieties as turnaround investments in which the investor invests in a troubled company that will need a great deal of work in order to turn it around and make it profitable.

There are also leveraged buyouts in which a group of management people get together and borrow a great deal money and put up a little equity to buy a company. This, too, is a special type of investing that takes a different type of investor.

You need to determine the stage of company development at which you wish to invest.

Specialty Investing

Some venture capitalists are generalists. They will invest in practically any area of industry and have an appetite for anything from oil wells to high technology. Generally speaking, most investors feel that they must specialize in an area in which they have some knowledge or they can learn quickly so that they can understand a specific area that they have decided to invest in. You too, will need to select a specialty area that you would like to invest in so that you communicate this to the outside world. Otherwise, you will be sorting through a wide variety of investment opportunities, many of which will be a waste of your time.

Timing of Your Investment Exit

Your investment timing may depend on the cycles you think the marketplace is in. If your ultimate objective is to take the company public then you will have to keep a sharp eye on which way you think the stock market is headed. If you are ready to invest in a company, but think the stock market is going to be down, then you may want to curb your appetite for investing in companies that need a public exit. If, on the other hand, you are going long term and you feel that the stock market will be strong in five years, you will invest for the long term when the stock market comes back.

Another idea is to invest in a company that you can sell to a larger company. When you invest in this mode you must pick several target companies you think will want to buy the company and try to judge when they might be willing to look at the company. Your timing is important because a very acquisitive company may, after several years, stop acquiring in order to digest what it has purchased. Timing in this regard will be more difficult to predict, but you should think about timing your exit before you invest. First, you want to decide whether you are investing for the short term or long term or if some part of your portfolio is in that time frame. Then you want to think about how you will exit, through a public offering or private sale of the company.

Size of Your Investment

You need to determine the size you will invest, that is, the amount of money you will be willing to risk in any one company. If you decided that you didn't want to invest more than $50,000 or $100,000, then this would place you in some very small companies and you might find yourself limited to investing in small businesses or in some very early stage companies. This will determine how you are going to invest your few dollars. On the other hand, if you only have a few dollars to invest, you may want to associate yourself with an investment group in which you can bring more to the table than just money. If you have specific expertise in a certain area, don't be shy about letting local venture capital funds know that you have this expertise area and money to invest. Let them know that you would like to coinvest with them in some deals and that you would be willing to do a lot of the work on the due diligence.

Geographic Preference

You must determine what distance you are willing to go to invest. Are you willing to invest only in your own backyard, or are you willing to board an airplane and fly to see a company. Generally speaking, if you are going to invest in early-stage companies, they should be within a very small circle around the area where you live because usually early-stage investments take a lot of time. In order to avoid riding airplanes all the time, you will want to invest in early-stage deals in your own backyard.

On the other hand, if you are getting ready to invest in a fairly large third-round financing in which you will not play a major role, you can travel a pretty long way in order to be an investor in a situation like that.

Liquidity Preference

Venture capitalists typically invest in companies that don't have much liquidity, but there are a number of "penny stocks" in which one may want to invest. This gives you the right to sell your stock at almost any time as long as there is a public market for it. This will give you liquidity, whereas most venture capital investments are illiquid.

Be careful, some small public companies are public for a time, then lose their trading status on over-the-counter system called NASDAQ, because they fail the net worth or earnings tests and get delisted. Stock in delisted companies is hard to sell.

Your Risk Profile

There is a wide spectrum of risk. You can go for a high risk, high return on investment or you can accept a low risk, low return. Generally speaking, there are some interesting ways to determine how high your risk is going to be, as discussed in previous chapters. You need to determine how much risk you are willing to take and communicate this to the outside world. If you are really interested in taking flyers, you will have a lot of early stage, start-up investments reaching your desk for money.

Your Activity Level

Determine how active you are going to be in the company you invest in. If you are going to play an active role managing the company, then you will be looking for companies that need someone like you to help. The typical ad in the newspaper for companies seeking financing will read, "Active Partner Needed." This might just suit you. If so, you will be looking for a different kind of investment than most venture capitalists. Typically, venture capitalists are involved in management, but not in a day-to-day fashion. They are called in from time to time to help out with problems. If you are interested in this level, then you will be more like most venture capitalists.

It is also possible for you to be a passive venture capital investor. Some venture capitalists play little or no role in the small companies they invest in. In fact, they make the investment, and then more or less sit back and hope that the investment comes out okay. These investors rarely invest in the company a second or third time. They invest once and hope for the best. You will have to follow your own vision here and determine how active you are going to be in any one company. Obviously, you can't be very active in many small businesses or there won't be enough hours in the day.

Timing of Return

You need to determine when you think you are going to have your money back in any company you are going to invest in. Most venture capitalists want to invest for five to eight years, whereas others want to invest for only three to five years. Some players will invest for ten years or more. You need to determine what your time horizon is for investing in any small business. When you invest, you want to make sure that your time horizon is congruent with that of the small business and the other investors.

Once you have analyzed each of these areas and written down your investment objectives, you will have a much clearer vision of what type of deals you should be looking for.

ORIGINATING INVESTMENT OPPORTUNITIES

Now that you have identified your basic objectives, you need to get the word out on what you are looking for. You should put together a one- or two-page letter that describes what you are interested in and what you are willing to consider. Then, you need to circulate it among the various sources of investment opportunities. Below are some sources of investment opportunities.

Banks

A bank can be of help in a number of areas. First, the lending department will be interested in showing you situations that need equity funds. Banks always have loans that need an infusion of equity. Second, bankers often have small businesses come to them looking for cash. But the commercial banker does not feel that the small business has sufficient collateral to justify a loan. The small business person may then tell his banker that if he runs across somebody that he thinks might be a good investment match, to send the investor his way. Commercial bankers run into a large number of small businesses looking for money and can help you find investments.

The workout department of banks is also a good place for problem loans. You may find the banker in a very precarious situation trying to get his money back and you may be the answer. If you like turnarounds, the bank workout department is a good place to visit. It usually knows of one or two companies that are in deep trouble and need some help.

The bank trust department also has tips on businesses for sale, usually because owners have died and left their small business in their estate. The bank would like to find somebody to buy the business and run it. Bank trust departments are trying to sell these businesses and you might be the right person at the right time. Make sure the bank trust departments in your town know what you are looking for. Also, the trust officer will be planning people's estates and if they have decided to sell, they have most likely communicated this to the bank trust department.

Even though you may not want to buy the business, you may well be the catalyst and the financial source needed to get the business sold.

Accountants

Small and large accounting firms run into an inordinate number of businesses for sale and many that need money. You may be just the right person to help an entrepreneur buy a business or you might be the right person to help out an entrepreneur who currently owns a business that needs money. Many accountants play the role of investment banker and help small businesses find money from individuals as well as institutions. You should make sure that you spend time with these accountants.

Attorneys

Attorneys are much like accountants. They spend time with their clients and understand what the client is going through. If it is an elderly client trying to settle an estate, the word will go out to the lawyer. You can back the existing management in the leveraged buyout of the company from the seller. You should communicate your interests to lawyers.

In addition, lawyers work with small businesses that need money because of operating problems or growing pains. They often know about the small businesses in their area that are in need of cash. You should let the lawyer know that you have money to invest in small businesses.

Investment Bankers/Stockbrokers

Almost every brokerage firm has a group of stockbrokers known as investment bankers. These are people who work for the brokerage house in a separate area, not buying or selling stocks, but acting as brokers on the sale of a business, or in the financing of businesses. Every department has a group of specialists in the small business area, and you should get to know these people because they can help you find investment opportunities in this area.

Business Brokers/Financial Brokers

There is a rather undefined group of individuals known as business brokers and financial brokers who help small businesses find buyers or investors. You need to associate with these small business brokers and become involved in helping them with their transactions. Somewhere along the way some company will need money and you'll

241

be there to put it in. You can locate these people by looking in the yellow pages under financial or business brokers. Also, you can look in the Sunday classified ads of your newspaper under business opportunities. There you will find dozens of business brokers listing businesses for sale. You should contact them and tell them you are interested in investing in small businesses. Ask if they know of any in which the entrepreneur doesn't have enough money. They will be eager to help you and some of their entrepreneurs get together because they stand to get a fee for selling a business.

Warning: There are many unethical brokers who are rip-off artists. Most have no association with financial sources. Make sure you are dealing with a quality broker who is affiliated in some way with a financial group. They will be your best brokers.

Consultants

Good consultants in the area of small business are few and far between. However, many of the big accounting firms have consultants who specialize in this area and some independent consultants in the marketplace also look at small businesses and try to help them with their problems. You should get to know some of these and tell them what you are looking for. These consultants often see small businesses that need money and could steer them to you.

Conventions

Many conventions around the country are oriented toward entrepreneurs and small businesses as well as venture capital. You should attend these fairs and try to determine if any of the small businesses participating are worth investing in. Unfortunately, it has been my experience that most of these conventions are not a good place to find investments. Who knows, maybe you will find something different in your town.

Economic Development Organizations

Every jurisdiction has an economic development organization whose investment officers are on the lookout for small businesses that might relocate in their area or might need help after relocating. Many of these businesses need equity capital and you could be the person to provide those funds. Determine who these economic development officers are and get to know them. Make sure they know what you are looking for.

Industrial and Professional Trade Organizations

Most cities have industrial and professional trade organizations to help their small businesses. Get to know these trade associations and let it be known that you have money to invest in small businesses in their industry. Each of these trade associations has contacts throughout their industry and they often know of small businesses that need money. They will be most happy to send you to the small business and earn brownie points for their members.

Local Chamber of Commerce

Like the economic development organizations, your local chamber of commerce will know of a lot of businesses in your area. Some of them will be looking for money. Make sure that you want to invest in the area and get letters and information in their hands so they can pass the word along.

Friends and Associates

In talking to the outside world, you should tell your friends and associates that you are very interested in small businesses and are looking for investment opportunities. They may run across a company looking for investment capital and may send them your way.

Venture Capital Companies

Although it is unusual for venture capital companies to syndicate their investments with individuals, it does happen, usually when the individual has special information or abilities in a certain area. They will want you for your expertise. You should let local venture capital companies know that you are interested in investing in anything they are investing in and would gladly play a more active role than they may have time to play. For example, you could sit on the board of directors and provide management with advice. Under that scenario you will find venture capitalists very interested in hearing about what you are looking for.

Cold Calls

From time to time you may hear of a small business in the area that sounds interesting. All you have to do is pick up the phone, call the company, ask who the president is, try to get through to him say you have investment capital and would like to invest in the company. You would be surprised how many cold calls get through when the caller is looking for an investment opportunity in the business. The next time your read about a company, don't say, "I wish I had invested." Call and see if you can invest.

Advertising and Direct Mail

Placing advertisements in newspapers, periodicals, and trade journals can sometimes help generate investment opportunities. The advertisement should specify certain requirements, such as the stage of development (like start-ups) or the level of investment, so as to ward off nuisance calls. Some venture capital companies have gained tremendous opportunities from such advertisements whereas others have had very little luck with them. The type of company and the type of investment you are looking for will determine whether you should use advertising. If you are looking for a very narrow investment opportunity such as radio stations, then advertising in periodicals that are mailed to radio stations will generate an opportunity list from the radio arena.

Direct mail can be used to solicit opportunities from specific business areas, but, like advertising, it also generates a large number of nuisance calls.

Suppliers

Sometimes suppliers to a specific industry such as electronic components, can help you find growing companies that need financing. Many of these suppliers have a vested interest in helping their customers obtain financing. Many years ago we worked out a relationship with drug wholesalers to finance a chain of drug stores that was growing rapidly at the time. It turned out to be a good investment for us. Similarly, you could select an industry and go to the suppliers in that industry to find investment opportunities.

Other Groups

There are some other groups you can contact from time to time to let them know you are looking for investments. These include employment agencies that may be recruiting for small businesses and thus could pass along your message.

Financial planners are another source. They frequently work with the heads of small businesses to plan their estates. They may be able to get through to the CEO when no one else can.

Now and then the staff of elected officials also hear from small businesses that are looking for money and might be able to send someone in your direction.

Universities, too, at times try to help small businesses and so are involved in the entrepreneurial process. Make sure that they know you are willing to invest in their small businesses.

Regional Small Business Administration (SBA) offices can be a source of small companies seeking venture capital. Most of these are start-up situations and many of them have contacted the SBA as a last hope. When you contact the SBA office, remember that here you will be seeing last-chance investment opportunities.

Pro-Activity

In order to succeed in finding good investments you must be pro-active. You must seek out investment opportunities whenever you can. You cannot sit in your office and hope that good investment opportunities will show up on your desk. Good investments come to those who are looking for them. If you want to be successful in the venture capital investment arena, you will have to hustle. They will not come into your office by chance.

HANDLING INVESTMENT OPPORTUNITIES

If you want to get a good reputation in the venture capital business, you should have a very quick method for handling the initial inquiries. You need to be able to review a business plan or listen to a presentation over the phone and decide immediately whether you have an interest or not. If instead you ask people to mail in a business plan and leave them waiting for weeks while you ponder to see if it is a good investment, you will get nowhere in the investment community. A quick "no" is much better than a "maybe" that turns into a "no".

However, quick analysis requires a quick screening process for initial inquiries. The screening list presented here is a condensed version of the entire due diligence process. It contains the key questions that you must ask about the business.

1. What is the business of the company (ten words or less)?
2. In twenty-five words or less, what is so great or unique about the business of the company?
3. Is the management knowledgeable and experienced in this industry?
4. Does the management consist of entrepreneurs, achievers, and aggressive and energetic people?
5. Is the management top quality?
6. Will you have to hire a new Chief Executive or Chief Operating Officer now or in the near future?

7. Is the company profitable? If not, why not? Is the cash flow positive?
8. What are the historical figures and projections? In thousands:

Year   _____   _____   _____   _____

Sales $
Profit $
Cash Flow $

9. What is the projected and actual sales growth rate in average % per year? Actual _____%. Projected _____%. Is it achievable?
10. Is there a company one can use as a role model? Has anyone else done this before? If so, who?
11. What is the deal you think you can get? What percentage ownership?
12. How much money will you make? How did you compute this?
13. What collateral will you have? What is the downside risk?
14. Why do you like this situation?
15. What is wrong with this situation?
16. Does this rate as a "Good Deal?" Why?

1		3	4	5	6	7	8	9	10
Junk		Needs		Possible			Good		Hot
		Something					Deal		Deal

USING BROKERS

Most investors and venture capital firms do not use brokers to help them find investment opportunities. That is, they do not hire investment bankers or brokers to find them deals. Investment bankers are generally hired by companies seeking capital. If you decide to align yourself with a broker, there are a number of things you will want to look for.

Qualities to Look for in a Broker

In any business arrangement you should look into the background of the person you are backing. After all this person will be working for you and representing your company to the outside world. The broker you work with should have the following qualities:

Experience: Extensive experience in helping finance business is usually a must. Without such a background a broker will not understand the problems of a small business. Nor will he understand the sources of funds that usually finance small businesses.

Professional: A business broker should be a true professional, one who is knowledgeable about your investment approach and the type of investment that you are looking for. He should be a full-time, and not part-time professional. It is unlikely that any part-time person can assist you.

Credentials: Any broker you have working for you should have a strong financial background. A degree from a recognized business school is a must. Experience as an investment banker or as an employee of a recognized brokerage firm is a plus. Experience in venture capital investment would be even better.

Special knowledge: If you are seeking investments in high technology or a specialty industry, the broker you are working with must have professional training in that special area. Without a degree from a technological school and knowledge of the technological area, the broker will not be able to gain the confidence of those in the industry and thus lead you to a potential investment opportunity.

The broker who meets most of the above qualifications is the one most likely to point you toward good financing opportunities.

Agreement with Broker

Your broker may want you sign a written agreement stating that if the small business concern is unwilling to pay his fee, you will be responsible for his fee. Such an arrangement between you and any financial broker should have all the elements of a good contract. Below are some of the items that it should contain:

Define the Service. In this section of the legal agreement, you should spell out in detail the service to be performed by the broker. Establish what is expected of you in the way of information. You should also clearly state the objective of this arrangement, such as, "a venture capital investment of $1,000,000."

Time Frame. Every legal document should specify the date that the relationship terminates. You should also specify intermediate dates by which certain milestones are to be completed. If you or the broker do not meet these intermediate dates, then the contract can be canceled by either party. You will be in a position to call the broker and ask what progress has been made. If none has been made, terminate your agreement by letter, stating that you are terminating it because the specified progress has not been made.

Termination Clause. The termination should be subject to written notices from one party to the other party. This clause will state how, and for what reasons, the agreement can be terminated.

Amount of the Fee. State the amount of the fee in detail. It can be a flat fee that covers all out-of-pocket expenses or it may be a fee plus out-of-pocket expenses. If you are agreeing to the latter, make sure you have in writing an estimate of the out-of-pocket expenses in excess of some named amount.

Reports on Progress. The agreement should state whether any progress reports are to be produced by the broker. Normally, the broker should report to you orally at least once every week and should frequently give you a written report of the work completed.

Ownership of Work Completed. Any work completed by the broker, such as charts or work on the business proposal, should be owned by you. You have paid for it; therefore you should own it. If you do not have this clause in your agreement, any work completed by the financial broker may belong to him. If you should terminate this agreement for just cause, he may keep everything. This will force you to duplicate a great deal of work.

Nondisclosure Clause. There should be another clause in your agreement specifying that the broker will not disclose any information divulged to him to any other persons without your prior written consent. This will prevent the broker, under any circumstances, from passing along information.

Indemnification. The broker should indemnify you in the agreement against any misrepresentations or wrongful doings by him while he is in your service. He should also indemnify you against violations of federal and state security laws. If he does not indemnify you for actions he has taken, he could conceivably misrepresent your situation to someone, and that person could sue you because of the misrepresentation. After all, he is your representative.

Complete Agreement. The agreement should state that this is the only agreement that the parties have entered into and that any oral understandings are null and void. This written agreement should supersede any previous agreements, and all future modifications should be in writing.

Once you have a full, written understanding of the relationship between you and the broker, you will be in a better position to use his services.

Some Tips on Dealing with Brokers

The soundest advice anyone can ever give you is to urge you to check out the broker. Obtain references from the broker and determine if he is legitimate. Call any companies that he claims to have helped. Call the presidents of those companies and ask about him. Also ask him for some names of companies that he was unable to help. Contact the president of those companies and ask them why he did not succeed. Any information you can develop about this individual will be useful in helping you to decide whether to hire him.

APPENDIX 1

QUESTIONS USED IN VENTURE CAPITAL INVESTIGATIONS

Investigation is an arduous task. Some people have a gift for investigating people and businesses, but most of us need help. We need help in organizing our approach. This means putting together lists of questions about the things we should be looking for.

Although no list is complete for every business situation, a long general list is better than no list at all. A general list of questions will obviously not fit the style of every investigator. You must therefore develop your own list of general questions and then adapt that list to each different business opportunity. The general list below is only a beginning. You must improve upon it by deleting those questions you believe are not important and adding questions that are not on the list.

There are a number of basic areas to investigate. Each one is like a flat stone. You have to turn up each stone to see if there is a snake under the stone. If you do not turn up each and every stone, you may leave a snake hiding that will come out one day and bite you. You never know which stone might be hiding a deadly snake that could someday kill a deal. It might be production or it might be finance. To repeat, when investigating business, you should leave no stone unturned.

Think of each of the areas below as a module that you must complete before your investigation is finished. The degree of detail you examine in each module will depend on the stage of development of the business, how much you know about the industry, how well you know the entrepreneur, and many other factors. Below is a guide to begin your search. Some of the same questions can be asked in each area to determine consistency. You need to modify this list of questions to suit your own needs.

MANAGEMENT AREA

Most venture capitalists say people are the most important part of any good investment. "Good management" are the watchwords of investors. But whether management is "good" seems to hinge on performance. That is, if the management team has made lots of money for the venture capitalists, then they are considered "good management." What is it that makes a venture capitalist believe a management team will succeed and therefore be good? What makes a good entrepreneur? Well, a billion pages have been written on these subjects in every type of publication imaginable, from psychology journals to popular self-help magazines. Judging people will be one of your most difficult tasks. Here are some questions to help you start thinking about the key people.

A. Chief Executive Officer

1. What achievements has the chief executive had in prior business? In personal affairs? In general? What makes you think the CEO will achieve the established goals in this business venture?
2. What other business ventures has this entrepreneur been in? How successful were they? Why were they unsuccessful?
3. What is the style of leadership of the chief executive? Will that style be effective in this business?
4. How does this person perceive his role relative to other members of the management team? Is the emphasis on one individual or on the team effort?
5. How well does the chief executive understand the details of this business? Is the entrepreneur a detail-oriented or a concept person?
6. Does the CEO know the details of the day-to-day operations of the business?
7. Is the CEO knowledgeable about all parts of his business, marketing, production, finance, etc.?
8. To what extent does the CEO rely on subordinates or other managers to analyze business operations?

9. Does the chief executive take a lead role in the company's planning efforts or rely on others to do the planning?
10. Is the chief executive innovative in dealing with existing or potential problems?
11. Characterize the CEO in terms of behavior, attitude, and approach to life? What behavior traits does the CEO have?
12. Is the CEO honest?
13. Does the entrepreneur have integrity?
14. Is the CEO knowledgeable about the industry?
15. What is the reputation of the CEO in the company, in the community, and in the industry?
16. What is the net worth of the CEO? Is he wealthy outside this business?
17. What is the age of the entrepreneur? Does he have the energy to run a small business?
18. What is the health of the CEO?
19. Is the CEO insurable?
20. What kind of home life does the CEO have? Is it stable? How will it effect his ability to run the business?
21. What does the CEO want to make in capital gains from this business? How much in salary?
22. There can be only one final decisionmaker in any company; is this CEO the final decisionmaker? Is the CEO in control of the decisionmaking process?
23. Is there a natural successor for the chief executive? Would the company be able to function smoothly without the CEO?
24. Does this entrepreneur need to achieve?
25. Is the CEO competitive?
26. What achievements are in the CEO's background?
27. Does the CEO have a high energy level?
28. Does this CEO give you straight answers to questions?
29. Does this CEO have a need for autonomy?
30. Does the entrepreneur seek independence?
31. Does the CEO need to dominate every situation?
32. Is the entrepreneur self-confident?
33. Is the CEO persuasive?
34. Does the CEO have a high tolerance for ambiguity?
35. Does the CEO change?
36. Is the CEO able to perceive risk well?
37. Does the CEO take excessive risk?
38. Does the CEO have good verbal ability?
39. Does the CEO have a good personality? Is the CEO easy to get along with or a difficult person to live with?
40. Is the CEO a leader or manager?
41. Does the CEO have a broad and deep knowledge of the industry or the market?

B. Number Two and Three in Management

1. Would the people in second or third command be able to fill the shoes of the CEO if the CEO should die or be disabled? Why do you believe this?
2. Are there any disagreements between the top executives? What kind of friction exists between them? Can they work as a team?
3. What are the backgrounds of the second- and third-level executives? How do they fit together as a team? Do their backgrounds complement each other? Does each have a specialty?
4. Ask the same questions of other key people as you did for the CEO above.

C. Management as a Team

1. Obtain an organization chart and job description indicating present management areas of responsibility.
2. How does management experience in the past and the responsibilities of each person in the team compare with present job requirements? How does salary level compare?
3. Are there any gaps in the present management structure? What are the company's plans for remedying these deficiencies? Should they be remedied before an investment is made?
4. Why do you think this team of managers will be successful? Have they worked together in the past?
5. What percentage of ownership or potential ownership does each member of the management team have? What was the amount of his cash payment for shares held? How significant is each person's investment position in the company relative to his overall financial resources?
6. Are there any loans to or from management or key stockholders?
7. Does the company have the right to repurchase shares held by employees if they leave or are fired? For how long does this right continue? Can the company repurchase share at cost?
8. What are the present salary levels of management?
9. Are there any kinds of incentive compensation?
10. Are there any employment contracts?
11. Have key employees signed noncompete agreements?
12. Is there presently any litigation or other potential liability resulting from management's previous relationship with another company?
13. What changes have there been in the management group in the last three years?

14. How is coordination between members of the management team achieved?
15. How do other members of management feel about the chief executives and their leadership style?
16. Does the company have a management development program?
17. How often is performance by members of the management team reviewed? By whom?
18. Is there a strong team spirit in top management? Is there esprit de corps?
19. Is there a strong work ethic? Do they work long hours?

D. Organizational Structure and Decisionmaking

1. Who exercises the principal authority?
2. What are the relative powers of the president, chairman of the board, vice-president of marketing, etc.?
3. Are there any functioning committees? What functions do they perform? Who sits on them? How often do they meet? What records are kept?
4. Who are the members of the board of directors? What recent changes have there been in board membership? What are their backgrounds and qualification? What compensation do they receive? What actual or potential stock ownership positions do they have?
5. Who are the people on the board of directors? What role do they play in the company? Do they attend board meetings?
6. What is the relationship between management and the board of directors?
7. What role do investors now play in the company?
8. What is management's attitude regarding the function of the board and the investors?
9. What other outside interests influence management's decisionmaking?
10. What are the individual duties, responsibilities, and authorities of each member of the management group? Who defines these? Do written job descriptions exist?
11. Are the basic rules of good organization being adhered to, such as delegation of authority, defined authority limits, defined responsibility limits, simple and flexible organization, separation of line functions, and staff functions?
12. Are successful and proven management personnel available to carry out plans, or does everything depend on one or two key persons? What happens if a key employee is not available for an extended period?
13. Is there a blend of youth and experience, or are most employees the same age and do they have the same experience?

14. Are there cohesive lines of authority and communication? Do all parts of the unit work closely together? Is there an integrated approach to all major problems?

15. Does any one individual excessively dominate operations and planning?

16. Have development plans been established for key managers and high-potential employees?

17. What is the strategy for filling key positions? Can internal development alone meet the requirements or will intercompany transfer or outside hiring be required? Are outside consultants used? What has been the company's past experience?

18. Are local laws prohibiting discriminatory hiring and advancement practices being complied with?

19. Is the compensation plan being administered so as to attract and retain top-quality personnel? Are salary levels competitive with industry norms?

20. Does the company have "key man" life insurance and disability insurance on any of its officers?

21. Do any voting trust arguments exist on any of the company's stock?

22. Does the company have a pension plan, profit-sharing plan, insurance plan, stock bonus plan, deferred compensation plan, or severance plan?

E. Questions Relating to Management Characteristics

1. What type of leader is successful in this industry? Is your entrepreneur like them? What type of leader is likely to be successful in this company? Does your entrepreneur fit?

2. What experience does the management team have in this industry?

3. How much energy does this management team have? Are they in good health?

4. How creative are they? How flexible are they?

5. How intelligent? What schools did they go to? What degrees did they receive? What did they achieve in college?

6. What successes have they had? What have they achieved in their lives?

7. What is the reputation of the management, the board members, and the company?

8. Have any of the officers, directors, or major stockholders been involved in legal proceedings? Criminal proceedings?

9. Has any officer, director, member of the management group, or the company, (including subsidiaries and/or affiliates) ever filed a petition under the Bankruptcy Code or State Receivership, or

made any assignment for the benefit of creditors? If so, describe.

10. Has any officer, director, member of management group, or the company (including subsidiaries and/or affiliates) ever been indicted or convicted of any crime other than a minor traffic offense? If so, describe.

11. Has a member of the management team left? If so, why? Contact this person and discuss the company and why he left.

12. Are there any actions, lawsuits, proceedings pending or threatened against the company or any officers or directors? If so, list.

13. Does the company have any management contracts?

14. Do any affiliated transactions exist between the company and any of its officers, directors, or their relatives other than in their capacity as an officer or director?

15. Have the company, its officers, or directors had any Securities and Exchange Commission problems or violations in the last twenty years? Also, do any exist at present, or are any pending or threatened?

16. Have any officers or directors violated any federal, state, or local laws (other than minor traffic regulations) in the past twenty years?

F. **Corporate Ownership**

1. How much of this company does the CEO own? After the financing will the ownership be enough to motivate the CEO to achieve long-term capital gains?

2. How much of this company does each member of the management team own? After this financing will they own enough to be motivated to sell long-term capital gains?

3. How much of the company do the outside/nonmanagement directors own? Are they motivated to achieve long-term capital gains?

4. Do any individuals outside the company own a large percentage of the company? What is their role in the company?

5. Does the company or any of its officers own 10% or more of the equity in any company other than the company you are looking at?

BASIC INFORMATION

A. **Documentation of the Management Area**

1. Management organization chart.
2. Details of management stock ownership.

3. Obtain detailed resumes (including past experience, salary and promotion history, and academic qualifications) and business and personal references for each key member of management and each department head.

4. Develop information on the CEO's family life, children, physical impairments, illnesses, and other personal data.

5. Copies of any employment agreements, noncompete agreements, or agreements with respect to the repurchase of shares owned by management.

6. Copies of any incentive compensation plans.

7. Copies of any litigation material.

8. Management checks:
   a. Personal reference
   b. Former employers of management
   c. Former employees of this company
   d. Former investors, shareholders, or business partners
   e. Retail credit reports
   f. Daily litigation reports
   g. Bishop's report
   h. Dun & Bradstreet on past business
   i. Past trade creditors
   j. Past suppliers.

9. At least five business and three personal references for each key member of management. Business references should correspond to most recent job, as indicated on resume.

10. The characteristics of the CEO and each of the members of the management team.

11. A complete list of the total compensation to the officers of the company including salary, commisssions, bonuses, fees, prerequisites, loans, advances, autos, club fee, pension, profit sharing, and other. What does each person cost the company?

B. Management Reports

1. What management reports are received by top management?

2. Which management reports are used by top management to "run the business"?

3. Does top management get performance reports on each functional area?

4. Does management receive sufficient, timely, and accurate reports so they know what is going on in the business?

C. Strengths and Weaknesses

1. List the five strengths of the CEO.

2. List the five strengths of the management team.

3. List the five weaknesses of the CEO.
4. List the five weaknesses of the management team.
5. What are the three greatest risks of backing this management?
6. What do you like or dislike about the CEO? About management?

D. Summary Analysis

1. In a very few words, how do you feel about the CEO? About management?
2. Can this CEO make this business plan happen? With this management team? Why do you believe this?
3. Are you willing to bet real money on this CEO and this management? Would you bet your career or job on this CEO and management?

PERSONNEL AREA

Personnel or human resources are a vital part of any company's long-range plan. Every company needs to put in place compensation systems that will motivate its employees to make the company successful. A company that ignores its personnel area will probably fail. Top management's ultimate task is to select and retain good people. You must determine that the company you are reviewing has a good personnel plan.

A. Corporate Organization

1. Does the company have a complete organization chart?
2. Are there job descriptions for each person in the organization?
3. Is there a complete list of officers and directors?
4. Is there a complete list of stockholders?
5. Is there a complete list of employees?
6. Is the organization consistent in its short- and long-range objectives?
7. Are savings available through consolidations or other restructuring?

B. Employee Compensation

1. Is there a list for all officers, directors and department heads, and other employees whose compensation exceeds $30,000/year?
2. What is the date and percentage wage increase of the latest general pay raise for all employees?

3. List the average salary and hourly wage level for the three categories consisting of officers, supervisors, and other employees. Is the average for each higher, the same as, or lower than it is for other local firms in the area and for the competition?
4. Does the company have a written procedure for determining beginning salaries, raises, promotions, etc.? Who set these policies?

C. Pension Plan

1. Does the company have a pension plan? If so, obtain a summary.
2. Is it fully funded? Through what date? Who is the actuary?
3. Do any Employee Retirement Income Security Act (ERISA) violations exist? If so, describe.
4. List the contributions for each of the past five years.
5. Is the plan overfunded so that termination of the plan will trigger a return of the surplus to the company?

D. Profit-Sharing Plan

1. Does the company have a profit-sharing plan? If so, obtain a summary.
2. Have all disbursements been made to the plan for the past year? If not, describe.
3. Can the plan be terminated at any time at the discretion of the company?
4. List the contributions for each of the past five years. Are they excessive?

E. Bonus Plan

1. Does the company have a bonus plan for any of its employees (including Christmas)? If so, describe.
2. Obtain a list of the bonuses paid last year. Are they excessive?

F. Other Employee Benefits

1. Describe medical and sick leave benefits and policies. Also determine the number, type, and cost of claims over the past three years, and specifically identify any significant open claims.
2. Describe vacation/holiday policies.
3. Describe stock option or related equity incentives.

4. Describe policies related to travel and entertainment expenses.
5. Describe policies related to the use of automobiles, airplanes, limousines, boats, etc.
6. Comment on escalation clauses or expectations, if any, within current fringe benefit programs. Expected higher levels of benefits and/or inconsistencies with the buyer should be highlighted.

G. Special Compensation Arrangements

1. Do any employment contracts, noncompete contracts, termination agreements, or other special employee agreements exist? If so, list.
2. Why does the company have such arrangements?
3. Who has signed these agreements? Who determines who must sign the agreements?
4. Who is responsible for obtaining these agreements?

H. Payroll Records

1. Obtain a copy of the weekly and monthly payroll record or printout for salaried and hourly, full-time and part-time employees. Identify the codes, departments, supervisors, and officers.
2. What payroll records exist for each employee? Why are they maintained?

I. Employee Books/Manuals

1. Does the company have a corporate policy handbook for the employees? If so, obtain a copy.
2. Does the company have an employee benefits handbook? If so, obtain a copy.
3. Does the company have a standard operating procedure manual for all departments and/or job functions? If so, review.

J. Union

1. Has a union represented any employee groups during the past ten years? If so, describe.
2. Is any union activity threatened or pending? If so, describe.
3. Does the company have a formal anti-union plan in existence? If so, review.

K. Work Stoppage

1. Has the company had a work stoppage for three hours or longer for any reason because of strikes, equipment failure, inventory shortages, or other reason during the past five years? If so, describe.
2. Has the company been threatened with work stoppage during the past three years?

L. Training Program

1. Does the company have a formal training program for its employees? If so, describe.
2. If no formal program exists, describe the procedure for training new employees and transferred employees.
3. Who is responsible for assuring that the company has a well-trained group of employees?
4. Describe the extent to which the employees in each department have been cross-trained to reduce problems when employees are absent.

M. Attitude and Morale

1. Has the company ever conducted an attitude/morale survey? If so, obtain a copy of the results.
2. If not, does the company plan to have one?
3. In touring the facilities, what did you think of the attitude and morale of the employees?
4. Is there a strong work ethic among the employers? Is there a team feeling, an esprit de corps?

N. Record Maintenance

1. Review the company reporting procedure for maintaining records regarding
   a. Hiring of new employees
   b. Employee evaluations
   c. Employee transfers
   d. Employee promotions/demotions
   e. Employee compensation changes
   f. Employee reprimands
   g. Employee disciplinary actions
   h. Employee training
   i. Employee tardiness
   j. Employee absenteeism
   k. Employee terminations

l. Procedure for building legitimate case for employee termination

m. Union organization activity.

2. Review several actual employee files.
3. Review personnel files for all officers, directors, department heads, and supervisors.

O. Reports

1. List the reports originating within the personnel department for other areas of the company and their value.
2. List the reports generated by outside personnel that you receive and their value to you.

P. Hiring Procedure

1. Review in detail your procedure for soliciting, interviewing, screening, evaluating, conducting reference and credit checks, and hiring new management personnel, and other new employees.
2. Does the company use lie detector tests? An honesty evaluation test?

Q. Motivation

1. What specific methods and techniques has the company found and applied to motivate hourly employees? Salaried employees? Can you quantify the effectiveness of each?
2. What monitory rewards are given for outstanding performance?
3. How is performance measured and used to communicate to employees?

R. Employee Litigation

1. Has employee litigation action occurred in the past twenty-four months, or is any threatened or pending now? If so, describe.
2. Why have some employees been fired and why have they sued?

S. Regulatory Agencies

1. Has the company experienced any regulatory problems or complaints within the past twenty-four months with any local, state, or federal agency? If so, describe.
2. Is the company in compliance with all federal, state, and local laws and with all rules and regulations of the agencies and commissions thereof, including but not limited to safety and

health, consumer products safety, environmental (air, water, waste treatment, land)? Is any threatened or pending? If so, describe.

T. Consultants

1. Has the company used any outside consultants within the past five years regarding any aspect of the company's personnel? If so, describe. Get copies of any reports.

U. Key Nonexecutive Personnel Department

1. Are the critical functions staffed with well-qualified people?
2. Are there special personnel or skill needs, e.g., related to technology, marketing, or manufacturing (short- or long-term)?
3. What are the plans to respond to skill needs or technical obsolescence?
4. Is there or will there be an excess of manpower in some functional areas?
5. Can excess people be retrained for other positions within the organization if the need arises?

BASIC INFORMATION

A. Documentation

1. The personnel manual given to each employee.
2. The company's rating for unemployment and workman's compensation.
3. A complete organization chart.
4. Job descriptions for various key jobs in the organization.
5. List of officers and directors.
6. List of the percentage of stock owned by all stockholders and the amount paid for their ownership.
7. Payroll listing by employee showing what each person makes.
8. Copy of pension and profit-sharing plans plus their financial statements.
9. Copy of any employment contracts.
10. Copy of noncompete and nondisclosure contracts.
11. Union contracts.
12. Personnel procedure's manual.
13. Written statement about any outstanding personnel or employee problems or suits.
14. Copy as the stock option plan.
15. List of all people with stock options, the number of options held, and the price of the options with the expiration date.

B. Personnel Reports

1. Obtain copies of reports used by the personnel department to "run" their department.
2. Obtain copies of reports given to top management.
3. Obtain a copy of the budget used in the personnel department.

C. Ratio Anaylsis

1. Calculate the *Average Salary* over time by dividing the Total Payroll by Total Number of Employees. This will tell you how much the average payroll has gone up per employee over time.
2. Calculate the *Average Salary per Employee by Division* such as Sales, Production, etc. This will show which divisions have high labor cost. Divide Total Payroll Expense for that division by the Number of Employees in the division.
3. Calculate *Total Payroll as a Percentage of Sales* by dividing Total Payroll and Benefits by Net Sales. This can show you if labor costs are going up relative to sales.
4. Calculate *Benefits as a Percentage of Sales* by dividing Benefits by Total Payroll. This will tell you if benefits are going up.
5. Calculate *Employee Turnover* by dividing the total Number of Employees who left in a year by the Average Number of Employees. This will measure the stability of the work force and perhaps reflect how satisfied employees are.
6. Calculate *Management per Employee* by dividing Number in Management by total Number of Employees. This can tell you if the organization is management top-heavy.
7. Calculate *Sales per Employee* by dividing net Sales by Number of Employees. This can give you a measure of efficiency.

D. Major Strengths and Weaknesses

1. Identify the company's five major strengths in personnel.
2. Identify the company's five major weaknesses in personnel.

E. Summary Analysis

1. In a very few words, how do you feel about the personnel situation?
2. Can the personnel policies of the company produce a winning team? Can they motivate the employees to win?
3. Are you willing to bet real money that this group of employees, working under these personnel policies, will be successful? Would you bet your career or job?

MARKETING AREA

The study of marketing is the study of how the outside world (external to the company) sees the company and how the company sees the outside world. Your task is to try to see the outside world as the entrepreneur's company sees it and then to compare that view with your own investigation of the outside world and how it sees the company. Your analysis should begin by looking at the marketing people.

MARKETING PEOPLE

In this section you are trying to understand who the marketing people are. It is a short list and you should ask these questions of personnel and management.

A. The Marketing People

1. Who is the head of marketing?
2. What is his background?
3. How long has the head of marketing been working for the company?
4. What is the head of marketing's salary? How is it divided into commissions and base salary?
5. Who are the top ten sales-people for the organization?
6. What are their backgrounds?
7. How long have these individuals been part of the company?
8. What salary and commissions have they received in the past twelve months?
9. What has been the sales volume of each individual during the past twelve months?
10. What has been the sales quota for each of the these individuals during the past twelve months? Did they make that quota?
11. What is the sales quota for each of these salespeople during the future? How does this compare with the projections?
12. What is your basic appraisal on a scale of 1 to 10 on each of the salespeople including the head of marketing?
13. What is the approximate age of each person in the sales force? How much energy do they have? How achievement-oriented are they?
14. Perform the same analysis of management here as used in the management area above.

B. Personnel and Organization

1. How many people are involved in the marketing function?
2. How many sales offices are there? Where are they located? How large a geographical area is served by each one? How many and what kinds of people are employed at each one?
3. What volume of sales is required to support the expenses of each sales office?
4. What is the number of people at each level?
5. What is the average wage or salary rate at each level?
6. What are the most recent annual sales production and compensation figures for salesmen? for sales managers?
7. What is the sales compensation plan? How does this compare with competitive plans?
8. What other benefits or forms of compensation are provided?
9. What is the relationship between past performance levels and performance levels required by projections?
10. What is the availability of required personnel?
11. How are hiring and firing decisions made?
12. How are employees trained? What is the cost of training?
13. How is productivity measured? How long does it take a salesman to become self-sustaining?
14. How are incentives provided for salespeople? Are sales quotas used? How do quota levels compare with sales forecast?
15. What are the procedures for promotions and raises?
16. How frequently and in what fashion are performance appraisals made and communicated to employees?
17. What has the rate of turnover been for each kind of employee?
18. Describe specifically the techniques and/or methods in which the marketing department motivates its employees and representatives.
19. List the name, years with the company, and reasons for termination for all salesmen and representatives who have resigned or were terminated during the past three years.
20. Perform the same analysis of marketing personnel that was used in the personnel area above.

C. Documentation of Marketing Personnel

1. Obtain resumes of the marketing people.
2. Check the background of key marketing people.
3. Obtain an organization chart from marketing.
4. Examine a typical personnel file to see how the procedures examined above are documented.

PRODUCTS

For each product, describe it in the terms set out below:

A. Product Description and Product Features for Each Product

1. What does the product do for its user? How does it work? What need does the product fill for its user? Is the need real, created, or imagined?
2. Give a complete physical and functional description of the product.
3. Does the product have any proprietary features?
4. Is the product or any aspect of it patented? When does each patent expire? How important is the patent to the success of the business?
5. What service goes with the product? Is the service the key to the sale?
6. Does a written procedures manual exist for the marketing department? If so, get a copy.
7. If one exists, is it followed closely?
8. Is it current? Date of last review?

B. Product Pricing

1. How is the product priced? What does management consider before making a pricing change?
2. How do prices compare with competitive products; end-user price, distributor price, OEM price, etc?
3. What have been the past price trends for this and other products?
4. What are expected future price trends? Why?
5. Will engineering and other features of this product make it more competitive or less competitive as these trends develop?
6. How are pricing decisions made? Who establishes the prices for each product? What is the rationale for the present pricing structure?
7. Describe the process you follow in establishing prices for your products.
8. Who is authorized to sell products at a price that differs from the approved price list? Who can discount?
9. How often are price changes reviewed?
10. Which products are the most profitable for the company?
11. What is the relationship between product profitability and incentives for salesmen?
12. How do pricing policies and structure compare with those of the competition?

13. What has been the price movement in relation to frequency of occurrence, magnitude of occurrence, elasticity of demand, and sales promotion?
14. What is the industry's ability to meet current and future product demand?
15. Does management believe cost increases could be passed on? Why?
16. Is the company sensitive to industry price changes?
17. Is there a price leader? Which company? Describe the circumstances?

C. Product Life and Reliability

1. When was each product introduced? When have major changes been made?
2. What stage of life cycle is the product in: new, emerging, mature, declining?
3. What is the estimated useful life of the product, stated in months or years?
4. What engineering changes are planned? What will be the effect on product cost and performance?
5. How reliable is the product? Give mean time to failure or some other specific statistical measure. Determine how this measure was arrived at. Compare this measure with the competition.
6. Is the product a standard product or does it require customizing? What is the cost of the basic product vs. the typical customization cost? How is the purchaser charged for customization? Can the product be mass-produced?
7. Is quality the key to the sale of the product?

D. Product Warranty

1. Describe your present warranty policy.
2. What was the warranty expense for each of the past three years?
3. What is the amount of the company's present warranty reserve? Is it adequate?

E. Product Development

1. What new products are planned for the company and what are the dates when they will be available to sell?
2. Does the company have any missing product to complete the product line? If so, describe.
3. What products are needed?

F. Promotion

1. What are annual advertising expenditure levels?
2. What is the advertising policy?
3. How does this relate to overall marketing strategy and objectives?
4. What other kinds of promotion are utilized?
5. What is the rationale for the overall mix of promotional activity?
6. How are the results of advertising and other promotional expenditures evaluated?

G. Product Packaging

1. What kind of packaging does the product have? Is the packaging a part of the promotion?
2. What is the cost of the packaging? Does the packaging cost more than the product itself?
3. What overall image is the package trying to project in the eye of the receiver? Is it well executed?
4. How could the packaging of the products be enhanced?

H. Documentation of Products

1. Sales literature describing product features and applications.
2. Technical literature describing product design and functioning.
3. Picture of product.
4. Copies of any patents or patent applications.
5. Samples of the products.
6. Get a copy of the procedures manual for the marketing department.

CUSTOMER DESCRIPTION

A. Customer Analysis

1. Who are the customers? What industry groups are they drawn from? What are the overall trends of this consumer? Is the buyer an individual or a corporation?
2. What is the procedure for making a buying decision?
3. How long does the purchase decision process take?
4. What are the key variables in the buying decision? Price, service, product features (enumerate), reputation of selling company, credit terms, delivery speed, or relationship with salesman?

5. Are buying decisions affected by advertising or sales promotion?
6. What is the degree of brand loyalty among customers? How is it measured or determined?
7. What methods are used to lock customers in?
8. What would be required to persuade the user of a competitive product to switch?
9. How much would a product switch cost the customer? What other inconveniences would be involved?
10. Why does the customer buy this product? What problem does it solve? What need does it fill? Does it save cost, improve efficiency, etc.?
11. Is this product a luxury item or a necessity?
12. What alternatives does the customer have? Are these substitutes for this product?
13. What factors affect the customers' need for this product? What would cause an increase in need? What would cause a decrease?
14. How are the needs of the customers or the makeup of the customer group changing? What are the reasons for the change?
15. Does the company have any contracts or special arrangements with the major customers, including consignments? If so, describe.
16. Has the company lost any major customers in the past two years, or is the company about to lose any? If so, describe.
17. What is the influence of overall business conditions on demand for the company's products? What is the importance of disposable income, consumer income, industrial production levels, population growth, and other broad economic trends to the company's business?
18. How important is personal selling to sell this customer? How good does the salesperson have to be?

B. Customer Complaints

1. List the five most common complaints received from the customers regarding the product.
2. List the five most serious or costly complaints received from the customers regarding product.
3. List the five most common complaints received from the customer regarding service.
4. List the five most serious or costly complaints received from the customer regarding service.
5. Describe the procedure for handling complaints.

6. Does the company have a monthly or cumulative complaint summary list? If so, review.

C. Customer Credit

1. Who establishes the credit limits for customers?
2. Describe the credit approval process.
3. Does the company have any special credit arrangements with customers? If so, describe.
4. What role does the marketing department have in the account collection process?
5. What are the normal terms of sales?
6. Are any sales invoices over $10,000 and are they under dispute?

D. Documentation

1. Obtain copies of any marketing studies, newspaper articles, magazine articles, etc., describing overall dimensions and configuration of markets and the customer.
2. List the ten largest customers by dollar sales volume and the ten largest customers by unit volume. Obtain the names, addresses, and telephone numbers of the largest customers.
3. Obtain a complete customer list.

CUSTOMER SERVICE

1. How is the company service function organized? Who does the service manager report to? How many people work in the service area? How are they recruited, trained, compensated, reviewed, etc.? What is personnel and salary structure within the department?
2. How many service offices are there? What is their relationship with the sales and marketing offices? How is the responsibility for customer relationships divided between these two groups? How is management responsibility divided?
3. What are the service requirements for each product? Can third parties be used to provide service for any products? What cost/performance tradeoffs are involved in the choice between using the company's service department and a third party?
4. How important is service capability to the customer? What are his most frequent service demands - repair of equipment, replenishment of usable supplies, etc.?
5. How is the customer charged for servicing? Is this a profitable operation for the company? If not, why not? What volume or other requirements are necessary in order to break even or turn a profit?

6. What are the logical follow-on products from a service standpoint? Can service personnel be used to provide service for other companies on a third-party basis?
7. How many employees are in the C/S department?
8. Who performs C/S work? Company employees, service reps, both?
9. Is there a C/S manual?
10. Describe the C/S operation.
11. List your ten major C/S problems.
12. What is the amount of the C/S budget for this year?
13. Describe the extent of product warranties and guaranties provided.
14. Does the company contract out any customer services/work? If so, describe the terms. Provide the names, addresses, telephone numbers, and contracts of contractors.

COMPETITIVE ANALYSIS

A. Competition

1. Who are the major competitors at present? Are there any expected new entries or other potential competitors?
2. What is the financial strength of the present competition?
3. What new entries are expected in the market?
4. What are the present and expected future competitive shares of market?
5. What is the relative ease of entry into the field? What are the capital and other requirements for entry? What is the importance of intangibles such as lead time, goodwill, patents, etc.? What are the barriers to entry in this industry?
6. How does the company compare with competition in each of the following categories: product features and capabilities, product price, present market share, marketing capability, production capability, financial resources, financial management, R & D capability, overall management strength, other strategic advantages?
7. If possible, construct a chart indicating the degree of competitiveness with each significant competitor on a 1 to 3 scale where 1 = superior, 2 = competitive, 3 = below average or not competitive.
8. Compare the company's product with that of the competition, stressing uniqueness of this company's product.
9. List the features and functions of all the products in the marketplace and then tick off those for each of the company's products and each of the competition's products.

10. Compare the company's price points against the competition's price points.

B. Documentation

1. Obtain a list of the company's competition with names, addresses, and telephone numbers.
2. Obtain product literature on the competitors.
3. Obtain annual reports and other literature on the competition.

INDUSTRY ANALYSIS

A. Industry Structure

1. What is the number of companies in the industry by size and category, national and international?
2. To what degree is the industry concentrated in one or a few companies.
3. Which way are mergers and acquisitions trending? Are they vertical, horizontal, or in some other mode?
4. What is the trend of business failures or successes? Are there a lot of failures? What are the causes of the failures?
5. How is the industry structured in terms of geographical location, product lines, channels of distribution, pricing policies, degrees of integration, and the type of customers?
6. What are the various barriers to entry by new companies into this industry?

B. Size and Nature of Market

1. How big is the overall market? Both domestic and international? List the total dollar size of the market at present by each product category.
2. What is the overall market annual growth rate for each product category? Both for the past three years and projected for the next three years?
3. What is the source of the information for questions 1 and 2 above?
4. How is the market segmented geographically, by type or size of customer, by applications, etc.? How is growth expected to be distributed among market segments?
5. What is the source of data on market size, growth rate, and market shares?
    a. Information supplied by company?
    b. Independent consultant's research report?
    c. Published data from other sources?

6. How were market estimates and other market data arrived at (market research methodology)?
7. What degree of reliability is attached to each market size estimate, growth rate projection, and market share estimate?
8. What are expected future trends in the market? Greater concentration of market share? More price competition? Why?
9. What are normal terms of sale?
10. What is the sale/lease ratio? How long is a typical lease? Are leases normally full payout leases?
11. Is this market typically a seasonal or cyclical one? Why?

C. Industry Growth

1. What are the annual growth rates for the industry for the past ten years?
   a. What has the sales growth been each year?
   b. What has the profitability of the companies in the industry been each year?
   c. How has market share changed?
2. What are the estimated annual growth rates for the industry for the next ten years?
   a. What is the sales growth in dollars and in percentage increase for the next ten years?
   b. What are the profit projections for the next ten years in total dollars and percentage increase?
   c. What market shared changes are anticipated for the industry?
3. What factors will affect growth in the future? Analyze each of the following:
   a. What are the demographic changes?
   b. What are the general economic trends?
   c. How will disposable income affect the industry?
   d. How will interest rates affect the industry?
   e. How will the composition of the industry change with respect to new business or failing businesses?
   f. How will the market size change?
   g. How will the market share change for each of the companies?
   h. What technological innovations are apt to spur growth?
   i. What production design changes will enhance productivity and perhaps spur growth?
   j. What economies of scale in the industry are likely to affect growth?
   k. What pricing differentials will occur, and what products will be priced differently?

275

l.   How will imports from foreigners affect the growth of the industry?

m.   How will exports of the product affect the growth of the industry?

n.   How will advertising and other forms of market development affect growth?

o.   What factors from government affect the industry? Will there be government demand for the product?

p.   How will government regulations affect the industry?

q.   How will government fiscal policy in general affect this industry?

r.   How will consumer buying power change and affect this industry?

s.   What environmental considerations could change the growth patterns of this industry?

D.   Competition

1.   What is the strategy for other companies in the industry?
2.   What competition will this industry have from substitute products from other industries?
3.   To what extent will trade practices and cooperation among businesses change this industry?
4.   What barriers to entry might change in order to increase competition?
5.   What key factors in success may change and allow the competition to get ahead?

E.   Customers of the Industry

1.   List all the major industries in which this product is sold.
2.   Estimate the health and welfare of these industries in the future.
3.   What major impacts on the industries to which these companies sell will change this industry directly or indirectly?
4.   Has there been any significant growth in new customers in the past five years?
5.   Has there been a trend toward integration of customers in this industry?
6.   Does this industry depend on a few key customers?

F.   Suppliers of the Industry

1.   List all the major industries from which this company must buy its products.

2. How have the industries from which this company must purchase products changed over the past five years?
3. What is the outlook for the suppliers of this industry over the next five years?
4. Has there been any significant growth in new suppliers for this industry for the past five years?
5. Has there been a trend in forward integration of suppliers during the past five years?
6. Does this industry depend on a few key suppliers?

G. Labor of the Industry

1. Is the supply of skilled labor adequate for this industry?
2. Are the pay rates in this industry competitive with those of other industries? Or are people leaving to join other industries?
3. Have there been any recent union negotiations in this industry?
4. Have there been any new labor contracts or renewals in this industry? What were the results of the settlement and negotiations?
5. To what degree is the industry as a whole unionized?
6. How influential is the union as a whole in the industry?

H. Government Regulation of the Industry

1. To what extent is the company regulated by the government? You should describe this in detail.
2. What regulatory agencies are responsible for regulating this industry?
3. Is there a trend toward more government regulation in this industry?
4. Are there any unique reporting requirements by this industry to government agencies?

I. Patents, Trademarks, Copyrights, and Other Intellectual Properties

1. Are any patents, trademarks, and copyrights important to the company's line of business?
2. To what degree do these patents, trademarks, and copyrights determine which company in the industry will succeed?
3. Are there any "household names" in this industry?

J. Cyclical Factors

1. What cycles does the industry go through?

2. What are the determinants of the cycle?
3. How easy is it to predict a cycle upturn or downturn?

K. Industry Associations and Trade Periodicals

1. Is the company a member of any trade or industry association? If so, list the name, address, phone number, and association manager.
2. Is the company represented at any trade shows? If so, list.
3. Is the company represented at any conventions? If so, list.
4. List the names of the three most important trade periodicals in the industry.

L. Documentation of the Industry

1. Obtain current periodicals, newspaper clippings, trade association releases, and company-prepared documents that will assist you in understanding the industry.
2. Obtain information from Standard Employee Reports, Value Line Surveys, Moody's Manual Extracts, and Security Research Reports that will help you understand the industry.
3. Obtain government data and publication and census studies that provide background information on the industry and the competition.
4. Determine who the trade associations are for the industry and contact them to obtain industrial information.
5. Determine who the experts are in the industry and contact them for additional information.

MARKETING STRATEGY

A. General Strategy

1. What are overall objectives in the marketing area? What are the top three objectives?
2. How are the objectives to be implemented? What are the details of the strategy?
3. What marketing effort is required? Is this a new product that requires extensive customer education and training?
4. Does the product replace a competitor's product or is it a new installation? If both, record the percentage of sales in each area.
5. Who does the marketing force consider to be the strongest competitors?
6. Obtain available sales breakdowns by territory, product, customer, industry, product end use, domestic, international,

etc. How do these compare with overall market segments? With future expected sales?

7. Obtain historical and projected percentages of sales to original equipment manufactures (OEMs), distributors, and end users.

8. What are the strengths and weaknesses of any OEMs or distributors?

9. How are potential customers identified? How are leads developed? What is the ratio of leads called to leads qualified? What is the ratio of leads qualified to leads closed?

10. What are the average dollar and time requirements to close a sale? How do these compare with projected sales levels and marketing expenses?

11. What is the size of a typical order? What has been the trend? What are the reasons for this trend?

12. What is the frequency and amount of repeat or follow-on orders? How many of the company's sales have been made as a result of follow-on orders?

13. What has been the trend in the rate of monthly orders?

14. What is the size and quality of present backlog? How much is released to production and shippable within six months to one year? How does this figure compare with projections?

15. How is backlog split between orders from existing customers and orders from new customers? How does this compare with projection assumptions?

16. What is the present geographical dispersion or concentration of product installations? How many installations are there per sales office and per service office? How is this ratio expected to change in the future?

B. Sales Projections

1. What input does marketing have in assisting the company in establishing budgets and forecasts?

2. How often are these budgets and forecasts reviewed?

3. If they exist, review them for the past three years for degree of variance from actual.

4. What does marketing think the results will be for this year? Either by product line or individual product, project sales for the next five years.

5. Why will sales go like this projection?

6. What backlog does the company have by product or product line? What has it been in the past? Is it increasing or decreasing? Why?

C. Advertising and Public Relations

1. Obtain the name and address of the advertising firm that the company employs.
2. Does the company have a written advertising program for this year? If so, obtain a copy.
3. What were the company's advertising expenditures for this year and each of the past three years?

D. Documentation

1. Obtain a copy of the marketing plan.
2. Determine who put the plan together.
3. Obtain promotional literature of this company for the future.

DISTRIBUTION OF THE PRODUCT

1. How many distributors are used by the company? How many salesmen per distributor?
2. How are distributors selected?
3. What is the availability of qualified distributors?
4. What is the geographical distribution of distributors?
5. What were the most recent annual volumes by each distributor?
6. How are distributors compensated?
7. What other products does the distributor sell?
8. What percentage of each distributor's sales do company products account for?
9. How does each distributor's compensation on company products compare with its compensation on the other products it distributes?
10. Does the distributor purchase products from the company or merely take a commission for selling products?
11. What credit terms are extended to the distributor?
12. How are the financial capabilities of distributors determined?
13. What sales support and other services (maintenance, customer financing, etc.) does the company provide for distributors?
14. How do distributors sell the products?
15. How does the company ensure a consistent sales approach by different distributors?
16. What are the other details of any distributor marketing agreements? Obtain a copy.
17. What is the rationale for use of a distributor organization vs. direct sales force or other type of marketing arrangement?
18. Under what conditions would a change in distribution methods be justified?

BASIC INFORMATION

A. Documentation of Marketing

1. Copy of written marketing plan.
2. Historical data on sales breakdowns.
3. Historical data on order rates and trends.
4. Data on backlog size and analysis.
5. List of sales and service offices by location.
6. Complete price list and service charge information for all products.
7. Copies of any promotional or sales literature.
8. Organization charts and salary structure for marketing group and service group.
9. Copy of representative distributor agreement(s).
10. Copy of typical service or maintenance contract.
11. Copy of any OEM contracts.
12. Customer list, including several references to contact.
13. Complete distributor list and names to contact.
14. List of reports generated by the marketing department.
15. Charts or graphs used by the marketing department.
16. Sales projections by product.
17. Make sure you obtain the documention items above under separate sections in the marketing area.

B. Marketing Reports

1. Obtain copies of the reports used by the marketing department to "run" their department.
2. Obtain copies of marketing reports given to top management.
3. Obtain a copy of the budget used in the marketing department to govern spending in that department.

C. Ratio Analysis

1. Calculate *Sales Per Salesman*, by dividing Total Sales by Number of Salesmen. This will measure the salemen's productivity.
2. Calculate *Selling Expense as a Percentage of Sales* by dividing Selling Expenses by Sales. This will measure the cost related to obtaining a sale.
3. Calculate *Salaries and Commissions as a Percentage of Sales* by dividing Total Salaries and Commissions by Total Sales. This will tell you what percentage of total sales accounts for payroll and will give you an indication of the human cost of a sale.

281

4. Calculate *Gross Profit per Salesman* by dividing Gross Profit by Number of Salesmen. This will let you measure the ability of salesmen to contribute gross profit to the company.
5. Calculate *Gross Profit as a Percentage of Marketing Expense* by dividing Gross Profit by Total Marketing Expense. This will give you a measure of the effectiveness of marketing in gross sales dollars.
6. Calculate *Marketing Expense as a Percentage of Sales* by dividing Marketing Expense by Sales. This will give you a measure of the cost of the marketing programs compared to the amount of sales generated.
7. Calculate *Discounts as a Percentage of Sales* by dividing Total Discounts by Total Gross Sales. This will indicate the discounts the company must be giving in order to accomplish sales.
8. Calculate *Returns as a Percentage of Sales* by dividing Total Returns in dollars by Total Sales before returns. This will give you a measure of the customer satisfaction and the quality of the product.

D. Strengths and Weaknesses

1. Identify the five major strengths the company has in marketing.
2. Identify the five major weaknesses the company has in marketing.
3. Are any of these weaknesses so great that the company cannot overcome them?
4. What could go wrong in marketing?

E. Summary Analysis

1. In a very few words, how do you feel about the marketing of the company?
2. Can the people operating the marketing section of the company accomplish their objectives?
3. Will this marketing strategy win?
4. Are you willing to bet real money that this group of marketing people will develop and execute a successful marketing strategy?

PRODUCTION AREA

The production area is a view from within the company. It's a review of how the company sees itself. It involves the production of the product or service and the value added by the company. Your task here is to determine the value added and how well the company performs. As usual, you need to understand the people before you dive into the production process.

A. Production Management

1. Who is the person in charge of production?
2. What is the background of the person in charge of production?
3. Does this person have the background and experience necessary to manage the production process?
4. Ask the same questions about production management that you asked in the management area above.

B. Personnel and Organization

1. Obtain or assemble an organization chart for production personnel.
2. What is the total number of employees? How many employees are there at each level?
3. What is the average wage or salary rate at each level? What other benefits or forms of compensation are provided?
4. What is the availability of each type of employee in areas where the company operates?
5. How are hiring and firing decisions made?
6. How are employees trained? What is the cost? How long does it take?
7. How is productivity measured? Are any incentive plans in effect?
8. How are promotion and raise decisions made?
9. How frequently are performance appraisals made? How are these communicated to employees?
10. What has the turnover rate been for each kind of employee?
11. What is the general appearance and attitude of workers?
12. If the company has several plants, answer questions for each plant.
13. What is the number of employees who report to top production management?
14. Does the company have any training manuals?

15. Describe the selection and training procedure for new supervisors. Hourly employees. Who does the training?
16. Identify the key production positions. What personnel backup does the company have for each?
17. What specific techniques does the company use to motivate employees?
18. How does the company specifically measure employee productivity and efficiency?
19. Review several completed employee evaluation forms. Do they seem to be in order?
20. Has the company experienced any problems with the Equal Employment Opportunity Commission during the past twelve months.
21. Review the written wage rate schedule for employee positions. What was the date of last revision?
22. Are the wage rates for the company high, low, or average in relation to the industry? Area? How does the company know this?
23. What is the date of the last general increase for all production employees?
24. Ask management to describe their five major personnel problems.
25. Does the company have a formal procedure for reporting employee absences, reprimands, promotions, transfers, etc., to personnel?
26. Does the company have an operating procedures manual for its various production departments? Review. Is it current and do the employees strictly adhere to it, or is it a nominal one? What is the date of the last revision?

C. If Union

1. How many employees are unionized?
2. What is the union?
3. When does the present contract expire?
4. Have there been any strikes in the past?
5. How are grievances handled?
6. How many grievances are outstanding?
7. What is the general status of union relationships?
8. Who is the union leader?

D. If Nonunion

1. Have there been any recent attempts to unionize employees?
2. What methods were utilized?
3. What was the outcome?

4. Are any additional efforts expected?
5. What specific plan has the company implemented to reduce the possibility of the employees becoming unionized?

E.   Staff Meetings

1. Do you have regularly scheduled meetings with all supervisors? When?
2. What regularly scheduled meetings does the company have for department heads?

PRODUCTION PROCESS

A.   Production Facilities

1. Where is each plant located?   Describe the location and construction.   Estimate the remaining useful life.   Evaluate its condition.
2. Is the plant leased or owned?
3. What is the mix of products produced there?
4. What is the production capacity of each plant?   What is the throughput for each production line?   At what capacity is the plant operating?
5. What are the reasons for the present distribution of production capacity?   How does it relate to customer distribution and shipment requirements?   To raw material and labor supply requirements?
6. What is the replacement value for each plant?   How does this compare with book value and liquidation value?
7. How much and what kinds of insurance are carried on each plant?   How does this compare with replacement value?
8. Is there a mortgage on the plant?   How much?   Have there been any recent appraisals?   What was the basis of the appraisal - replacement value, liquidation, etc.?   Obtain a copy.
9. How old is the existing plant?   What condition is it in?
10. What are the annual maintenance expenditure requirements? Are they expected to increase significantly as the equipment gets older?
11. What are the present maintenance procedures and replacement policies?
12. What is the estimated useful life of the plant and major pieces of equipment?   How do these compare with depreciation rates?
13. Does the company have a formal preventive maintenance (PM) program in effect?   If so, review the program including equipment maintenance scheduled for last month and this month.   Are the PM records current?   Make sure you review

the repair record and program for the critical pieces of equipment.

14. Who is responsible for PM?
15. Does the company prepare a monthly PM report? If so, who gets a copy? Review it.
16. Does the company anticipate any major repair or reconditioning work on its equipment in the next twelve months? If so, review items and amounts. Have these been included in the company's capital expenditure budget for this year?
17. Does the company need any new capital equipment items and/or production space during the next twelve months that will cost in excess of $5,000? If so, review the items and amounts. Have these been included in the company's capital expenditure budget for this year?
18. Assuming the company had no money constraints, what pieces of equipment would the company replace? What new equipment items would the company add to improve efficiency?
19. What equipment bottlenecks exist that limit the plant from increasing production?
20. What pieces of equipment can cause a production stoppage for a period of three hours or more if they fail to function properly? What plan exists if that situation occurs?
21. Is the equipment sufficiently modern so the company is not at a competitive disadvantage?
22. What is the company's capitalization versus repair expense policy?
23. Does the company have surplus or idle buildings or equipment valued at $5,000 or more. List.
24. Does a formal procedure exist for approving capital expenditures? If so, review. What is the company's ROI hurdle rate for new equipment? What is the payback period?
25. What alternate use could the physical plant be used for? Is it a one-use plant?
26. Is the company's plant and equipment in good repair?

B. **Manufacturing Process**

1. Obtain a plant layout sketch.
2. Is production a continuous process or a batch process?
3. What is the length of each production cycle? What are the setup times and costs for each one?
4. What are the key segments of the manufacturing process? What is the unit throughput rate for each one? How many employees are there in each segment?
5. Which segment is the bottleneck at present? What would be

286

required to increase the throughput of the segment? What would be the next bottleneck?

6. Is the production flow generally efficient? How could it be improved? How does this operation compare with other manufacturing operations in the industry?

7. Is the manufacturing process labor-intensive? What is the number of employees per sales dollar? What is the labor content per sales dollar?

8. To what extent is the production process now automated?

9. What is the capital investment per sales dollar? What is the value of equipment leased by the company for production use? What is the investment per sales dollar, including the value of leased equipment?

10. Are any computers or other electronic processing equipment used in the production process? What kinds? Where are they located? What functions do they perform? How much downtime has been experienced with each piece of equipment? What kind of backup system is available? How much production downtime has been experienced as a result of electronic equipment failures?

11. Is any of the production equipment highly specialized or custom-made?

12. Are there any backups in the event of failure of key elements? How long would it take to obtain replacement parts or equipment?

13. How much flexibility is there to shift production within each plant? Between plants?

14. To what extent could additional parts of the manufacturing process be automated? What would the capital requirements be? What would be the effect on overall product costs? On labor utilization? On labor content of product cost? On production flexibility? What other considerations are involved?

15. Are there any plans at present to replace or add equipment? Are they reflected in the budgets prepared by the company?

16. What kind of manufacturing process exists?
    a. Mass production or job shop-oriented?
    b. Product or process structured flow?
    c. Production to order or for stock?

17. Have the key components of the manufacturing process been identified?

18. Nature of operations:
    a. What are the major operations and their sequence (e.g., component fabrication and machining, component assembly, final assembly and testing)?
    b. What is the relationship of the cost of each operation to total product cost?

    c. What percentage of total factory floor space is used for each major operation?
    d. What is the degree of mechanization and automation for each major operation (highly automated machinery, semiautomatic, etc.)?
19. To what extent are finished products and components standardized?
20. What programs exist for increasing standardization and ensuring quality control?
21. What are the major components of total production cycle time?
22. Productivity:
    a. What are the current trends in manufacturing productivity?
    b. Are there indications of technical obsolescence?
    c. Does product design restrict the selection of the manufacturing process?
    d. Is the design conducive to an efficient manufacturing process (safety, degree of accuracy, etc.)?
    e. What degree of integration exists between product and manufacturing engineering?
23. Has the efficiency of this process been compared to competitors in the industry?
24. Does the plan layout appear efficient?

C. Complexity

1. How many component parts and raw materials are used in the production process? What are the annual requirements for each one? How are parts lists updated?
2. How many parts or components are available from only one supplier?
3. What are the lead times for critical components? Are they handled differently from routine inventory times?
4. What is the inventory reorder procedure? Is it computerized? How are usage rates monitored and matched with lead times?
5. Is any consideration given to reorder costs and carrying costs in determining the optimal time and amount of reorders?
6. Is there an identifiable trend in the recent relationship between inventory levels and order positions?
7. How are suppliers selected? Are current supplier relationships satisfactory? Are trade payables up to date? How often do suppliers fail to deliver on time? What effect has this had on production schedules? Obtain lists of supplier references.
8. What have price trends for components been? What are expectations?

9. Are any of the raw materials used by the company dependent on a harvest each year? What percentage of raw material costs do these items account for? What have recent (three years) price trends been for these materials? How does the company control the risks associated with the price fluctuation of these materials?

10. What are the inventory control procedures? Are inventory requisitions used? Is there a separate, enclosed area for inventory?

11. How often are physical inventories taken?

12. Trace the flow of raw materials from purchase to final product and document at each stage.

13. Visually examine the work-in-process areas. How do inventory levels appear to compare with book value? Do they contain any unfinished products that should be written off?

14. How is production coordinated with sales activities?

15. How much and what kinds of scrap or waste are generated by the production process? How is it disposed of?

16. What pollution control standards is each plant subject to? How are they expected to change over the next five years? What federal and local enforcement commissions exist? What is the company's current status with respect to pollution control requirements? How will future needs be met? Are any capital expenditures required? Are they included in the budget? Verify company status with appropriate agency officials.

17. What Ocupational Safety and Health Administration (OSHA) requirements is each plant subject to? What has the company's record been with respect to past OSHA inspections? What fines have been paid by the company as a result of OSHA inspections? Have violations been corrected?

18. How are production operations monitored? How does the production manager identify potential problem areas and inefficiencies? Does the monitoring system have a numerical base? How are these numbers generated?

D. Energy Requirements

1. What kinds of fuel does the company use? How much of each kind?

2. Where are energy supplies obtained? What companies supply energy? Do firm contracts or other commitments exist? Are there any questions about suppliers' ability to meet commitments?

3. Is the company or any of its suppliers subject to allocation regulations? What is the effect of these regulations on the company's ability to maintain or increase production levels?

4. What is the physical proximity of the company to raw material sources and sales markets? How are raw materials and finished goods presently transported?

5. What are the company's annual transportation expenses? How would a slowdown or reduction in transportation services affect the company's operations? Does it have any contingency plans in the event that one of these occurs?

E. Quality Control (QC)

1. What procedures does the company have for testing incoming raw materials and component parts?

2. What are the quality standards for each key component and material?

3. What has been the company's experience with each supplier of key components or materials?

4. What happens to parts or shipments that do not meet quality standards?

5. At how many points in the production process are tests made for quality or performance? What happens to items that do not meet tests? Can they be recycled? Are they disposed of? What is the average failure rate at each test point?

6. What do the final test and quality control procedures consist of? What is the average failure rate for products in final test? What happens to rejected products?

7. Does the company employ any full time QC people?

8. Who is in charge of the QC area?

9. How are the QC standards established?

10. Can the company match up product returns and can the QC inspector or production shift?

11. Describe in detail the company's QC programs, and obtain a copy of the QC procedures manual.

12. Is there a specification sheet for each product?

F. Engineering

1. What is the size, organization, and salary structure of the engineering department?

2. Who does the engineering section report to? What is its function within the overall corporate strategy?

3. What specific projects is the engineering group now working on?

4. How are engineering projects organized and monitored? How are efficiency and productivity measured?

5. How are engineering time schedules established? What is the

past record with respect to completion of engineering projects within scheduled times?

6. How are cost budgets established? How are costs monitored and controlled? What is the past record of performance vs. budget?

7. What is the relationship with production operations?

8. How are engineering change orders originated and implemented? Trace the cycle for an engineering order.

G. Regulatory Agencies

1. Is the company in compliance with all federal, state, and local laws and with all rules and regulations of the agencies and commissions thereof, including safety and health, consumer products safety, environmental (air, water, waste treatment, land)? Is any action threatened or pending?

H. Subcontract Work

1. Is any work subcontracted to others?
2. What problems are they having?
3. Is there a second and third source for this subcontracting work?
4. Are any critical parts obtained from a single subcontractor?
5. Is the subcontractor owed a lot of money?
6. Is the subcontractor a stockholder of this company?

I. Inventory

1. Is the current level of inventory at optimum levels? If not, describe. Who establishes the optimum inventory level?
2. What is the optimum inventory level for finished goods and raw materials?
3. Does the company have any inventory items that require delivery lead times in excess of thirty days? If so, list.
4. Do inventory items have only a single source of supply? If so, list.
5. Are any items in inventory obsolete, outdated, out of style, subject to markdown, etc.? If so, describe.
6. What was the inventory turn last year?

J. Production Stoppage

1. Has the company experienced a production stoppage of three hours or more during the past twenty-four months for any reason? If so, describe.

2. Is there a possibility that production will be stopped in the future? If so, from what?

K. Production Costs

1. Does the company have a detailed worksheet for determining direct labor costs? Indirect labor costs? Review.
2. Is a standard cost system used?
3. When was the date of the last standard cost revision?
4. How does the company monitor and control various costs of production?
5. Specifically, how does it use the information generated to keep costs under control?
6. What are the present and historical product costs? Obtain a complete list of labor and material costs, indirect costs, amount of overhead allocation, and other components of product cost, if any.
7. What are expected future costs? How do they compare in each category? What are the reasons for expected changes in costs?
8. What are the principal materials used in manufacturing each product? Where are they obtained? How many suppliers are there for each one? What are expected usage levels over the next three years? Obtain a list of suppliers to confirm availability and pricing of materials.

L. Production Level

1. How is the weekly/monthly production schedule established?
2. Is a copy of the monthly unit production summary for each of the past twelve months available? Obtain a copy.
3. How many shifts/day is the company now operating?
4. What is production capacity if we assume no new plant and equipment are added? At what percentage of capacity is the company operating?

PURCHASING, SUPPLIERS, SHIPPING, AND RECEIVING

A. Purchasing

1. Analyze purchases for the last year. Make a list of the ten largest suppliers during the past year. Get their names, addresses, telephone numbers, and the person to contact.
2. Are there any inventory items for which less than two suppliers are available?
3. Do any contracts exist between the company and any suppliers?

4. The company's objective is to maintain inventory levels to support how many months of production?
5. Do any inventory items have delivery lead times in excess of thirty days?
6. What are the normal credit terms from suppliers?
7. Does the company take purchase discounts?
8. How often are physical inventories taken?   Describe the procedure.
9. Who establishes the specifications for items purchased?
10. What is your purchase requisition/approval procedure? Obtain a requisition.
11. Is there a procedural manual for purchasing? If so, review. Is it current?   Does the company strictly adhere to it, or is it a nominal one?
12. What system is in place for reducing the possibility of internal theft?
13. Has the company experienced any inventory shortages exceeding $1,000 in the past three years. If so, describe.
14. Is there a formal system of reorder quantities and reorder levels or does the company use an informed approach based on communication received from production foremen, review of bills of materials generated for work orders, and review of raw material inventory records? Describe.
15. Obtain a copy of the company's purchasing procedures or, if not available, determine through discussion with management the informal procedures that may exist.

B. Suppliers

1. List the basic raw materials used in the manufacturing process.
2. List all suppliers who furnish 5% or more of the total material purchased for any of the facilities listed previously for the past three years and next three years. List the name, address, type of material, unit price, total purchased, and special terms.
3. Determine the economic condition of the suppliers' industry, including competitive structure, and the related possibility of significant raw material shortages, interruption of deliveries, or price fluctuations.
4. List and describe any long-term supply contracts and/or reciprocal buying agreements.
5. Summarize intracompany/intercompany purchases.

C. Receiving

1. Is there a procedures manual for receiving goods and services?

Is it strictly followed?   If not, describe.   Also, give date of latest revision.

2.   Describe the procedure for receiving goods and services.   How are requisition and receiving tickets reconciled?   Receiving hours?

3.   Is a receiving ticket signed and completed for every item received?

4.   Who is authorized to sign receiving tickets?   To accept returned damaged goods or unacceptable goods?

5.   What system is followed to ensure that items received are properly recorded in the company logs?

6.   What system is in place to reduce the possibility of internal theft?

7.   Describe the procedures for determining that the goods and services received meet the specifications and quality of those ordered.

D.   Shipping

1.   Is there a procedures manual for shipping products?   Review.

2.   Who signs the shipping tickets and how does the accounting department know the goods were shipped?

3.   Does the customer sign the shipping ticket to prove the merchandise was received?   If not, what record is there that it was received?

4.   What checks and balances does the company use to reduce the possibility of theft?

5.   Who is responsible for shipping cartons?

6.   Describe the methods of shipping - consumer carrier, UPS, company trucks, etc.

EFFICIENCY ANALYSIS

Does the company use any of the following methods for improving efficiency?   If so, how is it working out?

1.   Control of inventory using "ABC," zero inventory, and/or "just in time" inventory techniques.

2.   Setup and production line time reduction studies.

3.   Plant utilization and layout studies.

4.   Obsolescence reviews.

5.   Long-term supplier contracts.

6.   Responsibility accounting for inventory and scrap.

7. Value engineering (input from purchasing into decisions made by engineering regarding the components of new products).
8. Parts standardization.
9. Establishment of a cycle counting program.
10. Reduction of Engineering Change Notices.
11. Purchasing reviews (e.g., usage vs. substitution, competitive bidding, approved vendor list, etc.)
12. Vendor evaluation procedure (quality, timeliness, price).
13. Establishment of a routing system.
14. Time and motion studies.
15. In-line vs. batch manufacturing.
16. Make or buy analyses.

BASIC INFORMATION

A. Documentation of Production

1. Organization chart and salary structures for production and engineering personnel.
2. Copies of any union contracts and negotiation dates.
3. Plant layout sketch for each plant.
4. Diagrams of manufacturing process and production flow.
5. Copies of any recent appraisals of plant.
6. Useful life schedules for plant and major equipment.
7. Historical data on inventory trends.
8. List of supplier references.
9. Historical data on cost trends.
10. Pollution agency officials to contact.
11. Copies of any fuel supply or transportation contracts.
12. Historical data on quality control test results.
13. Resume on management of production.
14. A complete description of each physical plant or facility in terms of land acreage, building, square feet, cost assessed value, approved value, insured value, size, age, expansion dates, capabilities to expand leases, etc.
15. A copy of any appraisals.
16. A copy of any leases.

B. Production Reports

1. Ask for a copy of each management report generated outside of the production area that the company receives and have someone explain its value.
2. Ask for a copy of each management report generated in the production area and have its value explained to you. Who receives a copy?

3. Is a written shift report made out at each shift change? Review it.
4. Is there a production log report? Reivew it.

C. Ratio Analysis

1. Compute the *Hours Needed to Produce a Unit* by dividing Direct Labor Hours by Unit Produced. This will measure the units of labor it is costing for each unit produced and will measure employee productivity.
2. Calculate *Labor Cost as a Percentage of Total Production Cost* by dividing Labor Costs by Total Production Costs. This will measure the proportion of labor cost to the total production cost to give you an idea of the labor content in the production process.
3. Calculate *Material Costs to Total Production Costs* by dividing Cost of Material by Total Production Cost. This will measure the proportion of the production costs in the material side.
4. Calculate *Manufacturing Overhead to Total Production Costs* by dividing Manufacturing Overhead by Total Production Costs. This will measure the proportion of the total production costs and those consumed in manufacturing overhead.
5. *Idle Time Percentage* can be calculated by dividing the Total Idle Time by Total Available Direct Labor Hours. This will measure the efficiency the company is acheiving in keeping all employees busy.
6. Calculate the *Direct Labor Hours as a Percentage of Total Factory Hours* by dividing Direct Labor Hours by Total Hours of Factory Personnel. This will measure the amount of support personnel needed to complete the production process as opposed to the direct labor hours needed.
7. Calculate the *Percentage of Hours Worked on Overtime* by dividing Overtime Hours Worked by Total Hours Worked. This will measure the overtime and the percentage needed to complete the work and will indicate how well the employees are being scheduled.
8. Calculate *Machine Utilization* by dividing Productive Machine Hours Used by Total Available Hours. This will measure the efficiency of the equipment utilization as well as scheduling of the machines.
9. Calculate *Scrap Rate* by dividing the Number of Units Scrapped by Total Units Produced. This will measure the company's efficiency in producing good usable units without scrapping any of the pieces.

D. Strengths and Weaknesses

1. Describe the company's five major strengths in production.
2. Describe the company's five major weaknesses in production.

E. Summary Analysis

1. In a very few words, how do you feel about the production process.
2. Can management carry out the production plan?
3. Can the personnel involved in production be a winning team? Can the production people be motivated to be winners?
4. Are you willing to bet real money that this group of production employees working under this production situation will be successful? Would you bet your career or your job?

RESEARCH AND DEVELOPMENT

A. Management and Personnel

1. Who is head of R&D? What is that person's background? Why was that person chosen?
2. What backup does the company have in R&D management?
3. Does this person like being in R&D?
4. What is the size, organization and salary structure of R&D department?
5. Who does R&D report to? What is the function of R&D within overall corporate strategy?
6. Ask the same questions of research as you did for the management and personnel areas above.

B. Questions

1. How are projects chosen for research and development?
2. What marketing studies are completed before a R&D project is funded?
3. What specific projects is the R&D section presently working on? What are the timetables for their completion?
4. How are R&D tasks organized and monitored? How is productivity in this area measured?
5. How are time schedules established? What is the past record with respect to the completion of projects within scheduled time periods?
6. How are cost budgets established? How are costs monitored and controlled? What is the past record of performance vs. budget?

7. To what extent do future revenues projected in the present business plan depend on the results of R&D efforts?
8. How do budgeted cost and time requirements compare with successful efforts at developing similar products? What are the reasons for any projected variance?
9. If a formal R&D program has been adopted, what is the amount of your budget for this year and each of the past three years?
10. What specific projects are presently in progress? Why were they chosen? Who made the decision to proceed?
11. Has any formal market research been completed for any of the projects? Describe.
12. What outside consultants have been used?
13. Is the company involved in any basic research, such as "what is electricity"?
14. How do you ensure the secrecy of your projects?
15. Describe the company's procedure for capitalizing and expensing R&D activities.
16. Who do you report to?
17. What reports do you generate out of R&D and who receives them? Explain their value.
18. What is the estimated remaining life span of each of the company's major products? What is the company doing to sustain its past growth?
19. Does the company own any patents or have any patents pending? If so, describe the value and importance of patent positions.
20. Does the company produce any goods under patent licenses? If so, describe.

C. Major Programs

1. Describe the major programs completed during the past five years in terms of what they cost the company and the estimated benefit the company has received from the program.
2. Describe the major programs in progress now and estimate the costs that have been incurred to date. Estimate the amount of money that it will take to complete the project. Estimate the time it will take to complete the project. Estimate the benefits that will accrue to the company as a result of this project.
3. Describe in detail the proposed projects that are to be undertaken by the company, the costs it will incur, and the time it will take to complete them. Also, estimate the benefits that the company will derive from completing these research and development projects.

4. List any significant products recently developed and/or underway by the competition.
5. Compare the industry expenditures for R&D to those of the company, as well as those of competitors in the industry. Review the percentage of the expenditures for R&D as a percentage of sales during the last five years and try to determine why there have been any major variations.
6. What is the status of patents and trademarks regarding new products?
7. Are all of the company's proprietary rights protected by patents and trademarks?
8. Determine the current historical levels of research and development and the variations in those numbers. Determine why any research and development projects have been deferred or why costs have increased.
9. Evaluate the facilities and laboratories used for research and development? How convenient are they for management supervision? How related are they to the production process? What input does marketing have in research and development?
10. To what degree are those people involved in research and development "in touch" with the consumer or the marketplace that will ultimately buy the product?
11. To what degree are those involved in researchand development desirous of conducting "basic research" rather than developing products that can be brought to the market in the near term.

BASIC INFORMATION

A. Documentation

1. Organization chart and salary structure.
2. Resume of the head of R&D.
3. List of projects under way and those planned.
4. Marketing studies supporting the decision to produce a product.
5. A copy of the budget used by the research and development team to govern spending in that department.

B. R&D Reports

1. Determine which reports are prepared by the R&D department for managing the R&D process and obtain copies.
2. Determine which reports have been prepared and given to top management and obtain copies.
3. Determine from top management which reports it uses to manage the R&D process.

C. Ratio Analysis

1. Calculate the *Percentage of Gross Sales to Research and Development Spent* by dividing Research and Development Expenditures by Total Gross Sales. This should give you an idea of what percentage of sales is being plowed back into research and development.
2. Calculate the *Percentage of Employee Expenses as a Percentage of Total Employment Expenses by* dividing the Payroll for Research and Development by Total Payroll for the company. By analyzing the human side of research and development, you can obtain an understanding of the human cost of research and development.

D. Strengths and Weaknesses

1. Identify the five major strengths the company has in R&D.
2. Identify the five major weaknesses the company has in R&D.
3. What are the three critical aspects of this production process?

E. Summary Analysis

1. In a very few words write down how you feel about the research and development at the company.
2. Determine if the people operating the research and development section can accomplish their objectives.
3. Will this research and development strategy win? Is it the right product at the right time?
4. Are you willing to bet real money that this group of research and development people will develop the next great product for this company?

FINANCIAL AREA

Your financial investigation of the business will complement the work you have completed in the previous sections. All the qualitative investigation in the previous areas must now be verified by quantitative measures. Although it is difficult to restate your findings in numbers, that is just what you must do. In this case, if you can't count it, it doesn't count.

A. Management, Personnel, and Organization

1. Who is responsible for this section? Who are the people that will operate the financial side of this business? You should perform the same analysis of the key people here that you did in the management area above.
2. What is the size, organization, and salary structure of the finance section? You should ask the same question about personnel here that you asked in the personnel area above.

B. Management Reports

1. What financial reports are provided to the CEO and the top management?
2. Who is responsible for the management reports?
3. Are they prepared on time or are they late and useless?
4. Are the reports accurate or filled with errors?
5. Are performance reports prepared for all major areas of accountability? Do these reports relate actual performance to plans and budgets? Is adequate information provided to manage effectively and make informed judgments?
6. Describe the interface of subsidiaries, divisions, and departments with corporate headquarters concerning centralized reporting requirements.
7. Describe how the financial and management reporting systems work.

C. Budgeting and Controls

1. What are the company's budgeting procedures? How often are budgets assembled? Are they modified on an interim basis?
2. How are budget figures derived? What supporting schedules are available? What is the lowest unit component of the budget? Obtain or assemble a chart indicating the profit and cost centers on which the budget is based.
3. Does the company utilize a "top-down" budgeting process wherein goals are established by management? If not, how are corporate objectives integrated with the budgeting process?
4. Is the budgeting process an interactive one that allows for feedback and coordination between top management and line managers?
5. How has historical performance compared with budgets?
6. What kind of variance analysis does the company use? How does this help to improve its budgeting process?
7. How is overall coordination between budgeted goals and operations achieved?

8. How often is performance relative to budget measured?
9. What kind of accountability procedures does the company employ? Who is held responsible for deviations from budget? What corrective procedures are utilized?

D. Cash Management

1. What is the amount of cash flow handled by the company each month?
2. How many collection accounts does the company have?
3. How many depository bank accounts does the company have? What is the average amount of cash account?
4. What is the average amount of collected cash that is in the "float" and unavailable for company use?
5. What procedures does the company utilize to minimize the transfer time for collected cash balances?
6. How many cash disbursement accounts does the company have?
7. Who is authorized to make payments of company funds and what amounts are they authorized to disburse?
8. What procedures are utilized to ensure proper adherence to disbursement limits and authorization procedures?
9. Does the company take advantage of discounts when available? What procedures are utilized to avoid loss of discount due to late payments? What is the effective annual cost of funds when the discount is not utilized?
10. What is the minimum amount of cash balances which the company needs to maintain for transactions purposes? How was this amount determined?
11. How much is kept in short-term marketable securities? How are the amounts and maturities of the marketable securities determined?

E. Receivables Management - Credit and Collection Policy and Procedures

1. What percentage of the company's sales are on a credit basis?
2. What are the normal credit terms?
3. How do these terms compare with competition?
4. What are the reasons for the credit terms being established?
5. What credit information and credit analysis does the company use to determine the eligibility and amount of credit for individual customers.
6. How are credit extension procedures coordinated with sales activities?
7. How frequently is customer credit information updated?

8. What is the dollar amount and number of orders which have been declined for credit reasons? How are these divided between existing customers and new customers?
9. Does the company have a historical analysis with respect to the dollar amount and number of accounts on which credit losses have been incurred.
10. What percentage of sales have credit losses amounted to in each previous year? How does this compare with present and projected levels of bad debt expense?
11. How are delinquent accounts identified and monitored? How often are accounts receivable aging schedules prepared?
12. How long are accounts permitted to go unpaid before being considered delinquent?
13. What collection procedures does the company employ? What are historical and projected costs of collection?
14. What portion of the company's credit and collection procedures utilize electronic data processing techniques?

F. Inventory Management and Control

1. What procedures are utilized to minimize the cost of funds tied up in inventory?
2. How is this coordinated with the production manager's need for maximum flexibility? What are the tradeoffs between these two? Is the company able to quantify them?
3. How is the responsibility for inventory control divided between finance and production?

G. Investment Management

1. What capital budgeting procedures does the company employ?
2. Who makes the order decision for production equipment and machinery?
3. What is the minimum acceptable investment return on capital items?
4. To what extent is leasing utilized? How are lease vs. purchase decisions evaluated?
5. What is the amount of capital expenditures budgeted for the coming year? How is this different from past years?

H. Debt Management

1. Who is the company's lead bank? How many banks does it have relationships with?
2. Who in the company is responsible for banking relationships? Investment banking? Financial public relations?

3. Can all debt be assumed in the case of an asset purchase or liquidation? State restrictions on debt assumptions, if any.
4. What assets, if any, are pledged as collateral against the liabilities?
5. Does the company have an analysis of short-term borrowing patterns for the past five years (minimum and maximum levels, average amount, weighted average interest rate, etc.), and how does it compare to the cyclical nature of sales, inventory and production levels? Indicate interest rate and security required, if any.
6. Is there any "off-balance-sheet" financing and if so, obtain a summary of terms and restrictions.

I. Documentation

1. Organization chart and salary structure.
2. Chart indicating cost and profit-center structure.
3. Number and location of cash collection points and depository accounts.
4. Credit analysis forms.
5. Historical data on credit approvals and credit losses.
6. Copy of auditor's "management letter."
7. Copy of company operating manual indicating control procedures to be utilized - cash, credit, receivables, inventory, etc.
8. Obtain a complete history of all previous financings indicating date, amount, type of instrument, and price.
9. Obtain a complete list of all shareholders.
10. Obtain or assemble a complete description of the company's present capitalization.
11. Obtain a list of all common stockholders, the number of shares they hold, the price paid and the date acquired.
12. Obtain a list of all options or warrants.
13. Obtain a list of all preferred stock.
14. Obtain a list of all convertible debt.
15. List equity repurchase agreements such as puts, calls, and rights of first refusal.
16. List restrictions placed on equity securities.
17. Is any stock owned by management and other major stockholders (10% or more) pledged? List.
18. Any restrictions against the company repurchasing any of its equity?
19. List treasury stock. How and when acquired? Price? Reasons for acquisition?
20. Has the company ever filed SEC registration? If so, describe the circumstances.

21. Obtain the corporate policies and procedures manual, if any, and broadly assess comprehensiveness. Determine how compliance with these policies and procedures is enforced.
22. Obtain independent accountants' memorandum on accounting procedures and internal controls for the past three years.
23. Obtain internal audit department reports for the past three years and management response thereto.
24. Obtain a copy of the most recent aging schedule
25. List all banks with whom the company maintains a borrowing relationship by bank name, location, type of credit, maximum size, terms of commitment, interest rate, collateral and other significant terms.
26. Obtain loan agreements and indentures.
27. Describe financial covenants, and attach latest compliance computations and auditor's/officer's certification.

ANALYSIS OF FINANCIAL OPERATIONS

A. Accounting Policies

1. Have there been any significant changes in accounting principles, policies or estimates over the past three years?
2. Are any accounting policies unique to the company's industry?
3. What are the accounting policies that differ from industry practice, represent alternative methods where other preferable methods exist, or are excessively conservative or aggressive?
4. Are the interim financial statements prepared on a basis consistent with that of the annual report? Describe any differences.
5. Are there any proposed accounting pronouncements or government regulations that may have a significant impact on the company?

B. Accounting Methods and Costing Practices

1. What accounting procedures does the company use with respect to the recognition of revenue and expense? How does revenue and expense reporting compare with cash flows?
2. Are there any deferred costs or other intangible assets on the company's balance sheet? Over what period are they amortized? Obtain both amortization amounts and the amount of increases in deferred costs before amortization for the last three years.
3. What inventory valuation method does the company use? Has there been any recent change in inventory accounting

practices? What was the effect of this change on reported earnings and net worth?

4. When was the book value of inventory last reconciled with the present market value of inventory? Is any information available on the age of items presently in inventory?

5. How is inventory divided between raw materials, work in progress, and finished goods? What have recent trends been with respect to the amount of inventory in each of these categories?

6. How are work in progress inventory levels monitored? When was work in progress inventory last evaluated? How are work in progress or other inventory adjustments accounted for?

7. How are product costs established? Does the company utilize a job-order costing system or a standard costing system? Trace the flow of paperwork involved in establishing product costs and the relationship between paperwork and the manufacturing process.

8. Are burden rates used for indirect manufacturing expenses? How are burden rates determined? What is the rationale?

9. How are overhead expenses allocated to productive departments?

10. What depreciation method is used for fixed assets? Is the same method used consistently? What is the rationale for any difference in methods?

11. Have there been any recent changes in depreciation methods? What was the effect on reported net income?

C. Leverage Analysis

1. What are the average historical turnover rates for inventory, receivables, and accounts payable? How do these compare with projected levels?

2. What is the relationship between working capital needs and sales expansion based on these three turnover rates? That is, what is the effect of a $1 increase in sales on working capital needs?

3. What is the relationship between capital required for fixed assets and sales expansion?

4. What is the minimum feasible increment in the expansion of production capacity?

5. What is the incremental sales volume required to break even on incremental production capacity?

6. What is the incremental profit at full capacity?

7. What is the gross margin on sales?

8. What is the incremental pre-tax profit on a $1 increase in sales? How does this relationship change as volume increases?

306

9. What are the fixed and variable components of marketing costs and other overhead expenses?
10. Can these relationships be expressed as mathematical equations or put into chart form?
11. How does each expense category in past financials and projections compare with the sales figures suggested by this analysis?
12. What are the front-end costs required for an expansion of the marketing effort? How long does it take to recover these costs?

D. Lease Analysis

1. What percentage of the company's products are leased?
2. What is the typical term of a lease? Is it a full-payment lease?
3. How many months of lease payments are required for full recovery of product costs? Of products plus marketing and financing costs? Of full list price?
4. Does the company have any third-party leasing agreements at present? How many times monthly rental does this agreement call for? How are lease payments beyond this amount divided between the company and the leasing company?
5. What are the cash requirements for financing the company's leased products over the period for which projections have been provided? How are they to be financed?
6. What is the projected "if sold" value of equipment to be leased? What multiple of monthly rental is used?
7. How does the present value of any leases compare with current market prices?

E. Energy Intensiveness

1. What percentage of operating costs is accounted for by energy purchases? What portion of this is used directly in the manufacturing process?
2. What is the outlook for energy supplies in areas where the company operates?
3. Are any major customer groups significant energy users?
4. Is the processing of any raw materials heavily dependent on energy?
5. What ability does the company have to pass increased costs on to its customers without losing market share?

F. Impact of Inflation on Operations

1. Where FIFO is used to value inventory, has the company estimated the impact of restating costs based on current prices (i.e., elimination of "inventory profit") for each product line in order to determine the real gross profit?
2. Have sales price increases during the past year (and projected for the next year) been enough to offset the increase in costs? Has the gross profit percentage been maintained?
3. If depreciation or rental expense was calculated on the estimated replacement cost of property, plant, and equipment and leases rather than on the book value, what impact would this have on net income?
4. If interest on all long-term debt was at a current rate rather than the existing rate, what impact would it have on net income?
5. How does the company manage each of the following to ensure that current inflation is taken into account:
    a. Sales price increases to pass through increased costs?
    b. Speed in billing receivables, the use of lock boxes in key geographical areas, discount policy, and collection efforts?
    c. Fixed assets: financing methods, major replacement or expansion needs, appropriation procedures, and increasing/decreasing fuel costs on older, less efficient facilities?
    d. Accounts payable and accrued liabilities: deferral of payments, cash discount policy, and pension and tax payment timing?
    e. Labor costs: competitiveness of wages, influence of unions, pension-funding assumptions, and impact of possible relocation?
    f. Frequent review of insurance coverage?

G. Documentation

1. Actual historical profit-and-loss, cash flow, and balance sheet together with supporting schedules and list of assumptions.
2. Copy of recent audited statements, and audits for the past three years.
3. Security and Exchange Commission reports 10K, 10Q, and proxy, if public company.
4. Copies of any bank loan agreements.
5. A list of all shareholders by number of shares and price paid.
6. Company chart of accounts and accounting policy manual.
7. Copies of typical lease agreements.
8. A summary of significant accounting policies and procedures.

9. Auditor's report and management's representation letters for the past three years. Did any issues or events result in other than an unqualified opinion?

FINANCIAL STATEMENT ANALYSIS

A. Financial Statement Records

1. Does the company have monthly financial statements for the past thirty-six months?
2. Are there annual audited statements for the preceding three years?
3. Are any interim financial statements for the past months older than one month?
4. Are there individual financial statements for each major business segment, product line, or geographical location?
5. Does the company have a prospectus, annual report, or other SEC filings?

B. Assets

1. Cash
   a. What are the names and checking account numbers of all disbursement accounts?
   b. What has been the average cash balance in each account for the last year?
   c. Have all bank accounts been reconciled? Have unusual reconciling items been properly explained?
2. Receivables
   a. What is the recognition policy for recording revenues and establishing receivables?
   b. What are the credit terms given to purchasers?
   c. Describe the collection of accounts receivable.
   d. What is the discount policy?
   e. What is the returns policy?
   f. Which receivables are discounted or factored, and with whom, cost, terms, purpose, etc.?
   g. List all major receivables for amounts over 20% of the total.
   h. Are there accounts receivable that represent conditional sales?
   i. Does the company have a list of accounts receivable thirty, sixty, and ninety days old? Obtain an explanation of why accounts receivable over ninety days have not been collected. Are those over ninety days worthless?

309

3. Notes Receivable
   a. Is there a list of notes receivable, indicating the terms, such as interest rate, terms, etc.?
   b. Why was each material note receivable incurred?
   c. What is the company's bad debt reserve policy?
   d. What is the bad debt experience for the past three years and most recent interim period?
   e. Is the reserve balance adequate?
   f. Is there a list of receivables for the past three years?
4. Investments
   a. Is there a list of all marketable securities by original cost and carrying value?
   b. Why does the company hold these securities?
5. Inventories
   a. What is the breakdown for each major component such as raw material, work in progress, and finished goods, by each product line?
   b. What is the location of inventory (on hand, in transit, at outside warehouses, etc.)? Is it owned, on "bill and hold," or on consignment? Is it pledged as collateral for outstanding borrowing?
   c. Is labor and overhead counted in the dollar amounts for inventory? What are the percentages of material, labor, and overhead in inventory?
   d. How was the value placed on inventory? Is it market value, replacement value, or cost?
   e. How was the physical inventory that you saw on your tour?
   f. How are the inventory accounting records? Do perpetual inventory records exist?
   g. What are the dates of the last physical inventories? What were the amount and nature of adjustments? Are there book-to-physical reconciliations and analyses?
   h. What parts of the inventory are identified as excess, slow-moving, or obsolete? How do they identify such inventory?
   i. How do they determine realizable value of the inventory?
   j. What have the writedowns been for the past three years and most recent period?
   k. What are the seasonal inventory requirements?
   l. Is a standard or actual cost system used for inventory?
   m. How is job costing accomplished?
   n. What costs are included in overhead, and what overhead allocations are made to inventory?
   o. What capacity assumption is made about absorbing overhead costs into inventory?

p. How are returns, overruns, and scrap costs calculated?

q. Have variances been significant if a standard cost system is used? What have the variances been by product line for the past three years.

r. How reliable is the inventory valuation procedure?

s. Are there open long-term contracts? If so, what are their prices, terms, profit recognized, and total estimated cost? Have there been any variations in the open contracts?

6. Property, Plant, and Equipment

a. For each piece of land and building held, list the following: location, description, cost, current value on balance sheet, current market value, and liens.

b. For each piece of equipment list the following: location, description, age, cost, book value, estimated market value, and liens.

c. What significant plant, property, and equipment additions have occurred during the past three years? Are there any projects currently under construction or committed to?

d. Is there a list of all significant leasehold improvements, including original cost, accumulated amortization, and the period of amortization?

e. What is the accounting policy for depreciating capital assets? What changes have occurred in the policy during the last three years?

7. Does the company have a description and explanation of how other assets arose, capitalization and amortization policy, liens, and appreciation for each of the following: goodwill, deferred charges, research and development, organization costs, contract rights, patents and trademarks, and names?

C. Liabilities

1. Accounts Payable

a. Which companies constitute 5% or more of the current total accounts payable, or accounted for 5% or more of the average annual balance during the past year?

b. What are the regular and unusual credit terms (such as value discounts or extended payment terms) that exist with the companies listed?

c. Are discounts taken on normal credit terms?

2. Accrued Liabilities

a. What are the accrued liabilities outstanding and how did they arise?

b. Have all items been accrued? Look at professional fees, employee benefits, payroll, taxes, vacation pay, claims, severance and retirement benefits, warranty costs, pension liabilities and utilities.

3. Look at the notes payable. Does the company have a payee, description, interest rate, date, original amount, current amount, payment schedule, and explanation of why incurred?

4. Look at the long-term liabilities. Does the company have a payee, description, interest rate, date original amount, current amount, payment schedule amount, and explanation of why incurred?

5. Do any defaults or violations exist in any of the company's corporate obligations including loan agreements, notes, leases, etc.?

D. Stockholder Equity and Net Worth

1. Does the company have a list of all classes of stock in terms of type, shares authorized, shares outstanding, voting rights, liquidation preferences, dividends, terms of warrants and options outstanding, major owners, date acquired by major owners, major owner cost basis, market price range, and special terms?

2. Does the company have a complete shareholders' list?

3. What activity has occurred in treasury stock for the past three years?

4. Does the company have any stock option or purchase plans? If so, obtain details concerning each.

5. Do any restrictions exist on any of the company's common stock?

6. Do any preemptive rights exist on the company's stock? If so, list the dates and findings.

7. Do any options or rights of first refusal exist on any of the company's common stock?

8. Does the company have more than one class of stock?

9. Does the company have any stock purchase warrants, options, subscriptions, convertible instruments, contracts, or agreements for issuance of common stock, puts, calls, or other equity related instruments?

10. Does the company have any treasury stock?

OTHER ASSETS AND LIABILITIES

A. Unrecognized Liabilities

1. Is there a current review for unaccrued and unrecorded liabilities performed by the company?

2. Are there any truth-in-advertising problems?

3. Are there any product liability claims?
4. Are there adequate reserves for warranties?
5. Are there service guarantees?
6. Are there any employee-related deficiency letters issued by governmental agencies?
7. Are there any OSHA, EEOC or other employee violations? What actions has the company taken to resolve them?
8. Are there any employee occupational hazards inherent in the industry such as "black lung" found in coal mining?
9. Is the company a member of a pension plan, and if so have the funded and unfunded benefits been calculated?
10. Is the union due compensation for a planned plant shutdown?
11. Does the company have any unfunded pension costs or plans?
12. Have any environmental regulation violations or warnings been given to the company? If so, what actions does the company plan to take to resolve them, and what will the related cost be?

B. Contingent Liabilities and Commitments

1. Does the company have a list of all leases by description, years remaining, minimum annual payment, maximum annual payment, escalations, adjustments, renewals, and options to purchase?
2. Does the company have a list of the capital lease payments due for the next three years, and the imputed interest to derive the present value of such future lease payments? Has such amount been reflected as a liability? How has the related asset been reflected?
3. How does the present value of capital leases compare to their fair market value?
4. Are there sublease terms?
5. Has the company been involved in any significant litigation in the past three years? Is it threatened by pending or unsettled claims? Does the company have a list and description of the nature of those claims and the current status?
6. Are there any legal problems or potential litigation presently facing the industry (such as the asbestos industry), and if so, what effect might this have on the company?
7. Are there any potential antitrust problems?
8. Does the company have a list of all loans for which the company is a guarantor? What is the financial condition of the related companies?
9. Do subsidiary loans, guarantees, or exchange laws restrict dividend payments to the parent company?
10. Has the company promised to do other things or made any type of performance guarantees? What warranty guarantees exist?

Has the company entered into any guarantee to buy or sell merchandise? Are there contractual agreements to buy other companies? Sell or merge this company?

11. Does the company have any contingent liabilities, including but not limited to warranties, patent infringements, loss contracts, compensation for services, contracts subject to termination or renegotiations, etc.?

12. Does the company have a list of all open contracts? Describe the nature and potential cost, including informal agreements.

C. Undervalued Assets

1. Does the company have any patents, trademarks, copyrights, or licenses that are undervalued?

2. Does the company have a priority process that others would pay to know?

3. Does the company have undervalued real estate or equipment?

4. Are inventories understated?

5. Is the pension and profit-sharing plan overfunded? Can money be taken out?

TAXES

A. Federal Income Taxes

1. In general, what are the applicable federal, state and local income, property, excise and other taxes paid by the company?

2. What examinations have been conducted by federal tax authorities?

3. What is the last year examined by the government?

4. What is the amount of deficiencies and nature of adjustments in last years examined?

5. Have the results of the above reviews been reflected in the current reserve for taxes?

6. What is the status of the current examinations?

7. What are the tax years open and closed to future tax authority examination?

8. What tax loss carryforwards does the company have? Describe the amounts by year of expiration. Identify the type (i.e., net operating loss, capital loss, ITCs, FTCs, R&D credit, etc.)

9. Describe any special industry tax considerations such as depletion allowances, special credits or deductions, etc.

10. Can the company reconcile the effective income tax rate to the statutory tax rate for the past five years?

11. What are the deferred tax provisions for the past five years?

12. What are the current income tax requirements compared with the current income tax reserve?
13. What are the components of the deferred income tax reserve, and are they reasonable, and what are the future cash requirements?
14. Is the company current on all taxes owed (FICA, income, real estate, etc.)?

B. State and Local Taxes

1. Have state and local tax returns been filed for the past three years?
2. Have there been any state tax audits?
3. What is the amount of the deficiencies or adjustments in the past three years?
4. Have the results of the above reviews been reflected in the current reserve for taxes?
5. Have federal deficiencies been reflected in state and local tax reserves?
6. Does the company have state tax carryforwards? If so, what are the amounts by year of expiration and type?
7. Is the company complying with regulations regarding sales tax and payroll tax collection and remittance?

C. Tax Planning and Preparation

1. Is the company's tax planning adequate?
2. Has the company taken advantage of all potential tax savings?
3. Are aggressive interpretations adequately reserved for?
4. Does the company maintain adequate tax basis records?

D. Other Tax Considerations

Are there any other significant tax planning considerations of interest; include potential tax savings not currently achieved but that could be achieved, e.g., LIFO, accelerated depreciation, installment sales, accelerated pension or other expensing, etc., or proposed legislation that may adversely affect the company?

E. Buyout Specials Tax Questions

1. Does the company have an analysis of the tax basis of assets being acquired and an estimate of the fair value of the assets being acquired and liabilities assumed? What is the estimated recapture tax liability, assuming that such is triggered? Consider the following:

a. Depreciation
b. Tax credits
c. LIFO inventory reserves
d. Research and development
e. International, FSC or DISC earnings and profits
f. Previously expensed items, e.g., supplies, tools and dies, etc.
2. Are there deferred intercompany gains or nondeductible writeoffs that may result in additional taxes?
3. What is the expected transaction effect on net operating loss and tax credit carryovers?
4. What are the expected benefits of a taxable vs. nontaxable transaction?
5. Has the present value of step-up benefits been compared to the recapture and related tax liability cost?
6. What expense items can be added back to the income statement because the owner has been taking out excessive compensation? Consider:
a. Salaries
b. Bonuses
c. Pension and profit sharing
d. Loans
e. Airplanes
f. Expense accounts.

F. Documentation of Taxes

1. Obtain copies of federal and state tax returns for the last three years.
2. Obtain evidence that federal withholding taxes have been paid.

OTHER SECTIONS

A. Data Processing

1. What is the data processing equipment configuration?
2. Does the company have a description of the financial systems that have been computerized; i.e., sales, inventory, accounts receivable, accounts payable, payroll, general ledger and projections, etc.
3. Is the information produced by the computer accurate, reliable, and useful?
4. Does the company plan to make more extensive use of computerization? If so, describe areas in which computerization will be expanded.

5. Describe the computer facilities by type of machine, ownership, date installed, location and its application. Is it adequate for the company's needs?
6. Is an outside computer utilized?
7. How do users perceive the EDP function? How do user and EDP department perceptions differ? How effective is communication between EDP and user personnel?
8. Does the company have a recent evaluation of the EDP function and note significant weaknesses, problems and/or opportunities?

B. Insurance

1. Does the company have a list of policies in force on its property? If so, describe significant conditions, benefits, and frequency of review.
2. Does the company have a self-insurance plan?
3. What claims have been filed over the past five years?
4. What is the estimated replacement cost of assets held?
5. Is there adequate coverage for contingent liabilities?
6. Are there significant unaccrued costs on incurred but not reported claims?
7. Are increased premiums anticipated as a result of unfavorable trends or the need for increased coverage?
8. Are significant retroactive premium adjustments anticipated?
9. Does the company have life insurance on its key officers? Does it have disability insurance for the key officers?
10. What other insurance policies are in force, e.g., product liability, medical, etc.?

C. Long-Range Budgetary Planning

1. Do the managers develop the objectives and plans for their area and communicate them to the appropriate personnel?
2. Does the budgeting system monitor the accuracy of forecasts? Are there explanations of major variations (actual versus budget) on a current basis and over the past three years?
3. Does the company have a contingency plan in the event actual results will vary significantly from the budget?
4. Is profitability of individual business units and product lines monitored? Are financial ratios, controllable expenses analyses, contribution to overhead analyses, direct costing and other performance techniques employed?

317

D. Procedures and Organization Manuals

1. Does the company have procedures and organizational manuals? If so, provide a brief description, including the use of these manuals and personnel responsible for preparation.

ANALYSIS OF PROJECTIONS

A. Basic Assumptions

1. How were the projections and the assumptions put together? Are they realistic?
2. How much should they be discounted?
3. Has an accountant reviewed the numbers and assumptions?
4. Why do you believe they are achievable projections?
5. When you compute basic ratios in the projections, are they consistent? Does gross margin change year by year?
6. Are basic ratios consistent with industry figures? If not, why not?
7. How do these assumptions and projections differ from past projections?
8. Has the company achieved its projections in the past? If not, why not? If not, will it achieve its projections in the future?
9. Is there a model for this kind of growth in this industry, or are we being pioneers here?
10. Are there significant details in the projections to make them believable?
11. Is there enough reliable information behind the assumptions to make them believable?

B. Projected Financial Statement Analysis

1. What methodology is the forecasted growth based on (e.g., regression analysis, trend projection and extrapolation, economic or industry indicators, market studies, management estimate)?
2. Are the assumptions concerning sales growth (volume and price), gross margins, working capital requirements, operating expenses, capital expenditures, financing requirements and terms reasonably based on historical results, trends, industry, and overall business expectations?
3. Do the basic financial ratios (i.e., profit to equity and sales to assets) indicate that projected levels of growth are feasible without significant infusions of outside capital or changes in historical financial ratios? If not, how will increased

318

financing, faster asset turnover, and improved profit margins be accomplished?
4. Identify and describe any items that may not be recorded at fair market value:
   a. Lease agreements
   b. Long-term receivables
   c. Plant, property, and equipment
   d. Inventory
   e. Intangible assets, patents, copyrights, computer software
   f. Distribution agreements, customer lists, licenses
   g. Pension obligations and assets
   h. OSHA, EPA, and other regulatory deficiencies
   i. Severance costs (anticipated layoffs)
   j. Customer lists, licenses, franchises, air rights, easements
   k. Net-of-tax valuation adjustments (resulting from different tax vs. accounting valuations)
5. Identify potential future earnings adjustments:
   a. Excessive expenses incurred to reduce tax liability, i.e., personal expenses, excessive owner compensation, etc.
   b. Functions performed by parent for which no cost has been allocated
   c. Salary adjustments required for a more competitive wage, other employee benefit requirements
   d. Expected changes in material or other costs
   e. Incremental depreciation and amortization charges resulting from expected asset/liability revaluation, other effects of asset/liability revaluations
   f. Different tax provision due to new ownership structure and tax basis
   g. Cost savings from elimination of duplicate facilities, overhead, and "synergy"
   h. Reduction in interest income from excess cash
   i. Expected sales of facilities.
6. What are the anticipated industry changes/trends in accounting principles, and effect upon present and future operations?

C. Sensitivity Analysis

1. What effect does variation in key assumptions underlying financial projections have on P&L, cash flow, and projected balance sheet? Look at key assumptions: inventory and receivables turnover rate, gross margin on products, amount of sales expense required, rate of market penetration, variation in sales/lease ratio, variation in product mix, delay in production buildup, etc.
2. What are realistic best-case and worst-case projections?

3. Was a computer model used for this analysis?
4. Can the results be expressed in graph form?

D. The Risk

1. What is the probability that the company can meet its projections?
2. What major obstacles does the company have to overcome and what is the probability that they will?
3. What time pressures are management under and can they meet them?
4. Can you structure the investment as a debt instrument? As a secured debt instrument?
5. What collateral is available for your investment?
6. If the company is liquidated, what will you get?
7. Can the company be sold if it gets in trouble? Is there a ready buyer?
8. Who will put up more cash if the company needs it?

E. The Return

1. What is the valuation placed on the company under present investment terms? Pre-money and post-money? How does this value differ from other companies in this industry?
2. What are the best-case, worst-case expected returns, and your (vs. the company's) most likely projections?
3. What are the ROI, IRR, or NPV calculations based on your projected cash returns? Is this return sufficient for the risk you must take?
4. What return will the entrepreneur enjoy if the company meets projections? Other investors?
5. What is the probability that you will make the stated return?

BASIC INFORMATION

A. Documentation of Finance

1. Be sure you obtain the documents listed under documentation in other sections above.
2. Obtain a detailed schedule of the use of proceeds for the first six- to twelve-month period for one to three years.
3. Obtain P&L and cash flow projections for the next three to five years together with supporting schedules.
4. Obtain a complete list of all the assumptions used by management to make projections and budgets.

5. Obtain a sensitivity analysis of management's projection, so that you can understand their projections.
6. Obtain a complete written analysis of the return of the investment or internal rate of return on this business proposition.

B. Financial Reports

1. Obtain copies of reports used by financial people to "run" their department.
2. Obtain copies of reports given to top management by the finance department.
3. Obtain a copy of the budget used in the finance department to control costs.

C. Financial Ratio Analysis

1. *Gross Margin Percentage* can be calculated by dividing Gross Profit by Sales.
2. *Profit Margin Percentage* can be determined by dividing Net Income before Taxes by Net Sales.
3. *Return on Equity* can be determined by dividing Net Income by Total Shareholder Equity.
4. *Return on Assets* can be calculated by dividing Net Income by Average Total Assets out during the year.
5. *The Current Ratio* can be calculated by dividing Current Assets by Current Liabilities.
6. *Quick Ratio* can be calculated by dividing Current Assets minus Inventories by Current Liabilities.
7. To calculate the *Working Capital as a Percentage of Assets* divide Working Capital by Total Assets.
8. *Liquidity Ratio* can be calculated by dividing Total Assets by Total Liabilities.
9. *Debt Equity Ratios* can be computed by dividing Total Debts Outstanding by Total Stockholders Equity.
10. A similar ratio is *Total Liabilities to Stockholders Equity*, which can be computed by dividing Total Liabilities by Stockholders Equity.
11. *The Working Capital to Net Sales* can be computed by dividing Net Sales by Working Capital.
12. *Debt Coverage Ratio* is calculated by dividing Earnings before Interest and Taxes by Total Annual Debt Service.
13. *Cash Flow Debt Coverage Ratio* is calculated by dividing Earnings before Interest and Taxes plus Depreciation by Interest and Principal Due on all of the company's debts.
14. *Percentage Fixed Charges of Earnings* is calculated when you

divide the Fixed Charges by Earnings before Interest and Taxes plus Fixed Charges.

15. *Cash Flow Cycle* can be calculated by dividing Receivables plus Inventory by the Cost of Goods Sold.

16. Calculate the *Receivables Cycles* by dividing Net Credit Sales by Average Trade Receivables.

17. The *Past Due Index* is calculated by dividing Total Receivables Past Due by Total Receivables.

18. Calculate the *Bad Debt Expenses as a Percentage of Sales* by dividing Bad Debt Expenses by Total Credit Sales.

19. *Inventory Turns* can be calculated by dividing Cost of Goods Sold by the Average Inventory Outstanding in a year.

20. *Percentage of Cash Flow to Total Assets* can be calculated by dividing Net Cash Flow by Total Assets.

D. Strengths and Weaknesses

1. Identify the five major strengths the company has in finance.
2. Identify the five major weaknesses the company has in finance.
3. What could go wrong in the finance area?

E. Summary Analysis

1. In a very few words, how do you feel about the finance side of the business?
2. Can the financial people managing this company be a winning team? Can the finance people be motivated to succeed for the company?
3. Are you willing to bet real money that this group of financial employees working under the financial policies of this company will be successful? Would you bet your career or job that they can make it happen?

REFERENCE AREA

You still need to develop many other pieces of information. Some of it is general information and some is specific and can be obtained from various references. This is where you go outside the company to verify what you have learned about the company.

A. General

1. What is the exact corporate name and address?
2. Where (what state) and when was the company incorporated?
3. What are the states in which the company is qualified to do business?
4. Where are the minute books, bylaws, and certificate of incorporation?
5. List any predecessor organization or prior names of the corporation.
6. List corporate organizations - subsidiaries, division, and branches. Give name and location and describe operations. Draw a box chart to show relationships.
7. What is the fiscal year end for the company?
8. What is the Standard Industrial Classification Code for this company?
9. What is the IRS Employee Identification Number?
10. Have you reviewed the corporate minutes for the past three years?
11. Have you reviewed all past business plans? Operating plans? Marketing plans?
12. Does the company have any subsidiaries?
13. Does the company have any shareholder agreements?
14. Does the company need approval of any entity other than the board of directors regarding this financing?

B. Miscellaneous Questions for Management

1. Are there any actions, lawsuits, or proceedings pending or threatened against the company or any officers or directors? If so, list.
2. Is any broker entitled to a commission on this financing?
3. Do any defaults or violations exist in any of the company's corporate obligations including loan agreements, notes, leases, etc.?
4. Is the company current on all taxes owed (FICA, income, real estate, etc.)?
5. Is the company in compliance with all federal, state, and local laws and with all rules and regulations by agencies and commissions thereof, including but not limited to safety and health, consumer products safety, environmental (water, sewer, air, land) that are relevant to the ownership of its properties or operation of its business?
6. Are there any restrictions on any of the company's common stock?
7. Do any corporate guaranties exist?

323

8. Has the company acquired any operating entities or products within the past five years? Any divestitures?

9. Have any officers or directors violated (other than minor traffic laws) any federal, state, or local laws in the past twenty years?

10. Do any options or rights of first refusal exist on any of the company's common stock?

11. Does the company have any stock purchase warrants, options, subscriptions, convertible instruments, contracts, or agreements for issuance of common stock, puts, calls, or other equity-related instruments?

12. Does the company need approval of any entity other than the board of directors regarding this financing?

13. Has the company experienced any union-organizing activities during the past five years?

C. Reference List

1. **Bank:** List the bank's name, address, telephone number, and account officer for all banks the company has done business with for the past five years.

2. **Other Institutional Lenders:** Provide the same information as in item 1 for lenders who have loaned the company $100,000 or more.

3. **Accounting Firm:** List the firm's name, address, telephone number, and account manager for all accounting firms the company has used in the past five years.

4. **Law Firm:** List the firm's name, address, telephone number, and individual attorney for all law firms the company has used in the past five years.

5. **Suppliers:** List the supplier's name, address, telephone number, and contact person for the company's ten highest-volume suppliers and ten others.

6. **Customers:** List the customer's name, address, telephone number, and contact person for the company's ten highest-volume customers and ten others.

7. **Competitor:** List the competitor's name, address, telephone number, and chief operating officer for the company's five strongest competitors and five others.

8. **Independent Sales Representatives:** List the firm's name, address, telephone number, and representative name for your independent sales representative organization.

9. **Independent Service Representative:** List the firm's name, address, telephone number, and representative's name for your independent service representative.

10. **Directors**: List the names, addresses, and telephone numbers of all directors.
11. **Officers**: List all names, home addresses, and home telephone numbers of all officers.
12. **Principal Stockholders**: List the names and addresses of every stockholder owning more than 5% of the company's common or preferred stock, or anyone who has an option to buy more than 5%.
13. **Dissenting Stockholder**: List all dissenting stockholders.
14. **Investment Banker**: Get the names of all those used and call and discuss the company.
15. **Institutional Industry Analysis**: Get the name of the person in any large Wall Street brokerage house who follows this industry.
16. **Industry Consultants**: Obtain the names of industry consultants or "gurus" who are quoted frequently and are knowledgeable about this industry.
17. **Trade Associations**: Obtain the names of trade association executives in this industry.
18. **Trade Publications**: Obtain a list of trade publications in this industry and any newsletters covering this industry.
19. **Venture Capital Investors in the Industry**: Find out who else has invested in this industry.
20. **Public Companies**: Obtain public information on the public companies in this industry.
21. **Financial or Business Broker**: Obtain the name, address, and telephone number of any broker involved in this transaction.

D. **Questions to Manufacturing Representatives**

1. What products do you represent for the company?
2. How long have you been their representative?
3. What other products not made by the company do you represent?
4. How many of the company's products did you sell during the past twelve months? What does that represent in dollars?
5. Does the company have good-quality products? Do the customers like the products?
6. Have you had complaints about the products? If so, what kind of complaints?
7. How does the product compare in quality with competitor's products in the market?
8. Is the product priced right? Is it too high or too low compared with the competitor's prices? What price do you think the product should have?

9. Can you continue to sell the product? How many units can you sell in the next twelve months (dollar volume)?
10. How has the company treated you as a rep? Does it give you good support?
11. Has it paid commissions on time? How long does it take the company to pay commissions?
12. What changes would you like to see the company make?
13. What do you think of the management of the company?

E. Questions to Lawyers

1. Who is the lawyer? How long has he been on this client's work?
2. Any suits against the company outstanding?
3. Any suits against the company in the last two years?
4. Any potential suits against the company?
5. Has the company filed suits against others that are still open?
6. Has the company filed suits against others in the last two years?
7. Does company plan to file suits against others?
8. Any product liability suits or problems?
9. Any union suits or legal problems?
10. Any patent suits or problems?
11. If there is a suit then specify the following:
    a. Maximum settlement amount
    b. Minimum settlement amount
    c. Most likely settlement amount
    d. When it will be settled
    e. The nature of the suit
    f. Whether the suit has merit.
12. Is the company in compliance with all federal, state, and local laws and with all rules and regulations by agencies and commissions thereof, including but not limited to safety and health, consumer products safety, environmental (water, sewer, air, land) that are relevant to the ownership of its properties or operation of its business?
13. Are there any legal problems whatsoever?
14. What do you think of management?

F. Questions to Accountants

1. Verify the numbers in the audit on assets, sales, and profits.
2. Did they issue a management letter? If so, get a copy from the accountant or management.
3. Are the books and records in good condition for easy audit or do they need improvement?

4. Are adequate controls in place to foil misuse of funds?
5. How long have they been the auditors?
6. How long has the individual auditor been handling or working on the annual audit?
7. Is the financial officer good?
8. Is the company having operating problems?
9. Have accountants started this year's audit? If so, any material negative items?
10. Any significant or material changes in the numbers set out by management and the final audit such as
    a. Disagreement over inventory value?
    b. Disagreement over quality of accounts receivable?
    c. Disagreement over work in progress and cost of goods sold?
    d. Other material differences?
11. Did anything come to your attention during the audit that would indicate the company is having operating problems?

G. Questions to Suppliers

1. What do you supply the company?
2. What is the annual dollar volume you supply?
3. What credit limit do you have for the company?
4. Do you anticipate any shortage in the items you supply to the company?
5. How promptly are you paid by the company? Is it ever a problem?
6. Have you ever shipped the company anything COD?
7. What do you like about the company?
8. How would you describe your relationship with the company? How are you treated as a supplier?
9. Will you continue to supply the company?
10. Any other comments?

H. Questions to Customers

1. What products have you purchased from the company? How long have you been buying from the company?
2. How long ago did you purchase it?
3. What is your current outstanding order? Confirm this with the company's backlog of orders. Also confirm that the order in the backlog will be shipped in the next thirty, sixty, or ninety days. Are you a repeat user?
4. Do you like the product?
5. Has the company's product lived up to the quality that you had

originally perceived? Does the product perform as well as you expected?

6. Have you ever been shipped faulty goods? What happened?

7. Has the company lived up to the service representations it made to you before you bought the product?

8. Was the product overpriced or was it a bargain?

9. Do you think the product has brand-name recognition?

10. Have you purchased products from competitors of the company or other manufacturer brand names similar to the company's product?

11. How does the company's product compare in quality to products of competitors that you have either purchased or looked at?

12. Do you intend to buy from the company again?

13. Estimate how much you will purchase in the next twelve months.

14. What changes would you like to see the company make in the product?

15. What do you think of the people that you had contact with in the company?

16. Any other comments?

I. Questions to Landlords

1. How long have you been renting to the company?
2. How many square feet do they rent from you?
3. Where is the rental property located?
4. What is the monthly rental for property?
5. How timely are their payments?
6. Ever had to contact for failing to pay the rent?
7. What condition is the property kept in?
8. Would you rent to them again?
9. Who is your contact?
10. Any general comments?

J. Questions to Advertisement People

1. How long have you been advertising for the company?
2. How often do they advertise?
3. What is the average cost of their advertising?
4. Do you have a standing order?
5. What is the average cost of their advertising?
6. How timely are their payments?
7. Have you ever had to contact them for failing to pay?
8. Will you continue to run their ads?
9. Who is your contact?
10. Any general comments?

K. Questions to Bankers

1. How long has the company been banking with this bank?
2. Who did it bank with before?
3. How long has this bank officer been the company's loan officer?
4. What amount of credit (high and low) has the bank extended to the company?
5. What is the collateral for the loan?
6. Does the company pay as agreed? Has it ever been in default on a loan?
7. Has the company ever asked for credit and been denied? What was the amount?
8. Does the company have operating problems?
9. Is the management good?
10. Are they high livers?

APPENDIX 2

ACTUAL DOCUMENTS

The following documents are facsimiles of actual documents used by Allied Capital Corporation in a financing, except that they have been broadened in concept to include many of the standard "boilerplate" items used by most venture capitalists. After reading these documents, you will be well prepared for the ones you receive from the lawyers. All documents are for fictitious companies and people.

The following documents are covered in this appendix:

1. Commitment letter for a loan with options for stock on Ace Electromagnetic, Inc.
2. Legal Document 1: Loan Agreement on Ace Electromagnetic, Inc.
3. Legal Document 2: Promissory Note on Ace Electromagnetic, Inc.
4. Legal Document 3: Stock Purchase Warrants on Ace Electromagnetic, Inc.
5. Legal Document 4: Stock Purchase on Ajax Computer Genetics Corporation.
6. Legal Document 5: Exhibits to Stock Purchase on Ajax Computer Genetics Corporation.

COMMITMENT LETTER

Venture Capital Corporation
1666 K Street, N.W., Suite 901
Washington, D.C. 20006

Mr. O.K. Entrepreneur, President
Ace Electromagnetic Incorporated
1234 Main Street
McLean, Virginia 22102

Dear Mr. Entrepreneur:

The Management of Venture Capital Corporation (Venture) has approved a loan to your company (the Company) in the amount of $300,000. The approval was based on the following representations made by you:

    1.01   The Company is a corporation in good standing in Virginia.   You will provide Venture with a Certificate of Good Standing and a copy of the Charter and Bylaws and minutes of the organization of the Company.

    1.02   The Company is primarily engaged in the business of manufacturing electromagnetic equipment.

    1.03   There are no lawsuits against the Company, its directors, or its officers, personally, nor any you know of that may be contemplated.   If there are any suits outstanding or contemplated, your attorney will provide Venture with a letter stating the nature of such suits and a copy of the suits.   You will provide us with a copy of all lawsuits you have filed against others.

    1.04   The Company is current on all taxes owed and, in this regard, you will provide Venture with a copy of the last three years' tax returns for the Company.

    1.05   You have presented financial information showing that the Company, for the twelve-month period ending January 31, 1982, had: sales of $850,000 and pre-tax loss of $25,000; assets of $600,000; liabilities of $300,000; and a net worth of $300,000.

    1.06 The money borrowed will be used as follows:

        A. $100,000 to pay First National Bank
        B. $100,000 to pay accounts payable
        C. $100,000 to pay fees and working capital.

    1.07   Upon completion of Venture's loan, you will have approximately the following assets:

        A.   Cash, $100,000
        B.   Accounts receivable, $100,000
        C.   Machinery and equipment, $100,000
        D.   Land and building, $100,000

E. Other assets, $300,000.

1.08 With regard to leases, you will provide Venture with a copy of every major executed lease.

1.09 The information presented to Venture is correct and you believe the projections presented to Venture are reasonable.

1.10 You will pay no brokerage fees, legal fees, or other fees on this loan without Venture's written approval, and you will indemnify Venture against all such fees.

1.11 During the past ten years none of the directors has been arrested or convicted of a material crime.

2. The terms and conditions of the loan shall be:

2.01 A loan of $300,000 for six years at 15% per annum, paid monthly on the first of each month.

2.02 The loan shall be interest only for the first thirty-six months and, beginning with the thirty-seventh month, you will pay principal and interest sufficient to amortize the loan over the remaining thirty-six months. All principal and interest outstanding at the end of six years shall be due and payable in full as a balloon payment.

2.03 The loan may be prepaid at any time in whole or in part.

2.04 Takedown of the loan shall be $300,000 at closing.

2.05 Other terms standard for such loans.

2.06 In connection with this financing, Venture shall receive at closing separate options to purchase stock in the Company. Cost of the options to Venture will be $100. These options, when exercised by Venture and the other investment company, will provide stock ownership in the company of 35% at the time of exercise. The exercise price will be $100. The options will expire ten years from the closing. Venture will share pro rata in any redemption of stock by the Company.

2.07 There shall be an "unlocking" provision whereby if there is a bona fide offer to purchase the Company and Venture wishes to accept the offer and you do not, then you shall acquire Venture's interest on the same terms or sell the Company.

2.08 There shall be a "put" provision whereby any time after five years from closing Venture may require the Company to purchase its options or the resulting stock at the higher of the following:

A. Ten percent of sales for the year just ended times a price-earnings ratio of eight less Venture's debt times 35%.

B. Ten times cash flow for the year just ended less Venture's debt times 35%.

2.09 Venture shall have full "piggyback" rights to register its shares any time the Company (or its management) is registering shares for sale and such registration of Venture's shares shall be paid for by the Company.

3. Collateral for the loan shall be:

3.01 A second deed of trust on the land and building of the business, subordinated as to collateral to a mortgage of approximately $10,000, on terms acceptable to Venture.

3.02 A first secured interest in all of the tangible and intangible assets of the Company including, but not limited to, inventory, machinery, equipment, furniture, fixtures, and accounts receivable.

3.03 Pledge and assignment of all the stock of the Company and assignment of leases listed above.

3.04 Personal signatures and guarantees of you and your spouse.

3.05 Obtaining a life insurance policy on your life for $300,000 with the policy assigned to Venture and with Venture as the loss payee to the extent of its loan.

3.06 Adequate hazard and business insurance, which shall include federal flood insurance if your business is located in a designated federal flood area. All such insurance shall be assigned to Venture and Venture shall be listed as the loss payee to the extent of its interest. In this regard, you will supply Venture with a list of all business insurance and such insurance and coverage shall be acceptable to Venture.

4. Conditions of the loan are:

4.01 Provide Venture with monthly year-to-date financial statements in accordance with generally accepted accounting standards (including profit and loss and balance sheet) within forty-five days of the end of the month.

4.02 The president of the Company will provide Venture with a certificate each quarter stating that no default has occurred in the Loan Agreement.

4.03 If requested in writing, provide Venture with an annual certified audit within ninety days after the year's end from an accounting firm acceptable to Venture.

4.04 Before each year end, provide Venture with projections of the next year in the same format as the financial statements.

4.05 Within thirty days after they are filed, provide Venture with a copy of all documents filed with government agencies such as the Internal Revenue Service, Federal Trade Commission, and Securities and Exchange Commission.

4.06 There will be no change in control of the Company, nor will there be a change of ownership without the written approval of Venture.

4.07 Management will not sell, assign, or transfer any shares it owns in the Company without the written approval of Venture.

4.08 The Company will maintain in accordance with generally accepted accounting principles:

    A. A current ratio of one to one
    B. Sales of $500,000 per year
    C. Sales of $30,000 per month
    D. Sales of $105,000 per quarter
    E. Net worth of $50,000 or more.

4.09 The Company will have board meetings at least once each quarter at the Company's business offices. Although a Venture representative will not serve on the board, a Venture representative will have the right to attend each meeting at the Company's expense and Venture shall be notified of each meeting at least two weeks before it is to occur.

4.10 The Company will pay no cash dividends and the Company will not sell any assets of the business that are not part of the regular course of business without Venture's approval.

4.11 The Company will not expend funds in excess of $10,000 per year for capital improvements, and the like.

4.12 You will live in the general Washington, D.C. metropolitan area.

4.13 The Company will not pay, nor loan, nor advance to any employee money which, in total, is in excess of $25,000 per year, without the written approval of Venture. If (1) the Company is in default for nonpayment to Venture or any senior lien; or (2) the Company is not profitable for any quarter, then the Company will not pay, nor loan, nor advance to any employee money which, in total, is in excess of $20,000 per year, without the written permission of Venture.

4.14 The Company will not pay any brokerage fees, legal fees, or consulting fees in excess of $5,000 per year without the written permission of Venture.

4.15 Other conditions standard for such loans.

4.16 You will pay all closing costs and recording fees, which include all attorney's fees. You may use any attorney to draw the legal documents; however, they must be reviewed and approved by Venture's counsel. A simple review by Venture's counsel will not incur a fee; however, if the work done by Venture's counsel is beyond a simple review, a fee will be charged and the fee will be paid by you.

4.17 In connection with this financing, Venture will receive a 2% ($6,000) fee. Upon acceptance of this commitment letter, you will pay Venture $1,500 of this fee and the remainder at closing. Should closing not take place owing to the fault of Venture, then the fee will be returned less out-of-pocket expenses; otherwise, it is forfeited.

5.   This commitment is conditioned upon the following, which, if not attained, will make Venture's commitment void:

5.01   Acceptance by you of this letter and the return of one copy to Venture fully executed by you, with the fee set out in 4.17 above, before February 1, 1983.

5.02   Closing on the loan before March 31, 1983.

5.03   All legal documents being acceptable to Venture.

5.04   A favorable credit check of you and your business and no material adverse occurrences before closing.

5.05   A favorable visit by Venture to your business.

Sincerely,

A. V. Capitalist, President

VENTURE CAPITAL CORPORATION

AGREED: ACE ELECTROMAGNETIC, INCORPORATED

BY: _____ DATE: _____
O.K. Entrepreneur, President

_____ DATE: _____
Personally: O.K. Entrepreneur

Loan Agreement

DATE

WHEREAS, Venture Capital Corporation, a District of Columbia corporation (hereinafter "Venture") has committed under terms of a letter of January 31, 1983, to lend to Ace Electromagnetic, Incorporated, a Virginia corporation (hereinafter "Company") the sum of Three Hundred Thousand dollars ($300,000);

WHEREAS, the Company will issue VENTURE Stock Purchase Warrants (hereinafter "Warrants) for a total of 35 percent of the common stock of the Company,

NOW THEREFORE the Company and Venture agree as follows:

I. Parties

This Agreement shall bind and accrue to the benefit of the Company and its successors, the undersigned shareholders of the Company, Venture, and any subsequent holders of the Note, Warrants, or the stock issued thereunder (who are collectively referred to herein as "Holders"). The Note issued hereunder may be held by different persons, as may the Warrants. The terms of this Agreement as of the day the Company receives notice that a new party is holder of a Note or Warrant shall be binding between the Company and such new party, regardless of modifications that may subsequently be made between the Company and another holder.

II. Loan

The Company will borrow and Venture will lend the sum of Three Hundred Thousand Dollars ($300,000) to be repaid according to the terms of Promissory Note of even date herewith, (hereinafter "Note").

III. Use of Proceeds

The Company will use the proceeds of the loan only to fund commercial electromagnetic operations with approximately $100,000 to repay a line of credit at the First National Bank, $100,000 to pay accounts payable, and $100,000 for fees and working capital.

337

IV. Collateral

The Note and the Holders' rights herein shall be secured *pari passu* against the collateral below, provided that future advances in addition to the original $300,000 advanced to the Company shall not be considered in determining the secured parties' shares from sale of collateral. In regard to the items in subparagraph 2, the Company grants Holders a security interest to attach when the Company has signed this instrument and acquired rights in the property, and when Venture has made whole or partial disbursement of loan funds to the Company, the Company's designated payee, or an escrow agent. Although other parties may become holders of the instruments secured hereby, all security interests of record will remain in the name of Venture Capital Corporation, which will hold such interests in trust for the benefit of all Holders. The collateral shall be as follows:

1. A second mortgage on the Company's real estate in the Commonwealth of Virginia subject to a first mortgage to a financial institution according to terms of a separate instrument;
2. A second security interest in the furniture, fixtures, machinery, equipment, inventory, contract rights, licenses, and all tangible and intangible personal property of the Company subject to credit lines from financial institutions;
3. Assignment of accounts receivable, pledge of all the outstanding stock of the Company subject to bank lines of credit according to the terms of separate agreements therefor;
4. Collateral assignment of the policy number 1234567 issued by ABC Life Insurance Company insuring the life of O.K. Entrepreneur in the amount of $300,000.00;
5. Personal guarantees of Mr. and Mrs. O.K. Entrepreneur according to the terms of a separate instrument.

V. Representations and Warranties

To induce Venture to enter this transaction the Company represents and warrants that:

A. It is duly incorporated, validly existing and in good standing under the laws of Virginia, having Articles of Incorporation and Bylaws (all of the terms of which are in full force and effect) as previously furnished to Venture; it is not and does not intend to become an investment company or passive investment vehicle;

B. It is duly qualified to conduct business as proposed by it and is in good standing as a foreign corporation in all states in which the nature of its business or location of its properties requires such qualification;

C. It has full power and authority to enter into this Agreement, to borrow money as contemplated hereby, to issue the Warrants and upon exercise thereof to issue the stock pursuant thereto, and to carry out the provisions hereof; and it has taken all corporate action necessary for the execution and performance of each of the above (including the issuance and sale of the Warrants, the reservation of shares of stock, and the issuance thereof upon the exercise of the Warrants); and each document above-named will constitute a valid and binding obligation of the Company enforceable in accordance with its respective terms when executed and delivered;

D. The authorized capital stock of the Company is as set forth below, and all such stock has been duly issued in accordance with applicable laws, including federal and state securities laws:

Class	Par Value	Shares Authorized	Shares Issued	Shares Outstanding
Common	zero	5,000	3,200	3,200

E. The list of officers and directors of the Company previously submitted is complete and accurate. All representations made by the Company, its officers, directors, shareholders, or guarantors in any instrument described in this Agreement or previously supplied to Venture in regard to this financing are true and correct as of this date, and all projections provided are reasonable;

F. The Company has no debts, liabilities, or obligations of any nature whether accrued, absolute, contingent, or otherwise arising out of any transaction entered into or any state of facts existing prior hereto, including without limitation liabilities or obligations on account of taxes or government charges, penalties, interest, or fines thereon or in respect thereof except the debts to be paid off by the use of proceeds of this loan, and debts on open account; the accounts payable and the debts to be paid herewith have not changed materially since the date of the June financial statement previously submitted; the Company does not know and has no reasonable grounds to know of any basis for any claim against it as of the date of this Agreement or of any debt, liability, or obligation other than those mentioned herein;

G. The Company has not been made a party to or threatened by any suits, actions, claims, investigations by governmental bodies, or legal, administrative, or arbitrational proceedings except as set out in the Company counsel's letter of this date (hereinafter "litigation letter"); neither the Company nor its officers nor directors know of any basis or grounds for any such suit or proceeding; there are no outstanding orders, judgments, writs, injunctions, or decrees or any court, government agency, or arbitrational tribune against or affecting it or its properties, assets, or business;

H. Since the date of the Venture commitment letter the Company has not suffered any material adverse change in its condition (financial or otherwise) or its overall business prospects, nor entered into any material transactions or incurred any debt, obligation, or liability, absolute or contingent, nor sustained any material loss or damage to its property, whether or not insured, nor suffered any material interference with its business or operations, present or proposed; and there has been no sale, lease, abandonment, or other disposition by the Company of any of its property, real or personal, or any interest therein or relating thereto, that is material to the financial position of the Company;

I. The Company has duly filed all tax returns, federal, state, and local, which are required to be filed and has duly paid or fully reserved for all taxes or installments thereof as and when due which have or may become due pursuant to said returns or pursuant to any assessment received by the Company;

J. The Company is not bound by or party to any contract or instrument or subject to any charter or other legal restriction materially and adversely affecting its business, property, assets, operations, or condition, financial or otherwise;

K. Except for matters set out in the litigation letter, the Company is not in breach of, default under, or in violation of any applicable law, decree, order, rule, or regulation which may materially and adversely affect it or any indenture, contract, agreement, deed, lease, loan agreement, commitment, bond, note, deed of trust, restrictive covenant, license, or other instrument or obligation to which it is a party or by which it is bound or to which any of its assets are subject; the execution, delivery, and performance of this Agreement and the issuance, sale, and delivery of the Warrant and other documents will not constitute any such breach, default, or violation or require consent or approval of any court, governmental agency, or body except as contemplated herein;

L. The statements set forth in the *Size Stand Declaration* (SBA Form 480, Exhibit 4 hereto) and *Assurances of Compliance* (SBA Form 625D, Exhibit 5, herein), as previously provided, are complete and accurate; the Company is a small business concern as defined in the *Small Business Investment Act of 1958*, as amended ("the Act"), and the rules and regulations of the Small Business Administration (SBA) thereunder; there exists no agreement expressed or implied, no condition, state of facts or relationship between the Company and any other entity or entities which would prevent the corporation from qualifying as a small business concern;

M. Neither the Company nor any of its officers, directors, partners, or controlling persons is an "Associate" of Venture as such terms are defined in section 107.3 of the Regulations as amended promulgated under the Act, nor an "affiliated person" of Venture, as such term is defined in section 2(a)(3) of the *Investment Company Act of 1940* as amended;

N. To the best of the Company's knowledge, it has complied in all material respects with all laws, ordinances, and regulations applicable to it and to its business, including without limitation federal and state securities laws, zoning laws and ordinances, federal labor laws and regulations, the *Federal Occupational Safety and Health Act* and regulations thereunder, the *Federal Employees Retirement Income Security Act*, and federal, state, and local environmental protection laws and regulations;

O. There are no material facts relating to the Company not fully disclosed to Venture; no representation, covenant or warranty made by the Company herein or in any statement, certificate or other instrument furnished to Venture pursuant hereto or in connection with the transaction contemplated hereby contains or will contain any untrue statement of or omits to state a material fact necessary to make the statement not misleading;

P. The Company is primarily engaged in the business of commercial electromagnetic manufacturing and is not a franchise;

Q. The Company for the twelve-month period ending January 31, 1983, had: sales of $850,000; pre-tax loss of $25,000; assets of $600,000; liabilities of $300,000; and net worth of $300,000;

R. After disbursement of the subject loan the Company will have approximately the following assets: accounts receivable $100,000, machinery and equipment $100,000, land and building $100,000, other assets $300,000;

S. Copies of leases provided are true and correct;

T. During the past ten (10) years no officer or director of the Company has been arrested or convicted of any criminal offense;

VI. Affirmative Covenants

Until the Warrants are exercised and the Note repaid in full, the Company will:

A. Promptly make all payments of principal and interest as due under the Note and furnish from time to time to each Holder all information it may reasonably request to enable it to prepare and file any form required to be filed by Holder with the SBA, Securities and Exchange Commission, or any other regulatory authority;

B. Forward, or cause to be forwarded to Holders, its monthly accounting balance sheet and profit-and-loss statement within forty-five (45) days from the end of each month;

C. Forward, or cause to be forwarded to Holders, its final year end accounting balance sheet and profit-and-loss statement within sixty (60) days of such accounting year end, which if demanded by a Holder in writing shall be prepared at Company's expense by an independent outside accounting firm acceptable to a Holder, according to generally accepted accounting principles uniformly applied;

D. Maintain a net worth of $50,000 or more and a level of current assets (which shall be reflected in its books in accordance with generally accepted accounting principles) such that the amount of such current assets shall equal or exceed the amount of current liabilities; maintain sales of at least $500,000 per annum; $105,000 per quarter and $30,000 per month as reflected on its books in accordance with generally accepted accounting principles uniformly applied;

E. Provide to Holders in writing each quarter the certification of the President of the Company that no default has occurred under the Warrants, Note or this Agreement, or any debt or obligation senior to the debt of the Holders hereunder; or if any such default exists, provide Holders with a statement by the President of the Company as to the nature of such default;

F. Maintain such shares of its common stock authorized but

unissued as may be necessary to satisfy the rights of the Holders of the Warrants;

G. Perform all acts as required under the Warrants including without limitation, the re-issue of replacement Warrants to a Holder upon loss or destruction;

H. Permit any authorized representative of any Holder and its attorneys and accountants to inspect, examine, and make copies and abstracts of the books of account and records of Company at reasonable times during normal business hours;

I. Notify Holders of any litigation to which the Company is a party by mailing to Holders, by registered mail, within five (5) days of receipt thereof, a copy of the Complaint, Motion for Judgment, or other such pleadings served on or by the Company; and any litigation to which the Company is not a party but which could substantially affect operation of the company's business or the collateral pledged for this loan, including collateral securing any guarantees, by mailing to Holders, by registered mail, a copy of all pleadings obtained by the company in regard to such litigation, or if no pleadings are obtained, a letter setting out the facts known about the litigation, within five (5) days of receipt thereof; provided that the Company shall not be obliged by this paragraph to give notice of suits where it is a creditor seeking collection of account debts;

J. Prior to each accounting year end, provide Holders with projected financial statements for the coming year, in the same format as used for item C above;

K. Hold a meeting of the Board of Directors of the Company at least once each quarter; give Holders at least two weeks prior notice of such meeting; allow one representative designated by each Holder to attend such meeting at Company's expense;

L. Maintain all-risk hazard insurance on its assets, with mortgagee clause in favor of Holders, in such reasonable amounts and forms as required by Holders; this shall include federal flood insurance if any assets be in a designated flood plain; and supply Holders with a list of existing coverage prior to closing;

M. Give Holders notice of any judgment entered against the Company by mailing a copy to Holders within five (5) days of entry thereof;

N. Take all necessary steps to administer, supervise, preserve, and protect the collateral herein; regardless of any action taken by Holders, there shall be no duty upon Holders in this respect.

O. Within thirty (30) days of filing provide Holders with copies of all returns and documents filed with federal, state, or local government agencies including without limitation the Internal Revenue Service, Federal Trade Commission, and Securities and Exchange Commission.

P. Maintain an original or a true copy of this Agreement and any modifications hereof, which shall be available for inspection under subparagraph H above.

VII. Negative Covenants

Until the Notes are repaid and the Warrants exercised, the Company will not without the prior written consent of all the Holders:

A. Declare or pay any cash dividend of any kind on any class of stock; make any material change in its ownership, organization, or management or the manner in which its business is conducted; authorize, issue, or reclassify any shares of capital stock except as required under the Warrants;

B. Become a party to any merger or consolidation with any other corporation, company, or entity;

C. Make expenditures for capital improvements or acquisitions in any fiscal year in excess of $10,000;

D. Make loans, advances, wage payments including salaries, withdrawals, fees, bonuses, commissions direct or indirect in money or otherwise, to any officer, director, shareholder, partner, or employee in excess of $50,000 per year, or $30,000 per year if there is a default under this agreement;

E. Transfer, sell, lease, or in any other manner convey any equitable, beneficial, or legal interest in any of the assets of the Company except inventory sold in the normal course of business, or allow to exist on its assets any mortgage interest, pledge, security interest, title retention device, or other encumbrance junior or senior to Holder's liens except for liens of taxes and assessments not delinquent or contested in good faith;

344

F. Permit any judgment obtained against the Company to remain unpaid for over twenty (20) days without obtaining a stay of execution or bond;

G. Incur any declared default under any loan agreement pertaining to another debt of the Company;

H. Pay or incur any brokerage, legal, consulting, or similar fee in excess of $5,000 per year;

I. Create or incur any debt other than that incurred hereunder, trade debt or short-term working capital debt normally incurred in the ordinary course of business;

J. Incur any lease liability or purchase any additional life insurance from business income or assets;

K. Become a guarantor, or otherwise liable on any notes or obligations of any other person, firm, corporation, or entity, except in connection with depositing checks and other instruments for the payment of money acquired in the normal course of its business.

VIII. Investment Covenant

By accepting a Warrant, the Holder thereof represents, warrants, and covenants that it is an "accredited investor" within the meaning of section 4(6) of the *Securities Act,* or an "accredited person" within the meaning of Rule 242 of the *Securities Act,* or acquiring the Warrant and any stock issued thereunder for its own account for investment and not with the view to resale or distribution thereof except in accordance with applicable federal and state securities laws. Upon exercise of any conversion rights under the Warrant, this representation, warranty, and covenant shall be deemed to have been given with respect to the stock received.

IX. Fees, Expenses, and Indemnification

The Company shall reimburse Holders for reasonable expenses according to the terms of the commitment letter. The Company shall pay, indemnify, and hold any holders of the Warrants and Note harmless from and against any and all liability and loss with respect to or resulting from any and all claims for or on account of any brokers and from finder's fees or commissions with respect to this transaction as may have been created by the Company or its officers, partners, employees, or agents; and from any stamp or excise taxes that may become payable by virtue of this transaction or the issuance of any stock or modification hereunder. Venture warrants it has not contracted to pay any such fees.

X. Unlocking

If at any time after five (5) years from the date of this Agreement the Company or its shareholders receive a bona fide offer to purchase the assets of the Company or an equity interest in the Company, then the party receiving such offer (hereinafter offeree) will submit a copy of the offer and such information pertinent thereto as it may have to the Holders of the Warrants or the shares issued thereunder within three (3) days of receipt of said offer. Within ten (10) days of receipt of said copy each Warrant Holder will indicate in writing to the offeree its approval or disapproval of the offer. If a Holder approves the offer, then the offeree shall, within twenty (20) days thereafter or such shorter time if provided in the offer, accept or reject the offer. If the offeree rejects the offer then simultaneously with such rejection it shall be bound to purchase the approving Holder's Warrants or resulting stock in the Company under the same terms and conditions that such Holder would have received under the offer. If a Warrant Holder fails to communicate timely approval or disapproval, the Company may construe such failure to indicate disapproval.

XI. "Put" Rights

Beginning five (5) years from the date of this agreement ending ten (10) years from the date of this agreement, Warrant Holders may by written demand require the Company to purchase its Warrant or the shares of stock issued hereunder at a price of 35% of the higher of the following sums:

(a) Ten Percent (10%) of the Company's sales for the fiscal year immediately preceding the year of the demand times a price earnings ratio of twelve (12), less the aggregate principal balance of the Note on the day of demand; or

(b) Ten times the Company's cash flow for the fiscal year immediately preceding the year of the demand, less the aggregate principal balance of the Note on the day of demand.

XII. Default

A. If any of the below-listed events occurs prior to maturity of the Notes, then a default may be declared at the option of any Holder without presentment, demand, protest, or further notice of any kind,

346

all of which are hereby expressly waived. In such event the Note Holder shall be entitled to be paid in full the balance of any unpaid principal of its Note plus accrued interest and any costs thereof, including reasonable attorneys' fees, and to any other remedies which may be available under this Agreement, the Warrant, the Note, or any applicable law:

1. Occurrence of any default provision as set out in the Warrant or Note;

2. Any material representation made by the Company in writing herein or in connection herewith shall be untrue and shall remain so for thirty (30) days after written notice to the Company thereof;

3. The Company shall fail to comply with the covenants in this Agreement and such failure shall continue for a period of ten (10) days after receipt of notice thereof from any Holder of the Note;

4. The Company shall make an assignment for the benefit of creditors, or shall admit in writing its inability to pay its debts as they become due, or shall file a voluntary petition in bankruptcy, or shall be adjudicated as bankrupt or insolvent, or shall file any petition or answer seeking for itself any reorganization, arrangement, composition, readjustment, liquidation, dissolution, or similar relief under any present or future statute, law or regulation pertinent to such circumstances, or shall file any answer admitting or not contesting the material allegations of a petition filed against the Company in any such proceedings, or shall seek or consent to or acquiesce in the appointment of any trustee, receiver, or liquidator of the Company or of all or any substantial part of the properties of the Company; or the Company or its directors or majority shareholders shall take any action initiating the dissolution or liquidation of the Company;

5. Sixty (60) days shall have expired after the commencement of an action against the Company seeking reorganization, arrangement, composition, readjustment, liquidation, dissolution or similar relief under any present or future statute, law, or regulation without such action being dismissed or all orders or proceedings thereunder affecting the operations or the business of the Company being stayed; or a stay of any such order or proceedings shall thereafter be set aside and the action setting it aside shall not be timely appealed;

6. Sixty (60) days shall have expired after the appointment, without the consent or acquiescence of the Company, of any Trustee, receiver, or liquidator of the Company, or of all or

347

any substantial part of the properties of the Company without such appointment being vacated;

7. The Company shall be declared in default under an agreement in regard to the debts described in paragraph VI.E above;

8. Any guarantor or undersigned shareholder of the Company shall fail to comply with the terms of his undertakings to Holders;

B. No course of dealing between a Holder and any other party hereto or any failure or delay on the part of the Holder in exercising any rights or remedies hereunder shall operate as a waiver of any rights or remedies of any Holder under this or any other applicable instrument. No single or partial exercise of any rights or remedies hereunder shall operate as a waiver or preclude the exercise of any other rights or remedies hereunder;

C. Upon the nonpayment of the indebtedness under the Note or any part thereof when due, whether by acceleration or otherwise, a Note Holder is empowered to sell, assign, and deliver the whole or any part of the collateral for the Note at public or private sale, without demand, advertisement, or notice of the time or place of sale or of any adjournment thereof, which are hereby expressly waived. After deducting all expenses incidental to or arising from such sale or sales, Holder may apply the residue of the proceeds thereof to the payment of the indebtednesses, under the Notes, subject to the terms of paragraph XIII below, returning the excess, if any, to the Company. The Company hereby waives all right of appraisement, whether before or after the sale, and any right of redemption after sale. The Company shall have the right to redeem any collateral up to time of a foreclosure sale by paying the aggregate indebtedness under the Notes;

D. Holders are further empowered to collect or cause to be collected or otherwise to be converted into money all or any part of the collateral, by suit or otherwise, and to surrender, compromise, release, renew, extend, exchange, or substitute any item of the collateral in transactions with the Company or any third party, irrespective of any assignment thereof by the Company, and without prior notice to or consent of the Company or any assignee. Whenever any item of the collateral shall not be paid when due, or any part thereof has become due, Holders shall have the same rights and powers with respect to such items of the collateral as are granted in respect thereof in this paragraph in case of nonpayment of the indebtedness, or any part thereof, when due. None of the rights, remedies, privileges, or powers of the Holders expressly provided for herein shall be exclusive, but each of them shall be cumulative with and in addition to every other right, remedy, privilege, and power now or hereafter existing in favor of the Holders, whether at law or in equity, by statute or otherwise;

E.   The Company shall pay all expenses of any nature, whether incurred in or out of court, and whether incurred before or after the Notes shall become due at their maturity date or otherwise (including but not limited to reasonable attorneys' fees and costs), which Holders may deem necessary or proper in connection with the satisfaction of the indebtedness under the Notes or the administration, supervision, preservation, protection of (including, but not limited to, the maintenance of adequate insurance), or the realization upon the collateral.   Holders are authorized to pay at any time and from time to time any or all of such expenses, add the amount of such payment to the amount of principal outstanding, and charge interest thereon at the rate specified in the Notes;

F.   The security interest of the Holders and their assigns shall not be impaired by a Holder's sale, hypothecation, or rehypothecation of a Warrant or Note or any item of the collateral, or by any indulgence, including, but not limited to:

1.   Any renewal, extension, or modification which a Holder may grant with respect to the indebtedness of any part thereof, or,
2.   Any surrender, compromise, release, renewal, extension, exchange, or substitution which a Holder may grant in respect of the collateral or,
3.   Any indulgence granted in respect of any endorser, guarantor, or surety.   The purchaser, assignee, transferee, or pledgee of the Warrants, Notes, collateral, any guaranty, or any other document (or any of them), sold, assigned, transferred, pledged, or repledged, shall forthwith become vested with and entitled to exercise all powers and rights given by this Agreement to Holders, as if said purchaser, assignee, transferee, or pledgee were originally named in this Agreement in place of the Holders.

XIII.   Notice

All notices or communications under this Agreement of the Warrants or Notes shall be mailed, postage prepaid, or delivered as follows:

To Venture: 1666 K Street, N.W., Suite 901
                    Washington, D.C. 20006

To Company: Ace Electromagnetic, Incorporated
1234 Main Street
McLean, Virginia 22102

or, to such other address as shall at any time be designated by any party in writing to the other parties.

XIV. Entire Agreement

The Warrants, the Note, and this Agreement and the documents mentioned herein set forth the entire agreements and understandings of the parties hereto in respect of this transaction. Any prior agreements are hereby terminated. The terms herein may not be changed verbally but only by an instrument in writing signed by the party against which enforcement of the change is sought.

XV. Controlling Law

This Agreement shall be construed in accordance with and governed by the laws of the District of Columbia.

XVI. Headings

The headings of the paragraphs and subparagraphs of this Agreement and the Warrants and Note are inserted for convenience only and shall not be deemed to constitute a part of this Agreement or the Warrants and Note.

IN WITNESS WHEREOF, the undersigned hereby affix their hands and seals on the year and day first above written.

ACE ELECTROMAGNETIC, VENTURE CAPITAL
INC.   CORPORATION

By: _____   By: _____
    O.K. Entrepreneur   A. Venture Capitalist
    President   President

Attest: _____   Attest: _____
    John Smith, Secretary   Joe Smith
                            Assistant Secretary

Agreed Personally:

_____   _____
Mr. O.K. Entrepreneur   Mrs. O.K. Entrepreneur

Promissory Note

$300,000   Washington, D.C.
                                                                DATE

FOR VALUE RECEIVED the undersigned Ace Electromagnetic, Incorporated, a Virginia corporation (hereinafter "Company"), promises to pay to the order of Venture Capital Corporation, a District of Columbia corporation (hereinafter "Holder"), the principal sum of three hundred thousand dollars ($300,000) together with interest as set out herein at its offices in the District of Columbia or such other place as Holder may designate in writing.

Interest: From date of advance and thereafter until repayment, interest shall accrue hereunder at the rate of fifteen percent (15%) per annum.

Payments: Payments shall be due on the first day of each month after the date of this Note. Through the first thirty-six full calendar months after the date hereof, payments shall be for interest only ($3,750). Thereafter until maturity payments shall be $10,399.60.

Maturity: The entire indebtedness hereunder shall become due and payable in full six (6) years after the date the first payment is due.

Prepayment: Payment of any installment of principal or interest may be made prior to the maturity date thereof without penalty. Such prepayments shall be applied against the outstanding principal in inverse order of maturity.

Default and Acceleration:

A. In any of the below-listed events occur prior to maturity hereof, then a default may be declared at the option of the holder without presentment, demand, protest, or further notice of any kind (all of which are hereby expressly waived). In such event the Holder shall be entitled to be paid in full the balance of any unpaid principal amount plus accrued interest and any costs including reasonable attorney's fees, and to any other remedies which may be available herein in the Loan Agreement or under any applicable law:

351

1. Failure to pay any part of the indebtedness hereof when due;
2. Occurrence of any default as provided under the Loan Agreement pertaining hereto.

B. No course of dealing between the Holder and any other party hereto or any failure or delay on the part of the Payee in exercising any rights or remedies hereunder shall operate as a waiver of any rights or remedies of the Holder under this or any other applicable instrument. No single or partial exercise of any rights or remedies hereunder shall operate as a waiver or preclude the exercise of any other rights or remedies hereunder.

C. Upon the nonpayment of the indebtedness, or any part thereof, when due, whether by acceleration or otherwise, Payee is empowered to sell, assign, and deliver the whole or any part of the collateral at public or private sale, without demand, advertisement or notice of the time or place of sale or of any adjournment thereof, which are hereby expressly waived. After deducting all expenses incidental to or arising from such sale or sales, Holder shall apply the residue of the proceeds thereof to the payment of the indebtedness, as it shall deem proper, returning the excess, if any, to the Company. The Company hereby waives all right of appraisement, whether before or after sale, and any right of redemption after sale. The Company shall have the right to redeem any collateral up to time of a foreclosure sale by paying the aggregate indebtedness.

D. Holder is further empowered to collect or cause to be collected or otherwise be converted into money all or any part of the collateral, by suit or otherwise, and to surrender, compromise, release, renew, extend, exchange, or substitute any item of the collateral in transactions with the Company or any third party, irrespective of any assignment thereof by the Company, and without prior notice to or any consent of the Company or any assignee. Whenever any item of the collateral shall not be paid when due, or otherwise shall be in default, whether or not the indebtedness, or any part thereof, has become due, Holder shall have the same rights and powers with respect to such item of the collateral as are granted in respect thereof in this paragraph in case of nonpayment of the indebtedness, or any part thereof, when due. None of the rights, remedies, privileges, or powers of the Company expressly provided for herein shall be exclusive, but each of them shall be cumulative with and in addition to every other right, remedy, privilege, and power now or hereafter existing in favor of Holder, whether at law or in equity, by statute or otherwise.

E.   The Company will take all necessary steps to administer, supervise, preserve, and protect the collateral; and regardless of any action taken by Holder, there shall be no duty upon Holder in this respect. The Company shall pay all expenses of any nature, whether incurred in or out of court, and whether incurred before or after this Note shall become due at its maturity date or otherwise (including but not limited to reasonable attorneys' fees and costs) which Holder may deem necessary or proper in connection with the satisfaction of the indebtedness or the administration, supervision, preservation, protection of (including, but not limited to, the maintenance of adequate insurance), or the realization upon the collateral. Holder is authorized to pay at any time and from time to time any or all of such expenses, add the amount of such payment to the amount of principal outstanding and charge interest thereon at the rate specified herein.

F.   The security rights of Holder and its assigns shall not be impaired by Holder's sale, hypothecation, or rehypothecation of this Note or any item of the collateral, or by any indulgence, including, but not limited to:

1.   Any renewal, extension or modification which Holder may grant with respect to the indebtedness of any part thereof, or
2.   Any surrender, compromise, release, renewal, extension, exchange, or substitution which holder may grant in respect of the collateral, or
3.   Any indulgence granted in respect to any endorser, guarantor, or surety. The purchaser, assignee, transferree, or pledgee of this Note, the collateral, any guaranty, and any other document (or any of them), sold, assigned, transferred, pledged, or repledged, shall forthwith become vested with and entitled to exercise all the powers and rights given by this Note as if said purchaser, assignee, transferee, or pledgee were originally named as Holder in this Note.

Definitions: The term *indebtedness* as used herein shall mean the indebtedness evidenced by this note, including principal, interest, and expenses, whether contingent, now due, or hereafter to become due, and whether heretofore or contemporaneously herewith or hereafter contracted. The term *collateral* as used in this Note shall mean any funds, guarantees, or other property or rights therein of any nature whatsoever of the proceeds thereof which may have been, are or hereafter may be hypothecated directly or indirectly by the undersigned or others in connection with, or as security for the indebtedness or any part thereof. The collateral and each part thereof shall secure the indebtedness and each part thereof.

IN WITNESS WHEREOF, the undersigned has caused this Note to be executed and its seal affixed on the day and year first written above.

Seal: ACE ELECTROMAGNETIC, INCORPORATED

Attest:_____   BY:_____
          John Smith   O.K. Entrepreneur
          Secretary   President

LEGAL DOCUMENT 3
ACE ELECTROMAGNETIC, INCORPORATED
MCLEAN, VIRGINIA

Stock Purchase Warrants

DATE

I. Grant

Ace Electromagnetic, Incorporated, a Virginia corporation (hereinafter "Company") for value received hereby grants to Venture Capital Corporation, a District of Columbia corporation, or its registered assigns (hereinafter "Holder") under the terms herein the right to purchase that number of the fully paid and nonassessable shares of the Company's common stock such that upon exercise and issuance of stock hereunder the Holder will hold thirty-five percent (35%) of the outstanding common stock of the Company. On the present date such number is 1,724 shares.

II. Expiration

The right to exercise this Warrant shall expire then (10) years from the date hereof.

III. Exercise Price

The exercise price of this Warrant shall be one hundred dollars ($100.00).

IV. Effect of Redemption

Regardless of the above provision, if the Company shall redeem or otherwise purchase for value any of its shares of common stock prior to issuance of shares under this Warrant, the Holder shall be entitled to receive hereunder the same number of shares it could have received had the redemptions or purchases for value not occurred.

V. Exercise Procedure

This Warrant may be exercised by presenting it and tendering the purchase price in tender or by bank cashier's or certified check at the principal office of the Company along with written subscription substantially in the form of Exhibit I hereof;

The date on which this Warrant is thus surrendered, accompanied by tender or payment as hereinbefore or hereinafter provided, is referred to herein as the Exercise Date. The Company shall forthwith at its expense (including the payment of issue taxes) issue and deliver the proper number of shares, and such shares shall be deemed issued for all purposes as of the opening of business on the Exercise Date notwithstanding any delay in the actual issuance;

VI. Sale or Exchange of Company or Assets

If prior to issuance of stock under this Warrant the Company sells or exchanges all or substantially all of its assets, or the shares of common stock of the Company are sold or exchanged to any party other than the Holder, then the Holder at its option may receive, in lieu of the stock otherwise issuable hereunder, such money or property it would have been entitled to receive if this Warrant had been exercised prior to such sale or exchange.

VII. Sale of Warrant or Shares

Neither this Warrant nor their shares of common stock issuable upon exercise of the conversion rights herein, have been registered under the *Securities Act of 1933* as amended, or under the securities laws of any state. Neither this Warrant nor any shares when issued may be sold, transferred, pledged, or hypothecated in the absence of (i) an effective registration statement for this Warrant or the shares, as the case may be, under the *Securities Act of 1933* as amended and such registration or qualification as may be necessary under the securities laws of any state, or (ii) an opinion of counsel reasonably satisfactory to the Company that such registration or qualification is not required. The Company shall cause a certificate or certificates evidencing all or any of the shares issued upon exercise of the conversion rights herein prior to said registration and qualification of such shares to bear the following legend: "The shares evidenced by this certificate have not been registered under the *Securities Act of 1933* as amended, or under the securities laws of any state. The shares may not be sold, transferred, pledged, or hypothecated in the absence of an effective registration statement under the *Securities Act of 1933*, as amended, and such registration or qualification as may be necessary under the securities laws of any state, or an option of counsel satisfactory to the Company that such registration or qualification is not required."

VIII. Transfer

This Warrant shall be registered on the books of the Company, which shall be kept at its principal office for that purpose, and shall be transferable only on such books by the Holder in person or by a duly authorized attorney with written notice substantially in the form of Exhibit II hereof, and only in compliance with the preceding paragraph.   The Company may issue appropriate stop orders to its transfer agent to prevent a transfer in violation of the preceding paragraph.

IX. Replacement of Warrant

At the request of the Holder and on production of evidence reasonably satisfactory to the Company of the loss, theft, destruction, or mutilation of this Warrant and (in the case of loss, theft, or destruction) if required by the Company, upon delivery of an indemnity agreement with surety in such reasonable amount as the Company may determine thereof, the Company at its expense will issue in lieu thereof a new Warrant of like tenor.

X. Loan Agreement

This Warrant is subject to the terms of a Loan agreement dated today between the Company and the Holder, a copy of which is on file and may be examined at the principal office of the Company in Mclean, Virginia, during regular business hours.

XI. Unlocking

The Holder or its registered assigns shall have certain unlocking rights as set out in the Loan Agreement above-mentioned.

XII. "Put" Rights

Beginning five (5) years from today and ending ten (10) years from today, the Holder may by written demand require the company to purchase this Warrant or the shares of stock issued hereunder at a price of thirty-five percent (35%) of the higher of the following prices:

(a)   Ten percent (10%) of the Company's sales for the fiscal year immediately preceding the year of the demand times a price earnings of eight, less the aggregate principal balance of the Note on the day of demand; or

(b) Ten times the Company's cash flow for the fiscal year immediately preceding the year of the demand, less the aggregate principal balance of Note on the day of demand.

XIII. Registration

If the Company shall at any time prepare and file a registration statement under the *Securities Act of 1933* with respect to the public offering of any class of equity or debt security of the Company, the Company shall give thirty (30) days prior written notice thereof to Holder, and shall, upon the written request of Holder include in the registration statement or related notification such number of Holder's shares as Holder may request to be sold on a one-time basis; the Company will keep such notification or registration statement and prospectus effective and current under the Act permitting the sale of Holder's shares covered thereby to be sold on a time-to-time basis or otherwise; such inclusion, in any event, shall be at no cost to Holder and shall be at the sole cost and expense of the Company; in the event the Company fails to receive a written request from Holder with thirty (30) days after the mailing of its written notice, then the Company shall treat such failure with the same force and effect as if Holder's failure to respond constituted notice to the Company that Holder does not intend to include its shares in such registration statement or notification; the foregoing shall not apply to a registration statement relating to securities of the Company covered by an employee, stock option, or other benefit plan; in connection with any notification or registration statement or subsequent amendment to any such notification or registration statement or similar document filed pursuant hereto, the Company shall take any reasonable steps to make the securities covered thereby eligible for public offering and sale by the effective date of such notification or registration statement or any amendment to any of the foregoing under the securities or blue sky laws of Virginia and the District of Columbia; provided that in no event shall the Company be obligated to qualify to do business in any state where it is not so qualified at the time of filing such documents or to take any action which would subject it to unlimited service of process in any state where it is not so subject at such time; the Company shall keep such filing current for the length of time it must keep any notification, registration statement, posteffective amendment, prospectus, or offering circular and any amendment to any of the foregoing effective pursuant hereto; in connection with any filing hereunder the Company shall bear all the expenses and professional fees which arise in connection with such filings and all expenses incurred in making such filings and keeping them effective and correct as provided hereunder and shall also provide holder with a reasonable number of printed copies of the prospectus, offering circulars and/or supplemental prospectuses or amended prospectuses in final and preliminary form; the Company consents to the use of such prospectus or offering circular in connection with the sale of Holder's shares; in the event of the filing of any registration statement or notification pursuant to this Agreement or document referred to herein which includes Holder's shares, Holder shall indemnify the Company and each of its officers and directors who has signed said registration statement, each person, if any, who controls the Company within the meaning of the *Securities Act*, each underwriter for the Company and each person, if any, who controls such underwriter within the meaning of the *Securities Act*, from any loss, claim, damage, liability, or action arising out of or based upon any untrue statement or any omission to state therein a material fact required to be stated therein in writing by Holder expressly for use in such registration statement or required to be furnished by Holder.

XIV. Covenants of the Company

The Company covenants that until this Warrant is exercised or expires, it will:

(a) Reserve authorized but unissued 1,724 shares of its common stock or such additional number of such shares as necessary to satisfy the rights of the Holder;

(b) Not pay any dividends in cash or in kind unless written authorization is received in writing from the Holder;

(c) Furnish to the Holder consolidated financial statements of the Company, which statements shall include and be rendered as follows:

(1) Monthly year-to-date financial statements within forty-five (45) days after the close of the last previous month, which statements shall include a balance sheet and a statement of profit and loss for the period in question, and

(2) If requested in writing by Holder, within sixty (60) days after the close of each fiscal year a balance sheet and a profit-and-loss statement of Company relating to such year, certified by a firm of independent public accountants of recognized standing in McLean, Virginia, and approved by the Holder, accompanied by any report or comment of said accountants made in connection with such financial statements, and with a copy of all other financial statements prepared for or furnished to the Company.

(d) The President of the Company shall certify on each statement furnished to the Holder that no default exists hereunder, or, in the event a default does exist, the President shall submit his statement of such default.

(e) Maintain an office in the McLean, Virginia, area, at which its books and records will be kept and notices, presentations, demands, and payments relating to this Warrant, the Note, and the Loan Agreement may be given or made;

(f) Maintain books of account in accordance with generally accepted accounting principles;

(g) Permit the Holder through its designated representative to visit and inspect any of the properties of the Company, to examine its books and records, and to discuss its affairs, finances, and accounts with and be advised as to the same by the officers of the company at such reasonable times and intervals.

XV. Investment Covenant

The Holder by its acceptance hereby covenants that this Warrant is, and the stock to be acquired upon the exercise of this Warrant will be, acquired for investment purposes, and that the Holder will not distribute the same in violation of any state or federal law or regulation.

XVI. Law Governing

The Holder by its acceptance hereby covenants that this Warrant is, and the stock to be acquired upon the exercise of this Warrant will be, acquired for investment purposes, and that the Holder will not distribute the same in violation of any state or federal law or regulation.

XVII. Laws Governing

This Warrant shall be construed according to the laws of the District of Columbia.

IN WITNESS WHEREOF, Ace Electromagnetic, Incorporated, has caused this Warrant to be signed on its behalf, in its corporate name, by its President, and its corporate seal to be hereunto affixed and the said seal to be attested by its Secretary, as of this 31st day of January, 1988.

Seal: ACE ELECTROMAGNETIC,
                              INCORPORATED

                              By:_____
                                    O.K. Entrepreneur,
                                    President

Attest:

_____
John Smith, Secretary

LEGAL DOCUMENT 4

Ajax Computer Genetics Corporation
123 Main Street
McLean, Virginia 22102

DATE

Venture Capital Corporation
125 Main Street
Washington, D.C. 20006

Dear Sirs:

Stock Purchase Agreement

You have informed us that, subject to certain conditions, you are prepared to subscribe for and purchase, at a price of Ten Dollars ($10.00) per share, two hundred fifty thousand (250,000) shares (the "Shares") of our authorized but unissued Common Stock, One Dollar ($1.00) par value (the "Stock"). In this connection, we hereby confirm our agreement with you as follows:

    1. *Representations and Warranties.* ("Ajax" or "we") is a corporation duly organized and validly existing in good standing under the laws of the District of Columbia and is duly qualified to transact business as a foreign corporation under the laws of Florida and California, the only jurisdictions in which the nature of the business currently transacted by us requires such qualification.

    1.1 The authorized capital stock of Ajax consists of 2,000,000 shares of the Stock, all of one class, of which there are outstanding on the date hereof 972,515 shares and 27,800 shares are reserved for issuance pursuant to options held by key employees of Ajax and subsidiaries. Other than these shares there are no shares to be issued except (1) those reserved for stock options, and (2) the shares being purchased by you.

    1.2 Ajax has no subsidiaries, nor does it intend to establish any subsidiaries.

    1.3 There have been furnished to you the consolidated financial statements of Ajax as of and for the prior two years. These financial statements are complete and correct and present fairly the consolidated financial condition of Ajax and the consolidated results of their operations as of the dates thereof and for the period covered thereby. Such financial statements have been prepared in accordance with generally accepted accounting principles applied on a consistent basis throughout the periods involved, subject to any comments and notes therein. Since this date there

362

has not occurred any material adverse change in the consolidated financial position or results of operations of Ajax, nor any change not in the ordinary course of business.

1.4 There are no actions, suits, or proceedings pending nor, to Ajax's knowledge, threatened, before any court, agency, or other body which involves Ajax, wherein Ajax is a defendant.

1.5 This agreement and the issuance and sale of the Shares pursuant hereto have been duly authorized by appropriate and all required corporate action; such issuance and sale and Ajax's compliance with the terms hereof will not violate Ajax's articles of incorporation, bylaws, any indenture or contract to which Ajax is a party or by which it is bound, or any statute, rule, regulation, or order of any court of agency applicable to Ajax; and the Shares when issued and sold as provided herein will have been duly and validly authorized and issued, fully paid and nonassessable.

2. *Covenants.* We covenant and agree with you that:

2.1 Prior to your purchase of the Shares, we shall provide to you, your agents, and attorney access to the same kind of information as is specified in Schedule A of the Securities Act of 1933 (the "1933 Act"), and shall make available to you during the course of this transaction the opportunity to ask questions of, and receive answers from, ourselves and our officers necessary to your satisfaction to verify the accuracy of such information.

2.2 For a period of at least two years following the Closing Date, we will not apply more than twenty percent (20%) of the proceeds from the sale of the Shares to the business of any new products without the concurrence of all members of our Board of Directors who have been nominated by you pursuant to Section 2.3 or elected thereto pursuant to Section 5.4.

2.3 As long as you and your affiliates own combined a total of at least ten percent (10%) of the outstanding voting securities of Ajax, you and your affiliates together shall be entitled to nominate a total of two (2) persons for election as members of our Board of Directors and, if they are so nominated and legally qualify to serve in that capacity, our Board of Directors will support their election.

2.4 (a) If, at any time while you or your affiliates (collectively "you") hold any of the Shares, we shall decide to register with the SEC any issue of Stock (other than a registration of shares solely for the purpose of any plan for the acquisition thereof by our employees or for the purpose of a merger or acquisition), we will give you written notice of such decision at least twenty (20) days prior to the filing of a registration statement and will afford you upon your request the opportunity of having any Shares then held by you included in the registration if the request is made within ten (10) days after receiving such notice, to the extent and under the conditions upon which such registration is permissible under the 1933 Act and the Rules and Regulations of the Securities and Exchange Commission; provided, however, that we may exclude such Shares from a registration statement filed by us to the extent that, in the opinion of the managing underwriter of the issue being registered, the inclusion of such of the Shares or of more than a designated portion thereof would be detrimental to the public offering pursuant to such registration, and to the further extent that such exclusion is made applicable to sales by all holders of outstanding Stock, pro rata in proportion to their holdings. In the event in any registration we offer you the opportunity to sell such of the Shares which you propose to register to underwriters on a "firm commitment" basis (as opposed to a "best efforts" basis), you shall, as a condition of your participation in the registration, accept an offer to sell such of the Shares to the underwriters if the managing underwriter so requires or, in the alternative, agree not to sell such of the Shares pursuant to such registration within such reasonable period (not exceeding 120 days) as may be specified by the managing underwriter to enable those underwriters to complete their distributions; and in any event, shall enter into an agreement with us and such underwriter containing conventional representations, warranties, and indemnity provisions. You will comply with such other reasonable requirements as may be imposed by the managing underwriter to effect the offering and an orderly distribution of the shares, including your acceptance of the same offering price as shall be accepted by us for the Stock being sold by us pursuant to such registration statement. All expenses of such registration applicable to Shares offered by you shall be payable by us, to the extent permitted by Securities and Exchange Commission rules or policy, except for your pro rata share of the underwriters' discounts and commissions.

(b) Our obligation to accord you the right to register Shares pursuant to paragraph (a) shall apply to each and every registration which may be effected by us following your purchase of the shares, except if at the time you shall otherwise by, both as to time and amount, free to sell all the Shares held by you. Without limitation, for the purpose of this paragraph (b), you shall be considered to be free, both as to time and amount, to sell all the Shares held by you if all such Shares may be sold within a period of ninety (90) days pursuant to Rule 144 promulgated under the 1933 Act.

(c) In the event that any registration statement relating to any Shares shall be filed and become effective pursuant to any of the foregoing provisions of this Section 2.4, then at any time while a prospectus relating to such of the Shares is required to be delivered under the 1933 act, but not later than nine (9) months after the effective date of such registration statement, we will, at your request, prepare and furnish to you a reasonable number of copies of such prospectus and of such registration statements as may be necessary so that, as thereafter delivered to purchasers of any of the Shares, such prospectus shall comply with Section 10 of the 1933 Act.

(d) In the event that any registration statement relating to any Shares shall be filed pursuant to this Section 2.4, we will use our best efforts to qualify such of the Shares for sale under the laws of such jurisdiction within the continental United States as you may reasonably request and will comply to the best of our ability with such laws so as to permit the continuance of sales of and dealings in such of the Shares thereunder. The filing fees with respect to such jurisdictions requested by you shall be payable to you. We shall not, however, be obligated to qualify as a foreign corporation or file any general consent to service or process under the laws of any such jurisdiction or subject ourselves to taxation as doing business in any such jurisdiction or qualify under the securities laws of any jurisdictions which we reasonably deem unduly burdensome.

2.5 If the sale and purchase of the Shares shall be consummated, we will pay the reasonable fees and disbursements of your special counsel in connection with this agreement and the transaction contemplated herein and, in addition, will pay to you, a fee of twenty thousand dollars ($20,000.00) for services in connection herewith.

2.6 We shall indemnify you and any of your affiliates against any claim for any fees or commissions by any broker, finder, or other person for services or alleged services in connection herewith or the transaction contemplated hereby.

3. *Representations and Agreements of Investors.* By accepting this agreement you confirm to us that:

3.1 You and your officers have such knowledge and experience in financial and business matters that you and they are capable of evaluating the merits and risks of your investment in the Shares.

3.2 You represent that you will acquire the Shares for investment and without any present intention of distributing or otherwise reselling any of them.

3.3 You understand that the Shares will be "restricted securities" as that term is defined in the Rules and Regulations of the SEC under the 1933 Act and accordingly may not be reoffered or resold by you unless they are registered under the Act or unless an exemption from such registration is available, and you consent that any certificates for the Shares may be legended accordingly.

3.4 You represent that you have no knowledge of any fees or commissions due in this transaction, except those fees set forth in 2.5 above and any fee that may be due and payable to John Brown Brokers.

4. *Closing*. Subject to the terms and conditions hereof, the purchase and sale of the Shares shall take place at our office in Washington, D.C., on February 15, 1983, at 11:00 A.M. (the "Closing Date") by our delivery to you of a certificate or certificates for the Shares, registered in your name, and your payment to use of the purchase price therefore by wire transfer to our account with The First National Bank.

5. *Conditions*. Your obligation to take up and pay for the Shares on the Closing Date shall be subject to the following conditions:

5.1 Our representations and warrantees herein shall be true on and as of the Closing Date as though made on such date; we shall have performed all of our covenants and agreements herein required to be performed on or before the Closing Date; and we shall have delivered to you a certificate to such effects, dated the Closing Date and executed by our President or Executive Vice-president.

5.2 There shall have been delivered to you a letter dated the Closing Date, from our accountants to the effect that, (i) nothing has come to their attention which would require them to withdraw or modify their report dated January 15, 1983, on your consolidated financial statements as of and for the two prior years. And (ii) they have performed a review of the interim consolidated financial statement of Ajax as of and for the month ended in accordance with the standards established by the American Institute of Certified Public Accountants. Such a review of the interim financial statements consists principally of obtaining an understanding of the system for the preparation of interim financial statements, applying analytical review procedures to financial data, and making inquiries of persons in accordance with generally accepted auditing standards, the objective of which is the expression of an opinion regarding the financial statements taken as a whole. Accordingly, no such opinion is expressed.

5.3 There shall have been delivered to you a favorable opinion, dated the Closing Date, of our general counsel, John Paul, Esquire, as to the questions of law involved in Section 1.1 through 1.4 and 1.5 and covering such other questions of law as you or your special counsel may reasonably request.

5.4 There shall have been elected as a member of our Board of Directors, subject to the purchase and sale of the Shares, your President, Mr. A. V. Capitalist.

5.5 The certificates, accountants' letter, and legal opinion delivered on the Closing Date shall be deemed to fulfill the conditions hereof only if they are to your reasonable satisfaction and to that of Mr. M. S. Smith, your special counsel for the purpose of this transaction.

6. *Miscellaneous*.

6.1 All notices required or permitted by this agreement shall be in writing addressed, if to us, at our address appearing at the head of this letter and, if to you, as this letter is addressed. Either party may, however, request communications or copies thereof to be sent to a different address and you may direct us to pay any dividends on the Shares to a bank in the United States for your account.

6.2 All representations, warranties, and covenants made by all the parties herein shall survive the delivery of and the payment for the Shares.

6.3 This agreement shall be binding upon and inure to the benefit of the parties hereto and their respective successors and assigns.

6.4 This agreement shall be construed in accordance with, and the rights and obligations of the parties hereto shall be governed by, the laws of the District of Columbia, U.S.A.

6.5 This agreement supersedes any prior agreement, written or oral, between the parties hereto or their affiliates regarding the subject matter hereof.

6.6 In the event the closing described in section 4 hereof has not taken place in one year from closing this Agreement shall terminate unless the parties agree in writing to further extend the same. In the event of termination, all rights, duties and obligations of each of the parties shall cease and terminate, and this Agreement shall be considered cancelled and of no effect or validity thereafter.

If the foregoing accords with your understanding of our agreement, please sign and return to us the enclosed copy of this letter.

AJAX COMPUTER GENETICS CORPORATION

By:_____
    O.K. Entrepreneur, President

ACCEPTED: VENTURE CAPITAL CORPORATION

By:_____
    A. V. Capitalist, President

LEGAL DOCUMENT 5
SCHEDULE A: EXHIBITS TO
STOCK PURCHASE AGREEMENT

1. Ajax (the "Company") is a Virginia corporation with its principal office at 123 Main Street, McLean, Virginia, 22102.

2. A. Exhibit 1A enclosed herewith is a copy of the Annual Report of Ajax for the fiscal year ending the past year, and included in said report under date of, is a copy of the Certified Audit of the Company made by its current accounting firm for the above fiscal year. Also, Exhibit 1B enclosed herewith is a copy of the preliminary unaudited Financial Statements of Ajax of the one month ended this month.
   B. A list of Officers and Directors of the Company and their addresses is enclosed as Exhibit 2 hereof.

3. O.K. Entrepreneur, the President of the Company, is the sole owner owning 10 percent or more of record and beneficially of stock of the Company.

4. As of this date, Mr. Entrepreneur owns of record and beneficially 200,000 shares of stock of the Company.

5. The Company is not a holding Company and has no subsidiary corporations.

6. Ajax has 2,000,000 authorized shares of stock, all common, with a par value of $1.00 per share and presently issued and outstanding there are 300,000 shares of stock. In addition thereto, there are options to purchase 100,000 shares of stock issued to and held by existing employees. The company has a stock option plan with 100,000 remaining unissued shares.

7. See Exhibit 3 pertaining to a list of Stock Options outstanding that have been granted to employees of the Company.

8. The Company intends to sell not less than 250,000 shares of stock in this private placement at an offering price of $10.00 per share. The Company may sell additional shares of stock to a secured venture capital firm at a price of not less than $10.000 per share, which transaction would take place in the near future if consummated.

9. Proceeds of the private placement will be used as follows; $1,000,000 in research and development, $1,000,000 in plant expansion, and $500,000 in salaries and working capital.

10. For the period just ending, the Company paid salaries, bonuses, and director's fees to O.K. Entrepreneur in the amount of $51,000.00. For the current fiscal year, Mr. Entrepreneur is being paid a base salary of $50,000.00.

11. The net book value per share of Ajax is $5.00 as of this month. The Company anticipates receiving the entire net proceeds, with the exception of commissions and legal expenses

that might be incurred under 12 below, derived from the sale of the securities being offered at $10.00 per share.

12. Commissions being paid for service rendered in the sale will be $20,000.00 to the Venture Capital Corporation.

13. The Company has:

A. Employment Contract with O.K. Entrepreneur entered into two years ago for a period of five years providing for annual compensation of not less than $50,000.00.

B. The other basic contracts that the Company has are for leases for office space where it maintains its offices in McLean, Virginia.

14. Enclosed herewith is Exhibit 4, a copy of the Articles of Incorporation together with all Amendments thereto of Ajax, and Exhibit 5, a copy of the existing Bylaws of the Company.

APPENDIX 3

LIST OF TRAITS FOR ANALYSIS OF PEOPLE

Use this list to crystallize your thinking about an entrepreneur. After you have gotten to know him, go through the list and circle the adjectives that best describe him. After you have been in the investment for two years, go back and select traits again. I'll bet they won't be the same.

Adjective	Definition
accomplishing	successful, bringing to completion
accurate	correct, clear-cut, beyond doubt
achieving	accomplishing, persevering, striving
active	energetic, lively, dynamic
adaptive	able to adjust, fits in, flexible
adventuresome	daring, willing to take chances
affiliative	associated, connected, a joiner
aggressive	forceful, assertive
ambitious	enterprising, striving, eager
apologetic	sorry, regretful, makes excuses
apprehensive	fearful, worried, afraid
approval-seeking	wanting acceptance and praise
carefree	free of worry or responsibilities
charitable	generous, kind, giving
comforting	soothing, relieved, consoling
competitive	seeking to win, ambitious, achieving
concerned	aware, caring, interested
conforming	compliant, obedient
conservative	moderate, prudent, cautious
consoling	offering solace, cheering up

creative	imaginative, inventive, innovative
cultured	refined, showing gentility, taste
defenseless	protective, shielded, careful
dependent	needing aid or assistance
distant	remote, inaccessible, removed
educated	knowledgeable, informed, cultured
egotistic	self-centered, individualistic
empathetic	aware of another, compassionate
energetic	inexhaustible, vigorous
envious	resentful, discontented, jealous
fun-loving	playful, carefree, spontaneous
goal-oriented	seeking success and achievement
good-natured	amicable, pleasant, happy
guarded	kept safe, protected, watched over
hard-working	eager, responsible, go-getter
help-seeking	looking for assistance or comfort
honest	truthful, respectable, sincere
hospitable	welcoming, warm, receptive
humble	reserved, self-conscious, modest
idealistic	daydreamer, imaginative, visionary
impatient	excitable, unable to wait
independent	self-reliant, autonomous
individualistic	one-of-a-kind, independent
innovative	creative, new, original
insecure	inadequate, unsure, shaky
intellectual	rational, smart, quick-witted
jealous	envious, vigilant, fearful
joking	witty, wisecracking, jesting
kind	gentle, considerate, warmhearted
knowledgeable	exhibiting knowledge or intelligence
law-abiding	tends to obey the law
leadership	has the capacity to lead
liberal	tolerant, generous, unrestrained
likeable	pleasant, enjoyable, attractive
loving	affectionate, devoted, caring
loyal	steadfast, faithful, devoted
meek	humble, submissive, patient
meticulous	extremely careful, scrupulous
neighborly	friendly, amicable, familiar
nurturing	nourishing, supporting, fostering
obedient	compliant, amenable, dutiful
open-minded	aware, unbiased, receptive
optimistic	hopeful, positive, enthusiastic
outgoing	sociable, friendly
passive	submissive, compliant, inactive
persistent	determined, persevering, stubborn

pessimistic	gloomy, negative, depressed
playful	impish, mischievous, frivolous
pleasure-seeking	seeking gratification or delight
precise	clearly defined, exact
protective	defended, guarded, careful
quick-thinking	bright, perceptive, alert
quiet	still, silent, not talkative
religious	pious, scrupulous, devout
reserved	restrained, self-controlled, shy
responsible	accountable, trustworthy
rigid	stiff, unchanging, inflexible
sarcastic	joking in a biting or cynical way
secretive	covert, underhanded, concealed
seeks attention	wanting to be noticed
seeks recognition	wanting to be praised
self-blaming	guilt, fault finding
sensitive	perceptive, touchy, nervous
serious	grave, earnest, weighty
silly	lacking good sense, frivolous
sincere	true, honest, natural
socially striving	seeking respectability
status-conscious	attentive to position and wealth
stealing	thieving, dishonest
striving	contending, exerting effort
suspicious	doubtful, distrustful, showing uncertainty
sympathetic	comforting, understanding
talkative	chatty, always speaking
tidy	neat, orderly, clean
trusting	confident, committed
truthful	honest, trustworthy
uncaring	lacking in warmth or sympathy
unconventional	unusual, not the norm, rebellious
virtuous	pure, moral, good
warm	friendly, sincere, cordial
wary	cautious, watchful, on guard
wise	profound, judicious, sensible, prudent
yielding	deferring, relenting, gives in

APPENDIX 4

EVALUATION OF AN ENTREPRENEUR BY AN INDUSTRIAL PSYCHOLOGIST

Name: O.K. Entrepreneur

By: Industrial Analysis, Inc.
Washington, D.C.

Summary and Recommendation

Mr. Entrepreneur possesses many outstanding qualities for a chief executive officer's position. He is intelligent and empathic and so will receive good feedback from subordinates. He is open and flexible enough to use that feedback in a constructive way, making use of the ideas and suggestions of people.

Further, he does possess reasonably strong persuasive motivation. Since the chief executive officer often is in a situation in which he must persuade, e.g., dealing with the Board, with unions, with department heads, et al., this ability to persuade to his point of view can be extremely valuable. Finally, on the plus side, Mr. Entrepreneur is extremely well-organized, and although he does not love detail, he is an individual capable of both planning and organizing his own work exceptionally well, and planning, organizing, coordinating, and following up on the work of others.

His only real drawbacks relate to his aloofness and his somewhat inconsistent assertiveness. As to the former, despite the fact that he has exceptionally good empathy and is able to understand people very well, he does tend to keep them at a distance. He is a bit cool and aloof, and so could be perceived as cold and uncaring despite his real understanding of his subordinates.

375

It is very important that he be made aware of this and that he work to warm up his relationships to convey the notion that he does understand people in order to do the most effective job. As to the latter, there are many occasions in which he can be strongly assertive, but there are other times when he may back down inappropriately and not push strongly enough for his point of view. He is not by any means unassertive, but more consistency here would help a great deal.

In short, Mr. Entrepreneur is definitely an individual who can handle a chief executive officer's responsibility for the firm. Some improvement in the two weaker areas discussed would allow him to perform on an exceptionally good level.

Ego-drive

His ego-drive is moderately strong. He does have, to some extent, the inner personal need to persuade others. He is somewhat challenged when he convinces other people, since he does enjoy the conquest of others both for its financial rewards and for his own sense of achievement. However, persuading others does not gratify him in the same personal way it would if his ego-drive were more intense.

> Note: Ego-drive is the *inner need to persuade* another individual as a means of gaining personal gratification. The ego-driven individual wants and needs the successful persuasion as a powerful enhancement of her or his ego. His/her self-esteem is enhanced by successfully persuading another, and diminished when he/she fails to persuade. Ego-drive is *not ambition*, aggression, energy, or even the willingness to work hard. The ego-driven individual wants and needs to persuade not primarily for the practical benefits that might be gained, i.e., money, promotion, or other rewards, but, more importantly, for the feeling of satisfaction that comes from the victory. Successful persuasion, then, is the particular means through which the ego-driven individual gains pleasure and ego-gratification.

Empathy

His empathy is above average. He has good ability to relate effectively to others, accurately sensing their ideas and reactions. He is able to objectively understand the other person's point of view and use this knowledge to good advantage. He is thereby able to make adjustments in his own behavior in order to deal most appropriately with the other person.

This good empathy gives him the ability to deal sensitively with others, and so develop good relationships with them.

> Note: Empathy is the ability to accurately sense the reactions of another person. Empathy is the capacity to recognize the clues and cues provided by others in order to relate effectively to them. Empathy is *not sympathy*. Sympathy involves overidentifying with another person, thereby losing sight of one's own objectives. Sympathy can block the ability to deal effectively with others. The individual with empathy is able to *accurately* and *objectively perceive* the other person's feelings without necessarily agreeing with them. This invaluable, *indispensable ability* to get powerful feedback enables the individual to appropriately adjust his/her own behavior in order to deal effectively with others.

Growth

His empathy provides the key to his ability to learn and adapt to new situations. He is quite intelligent, and this, linked with his empathy, enables him to grow steadily in the understanding and performance of his job. He is an open, flexible human being who is not only capable of learning and growing, but welcomes challenges and adapts readily to new methods and ideas.

Thus, his potential for growth personally and on the job is excellent both in terms of his motivation for growth and his ability to achieve growth.

> Note: The ability to learn and grow requires considerably more than the possession of good intelligence. It needs the combination of native intelligence with sufficient empathy and flexibility to permit an individual to use her/his intelligence to acquire new ideas and formulate new methods. In many cases, even people with well above average intelligence lack the capacity to grow because they use their intelligence to rigidly defend and justify their preconceptions rather than to genuinely seek or accept new approaches. On the other hand, many individuals with only average *intelligence* have the potential for growth because their *openness, flexibility*, and *empathy* permit them to make full use of the abilities they do have to acquire new knowledge and skills. Thus, for an individual to have good growth potential, she/he should combine native intelligence with the openness and flexibility to seek and acquire new ideas and integrate and utilize them in day-to-day life and work.

Leadership

This man's leadership ability is reasonably good. He has some ability to assert himself, and is capable of exhibiting real strength on some occasions. However, he does not have the consistent overall assertiveness possessed by most strong leaders, and so might tend to vacillate in a leadership role.

His empathy, intelligence, overall flexibility and genuine interest in people will most often allow him to lead effectively. Some improvement in his assertiveness, in his willingness to act strongly and decisively, combined with the important assets he does possess, would give him all the attributes of a good leader.

> Note: Leadership is the ability that enables an individual to get other people to do willingly what they have the ability to do but might not spontaneously do on their own. Leadership implies that an individual has a special effect on others which commands their respect, admiration, or affection, and causes them to follow that individual. In other words, leadership consists of getting a positive response from others and utilizing that response to bring about a desired attitude or course of action. This implies a certain amount of assertiveness in the sense that the leader projects some part of his/her personality or will on others. It does *not* mean aggression, force, or coercion. Whether the leader influences by *personal* example, persuasion, or empathic feedback, he/she wins others over the influencing their *willingness* to act rather than by forcing their compliance. The good leader strives to become aware of the abilities of subordinates or associates, so as to guide them only toward goals that they realistically are capable of attaining.

Decision Making

His leadership capacity is further enhanced by his ability to balance a strong sense of responsibility with enough impulsiveness to permit him to make decisions on his own. He is willing to risk the possibility of occasionally being wrong by acting quickly and positively when necessary. He is not likely to be wrong too often since he has sound judgment and the ability to sense how his decisions will affect others.

Further, he possesses the intelligence and flexibility to learn from any mistakes he might make and adjust his future behavior. Rarely will he make the same mistake a second time.

> Note: The competent decisionmaker possesses a strong sense of personal responsibility and the willingness to make quick

decisions where called for. His decisions must be thoughtful and should be based on knowledge of all the available data and possible consequences of his action. On the other hand, he must be willing to take the risk of occasionally being wrong in order to act with the speed and decisiveness that many situations require. The overly impulsive decisionmaker is likely to make decisions too quickly without sufficient thought about their long range implications. The overly cautious individual is likely to be so fearful of being wrong that he would prefer not to act at all rather than take that risk, and so may miss many opportunities owing to his indecisiveness. The *ideal* decisionmaker, therefore, combines *thoughtfulness* and *responsibility* with *courage to act*, even to take a risk, with the *intelligence* and *flexibility* to make generally sound judgments and learn from any mistakes he/she might make.

Delegate

He is very well able to delegate responsibility to others. He is not so consumed with his own drive that he has to do everything himself. Rather, he derives a good deal of satisfaction from the achievements of others, and so is willing to allow them to do their own jobs, to grow, and to achieve their own successes.

He is, moreover, well able to correctly assess the ability of another to do a particular job, and so can make good judgments as to the advisability and appropriateness of delegating a specific responsibility.

In short, he possesses the prime requisites of a good delegator. He combines the willingness to delegate with the ability to do so appropriately.

> Note: The ability to delegate effectively involves the capacity to judge whether another person can perform a task, the ability to correctly evaluate whether it is advantageous to let him do it, and the willingness to let him try. The capable delegator is an individual who, although he may personally be as well or better able to do a certain job, realizes that keeping the work to himself may involve the inefficient use of his time or ability, and possibly interfere with the development and best utilization of others. There are two types of individuals who strongly resist delegating: 1. the highly impulsive ego-driven individual who wants the gratification of doing the job, and so convinces himself that he can do it faster and better than anyone else, and 2. the overly cautious perfectionist who fears that no one will do the job as carefully and responsibly as he himself. Good ability to delegate combines the willingness to

allow others to do a job with the capacity to accurately assess
their ability to do so.

Detail Ability

He dislikes detail work, but probably can handle it competently when
necessary. He is likely to be restless if he is continually confronted
with routine tasks, or jobs that are repetitive in nature.

Although he will always see detail as a chore, as the least
desirable aspect of any job, his sense of responsibility is sufficient
to motivate him to do what is necessary despite these feelings. He
possesses the self-discipline to allow him to deal with the details
when necessary to complete a job.

> Note: The ability to handle detail requires that combination of
> personality dynamics that enables an individual to organize
> work in a systematic way. It also enables him/her to deal
> effectively with activities that are repetitive and structured.
> At one extreme, a person with too deep-seated a need for
> personal organization and structure may tend to become so
> overly involved in day-to-day detail that he/she may lose sight
> of the real meaning of the activity. At the other extreme, a
> person may be so impatient and intolerant of order that he/she
> will be undisciplined in the planning and execution of his/her
> work. This lack of self-management could hamper the
> individual even in functions not normally requiring a great deal
> of detail involvement. The individual with good ability to
> handle detail enjoys, or at least is comfortable with, order or
> structure and yet is not so enmeshed in detail that he/she
> loses sight of the broader picture.

GLOSSARY

This glossary contains some of the more colorful terms used by venture capitalists. It does not include a large number of standard accounting or business terms that you should know. If you find that you do not recognize some of the terms in this book and they are not covered in the glossary, you should refer to a standard business text or your accounting book in order to find definitions of the words being used.

Arm's length Refers to business transactions in which neither the buyer nor the seller is influenced by the other. In a non-arm's length transaction you might sell a family member some assets of the business at a low price to move assets out of the business.

Board Meaning board of directors of a corporation. These are the individuals who control a corporation for the benefit of the stockholders. They listen to management's recommendations and set policy for the corporation.

Boilerplate Boilerplate paragraphs are the standard paragraphs in most venture capital and investment documents.

Bricks and mortar The assets of your company. The term is derived from a building that is built of bricks and mortar.

Bridge financing Medium-term investment designed to finance a company until it can go public and raise equity capital.

"Burn rate" The monthly rate at which a company is spending cash.

Buy out The term refers to the sale of a business; for example, when the buyer of a business buys it, he "buys out" the seller.

Buy-Sell A buy-sell agreement is one in which, under certain circumstances, the first party in a partnership must agree to buy out the second party, or the second party must agree to buy out the first party. Buy-sell arrangements usually are negotiated between two partners such as an entrepreneur and a venture capitalist.

Cash flow The most important aspect of any small business is the cash flow. The money coming in and the money going out constitute the flow of cash that determines whether a business will survive.

Cash in When you sell all or part of your stock for cash. Cashing in is an extremely exciting moment because it usually means you are rich.

Closing The event that occurs when you sign legal documents binding your company and transferring cash from the venture capitalist to your company.

Collateral The assets you pledge for a loan made to your company. If you do not repay the loan, the collateral can be sold.

Compounding The effect of adding the interest on an investment to the principal each month or year so that interest is earned on interest.

Control Owning 51% of the stock of a company or, from another perspective, owning enough stock in the company to control what management will do.

Convertible Usually refers to debt or preferred stock, each of which is convertible into common stock of the company. Obviously, it is possible to have debt convertible into preferred stock and it is even possible to have preferred stock convertible into debt, although the latter is unusual.

Covenant Paragraphs in the legal documents stating the things you agree you will do and paragraphs stating what you will not do.

Current ratio The ratio of current assets over current liabilities. Less than 1 to 1 usually means a problem.

Current return Income that is received monthly, quarterly, or annually as interest or dividends as opposed to the capital gain portion received on an investment at the end of the investment period.

Deal The bargain struck between the venture capitalist and the entrepreneur. In more general terms, any agreement between two individuals, especially a buyer and a seller.

Debenture Another word for a debt, note, or loan.

Debt service The amount of money you have to pay on a debt in order to keep it from being in default. If you make the payments that are called for under a note or loan, then you are servicing the debt.

Default When you have done something you told your investor you would not do, which is written down in the investment agreement, then it is a default.

Discount rate The rate used in present value calculations to convert future cash flows into present dollars.

"Down and dirty" round of financing A highly dilutive equity round of financing when the company's performance is poor.

Downside The amount of risk an investor takes in any venture is called the downside. If you stand to lose half your money if a business goes under, the downside risk is said to be 50%.

Due diligence The process of investigating a business venture to determine its feasibility.

EBIT (earnings before interest and tax) The bottom line before interest and tax payments.

Earn out The contract between the entrepreneur and the buying corporation that provides for the entrepreneur to earn additional money on the sale of his company, if operating earnings are in excess of a specified amount during the future years.

Equity Normally it describes the preferred and common stock of a business. Also, it is frequently used to describe the amount of ownership of one person or a venture capitalist in a business.

Equity kicker Equity participation that accompanies debt securities such as warrants, convertibility features, or common stock.

Exit The sale of equity or ownership in the business for cash or notes.

Fully diluted ownership Ownership assuming the exercise of all common stock options, warrants, and the conversion of any convertible securities.

Good idea A good idea is one that makes a large amount of money.

Good people The supreme compliment to an entrepreneur by a venture capitalist. It means the entrepreneur is honest, loyal, and a straight shooter.

Grace period The period of time you have to correct a default. *See* Default, above.

Hurdle The ROI necessary to compensate the investor for the risks involved in the particular investment.

Internal rate of return (IRR) The discount rate that equates the present value of cash outflows with the present value of cash inflows.

IPO (initial public offering) The initial offer and sale of a company's stock to the public.

Junior securities Securities with claims that are subordinated to the senior creditors in liquidation.

Lead investor The investor who leads a group of investors into an investment. Usually one venture capitalist will be the lead investor when a group of venture capitalists invest in a single business. *See* Syndication, below.

Leverage Another term for debt. Debt is usually referred to as leverage because in using debt, one does not have to give up equity. So for a very small amount of equity and a large amount of debt, one can leverage a business on the basis of its assets.

Leverage buy-out (LBO) An acquisition of a business using mostly debt and a small amount of equity. The debt is secured by the assets of the business.

Mezzanine financing The level of financing between senior debt and the equity, usually subordinated debt or preferred stock with an equity kicker.

Multiple Sometimes called PE for price earnings. The multiple of earnings, EBIT, or cash flow used to estimate the future value of a company.

Net present value The discounted present value of an investment minus the required initial investment.

NOL (net operating loss) Cumulative operating losses that may be carried back and/or forward to other tax years to offset taxable income for those years.

Options The right given to someone, say the venture capitalist, to buy stock in your company. *See also* Warrants, below.

Paper The notes you receive for the sale of your stock or the assets in your company. These are called paper because paper is fairly worthless. Many of the notes received by entrepreneurs from the sale of their company to someone else have turned into worthless paper.

Payback period Measures the number of years required to recover the initial cash investment.

PE *See* Price-earnings ratio, below.

Pool Usually a venture capital limited partnership in which each investor has "pooled" his resources by purchasing a limited partnership interest in the venture capital partnership. The partnership then invests in small businesses.

Post-money valuation The post-investment valuation of the company. Equal to the amount of the investment divided by the percentage ownership that such investment purchases.

Pre-money valuation The pre-investment valuation of the company. Obtained by subtracting the dollar amount of the investment proceeds received by the company from the quotient of the amount of the investment divided by the percentage ownership that such investment purchases.

Present value The discounted value of a series of future cash flows so as to account for the time value of money. Alternatively, the value of a future series of cash flows stated in terms of current dollars.

Price-earnings ratio   The number you multiply times the earnings per share number, in order to determine a fair price for a stock. For example, if a stock is earning $.50 a share and a price-earnings ratio of eight is used, then the stock is worth $4 per share.

Pricing   The determination of the price that an investor will pay to purchase shares of stock in the business.   Pricing is determined on the basis of the full value of the company.   Every time one share of stock is sold, the sale determines the value of the company and in this way, pricing occurs.

Promoter's equity   Represents the higher effective price paid by an investor than that paid by the originator of the transaction.

Proposal   The document that must be put together by an entrepreneur in order to propose an investment to a venture capitalist or other investors.

Public offering   The selling of shares to the general public through the registration of shares with the Securities and Exchange Commission.

Raising capital   Raising capital refers to obtaining capital from investors or venture capital sources.

Reality   What every individual should make sure he understands before jumping into the small business area.

Recapture tax   The "recapture" of the tax benefit of certain deductions or credits previously taken as ordinary income instead of capital gain.   Major types are LIFO Inventory, Investment Tax Credit, and Accelerated Depreciation Recapture.

Representations   These are the facts about your company that you represent to the investor to be true.

Restricted stock   Stock acquired directly from the company in a private sale and not pursuant to a registration statement.

Return on investment (ROI)   The internal rate of return on an investment.

Rule 144 SEC rule that governs the sale of "Restricted Stock" once a public trading market in the securities exists.

Second- and third-round financing The later rounds of expansion financings that follow the start-up round of financings.

Sensitivity analysis Analysis to determine how sensitive the ROIs are to variances from the expected values of the key variables (sales growth, margins, interest rates, exit multiples, etc.)

Situation General term used to refer to any business deal. It is common to refer to a business opportunity as a "situation."

Structure Term referring to the type of financing that will be used to finance a small business. The structure might be $100,000 in common stock and $500,000 in debt at 15% for ten years.

Syndication The process whereby a group of venture capitalists will each put in a portion of the amount of money needed to finance a small business.

Take back Term referring to the situation in which the seller of a business must take back something rather than cash. The take back usually refers to a note with reasonable terms and conditions.

Turnaround This word is used to describe businesses that are in trouble and whose management will cause the business to become profitable so they are no longer in trouble.

Underwriter The brokerage house used to raise funds for a small business in a public offering. In a public offering the brokerage house that underwrites the small business is the one that buys the shares from the small business and sells them to the general public.

Unlocking agreement A legal agreement between two parties meaning that one party may require the other to buy it out under certain circumstances; thus, the so-called unlocking of the partnership.

Upside The amount of money that one can make by investing in a certain deal is called the upside potential.

Warrant A stock option given to someone else that entitles them to purchase stock in your company.

Warranties These are items concerning your company that you have told the venture capitalist or investor are true.

Workout Situation in which a company's financial troubles necessitate an additional financing, reorganization, restructuring, or renegotiation.

INDEX